KU-520-631

THE CHANGING FACE OF GLOBALIZATION

Edited by
SAMIR DASGUPTA

SAGE Publications
New Delhi | Thousand Oaks | London

Copyright © Samir Dasgupta, 2004

All rights reserved. No part of this book may be reproduced or utilized in any form or by any means, electronic or mechanical, including photocopying, recording or by any information storage or retrieval system, without permission in writing from the publisher.

First published in 2004 by

Sage Publications India Pvt Ltd
B-42, Panchsheel Enclave
New Delhi 110 017

Sage Publications Inc **Sage Publications Ltd**
2455 Teller Road   1 Oliver's Yard, 55 City Road
Thousand Oaks, California 91320   London EC1Y 1SP

Published by Tejeshwar Singh for Sage Publications India Pvt Ltd, typeset in 10/12 Galliard BT at S.R. Enterprises, New Delhi and printed at Chaman Enterprises, New Delhi.

Library of Congress Cataloging-in-Publication Data

The changing face of globalization/edited by Samir Dasgupta.
    p. cm.
Includes bibliographical references and index.
    1. Globalization—Moral and ethical aspects. 2. Globalization—Moral and ethical aspects—Developing countries. I. Dasgupta, Samir, 1949–
    JZ1318.C52   909.83—dc22   2004   2004018544

ISBN: 0-7619-3290-9 (Hb)   81-7829-416-8 (India-Hb)
      0-7619-3291-7 (Pb)   81-7829-417-6 (India-Pb)

Sage Production Team: Jai S. Prasad, Mathew P.J. and Santosh Rawat

Dedicated to Sumitra
for her silent expression of inspiration,
my son, Diba
for his best assistance and
my little grand daughter, Bristi,
for her sweet melody.

CONTENTS

TABLES

FIGURES

ABBREVIATIONS

APEC	Asia-Pacific Economic Council
ASEAN	Association of South-East Asian Nations
CENTO	Central Treaty Organization
CNN	Cable News Network
EU	European Union
FAO	Food and Agriculture of United Nations
FDI	Foreign Direct Investment
G7	Group of Seven Leading Industrial Economies
GATT	General Agreement on Tariffs and Trades
GDP	Gross Domestic Product
ILO	International Labour Organization
IMF	International Monetary Fund
INGO	International Non-Government Organization
ISA	International Sociological Association
MNC	Multinational Corporation
MNE	Multinational Enterprise
NAFTA	North American Free Trade Area
NATO	North Atlantic Treaty Organization
NCA	Norwegian Church Aid
NGO	Non Governmental Organization
NIC	Newly Industrializing Country
NIDL	New International Division of Labour
NIEO	New International Economic Order
OECD	Organization for Economic Co-operation and Development
OPEC	Organization of Petroleum Exporting Countries
SEATO	South-East Asia Treaty Organization
TNC	Transnational Corporation
TRIP	Trade Related Intellectual Property

UNCTAD	United Nations Council for Trade and Development
UNDP	United Nations Development Programme
UNESCO	United Nations Educational, Scientific and Cultural Organization
UNICEF	United Nations International Children's Emergency Fund
UNO	United Nation Organizations
WHO	World Health Organization
WTC	World Trade Centre
WTO	World Trade Organization
WWF	Worldwide Fund for Nature

ACKNOWLEDGEMENTS

Professor Jay Weinstein of Eastern Michigan University has immense influence over my intellectual landscape. His appreciation and encouragement has inspired me to explore contemporary sociological issues for a brighter tomorrow. I would like to thank Professor Nityananda Saha, Vice-Chancellor, Kalyani University; Professor Pujan K. Sen, Professor Himanti Dasgupta, Sri Chaitanya Chand Chattopadhyay and Professor Debabrata Dasgupta, Vice-Chancellor, Bidhan Chandra Agricultural University, for their inspiration and good wishes.

I am very much indebted to Professor Peter Kivisto, Professor Vijayan K. Pillai, Professor Abbas Mehdi, Professor Robyn Driskell, Professor Emily Schultz, Professor Nicola Yeates, Professor Pabitra Sarkar, Professor Alok Majumdar, Professor Buddhadev Choudhury, Professor Dibyendu Hota and Professor Ajit K. Danda for reading the Introduction for this book very carefully and giving helpful and valuable suggestions.

I am grateful to my friends, colleagues, students and members of my family who have always encouraged me to do my best for sociology.

I am very much indebted to all contributors of this volume for their chapters. I want to thank them all for their unflagging encouragement.

Thanks are also due to Dr Jarrod Wiener, Director and former Editor of the Journal, *Global Society* for permission to publish the chapter by Sing C. Chew, and distinguished Professor Immanuel Wallerstein to publish his brilliant Y.K. Pao lecture in the volume. I am especially grateful to all at Sage India. It has been my pleasure to work with Sage.

Samir Dasgupta

INTRODUCTION

Samir Dasgupta[1]

You may not be interested in globalization but globalization is interested in you. It has become the focal point of attention in the social sciences since the late 1980s, and appeared as a paradigmatic concept in analyzing the economic, social, political, environmental, ecological, and cultural metamorphoses occurring across the modern world. The currency acquired by the concept reflects the agenda that the world today is unprecedently interconnected and interdependent. This is mainly a result of changes in the global economy and information and communication technology, which have had a great impact on this cultural, social, and political shift. Globalization, as a concept, is used to describe the process by which the world is transformed into a single arena. At the core of this understanding, is the contention that it should be applied to the concrete structuration of the world as a whole. Globalization is not merely an economic phenomenon, rather it covers all the aspects of modern life: the economic, the cultural, the political, the humanitarian, the social, and the ecological. In relation to these aspects, the social scientists today increasingly concentrate on global phenomena. In simple words, globalization can be defined as a process which denotes a transformation in the spatial organization of social relations and transactions. The prime features of this process is associated with several historical trajectories such as, universal adoption of the state system and emergence of a globally interdependent economic, political, cultural, technological, and communication system. But, simultaneously, it is also associated with the feeling of powerlessness and economic depression. The speed and scale of current global socioeconomic change appear to overwhelm political leaders, planners, policymakers, and academics. The unevenness of globalization compounds such dejection as the strong seem to be growing stronger and the weak, even weaker. So, we might say that globalization is an uneven process, which divides winners and losers. For the most affluent it entails a shrinking world but is very deceptive for the destinies of the deprived majorities. Globalization is like an American child whose glittering eyes are fixed on the enchanting Disneyland but also presents a tragic picture of a dejected child beggar. The inter-connection between globalization and inequalization shows a headspinning glimpse of alien future, as we are confronted with two contradictory forces: globalization and localization on one hand and progress and misery on the other. As the 20th century came to an end, we all felt the incredible and positive change of mindset among people and nations on the one hand, and the tale of tragedies, fear of identity, and uncertainty on the other. As we move beyond the dichotomies of globalization and localization, developed and rejected, we are becom-ing an increasingly interconnected "global village." And there is a glo-bal village—which we have not yet visited. We can only imagine what would be the physical and socioeconomic realities of a global village and how the structural and functional components would interact. We are, however, afraid of thinking about the future of such a global village. What would be its identity? What would be its nature of inter-action? What would be its economy, culture, environment, and pol-ity? It is true that our planet is one but it is also a grim reality that on our planet "... 22 children die of starvation every minute ... one mil-lion dollars are spent on arms every minute ... in the meantime three children died and the arsenal of the instruments of murder in the hands of adults grew by $150,000" (Dadayan, 1988). Would the glo-bal village be able to counter such contradictions and evolve a single economy, single culture, single society, and a single polity? Unifica-tion is not a process of averaging out. If some values become universal—for instance, all people the world over equally value peace and hate violence, then such unification is welcome, and we don't see in what way it can contradict such concepts as individuality or per-sonal freedom.

GLOBALIZATION DISCOURSE

The term "global" is an indicator of change. In the 1960s, this came to be used to mean "belonging to the world" or "worldwide." Marshall McLuhan (1964) uses the term "the global village," capturing a prop-erty of the modern culture, like the possibility of global communica-tion, and suggests that the instant reception of far-off lights and voices has changed the very concept and content of culture. His idea focuses on the worldwide network of communication as a key organ of transforming local life. This is also of equal significance to assess the impact of capitalist markets worldwide. The advent of the global village as an imagined community is a sign of not only integration and co-existence but also of differences and dissonance.

The concept of globalization dates back to the voyages of discovery in the 15th century. The capitalist economic foundation was laid in the 16th century. Wallerstein (1974) analyzes his "World System Theory" in terms of the powerplay which the center or core extends and links to the periphery i.e., extension of power from the "metropolis" to the "satellite." This image of exercised influence in the idea of global culture gives impetus to those who identify culture as an independent factor in the creation of one world (Robertson, 1990).

Robertson (1992) develops a paradigm to denote the historical–temporal aspects of globalization, apparently intellectually inherited from Rostow. Considering political inputs, Robertson directly analyzes the canvas of development in terms of the globalization process, which ties the question of reality. This is linked to the growth of communication, on which globalization depends. Robertson claims that globalization refers both to the compression of the world and the intensification of the consciousness of the world as one whole. The European commission defines globalization as the process by which markets and productions in different countries are becoming increasingly interdependent due to the dynamics of trade in goods and services and flows of capital and technology. This indicates a new type of capitalism known as "flexible accumulation" (Harvey, 1989). Marx in his *Communist Manifesto* suggests that the need of a constantly expanding market for their product, chases the bourgeoisie all over the world. It must nest, settle, and establish connections everywhere possible (Marx and Engels, 1848). Wallerstein's (1990) world system theory has widened the Marxist version of understanding global capitalism. The "global capitalist class" generally operates from a nation state of hegemonic type that dominates the transnational practices in economic, political, and cultural spheres. Castell's (1996) interpretation rejects the concept of a global capitalist class and accepts the view of an integrated global capital network. Albrow (1996), on the basis of the debates of globalization, raises the issue of using sociology to enhance the global network and thus, pleads for a global sociology.

The term globalization has come to be emotionally charged in public discourse and has become a buzzword now. In fact, the hallmark of globalization is the emergence of a single social system—the process hastened by a worldwide network of economic, political and social relationships—able to produce a unique social order. Present day globalization, as we see it or as we feel it, is a collection of processes in which economic, political, cultural and other ties are made between different countries. This interdependence has been contributory in forming a new pattern for our daily lives. Now-a-days, internet and fax machines are connecting people world over job availability for a person is widening, cross-border monetary transaction is increasing by many folds, trade patterns are altering quickly and the aftermath of an event are not confined within the national boundary but considerably affecting other countries too. The economic action patterns of local actors and institutions are moulded by external agencies, which epitomizes the global changes in this regard. But the concept does not just point out the concern of interconnectedness. Globalization is best perceived in terms of a time–space distanciation. Giddens (1991) states that globalization concerns the intersection of presence and absence, the interlacing of social events and social relations at a distance with local contextualities. Today globalization indicates a phenomenon identified interchangeably as a process, an historical event or the end result of shifting "ethno-, techno-, media-, finance-, and ideo-scapes" (Appadurai, 1996). Contemporary social scientists discuss globalization as a process by which the world is becoming increasingly interconnected and unified, subject to homogeneous and uniform processes of cultural, technological, and economic unification. This process replaces the concept of modernization, which mainly depends on the dualistic interpretation like "Center–Periphery," "North–South" "Developed–Third World" distinctions. But Martin Albrow (2001) emphasizes that globality is not the latest form of modernity. Globality is non-teleological and, in fact, consists of multiple globalizations without the totalizing character of the "modern" project which neglects everything that resists the advance of modernity. Theoretically, the concept of globalization may be viewed as the expansion of the world system, accompaniment of modernity, creation of a single world market and a resultant of modernity. Of course, Beck (1993) refers to it as a "second modernity." Social scientists have to accept the intensified impact of globalization not simply as an imaginative jargon but as a contemporary social reality.

While globalization is progressing at an unprecedented pace and intensity, the pervasiveness and depth of local identities have resurfaced. The ideal type global village which was created with the imagination of an open discourse of integration, interaction, and harmony has failed to triumph over discord, differences, demarcation, discrimination, and dissonance of local villages. However, people in the Third World have been misled into believing that the world has changed and globalization means homogenization. The hegemonies and domination of the globalists indicate the blackhole of exclusion and threats. It is a very debatable concept, explained in all sorts of different ways. But the rhetoric of debate often hides more than it expresses. So the debate over the merits and demerits of globalization continues. Behind the architecture of a new world order, (benign globalization?), malignant globalization creates a three-tier structure across national boundaries. The globalists represent the core of the circle, in the second circle are the people who "labor in insecure forms of employment are and thrown into cut-throat competition in the global market," and the outer ring represents the excluded ones. If the world were a global village of a 100 people, 70 of them would be unable to read, and only one would have had any college education. Over 50 would be suffering from malnutrition and over 80 would live in what we call substandard housing. If the world were a global village of 100 residents, six of them would be American. These would have half the village's income while the other 94 would exist on the other half. How would the wealthy six live "in peace" with their "neighbours"? (Huizer, 2003). To some observers, the process of globalization is linear, unidirectional. However, this is a superficial perspective, as its clear that inconsistencies and disharmony characterize the process. At its root, there are profound contradictions between globalization in progress and globalization in conflict. What seems to be globalization for some appears to be localization for others. Under these circumstances, a key question is whether globalization is bringing people new freedom to act or if it portends an uninvited, unwanted, and cruel fate for the majority of the world's population. The clash continues between fear, anxiety, and uncertainty for the dejected majority and freedom, comfort, and happiness for the few elites.

The present volume is the product of the unfolding debate about globalization. Zygmunt Bauman (1998) notes that being local in a globalized world is a sign of social deprivation and degradation. Those local areas where global inputs exert the most pressure are losing their "meaning generating" and "meaning negotiating" capacities. The people in those areas are increasingly dependent on the economic and cultural hegemony of global powers. The gap between the global and the local, although often unobtrusive and dynamic, is potentially explosive. In brief, globalization is now oscillating between global winners and losers. Thus, globalization has to be perceived as a process which both includes and excludes peoples and nations. The process is embedded in a hierarchical system of power, exchanges, and benefits (Petras, 1999). Can globalization lead us to a brighter world or will it generate more conflicts, poverty and contradictions in our already anxiety-ridden world? Dialogue is the only instrument to understand the present status of globalization. Thus, the need for discourse among the people of different nations has never been more acute. The focus of this book is on globalization as a worldwide phenomenon and attempt has been made to draw theoretical and applied illustrations from different parts of the world. The emphasis of this volume is mainly on environment and ecology, altruism and humanity, culture, polity, and economic issues related to globalization. The ongoing debate and research on globalization have also been incorporated in the book.

THE DIALECT OF GLOBALIZATION

Until recently, the leading philosophical perspective on globalization emphasized crossing the economic and cultural divide. Ethically and morally, the purpose of globalization was to bring different races, cultures, ethnic groups, and socioeconomic classes into closer contact with each other. The rationale for the movement was altruistic: to replace hatred with love, violence with peace, destruction with construction, "their" culture with "our" culture, and an "either" with an "or" mindset. The elements of this paradigm were the elimination of hostility, construction of an ideal type civil society, restructuring of a sick economy, and the integration of all cultures.

Now, however, we fear the injuries that globalization can inflict in each and every facet of our economic, cultural, political, and social lives. The concept demands revision, re-assessment, re-evaluation, and re-projection. It demands reflections on diversity, an open vision of humanity, and free discourse. It is a grim fact that many nations and peoples are now confronting reality with what appear to be two contradictory faces: the global and the local. Along with the increasing pace of globalization in science, technology, economy, culture, education, empowerment of women, communication, local conflicts are also increasing unprecedently. This situation weakens the positive potentials of globalization.

According to Martin Albrow (2001), nothing better illustrates the difference between globalization on one hand and modernization on the other than the debates about the relationship between global and local interests. From Albrow's perspective, the local is always defined in contrast to a specific frame of reference. That is, the local is the neighborhood in relation to the community; it is the community in relation to the nation-state; and it is the nation-state in relation to the international system. Conflicts emerge with the metamorphoses of localism into globalism. This is the locus of economic, cultural, and political marginality, which can easily create a situation of crisis, adoption–rejection conflict, disintegration, chaos, and disorder.

It was once believed that the primary mission of globalization was to integrate the parts into whole. But, in fact, the parts have lost their sociocultural, economic, and political identity. The result is severe economic disparity, painful cultural identity crisis, loss of the sense of belonging, ethnic violence, secessionism, and ultimately civilizational shock. The tragedy of globalization is that it began with the aim of restructuring and rebuilding civilizations; yet the mission has produced discord, even more separatism, and identity crisis. The global village, once a symbol of integration, unification, and harmony, now denotes difference, differentiation, demarcation, discrimination, and dissonance. The world, compressed into a single economic, ecological, cultural, electronic, and political system has never been so highly stratified (Picco, 2001). Charlie Chaplin in his excellent film *The Great Dictator*, expresses the true spirit of democracy and altruism: "We want to live by each other's happiness, not by each other's misery. We don't want to hate and despair one another … in the name of democracy…. Let us all unite. Let us fight for a new world—a decent world that will give men a chance to work—that will give youth a future and old age security. Let's fight to free this world, to do away with national boundaries, to do away with greed, with hate and intolerance…."

Chaplin sings a melodious *raga* about an ideal type of globalization. But 40 years have passed since the coinage of the term "global village" by Marshall McLuhan, and our society remains as it was. In terms of disparity, we remain parts rather than wholes. In terms of a single humanity, we are divided. In terms of possessions, we are either rich or we are destitute. From the porthole of a space vehicle high above the earth, it is obvious that the divided and rival peoples comprise only one human race; for the borders that separate nations are not visible from the outer space. But in the inner space of the earth, we see the tragic division of humanity into hostile groups. Terrorism, sectarianism, bigotry, fundamentalism, and its horrible descendant, fanaticism, have possessed this beautiful planet. They have filled the earth with violence, drenched it often with human blood (Vivekananda, 2001). Does this represent altruism and humanism? Does it indicate the philosophical, idealistic spirit of the globalization mission?

The catalog of horrors attests not only to the failures of the ideals of globalization, but even more vividly to the harsh, unintended consequences the process has produced. Consider, for example, the severe famine in Somalia, extreme economic genocide in Rwanda, the rise of fundamentalism and fanaticism in India and Pakistan, and moral and ethical corruption and political and economic turmoil in Bangladesh. Recall, too, the debt burden in Brazil, Argentina, and Bolivia, and economic disintegration in Peru. In these and related instances, globalization has brought depression, disparity, and ethnic explosion.

THE ECOLOGICAL DIMENSION

The essays in this book demonstrate that globalization is indeed a multidimensional and often self-contradictory process. The topics covered include much that is familiar, but our main aim is to examine previously unexplored aspects of globalization and its impacts. This has produced a wide-ranging approach that blends ecology and environment, culture and economy.

The spatial dimension of globality/locality corresponds to cultural particularism on one hand and creation of new cultural spaces on the other. This consciousness of the world as a single place (Robertson, 1992) conceives the globe as a natural entity. Sociologists often view society as a set of nations; but this concept needs to be complemented with an explicitly ecological perspective. It is assumed that biophysical reality shapes social reality, which ultimately creates a diverse ecosystem. Thus, it is difficult to consider all nations as part of a single global system (Yearley, 1996). The differences between warm and cold climates and natural topographical and climatological differentiation appear to deny the possibility of globalization. The ecologically linked notion of time and space has been transformed into another neo-ecological dimension of late modernism, which is a source of globalization in conflict. Ecological disequilibrium as a universal phenomenon appears to deny the possibility of a global culture and humanism.

One might deny the fact that our bodies are restricted in time and space. This prospect is related to the crucial issue of global warming. Many social scientists who fear threats to the global environment e.g., Offe (1985) and Archer (1991) seek a global identity in relation to environmental issues. Yet, little has been done to explore ecological problems in most contemporary works on globalization. An exception to this trend is Robertson (1992), who stresses the need to study globalization–environmental problems in terms of "species threatening phenomena."

Sing C. Chew's essay on globalization, ecological crisis, and Dark Ages examines the relationship between culture and nature, a relationship that has been punctuated by periods of ecological crises. These crises moments or Dark Ages exhibit conditions of ecological degradation, climatic changes, and reorganization of socioeconomic and political structures. M. Tolba and El Kholy (1992) point to a number of major themes as symptoms of the global ecological crisis. These include climate change, biodiversity loss, population growth, freshwater pollution, contamination, air pollution, the greenhouse effect, deforestation, land degradation, and desertification.

Globalization experts advocate technological inputs as the savior from global ecological degradation. However, the introduction of technology and electronics, from the kitchen to the bedroom, not only conserves human energy, it also creates environmental hazards. Meadows identifies the major factors that are likely to present insurmountable barriers to future economic growth. These include the limited volume of food production and constraints on the extraction of nonreplenishable natural resources, together with the pollution of the environment resulting from technology (Dadayan, 1988).

What has globalization given to the Third World countries? What things have really been globalized? Are these stockpiling of thermonuclear weapons, the creation of neutron, biological, laser and chemical weapons, and fear of global nuclear catastrophe? The gifts that the Third World countries have received thus far from the globalizers are anxiety, poverty and inequality, hunger, disease and illiteracy. The preservation and development of the environment are continually being sacrificed in the name of ecological modernization.

Ulrich Beck in his excellent work *The Risk Society*, examines the impact of dominant global economic forces and the postmodern culture. According to him, these will lead to uncertainty and loss of control. Beck observes:

> Forests have also been dying for some centuries now—first through being transformed into fields, then through reckless overcutting. But the death of forests today occurs globally, as the implicit consequence of industrialization...it is nevertheless striking that hazards in those [early] days assaulted the nose or the eyes and were thus perceptible to the senses, while the risks of civilization today typically escape perception and are localized in the sphere of physical and chemical formulas.... In the past, the hazards could be traced back to an undersupply of hygienic technology. Today they have their basis in industrial overproduction. The risks and hazards of today thus differ in an essential way from the superficially similar ones in the Middle Ages through the global nature of their threat. They are risks of modernization (1992: 21).

This is the tragic tale of the impact of globalization on the environment. In the past also people lived with environmental hazards and were at risk. But today the influence of globalization has also threatened their biological security. The transformation of premodern to modern social risks has led to a total lack of control over our destinies. Beck's thesis poses some serious questions concerning what type of "development" developing countries should pursue (Salih, 2001).

In considering the current concern about ongoing global environmental crisis and its impact on sociocultural change, Sing Chew observes that the past can help us understand the likely possible futures. His essay examines past trends, such as deforestation, soil erosion, pollution, trade and economic disruptions, de-urbanization, political regime and climatological changes, during the Dark Ages. These, he argues, provide insights on the conditions that give rise to system transformations, and the possibility that we might be about to experience another Dark Age phase.

THE CULTURAL DIMENSION

Environmental problems are increasing rapidly with the ever-accelerating pace of globalization. Environmentalist concerns (Yearley, 1996) are now an accepted matter of discourse. Yet the linkage between environmental consciousness and "species consciousness" remains problematic. To some extent, people of the world share a global culture (here defined as "communicable intelligence"). However, it is a culture in conflict, as opposed to a universal consensus, because of the confusion between globally local and locally global phenomena. Some critics note that globalization in its current phase is thus a product of "triadic cultural hegemony."

The cultural homogenization model does not fit the Third World countries, mainly for economic reasons. Economy and culture are intimately interrelated. Our age of cultural realism is tied to the current stage of market capitalism. Monopoly capitalism links cultural modernism; and postmodern cultural phenomena constitute the denominator of managerial capitalism. Thus, capitalist hegemony continues. Those who promote globalization conceal questions of economic particularism and domination behind their programs of global culture. "[T]here is a significant political link between culture and economy [which]proves very difficult to analyse...." (Tomilson, 2001).

The issue of universalism has an intimate connection with globalization; it promises to create global homogeneity. But for J. Grey (1997), both the social processes of globalization and the cultural and political norms of universalism are negative. Universalism is "One of the least useful and indeed most dangerous aspects of the western intellectual tradition...the metaphysical faith that local western values are authoritative for all cultures and people" (Grey, 1997). Such "progressive individualism" (another name for universalism) aims to make the rest of the world—the rejected world—de-traditionalized and disenchanted. Cultural globalization is also malignant in the form of the ever-expanding electronic culture and the ever-proliferating fast food outlets—the process that George Ritzer refers to as *McDonaldization*. Ritzer notes that these restaurants are the new "cathedrals of consumer culture" (2001). The result is a clash between new cultural spaces and traditional cultural spaces.

A binary cultural fusion arises from this imposition. Yan Yunxiang writes:

> ...during the 1999 student demonstrations against the NATO bombing of the Chinese embassy in Belgrade ... many young protestors were drinking Coca Cola as they chanted "down with American imperialism" in front of the U.S. embassy in Beijing. The irony goes much further, when some young activists sent messages over the Internet calling for a resistance movement to the invasion of western culture ....

Others went to eat at a KFC outlet immediately after parting anti-McDonald's slogans on the streets.... (2002: 19).

This observation reveals the phenomenon of "managed globalization." Older explanatory schemes, such as Talcott Parsons' *Pattern Variables*, fail entirely to account for such dual cultural functions. *Particularism*, according to Parsons, is a cultural emphasis on familiar and familial values; i.e., loyalty to one's society. *Universalism*, on the other hand, emphasizes the organization of interaction according to general, cosmopolitan standards; i.e., loyalty to humanity as a whole. Whether such universalism is harmful or not is a matter of debate. But a metamorphosis of the universal into the particular has occurred, and with it the transformation of emotion into a disciplined cultural reality.

In his contribution, Immanuel Wallerstein emphasizes that the term globalization emerged with end of the Cold War, and a new concept of culture became part of international discourse. Wallerstein analyzes multiculturalism in terms of the interplay of *Universalism, Particularism,* and *Time*. The result of this interplay is a clash between "we" and "others," which according to Wallerstein, turns benign cultures malignant.

A fundamental re-organization of our epistemologies may help us understand this multiple universalism. A multicultural society is one made up of people belonging to different cultures. Under such circumstances, culture clash is likely if those who share "their own" values and standards unintentionally accept the culture of the "others." At the extreme, this can result in genocide, Holocaust, and ethnic cleansing. Globalization creates a distance between the particular and universal cultures. Slavoj Zizek (1997: 44) notes, "Multiculturism is a disavowed, inverted, self-referential form of racism, a racism with a distance—it respects the other's identity, conceiving the other as a self-enclosed 'authentic' community towards which he, the multiculturist, maintains a distance rendered possible by his privileged universal position. The multiculturalist respect for the other's specificity is the very form of asserting one's own superiority."

In this context, conflict can also occur between "privileged universality" and "shared universality" (Bharucha, 1999). In other words, it is a clash between multiculturalism and interculturalism. Whereas multiculturalism works within the "cultural logic of multinational capitalism" (Zizek, 1997), interculturalism opposes such a logic (Bharucha, 1999). True universality can occur when, in a socially constructed world, "we" are the constructors. This is perhaps the true form of benign global culture.

Most promoters of globalization, according to Wallerstein, favor hierarchies as they are the beneficiaries of the wealth and power thereby accumulated. They attempt to command intelligence and knowledge; that is, they seek hegemony. But these groups represent the numerical minority of world's populations. Their quest for control is largely unpopular. Their victory is not guaranteed. The cultures and ethnicities of most people in the world are viewed as subordinate by the globalizers. This leads to confusion, but also to a kind of solidarity among the majority and its representatives. In this context, the clash of cultures follows two tracks: (*a*) multicultural particularism in conflict; and (*b*) conflict between multiple universalism and multiple particularism. Wallerstein refers to the blend or synthesis as a "rainbow coalition." No doubt, the creation of such a global coalition is a formidable political task. But the increasing rate of economic disparity between the minority and the majority renders a dialogue of inclusion increasingly unlikely.

THE MORAL DIMENSION: CREATIVE ALTRUISM

A prime item on the political agenda of the majority is the reconstruction of ethical and knowledge systems. Until this is undertaken, it will be difficult, if not impossible, to confront such phenomena as multiple temporalities, multiple universalism, and multiple particularism. Fortunately, this project is already underway. It is part of current reflections on the vision of our common humanity and the search for universal dialogue (Annan, 2001). It is related to the expanding search for altruism and a sense of humanity that can dissolve the "either/or" mindset and the "us" and "them" mentality. A new knowledge system, informed by an altruistic sense of humanity, can help produce a global ethic that provides a new and revised sense of belonging.

Based on the practice of "aidocracy" (rule through helping others), such a global ethic would begin and end with humanity. For, "we appeal as human beings to human beings to remember your humanity and forget the rest. If you can do so, the way lies open to a new paradise" (Russell and Einstein, cited in Picco, 2001: 38).

An inventory of the effects of globalization on the "other" world reveals disparity, dejection, faceless universalism, hegemonic control and monopolistic behavior, ethnocentric bigotry, religious exclusivism, and cultural chauvinism (Picco, 2001). Thus, Joseph Stiglitz in his excellent work *Globalization and its Discontents* makes the following observation:

> [T]he way globalization has been managed, including the international trade agreements that have played such a major role in removing those barriers and the policies that have been imported on developing countries in this process of globalization, need to be radically rethought.... Decisions were made on the basis of what seemed a curious blend of ideology and bad economics, dogma that sometimes seemed to be thinly veiling special interests.... Rarely did I see forecasts about what the policies would do to poverty.... We are a global community, and like all communities have to follow some rules so that we can live together (2002: IX–XV).

What are these rules to which Stiglitz refers? Are they merely a few lines on economic conduct or policy resolution? These are hardly adequate. No, they must be principles of conduct for a common humanity, for an unprecedented and authentic form of altruism. Learning to be humane is a profoundly meaningful challenge in the contemporary world. For true altruism—perceived inclusively and holistically—is applicable to every person under all circumstances. Reciprocity and altruistic love underlie the Golden Rule. Positively stated, it directs one to "do unto others what you would want others to do unto you." In its negative form, it warns, "do not do unto others what you would not want others to do unto you."

The Golden Rule, like the *Bhagvadgita* in Hindu philosophy, identifies all the altruistic and humane qualities that result in awareness, recognition, inclusion, and love. This is the "species consciousness" that Jay Weinstein and Elvira del Pozo mention in their essay. Weinstein and del Pozo argue that the most complete and effective realization of a truly global sociocultural system involves the coming to species consciousness by all of humanity (much as Karl Marx stressed that meaningful social change could not occur without the workers coming to true class-consciousness).

Marxist humanism is founded on such principles. Labor, according to Marx, is the main ingredient in the humanization of nature and humanity itself. In *The German Ideology* (1844) Marx suggests that we must avoid postulating society as an obstruction vis-à-vis the individual. The individual is always to be seen as the social being. His manifestations of life as expressions and confirmations of social life itself.

Our adaptive possibilities have increased substantially through the use of technology and the resulting "artificial intellect." Will these alter our species nature? Will *simulacra* replace homo sapiens? For our species, consciousness is inherent in the mind, and is not a matter of biological determinacy. The Dutch philosopher Spinoza (1677) states that every definition of man is a negation, a negation of its own, inevitably limitedness, abstractness and one-sidedness. Spinoza emphasizes that human action is determined by interactions with fellow humans, guided by reason.

Others who have stressed the need for altruism as a prerequisite for authentic globalization include Auguste Comte, Emile Durkheim, James Ozinga (1999), and Pitirim Sorokin (1950). In the present volume, Weinstein and del Pozo connect an altruistic social order with the prospects of a common humanity. Samir Dasgupta in his essay analyzes social altruism as the prime agenda item in our quest for true globalization. Analyzing Indian society in terms of Vedic thought, Dasgupta defines the center of the global village as the universal self. The philosophy of altruism, according to him, can lead to a world in which trade in love is a sin. In this context, he seeks out the roots of sociology of humanity and its impact on the process of globalization. Adoption of a global policy of benign altruism, he argues, can help to solve the problems of religious dualism—between peace and violence, and between tolerance and aggressiveness. Globalism, according to Dasgupta, involves sublimation. The synthesis represents the true nature of *Karma* (deed), which ultimately leads to *Moksha* (salvation).

In assessing the prospects for a common humanity, Weinstein and del Pozo reflect on why altruism is considered deviant behavior in modern and postmodern cultures. This assessment is deeply rooted in the two worldviews. Modernists focus on variables such as capitalism, industrialism, surveillance capacity, and rise of military power (Giddens, 1990). All of these are faceless phenomena, representing only shadows of human interaction. The postmodernists perceive the cultural logic as a metamorphosis of form into anti-form, purpose into play, design into chance, hierarchy into anarchy, presence into absence, genre into text, and root into rhizome or surface (Ihab Hassan, 1982). In the postmodern age, there is no linguistic normality, only "pastiche." In this context, it is important to note Baudrillard's (1970; 1980) comments. In his *Vanishing Point* he defines postmodernism as the death of meaning, the death of reality, the death of the social and political and the death of sexuality.

These are hyper-rational (Ritzer, 1996) or hyper-real expressions; that is, the "irrationality of rationality." The inclusion of mind, culture, civilization, reality, and the whole, on the one hand, and repression of body, nature, tradition, appearance, and the part, on the other, signifies the state of uncertainty that Ulrich Beck (1992) referred to as "risk society." Modern and postmodern cultures, each in their own way, thus reject the possibility of species consciousness. True altruism is excluded from the discourse of both because both attend to the surface of the road to the future, not to the underlying foundation of humanity on which the road is constructed. Thus, the obsession with our "body" and the denial of our "mind" render as deviant the very act of *being* human.

THE POLITICAL ECONOMY OF GLOBALIZATION

By marginalizing the prosocial behavior, modernist and postmodernist accounts of the globalization process have diminished the sacredness of altruistic humanity, especially for those who live in the Third World countries. The prime virtues of an authentic global ethic are liberty, justice, and love for a human world—a world without gender inequality, racial discrimination, stark income discrepancies, illiteracy, ethnic conflict, and religious bigotry. But the increasing economic disparities created by globalization generate fanaticism, terrorism, moral indignation, and aggressive suffering. The severity of the contrast between the elite and the rejects feeds a pervasive mood of uncertainty. It divides the world into hegemony and domination on one hand, and exclusion and threat on the other.

From this perspective, globalization can then be defined as "how the multinationals are taking over the world." In the year 1998, numerous globalization conferences were held. In Paris they centered on the Multilateral Agreement on Investment (MAI), in Geneva on the World Trade Organization (WTO), in Cardiff on the Single European Currency (SEC), in Birmingham, U.K., on the G-8 Summit, IMF reforms, APEC etc. The mission of such summits was to promote a new world order with deregulated free trade and capital flows. Advocates of neo-liberal economies claim that the market will stimulate economic growth, which will gradually trickle down to all sections of society, creating new consumers worldwide, enjoying a higher standard of living (CTA, 1999).

Such are the claims, but what is the reality? The reality depicts a rather more sordid picture. The transnational corporations (TNCs), with their enormous economic resources and political power, bypass the poorer states of the Third World in order to dominate them. What kind of globalization is this? Kiely (1998) suggests that the globalization of production thesis exaggerates the degree of capital mobility in the world economy, which has important (and largely negative) implications for much of the so-called Third World today. By the early 1990s, there were approximately 37,000 TNCs. They controlled more than 200,000 foreign affiliates worldwide, generating sales of more than $4.8 trillion (UNCTAD, 1994). Today, the TNCs enjoy an enviable 50 percent share of the world's largest economic sales units. Seizing the opportunities provided by this type of globalization process, the giant companies entirely or partly control national economies all over the globe, and are now able to move capital freely across national boundaries. With these trends, the economic sovereignty of the Third World has been lost.

According to Verghese Chirayath and Ernest de Zolt, additional adverse consequences have arisen for the local economies of the world in their interactions with multinational corporations. In their contribution to this volume, these authors underscore the ways in which TNC-oriented globalization results in further opportunities for the expansion of global capitalism; and false promises for developing nations. The TNCs sought a ticket to enter the arena of the Third World to ensure the rapid circulation of their products. One result was the emergence of newly industrializing countries of East Asia, South Korea, Taiwan, Hong Kong, Singapore, and India (Frank, 1981). Yet this is largely a byproduct of a quest whose motives were far more self-serving. For TNCs, investment in the poor countries has in fact been motivated by (*a*) the utilization of lucrative domestic markets; (*b*) the availability of cheap raw materials and cheap labor; and (*c*) avoidance of stringent state regulation.

Chirayath and De Zolt cite research on infant mortality throughout the Third World, the Union Carbide disaster in Bhopal (India), and the Enron scandal in the USA and India. Using these studies, they show that the lucrative financial terms, weak environmental regulations, and low wages that attract multinationals, rarely, if ever, contribute to the economic self-sufficiency of host nations. Instead, in their view, transitional economies serve as platform for corporate criminality. They explain transition economics in terms of three prime dilemmas:

i.e., internal dilemmas, ownership of projects, and necessity of a guarantee of project completion.

Chirayat and De Zolt define the role of TNCs in terms of white-collar criminality. Here is an authentic instance of deviant globalization, far removed from true altruism, species consciousness, and a common humanity. In his powerful book on globalization Joseph Stiglitz (2002) makes a similar point in locating corporate crimes such as corruption throughout the private sector. He also refers satirically to such practices as "briberization." Such criminal activities help the TNC's to increase their profits and simultaneously to victimize the Third World with economic depression. And if governments are also corrupt, it is unlikely that privatization will solve these problems (Stiglitz, 2002).

GENDER INEQUALITY IN A GLOBAL CONTEXT

The impact of globalization on gender relations is far-reaching. Increasingly involved in the world's production and consumption processes, women have been affected by globalization in the most diverse aspects of their lives and in the farthest reaches of the world (Afshar and Barrientos, 1999; Villareal, 1994). Women's lifestyles have been dramatically affected, as have their decision-making power and their decision-implementing roles in the family. In principle, globalization also does—or ought to—challenge the traditional subordinate status of women virtually everywhere. But the potential empowerment of women is contradicted by the realities of continuing male domination of major social institutions. Thus, it is necessary to review and rethink the extent to which women today have authentic "biopower," economic power, cultural power, and power in making and implementing political decisions.

More than a century ago, the early feminist, Elizabeth Cady Stanton observed that the actual size of the movement for gender equality (in her case, suffrage) is readily underestimated. "[T]he number is larger than appears on the surface, for the fear of public ridicule, and the loss of private favors from those who shelter, feed, and clothe them, withholds many from declaring their opinions and demanding their rights" (Stanton, et al., 1881 cited in Dale, 1982: 2). Because men have power, notes Dorothy Smith (1978: 2), they have the power to keep it.

These and other related issues indicate a continuing and underlying dilemma between the reality and ideology of empowerment. In one sense, empowerment refers to the capacity of women to become more self-reliant and to increase their internal strength. This entails the right to determine life-choices and to influence the direction of change through control over material and non-material resources. Yet, women still have subordinate social positions. They suffer from extensive abuse, psychosocial stress, and somatic complaints. Poor women especially—that is 70 percent of all women—have the greatest responsibility for child rearing, suffer from the consequent overwork, and experience more domestic violence and sexual mistreatment. Much of this is traditional, but much can also be traced to the colonial experience.

A United Nations report (1989) observed that economic progress for women has virtually stopped, social progress has slowed down and social well-being in many cases has deteriorated. Citing Indian cases, Jean Drèze and Amartya Sen (1995) identify four main dimensions: (*a*) extraordinarily high levels of gender inequality and female deprivation persist; (*b*) gender inequality does not diminish automatically with economic growth; (*c*) gender inequality is not merely a social problem in itself, it also leads to other social problems; (*d*) the agency of women as a force for change is one of the most neglected aspects of the development literature.

The emergence of feminism as an international movement has introduced the prospect of change. With it has come an alternative conception of the role of women in the process of socioeconomic development (McMichael, 1994). The first UN World Conference on Women, held in Mexico City in 1975, focused specifically on the connections between empowerment and development. Attention thus shifted from an integrationist to an agenda-setting approach. In terms of globalization ethic the women should not be suppressed from social, economic, and political life. In these terms, real empowerment means growing awareness—emancipation in the true sense.

In the present volume, Driskell analyzes the concept of women's empowerment in terms of economic development. Recent research indicates that the nutritional well-being of children, as reflected negatively in low body weight, wasting, and stunting, betters with improvement in economic conditions. All members of a society are ultimately benefited when the economy grows: economic growth leads to an increase in wages, which in turn are spent on more and higher quality food. Thus, Driskell notes, empowerment of women in development planning involves the linkage between improvement in the lives of women and the health of their children.

Unfortunately, the economic status of women in the Third World countries remains extremely low. Questions of gender have long been ignored within mainstream economics. And the few studies that have considered the issues have not been very powerful in shaping the discipline's theoretical treatment of gender (Grapard, 2001). The inclusion of gender issues in formal economics practically began with the emergence of globalization. Yet, early in the 20th century, Charlotte Perkins Gilman (1966) challenged the accepted gender roles and domestic relations. In response to criticism of her work as "socialist" and "feminist," she countered: "The anti-suffrage masses, had me blankly marked 'suffragist,' while the suffragists thought me a doubtful if not dangerous ally on account of my theory of the need of economic independence of women (p. 198)." In another passage she writes: "Without the economic dependence of the females, the male would still be merely the hunter and fighter, the killer, the destroyer; and she would continue to be the industrious mother without change or progress (p. 132)." Gilman's evolutionary concepts reveal the consequences of women's subordination.

The twin struggle for gender equality and economic justice has for generations brought together the women's movement and the labor movement (Grapard, 2001). Women are naturally the bearers of children and to some extent necessarily involved in their care. Since time immemorial and in every conceivable cultural context, it has been argued that women who are economically independent can be neither good housekeepers nor ideal mothers. It is a fact that women, at least in the industrialized nations, are becoming economically independent. But it remains to be shown that this is at the cost of their child care or household work.

In this light, Driskell explores a new concept of feminism. Empowerment, according to Driskell, means living autonomously, freedom from male entrapment, and the achievement of self-esteem and productive roles. Her empirical analysis, using data from the World Bank, reveals some significant relationships among empowerment and development variables. The study also indicates that women's empowerment has a somewhat more significant impact on children's nutritional well-being than economic development.

The Question of Development and the Debt Crisis

Issues of socioeconomic development have a central place in the globalization debate. Development can indeed bring benefits, and globalization does not necessarily deny the possibility of individual and ethnic identities. Then, one might ask, what is the source of tension between those who promote globalization and the people of the Third World? Why do globalization and development appear to be at such odds? Wolfgang Sachs (1992) has provided the answers to these questions, at least in part:

> Like a towering lighthouse guiding sailors towards the coast, development stood as the idea, which oriented emerging nations in their journey through postwar history. No matter whether democracies or dictatorships, the countries of the South proclaimed development as their primary aspiration, after they had been freed from colonial domination. Today, the lighthouse is starting to crumble. The idea of development stands like a ruin on the intellectual landscape. Delusion and disappointment, failures and crimes have been the steady companions of development and they tell a common story; it did not work (p. 1).

Such pessimistic views have caused many social researchers to declare the concept of development dead. Ankie Hoogvelt, in an interview asserted that in the era of globalization there is no longer any purpose for development studies, on both theoretical and conceptual grounds. Changes in the world economy have dissipated and fragmented development studies into several different approaches. The most important of these changes is that the Third World, or the periphery, as a unitary category has disappeared. Some Third World states (e.g., in East Asia) have become developed, while others have become completely marginalized: Africa can hardly be included in the same periphery as Latin America.

Hoogvelt (1997) views the sociology of globalization as an intensification of human relations. Relations extend across borders, but they do not necessarily reach out and touch all parts of the globe. In this respect, globalization is merely an extension of capitalism to ever more remote parts of the world—essentially an expression of capitalist implosion (or explosion). This is most evident in the rapidly increasing disparities between the poor majority, on one hand, and those that share in the profits and accumulate capital, on the other. At the same time that capitalism is expanding its reach, it is contracting its scope. As it spreads geographically, it expels more and more people who are structurally irrelevant to the system, who are irrelevant to production, trade, or consumption. Development studies are relevant only in the few remaining places that are outside the orbit of the global economy. Most Third World countries, including India, have already exchanged development for globalization.

In their essay in the present volume, Samir Dasgupta and Kaushik Chattopadhyay view globalization as a dangerous prospect for the Third World. They point to numerous contradictions: progress alongside of hunger, the blessings of wealth combined with the abomination of destitution, the pleasure of achievement along with the pains of failure, and the slogan of equality linked to cries of disparity. Using data from the *World Development Report* and other secondary sources, they conclude that severe poverty remains the main characteristic of the world's population as a whole. They identify the source as the unbalanced policies of those who promote globalization. "To them," Stiglitz explains, "globalization (which typically is associated with accepting triumphant capitalism, American style) is progress; developing countries must accept it.... But to many in the developing world, globalization has not brought the promised economic benefits" (2002: 5). Rather, the Third World countries are left with economic disparity, localized wars, environmental degradation, a heavy debt-burden, religious bigotry, ethnic violence, and sociopolitical dislocations.

Two other case studies have been included in this volume. One is about globalization and the Arab World and the other discusses the impact of globalization on African societies. During the 1960s and 1970s, Arab nations were able to adapt to the times and consequently experienced the most rapid economic growth in the world. Since the mid-1980s, their record of economic growth has been dismal. Abbas Mehdi's essay discusses this economic decline in the Arab World, where the threats and opportunities prevented by globalization are particularly acute. Mehdi argues that it would be wise for the Arab people to take a more measured look at the effects of globalization, especially taking into account their nations' changing patterns of migration, the role of their public sectors, and the complexities of their labour markets.

There is a commonly held view that globalization will come to the rescue of failing Arab economies which, since 1985, have been suffering from reduced oil revenues. The Middle East, primarily the Arabian peninsula, is known for its huge energy reserves. But globalization has not helped to employ these resources to the benefit of the local people. To the contrary, those who promote globalization seek to establish control over the Arab World. For the region has a stupendous source of strategic power and one of the greatest material prizes in world history.

Mehdi underscores the impact of shortsighted domestic prices as well as the flaws that lie within the framework of the new global economy. He does hold out hope for a more positive, inclusive form of globalization. For, in his view, integration into the world economy is not only economically desirable for Arab nations, but it will help to avoid widespread social chaos.

Alemazung's contribution to this volume explores the impact of globalization in Africa, a case that bears both positive and negative lessons. He reminds us of how colonial decisions involving the demarcation of territory divided people from their neighbors and kin. Goldsmith (1994) points out that the colonial powers inflicted profound damage on that continent, driving frontiers straight through the ancestral territories of nations. This "damage" includes ethnic conflict, economic collapse, and identity crisis. During the 1950s, questions were raised by anti-colonialists about the appropriateness of nation states for a postcolonial Africa (McMichael, 1996). In reviving the issue, Alemazung assesses the effects of nationalism as both inclusive and exclusive.

Western-dominated globalization has helped to transform Africa into a *cultural Chernobyl* and a socioeconomic *Disneyland*. With it has also come anxiety over the loss of cultural identity and a clash between local and overseas Africans. Setting aside the causes and consequences of economic destabilization, Alemazung focuses on the effects of the very high rates of migration from Africa to the West, especially the cultural changes that have made Africa a mosaic of the old and the new. The new cultural inputs have undoubtedly improved Africans' style and quality of life. But the influence of global culture on their local cultures has also created marginality. This has now raised questions about cultural exclusion and, ultimately, about Africa's participation in setting the development agenda. In contemporary Africa the forces of globalization and its opposite, localization—between homogeneity and heterogeneity, are exerting tremendous pressure on individuals (Picco, 2001).

Those who promote globalization are unconcerned about the historical and anthropological aspects of the cultures of Africa. Africa has a long-standing, close connection with the West and has for generations been subject to cultural influence emanating from Britain, the United States, and elsewhere (Bernstein, 2002). Thus, these societies are well along the way to adopting an "economic production culture." In addition, the penetration of African markets by the multinational companies contributes to the already widespread identity crisis. For, in addition to dilemmas posed by local versus global values and norms, people are now forced to chose between adoption and rejection of foreign innovations and consumer items. The institutionalization of corporate capitalism in Africa and domination of its political economy by the TNCs have created a peculiar type of universalism: "the vicious category of universalism" (Tomilson, 2001). Cumulatively, these assaults amount to cultural genocide.

In the developing world, the burden of the external debt has now reached around $2 trillion. Entire countries have been destabilized as a consequence of the collapse of national currencies, often resulting in the outbreak of social strife, ethnic conflict, and civil war (Chossudovsky, 2001). Structural reformers promote trade liberalization, the main result of which is the closure of domestic manufacturing in the Third World countries—and thus, the exacerbation of their debt burden. The unspoken motive of the trade-liberalization agenda was quick disbursement of loans to the Third World that would allow them to continue importing goods and commodities on the international market. This has let to complete economic stagnation, development crises, and the destruction of entire domestic economies.

NEO-LIBERALISM AND THE ANTI-GLOBALIST RESPONSE

The globalization conferences held during the late 1990s emphasized promotion of a New World Order with deregulated "free" trade and capital flows. According to the underlying neo-liberal economic principles that guided these talks, the market will stimulate economic growth and the newly generated wealth will then gradually trickle down to all sections of society. The new consumers, created worldwide, will ultimately enjoy a higher standard of living. The neo-liberals also argue that a globalized "free" market benefits the environment because it provides incentives for development and transfer of technologies that have fewer negative impacts than the existing system does (CTA, 1999). The neo-liberalism that has dominated globalization policy during the past quarter century is characterized by its emphasis on deregulation, privatization, and free competition. But its hidden aim is to de-politicize the state. "And [the local populations'] claims on the state's resources were treated as an unfortunate burden on the grand designs of global economic growth" (Kalhan, 2002: 21).

The political agenda dictated by the World Bank, IMF, and the WTO is essentially globalization from above. In response, a movement to resist this agenda has emerged anti-globalization protest movements. Participants include left wing intellectuals, trade unionists, youth and women activists, and NGO workers. The Earth Summit in Rio de Janeiro in 1992 directed international attention to the need to control greenhouse gases. The slogan, "fifty years is enough," echoed by the anti-globalization campaigners before World Bank anniversary meeting in 1994 and the anti-globalization campaigns against land mines, Nike shoes, Nestle, Enron, etc., served to articulate the movement's program. The 1999 "Battle in Seattle" against the WTO was the first major victory for the movement. Since these events, the movement has sought to lay the foundation of a global civil society that can derail globalization.

Protests occurred at the G-8 Summit meeting in Genoa in 2002, following the arrest of anti-globalization activists—known as the "black block." Tens of thousands of delegates from several countries participated in the historic four-day demonstration. Their mission was to focus international attention on issues regarding debt reduction, equitable distribution of wealth, and the global growth of corporate power. Paolo Cento, Member of Parliament from the Italian Green Party, described the arrest of the protestors as "the gigantic provocation aimed at the anti-globalization movement."[2]

In his contribution to this volume, Ray Kiely examines the rise and significance of the "so called anti-globalization movement" in the late 1990s. Kiely views it as part of a "double movement" that constitutes an attempt to restore social control over the market. Examining the politics of the movement, he discusses its critique of globalization from above and the role of direct action and its non-hierarchical organization. He notes that the movement organizers argue that the globalization of capital has led to a new international class divide between a transnational bourgeoisie, which enjoys unprecedented capital mobility, and the exploited "mass." For Kiely, convergence has occurred across nations and so anti-globalization struggles now take similar forms throughout the world. He points out that global capital has not led to socioeconomic equality but has actually intensified uneven development.

If the anti-globalization movement prevails and the globalization project of the TNCs is defeated, Kiely asks, can an alternative be constructed? Is it after all "socialism," guided by the philosophy of historical materialism, for which many on the left argue? (see Petras, 1999). Will a socialist transformation be operative through the process of either "de-linking" or developing "market socialism"?

DILEMMAS AND DUALITIES

In their essay in this volume Ritzer and Ryan argue that globalization is not *nothing*. Rather, *nothing* is being globalized, and this process is important. They define *nothing* as a social form that is generally centrally conceived and controlled and comparatively devoid of distinctive substantive content. This stands in contrast to *something*, which is a social form that is generally indigenously conceived and controlled and comparatively rich in distinctive substantive content.

The confrontation between the *nothing* and the *something* of globalization, according to Ritzer and Ryan, leads to a *nothing–something* continuum. In this light, they focus on two main themes: (*a*) globalization in the arena of consumption; and (*b*) the impact of local culture on global consumption. They cite shopping malls and the Internet as the key agencies of consumer behavior, which—as noted earlier—Ritzer describes as "Cathedrals of Consumption."

Social scientists have long been interested in globalization as a process of transforming heterogeneity into homogeneity, diversity or difference into sameness, local systems into global systems, and tradition into modernity. In this respect, globalization is certainly *something*. Thus, Ritzer and Ryan assess the role of consumer behavior, whose universal form is seen in the shopping mall, the fast-food restaurant, and the cyber café. But the content of this behavior has not been fully globalized; rather, it varies greatly according to local social-networks and lifestyles. Here, issues of production are central, especially those that underscore the difference between that which is mass produced and that which is more individualized.[3]

The *nothing–something* dichotomy begins at the global level, but its end is local. As Arie de Ruijter (2001: 31) observes:

We ask ourselves…[w]hether we view homogenization as an ideal or a nightmare. Some of us applaud the increase in diversity as a source of alternative behaviors or as empowerment of indigenous peoples and marginalized groups. Other regrets this diversity. They refer to the growing complexity and uncertainty of our existence. We must after all, live in this reality and this reality is characterized by just such diversity…. The twofold action between the processes which constitute and feed each other, that is, globalization and localization is responsible for this.

Social scientists have introduced various synonyms for globalization (Robertson, 1992). These include "creolization" (Hannerz, 1992), "hybridization" (Latour, 1994), and "second modernity" (Beck, 1993). Ritzer and Ryan in this volume, add the term "grobalization." At an ever-increasing rate, the transnational system promotes mutual reciprocity and the leveling of interaction among a growing number of actors (Appadurai, 1990). The multinationals have seriously disrupted the traditional styles of living, behavior patterns, and consumption orientations in most countries where they operate. This is the main impact on local actors of the something–nothing continuum: a new culturally specific consumerism. It reflects an ongoing dialectical process (de Ruijter, 2001). The diffusion of increasing oneness, which is the prime rationale of McDonaldization, also leads to divergence— a process of cultural copy-and-paste.

Ritzer and Ryan introduce the neologism, grobalization in order to emphasize a feature that globalization ignores or downplays. For the process is not an unmitigated source of *nothing* (it can involve *something*) and—another of their new terms—"glocalization" is not solely a source of *something* (it can involve *nothing*). Grobalization is the outcome of imperialistic ambitions of nations, corporations, and organizations and of their desire or need to impose their will in geographic areas throughout the world. This is, after all, a revised version of mercantilism, which always emerges when power and profit are at stake.

In the modern era, the multinational consumer club or mall culture—a peculiar form of Disneyland-fashioned global culture—influences the lifestyles and enforces Western patterns of behavior among the people of the Third World. Yet, traditional consumer behavior often prevails. Even the US–style business practices of local actors or local leaders of a multinational corporation are affected. The management and administrative orientation of a fastfood restaurant like McDonalds, which serves 20 million people worldwide each day, maintains a specific style of providing clean, hygienic, and cheap food.

It stresses the need to have the customer exit the restaurant promptly, so as to save time and sell more. But in India, for example, the orientation is shaped by local styles. Customers and sellers enact more traditional roles, in which interaction includes expressive as well as instrumental elements. In such cases, universalism gives way to particularism. "This localization is particularly interesting because it has obvious economic consequences to which McDonalds's management has had to adapt" (Berger, 2002: 10). Here is another instance of the clash between strong, traditional local culture and imposed modern Western culture.

Ritzer and Ryan develop four "ideal types" to clarify the operation of the grobalization–glocalization and the *something–nothing* continua. With these, we see the connection between their perspective and the modernist and postmodernist movements. The metamorphoses of form to anti-form, purpose to play, design to chance, centering to disposal, genre to text, depth to surface, root to rhizome, and presence to absence (Hassan, 1982) are reinterpreted by Ritzer and Ryan. For them, they key shifts are from place to non-place, thing to nonthing, person to non-person, and service to non-service. They argue that development and diffusion tend to occur together. The extension and expansion of global markets thus, through a spontaneous force, transform the grobal from the glocal and the *nothing* from the *something*. They suggest that it is far easier to grobalize nothing than something, whereas the development of grobalization creates a favorable ground for the development and spread of *nothing* (and *nothing* is easily grobalized and *something* is easily glocalized).

Ritzer and Ryan cite the ultimate example of the globalization of nothing using the model of "consumption on the Internet." The companies that use various Websites are mainly consumption and trade-promotion oriented. This signifies *nothing*—as empty forms, and it is a global phenomenon. But direct interaction is formal and localized. Thus, the philosophy of absence dominates face-to-face interaction. Websites, instead of establishing face-to-face interaction, transform at the speed of light the global products to the Internet users. The Internet is global but its content is the globalization of nothing? According to Ritzer and Ryan, we have two options: either to support the local as an alternative to the global or to accept global culture and with it cultural innovation.

THE TOOLS FOR RETHINKING GLOBALIZATION

The essays in this volume abound with concepts, principles, and theories with which to challenge and to help reshape the commonly held views about the process of globalization. The comments of Ritzer and Ryan, Wallerstein, Weinstein and Pozo, Driskell, and the other contributors clearly refute such oft-repeated claims to the effect that the process is unidirectional, or that it is uncontested, or that it is ultimately in the interests of all of humanity. And, although it is difficult not to accept the near-universal verdict that globalization is inevitable, the authors all have something to offer that tempers this kind of forecast. *When* does the inevitable occur? *Whose* globalization is inevitable? *Which* dimensions of globalization are inevitable? And, the globalization of *what* is inevitable?

Begged questions, semantic traps, and ideological distortions burden the rhetoric and discourse in this field. The word *globalization* itself is as much a weapon of political combat as it is a descriptor of a social process. In this light, one of the most useful features of the essays in this volume is the care that the authors have taken in examining meanings and defining carefully the terms they use. As the philosopher Ludwig Wittgenstein observed around 50 years ago, the most valuable service that a contemporary scholar can perform is to help dissolve (i.e., rather than solve) humanity's problems by examining the language in which they are expressed. The contributors to the volume have performed this service with great skill, and in this way have helped us see through the dilemmas, real and imagined, that attend globalization.

Of greatest significance, perhaps, this collection is not merely about the functions and dysfunctions of globalization. It is also a handbook of social action. Each essay provides some guidance for social activists and social scientists concerning the things that can be done to mitigate the disasters and to amplify the benefits that attend this complex process. Globalization and impacts are the products of human acts, undertaken with intent and punctuated by unintended consequences. Despite the appearance of the process as a juggernaut, it is not too late for those of us who care about the human prospect to exert control over it—intellectual and political—and turn it to the human interest. These essays provide numerous sound strategies, suggestions, and programs to assist in such an effort—momentous, as it may seem.

As Ray Kiely and some of the other contributors note, the destructive tendencies of globalization have spread to all corners of the world. But so, too, has the opposition to these tendencies, in the form of scholarly criticism and social movements. The fact that the authors of the following essays represent four continents and several countries, bears testimony to this *globalization* of anti-globalization. Beyond all that is written here, this is the most profound sign that all hope is not lost for those who place universal human values above transnational power and profit.

NOTES

1. I am grateful to Professor Jay Weinstein of Eastern Michigan University and President, Society for Applied Sociology (SAS) USA, for the patience and care with which he read and commented on the Introduction. I would also like to thank for helping me improve the language of the text.
2. Joseph Stiglitz (2002: 5) has examined extensively how and in whose interest structural adjustment policies were evolved, and the effects that they have had on the Third World economies. He notes, "Despite repeated promises of poverty reduction made over the last decade of the 20th century the actual number of people living in poverty has actually increased by almost one hundred million. This occurred at the same time that total world income actually increased by an average of 2.5 percent annually."
3. Here, one might speak of the mass production of individuality.

REFERENCES

Afshar, Haleh and Barrientos, Stephenie. 1999. "Introduction: Women, Globalization and Fragmentation" in Afshar, Haleh and Barrientos, Stephanie (eds). *Women, Globalization and Fragmentation in the Developing World*. London: Macmillan.

Albrow, Martin. 1996. *The Global Age*. Cambridge: Polity Press.

_____. 2001. "Globalization after Modernization: A New Paradigm for Development Studies" in Frans J. Schuurman (ed.). *Globalization and Development Studies*. New Delhi: Vistaar Publications.

Allen, Tim and A. Thomas (eds). 1992. *Poverty and Development in the 1990's*. Oxford: Oxford University Press.

Annan, Kofi A. 2001. "Foreword" in Picco, Giandomenico (ed.), *Crossing the Divide*. New Jersey: School of Diplomacy and International Relations, Seton Hall University.

Appadurai, Arjun. 1990. "Disjuncture and Difference in the Global Cultural Economy" in Mike Featherstone (ed.). *Global Culture: Nationalism, Globalization and Modernity*. London: Sage.

_____. 1996. *Modernity at Large: Cultural Dimensions of Globalization*. Minneapolis: University of Minnesota Press.

Archer, Margaret S. 1991. "Sociology for One World: Unity and Diversity" in *International Sociology*, vol., no. 2.

Baudrillard, Jean. 1970. *La Societe de consommation*. Paris: Gallimard, English citation in Powel, Jim. *Postmodernism for Beginners*. India: Orient Longman.

_____. 1980. *De la seduction*. Paris: Galilee, English citation in Powel, Jim. *Postmodernism for Beginners*. Hyderabad: Orient Longman.

Bauman, Zygmunt. 1998. *Globalization: The Human Consequences*. Cambridge: Polity Press.

Beck, Ulrich. 1992. *Risk Society: Towards a New Modernity*. London: Sage.

_____. 1993. *Die Erfindung des politischen*. Frankfurt: Suhrkamp, as cited in Schuurman, Frans J. (ed.) 2001. *Globalization and Development Studies*. New Delhi: Vistaar Publications.

Berger, Peter L. 2002. "Introduction: The Cultural Dynamics of Globalization" in Peter L. Berger and Samuel P. Huntington (eds), *Many Globalizations—Cultural Diversity in the Contemporary World*. New York: Oxford University Press.

Bernstein, Ann. 2002. "Globalisation, Culture and Development: Can South Africa be more than an offshoot of the West!" in Peter Berger and Samuel Huttington (eds). *Many Globalizations: Cultural Diversity in the Contemporary World*. New York: Oxford University Press.

Bharucha, Rustom. 1999. "Politics of Culturalisms in an Age of Globalisation." *Economic and Political Weekly*, Feb. 20, 1999.

Castells, M. 1996. *The Risk of the Network Society*. Oxford: Blackwell.

Chomsky, Noam. 1994. *World Orders: Older and New*. New York: Oxford University Press.

Chossudovsky, Michel. 2001. *The Globalisation of Poverty*. Goa: Other India Press.

Choudhury, Biswajit. 2002. "A Storm of Protests," *Frontline*, vol. 19, no. 16, Dec. 7–10.

CTA (Technical Centre for Rural and Agricultural Cooperation) 1999 Report.

Dadayan, V. 1988. *The Orbits of the Global Economy*. Moscow: Progress Publishers.

Dale, Spender. 1982. *Women of Ideas*. London: Pandora.

Dasgupta, Samir and Chattopadhyay, Kaushik. 2002. *Global Malady in the Third World—A Reflection*. West Bengal (India): Prateeti Publications.

Davids, Tine and Francien Van Driel. 2001. "Globalization and Gender: Beyond Dichotomies," in Frans J. Schuurman (ed.). *Globalization and Development Studies*. New Delhi: Vistaar Publications.

Drèze, Jean and Amartya Sen. 1995. *India: Economic Development and Social Opportunity*. New Delhi: Oxford University Press.

Frank, Andre Gunder. 1981. Crisis in the Third World. New York: Holmes and Meyer.

Gelinas, Jacques, B. 1998. *Freedom From Debt*. Dhaka, Bangladesh: The University Press Limited.

Giddens, Anthony. 1990. *The Consequences of Modernity*. Cambridge: Polity Press.

_____. 1991. *Modernity and Self-Identity*. Cambridge: Polity Press.

Gilman, Charlotte Perkins. 1966. *Women and Economics*. New York: Harper and Row.

Goldsmith, James. 1994. *The Trap*. New York: Carroll&Graf.

Grapard, Ulla. 2001. "The Trouble with Women and Economics" in Stephen Cullenberg, Jack Amariglio, and David F. Ruccio (eds). *Post Modernism, Economics and Knowledge*. London/New York: Routledge.

Grey, J. 1997. *Endgames: Question in Late Modern Political Thought*. Cambridge: Polity Press.

Hannerz, U. 1992. *Cultural Complexity: Studies in the Social Organization of Meaning*. New York: Columbia University Press.

Harvey, D. 1989. *The Conditions of Post Modernity*. Oxford: Blackwell.

Hassan, Ihab. 1982. *The Dismemberment of Orphans: Toward a Postmodern Literature*. New York: Oxford University Press.

Hoogvelt, Ankie. 1997. *Globalization and the Postcolonial World: The New Political Economy of Development*. London: Macmillan.

Huizer, Gerrit. 2003. *Globalization From Above and From Below: A Dialectical Process*. Inhoud.

Kalhan, Anuradha. 2002. "Globalization of Protest," *One India One People*," vol. 5/6, January.

Kiely, Ray. 1998. "Introduction: Globalisation, (Post)Modernity and the Third World" in Kiely Ray and Phil Marfleet (eds). *Globalisation and the Third World*. London: Routledge.

Latour, B. 1994. Wij Zijn Noit Modern Gewest. Rotterdam: Van Gennep.

Marx, Karl and Engels, Fredrich. 1848. *Communist Manifesto*. Moscow: Progress Publishers.

McLuhan, Marshall. 1964. *Understanding Media*. London: Routledge.

McMichael, Philip. 1994. *Development and Social Change: A Global Perspective*. Thousand Oaks: Pine Forge Press.

Offe, Claus. 1985. "New Social Movements: Challenging the Boundaries of Institutional Politics" in *Social Research*, vol. 52, no. 4.

Ozinga, James R. 1999. *Altruism*. Westport, Conn.: Praeger.

Petras, James. 1999. "Globalization: A Socialist Perspective" in *Economic and Political Weekly*, 20, 1999.

Picco, Giandomenico (ed.). 2001. *Crossing the Divide*. New Jersey: School of Diplomacy and International Relations, Seton Hall University.

Powel, Jim. 2001. *Postmodernism for the Beginners*. India: Orient Longman.

Ritzer, George. 1996. *Modern Sociological Theory*. McGraw Hill. (fourth edition).

———. 2001. *Explorations in the Sociology of Consumption*. New York: Sage.

Robertson, Ronald. 1990. "After Nostalgia?" in Bryan Turner (ed.). *Theories of Modernity and Postmodernity*. London: Sage.

———. 1992. *Globalization: Social Theory and Global Culture*. London: Sage.

Ruijter, Arie de. 2001. "Globalization: A Challenge to the Social Sciences" in Schuurman, Frans J. (ed.). *Globalization and Development Studies*. New Delhi: Vistaar Publications.

Russel, Bertrand and Einstein, Albert. 1955. *Signatories*. Manifesto.

Sachs, Wolfgang. 1992. "One World" in Wolfgang Sachs (ed.). *The Development Dictionary*. London: Zed Books.

Sandler, Todd. 1997. *Global Challenges*. Cambridge: Cambridge University Press.

Salih, M.A. Mohamed. 2001. "Globalization, Sustainable Development and Environment: A Balancing Act" in Frans J. Schuurman (ed.). *Globalization and Development Studies*. New Delhi: Vistaar Publications.

Sen, Amartya.1981. *Poverty and Famines*. New Delhi: Oxford University Press.

Smith, Dorothy. 1978. "A Peculiar Eclipsing: Women's Exclusion from Man's Culture" in *Women's Studies International Quarterly*, vol. 1, no. 4.

Sorokin, Pitirim.1950. *Altruistic Love: A Study of American "Good Neighbors" and Christian Saints*. Boston: Beacon Press.

Spinoza, Baruch Benedict de. 1677. *Ethics*. Translated from the Latin by R.H.M. Elwes (1883). MTSU *Philosophy WebWorks*. Hypertext edition. 1997.

Stanton, Elizabeth Cady, Susan B. Anthony and Matilda Joslyn Gage (eds). 1881. *History of Woman Suffrage*, vol. 1, New York: Fowler and Wells.

Stiglitz, Joseph. 2002. *Globalisation and Its Discontents*. New Delhi: Penguin Books.

Tolba, M. and El Kholy. 1992. *The World Environment 1972–1992: Two Decades for Challenge*. London: Chapman and Hall.

Tomilson, John. 2001. *Globalization and Culture*. Cambridge: Polity Press.

UNCTAD. 1994. World Investment Report. New York: United Nations.

Villareal, Magdalena. 1994. Wielding and Yielding: Power Subordination and Gender Identity in the Content of a Mexican Development Project. Wageningen, Ph. D. Dissertation.

Vivekananda, Swami. 2001. *Chicago Address (1893)*. Kolkata (West Bengal) India: Advaita Ashrama Publications Department.

Wallerstein, Immanuel. 1974. *The Modern World System*. New York: Academic Press.

————. 1990. "Societal Development or Development of the World System?" in Martin Albrow and Elizabeth King (eds). *Globalization, Knowledge and Society*. London: Sage.

World Development Report. 2000–2001. *Attacking Poverty*. New York: Oxford University Press.

Yan, Yunxiang. 2002. *Managed Globalization: State Power and Cultural Transition in China* in Peter L. Berger and Samuel P. Huntington (eds). *Many Globalizations: Cultural Diversity in the Contemporary World*. New York: Oxford University Press.

Yearley, Steven. 1996. *Sociology, Environmentalism, Globalization*. London: Sage.

Zizek, Slavoj. 1997. "Multiculturalism or The Cultural Logic of Multinational Capitalism," in *New Left Review*, 225, September/October, 1997.

1

GLOBALIZATION, ECOLOGICAL CRISIS, AND DARK AGES[1]

Sing C. Chew

INTRODUCTION

Explanations of long-term global transformations to date have been based primarily on socioeconomic and political factors. As we increasingly question whether there are physical and environmental limits that would affect the reproduction of the world-system; socio-economic and political factors might not necessarily be sufficient to explain long-term global transformations. What is needed is the inclusion of ecological and climatological changes as important dimensions in our understanding of long-term global transformations. Given these parameters, global transformations are outcomes not only of political and economic interactions, but are also consequences of the relationship between society (culture) and nature; they are about climatological changes.

Over world history, the relationship between culture and nature has been punctuated with periods of ecological degradation and crisis (Chew, 2001a). Given these outcomes, the history of human civilizations can therefore also be described as the Ahistory of ecological degradation and crisis (Chew, 1997, 1999, 2001a). It is the latter moment, that of ecological crisis commonly known to historians as the Dark Ages, that is of interest to us. During these periods of Dark Ages or ecological crisis, we find political–economic and ecological patterns and trajectories that are very different from crisis-free periods. In this regard, Dark Ages are times exhibiting ecological degradation, climatic changes, reorganization of socioeconomic and political structures, and hegemonic challenges. On this basis, Dark Ages offer us a window into moments of system crisis and transformations.

Given the current concern about the ongoing global environmental crisis having an impact on global transformations, our consideration of patterns of the past (such as Dark Ages) can provide a comprehensive understanding of likely possible futures. This chapter is an attempt to examine past trends and tendencies during Dark Ages for insights on the conditions that can give rise to system crisis and transformations. With this understanding and mapping of the contours of Dark Ages and their recurring nature, I pose the question of whether we are again moving into another Dark Age of human history in view of the contemporary ecological crisis conditions. To explore this possibility, I identify some trends, tendencies, and indicators (such as deforestation, soil erosion, species endangerment, pollution, trade and economic disruptions, deurbanization, political regime, and climatological changes), depicting the conditions underlying prior Dark Ages to highlight the possibility that we could be entering another such phase. Our effort here is to understand current global systemic trends within the dynamics of an evolving world system over the *longue duree*.

THEORETICAL CONTEXT

Over world history since the Bronze Age, the political–economic connections between communities, kingdoms, and civilizations from Asia to Europe have exhibited certain economic rhythms and trends that seemed to have circumscribed the socioeconomic developmental trajectories of regional and world transformations (Chew, 1997, 2001a; Kristiansen, 1993, 1998; Modelski and Thompson, 2001; Sheratt, 1993). Periodizing these rhythms has been based overwhelmingly on economic conjunctures of expansion and contraction over long periods of time, contingent on kingdom, regional, and civilizational reports of economic conditions in the areas of trade, manufacturing and natural resource extractive activities, agricultural productivity, etc (Frank, 1993; Modelski and Thompson, 1996; Sheratt, 1993). Beyond these political and economic cycles, there are also certain long phases of socioeconomic and political downturns that have been labeled as Dark Ages by historians and archaeologists. These phases are periods, in some cases, of contraction and/or collapse of human communities and civilization. They exhibit conditions of acute social, economic, and political disruptions, such as economic slowdowns, structural social a political breakdowns, deurbanization, increased/reduced migration, population losses. Unfortunately, such long-term socioeconomic analyses of these Dark Ages, most often fail to account for the condition of the environment during such times. During these Dark Ages we find ecological degradation on a world scale (Chew, 1997, 2001a). The latter is brought about by the numerous collisions with the natural environment as civilizations, empires, kingdoms, and nation states seek to reproduce themselves (Chew, 1997, 2001a; Hughes, 2001).

From an ecological point of view, this makes Dark Ages interesting periods in world history. During these phases, Culture–Nature relations exhibit trends and tendencies that are significantly different from expansionary phases when socioeconomic activities assume an intensive natural resource extractive trajectory. The socioeconomic patterns that emerge during these Dark Ages veer away from the usual intensive exploitation of nature that normally characterize periods of economic expansion (though initially the landscape exhibits devastation only to recover in the later periods of the Dark Ages). During Dark Ages all expansionary trends that are typical reproductive features of human communities display negative trajectories and tendencies, especially in the core areas of the world system. We find several Culture–Nature trends and patterns that are subdued: fall in population levels, decline or loss in certain material skills, decay in the cultural aspects of life, fall in living standards and thus wealth, and loss of trading contacts (see Desborough, 1972; Snodgrass, 1971).

From an anthropocentric point of view, such socioeconomic and political trends would spell disaster for human communities and socioeconomic progress. Hence the use of the adjective, "dark," to depict these specific phases of world history. Ecocentrically speaking, Dark Ages should be appreciated as periods for the restoration of the ecological balance that has been disrupted by centuries of intensive human exploitation of nature. The anthropocentric evaluations of Dark Ages in terms of conditions and factors leading to the onset of these periods are found quite commonly among the historical and archaeological literature, especially for the Dark Age that occurred in the second millennium B.C. They ranged from cultural decadence, invasions and conquests by "barbarians" and nomadic tribes, internal conflicts, overcentralization of authority, famine and diseases, climate changes and tectonic shifts (see Bintliff, 1982, Bryson et al., 1974; Carpenter, 1968; Childe, 1942; Desborough, 1972; Neumann and Parpola, 1987; Renfrew, 1979; Shaffer, 1982; Snodgrass, 1971; Toynbee, 1939).

On the whole, most explanations for the onset of Dark Ages have focused overwhelmingly on anthropocentric causes related to social and economic conditions, and to some extent, on climatological changes and earthquakes. There seems to be less emphasis on analyzing ecological conditions and the relationship between human communities and the ecological landscapes to account for the onset of the Dark Ages. There are, however, some exceptions. Kristiansen and I have suggested that ecological relations between human communities and nature have impacted on their economic reproduction, and have also caused socioeconomic organizational changes, and perhaps even their collapse (Chew, 1997, 2001a; Kristiansen, 1993, 1998). In this respect, I have further suggested that extreme ecological degradation over prolonged periods have led to system crisis, and in some cases collapse, followed by Dark Ages (Chew, 2001a, 2001b).

If one thinks along the lines Kristiansen and I have pursued, ecological limits become also the limits of the socioeconomic processes of the world system, and the interplay between ecological limits and the dynamics of the system define the historical tendencies and trajectories of the human enterprise (Kristiansen, 1998). Therefore, perhaps the usual dictum, "economy in command," is the sole underlying force underlining global transformation in the long-term needs to be reconsidered. Along the type of argument I have been stating in my previous works, we might need to file down further the key for understanding and explaining world system dynamics and transformation (Chew, 2001a, 2001b). The operating dimension should be "ecology in command," interpolating with the often accepted "economy in command". This means if we shift our focus to Culture–Nature relations and examine the outcomes of these relationships we might obtain a better understanding of the rise and fall of political–economic systems. In this regard therefore, Dark Ages are interesting because these are periods which can reveal the extent of the dependency of the socioeconomic realm on ecological relations in the reproduction of political–economic systems.

Notwithstanding the visible impacts on socioeconomic life as a consequence of the onset of the Dark Ages, these impacts do not extend necessarily and evenly across geospatial boundaries of the system. Depending on the systemic connections of the world economy at a particular point in time, and the level of intensity of the Culture–Nature relations experienced by a given region, the extent of impact of a Dark Age period is uneven. The state of crisis and/or transition appears to have its greatest impact on the regions of the world system that are considered the core/s of the system at the specific point in time. No doubt, this is related to the fact that it is in the core region(s) where Culture–Nature relations are at their most heightened levels. This does not imply that the periphery does not experience any crisis type conditions. The connections that the core has with the periphery via several economic and political processes assure that at least some (if not all) crisis conditions will be felt. The extent, of course, is based on how incorporated the periphery is in the productive processes of the core/s.

To some extent, the crisis/transition also offers opportunities for some in the periphery to re-articulate themselves within the hierarchical matrix of the zonal production and reproduction processes. One would suspect that the conditions and impacts of the Dark Age occur in different phases for the core and the periphery/margins, and the simultaneity and synchronicity of these conditions are contingent on the connectivity of the world system at a particular point in time. As human history evolved and with the increasing systemic connectivity between regions and the development of new technologies, these long ecological swings of Culture–Nature relations (Dark Ages) are more systemic and impactful when they occur. Such is the danger we face at this point in world history when the process of globalization has been quite extensive.

The articulations of the connections between and within regions during certain periods of world history reveal further the characteristic of Culture–Nature relations especially those perpetrated by the dominant core for a certain period in time on the periphery of the world system. In this regard, ecological degradative shadows are cast by the dominant core over wide areas of the world system. These shadows thus are a consequent of core–periphery relations beyond those ecologically degradative effects that might be generated by the periphery itself.

Besides these devastating ecological outcomes, climatological changes are also associated with Dark Ages, Climatological changes and natural calamities when they occur during Dark Ages generate further challenges to social system reproduction. Their occurrences and impacts on social systems have been noted during periods of the Dark Ages (Chew, 1999; Keys, 1999; Weiss, 1982, 2000; Weiss and Bradley, 2001). Higher than normal temperatures can generate salinity problems for agricultural cultivation, especially in areas where irrigation is extensively used, and can also lower harvest yields. The aridity that commonly occurs with high temperatures has often generated severe problems for pastoral herds, which have led to nomadic migrations thus causing further pressures on core centers.

Dark Ages, therefore, should be utilized to refer to those periods of systemic socioeconomic collapse characterized by severe ecological stress and losses. They reflect long centuries of exploitative relationship (via accumulation, urbanization, etc.) between Culture and Nature (leading to excessive ecological scarcity and degradation), especially when this historical relationship is coupled with natural calamities (tectonic shifts, volcanic eruptions, etc.) and climatological changes during a specific conjuncture (Chew, 2001a). These are moments of crisis that can even lead to systemic collapse, depending upon the state of the natural environment at that point in time, the cultural willingness and foresight to make changes in lifestyle and social organization, and the level of technology and knowledge available to address the conditions of the ecological crisis. The rarity of such occurrences in the last 5000 years of world history suggests the resilience of ecological landscape against human assault. Besides, it underscores the different time frame for our understanding of the interaction between culture and the natural environment. This must be measured along ecological time compared with political and economic activities, which are necessarily gauged along social time.

Dark Ages, therefore, depict very specific moments in world history when system reproduction is in a state of crisis and/or transition. Resolution of the crisis requires an extended period of time (historically at least 600 years) as the length of occurrence of a specific Dark Age has revealed. Such an expanse of time (ecological time) provides the opportunity for a restoration of the ecological balance so as to enable sustained economic productive capacities. Especially in the case of resource depletion, their is a need for innovation in social organization and technology. If restoration of the ecological balance and related trade networks is not possible then new ecological assets have to be located and/or the replacements of much depleted natural resources need to be adopted. Furthermore, technological innovations could also occur to address the issue of depleted natural resources so that some level of economic production can continue.

Related to the aforementioned developments various social, political, and economic processes come into play during such moments of systemic crisis and/or transition. They range from social upheavals (revolts, wars, etc.) and dislocations (such as migrations), to cultural/

ideological shifts, along with political and social reorganizations, etc. In certain circumstances, resolution of a systemic crisis might not necessarily lead to a system transition. In that case, the crisis is resolved due to restoration of the ecological balance, allowing for social reproduction on the extended scale to occur. Also, the state of the socioeconomic organizations and political hegemonies present show the capacity to meet the contingencies of a restored ecological balance. If, however, these conditions are not in place, a new set of organizing and learning principles are needed in order to meet the contingencies of the transformed terrain generated by the crisis conditions of the Dark Age. In such a context, qualitative changes ensue and a systemic transition occurs.

Hence, Dark Ages are important moments in world history for they provide opportunities for the ecological balance to be restored, political and economic opportunities for some peripheral groups to advance in the zonal power matrix, and for reconfiguration of the hierarchical division of political–economic power of the world system at specific junctures of world history.

DARK AGES OVER WORLD HISTORY
(2200 B.C.–A.D. 900)

Given the current concern over the deteriorating conditions of the environment and the considerable analytical attention given to the impacts and outcomes of contemporary globalization processes, directing our efforts on past periods of ecological stress can provide some sense of the future trajectory of socioeconomic and political processes of the world system. For some, the current globalization process and its impacts have been an ongoing process for at least the last five millennia and cannot be considered a *stage* that is reached in world development (Chew, 2001a; Modelski, 1999; Thompson, 2000). This means that human impact on the environment has had a very long history (Chew, 2001a; Hughes, 2001; Williams, 2000).

To date, social historians and archaeologists have noted of various occasions in world history of periods of long socioeconomic decline commonly termed as Dark Ages. These periods cover centuries, with the very earliest starting during 2200 B.C.–1700 B.C.[2] This downturn was followed by another period 1200 B.C.–700 B.C., and A.D. 300–A.D.

900. The extent of the impact of Dark Age conditions in terms of geographic limits of the world system is difficult to map completely, especially with the limited amount of data available and our understanding of the level of connectivity of the world system. To be sure, as the world system evolves we can see the extent of these trends and tendencies. Rather than being comprehensive in coverage, instead I will identify selectively the simultaneity and connectivity of the different areas of the world system that are impacted by Dark Age conditions. One should also realize that not all regions/zones of the world system are impacted simultaneously during the same time period.

If we perceive Dark Ages as periods of ecological crises—besides being characterized by depressive socioeconomic and political conditions as maintained by anthropologists, historians, and archaeologists—we would expect to find some proxy indicators of ecological degradation, such as deforestation levels, soil erosion, and species endangerment, that would correlate with characteristic features commonly depicted for Dark Ages such as population decreases, trade and economic disruptions, de-urbanization, and political regime changes. Coupled with these anthropogenic and ecological correlations, one would also expect to find climatological changes, such as temperature and rainfall, interacting with the former trends and tendencies.

Ecological degradation levels are outcomes of the expansionary dynamics of the process of accumulation in the world system. With long cycles of economic expansion we would also expect to see extreme signs of ecological degradation, such as deforestation, following these expansionary phases. The scope of degradation is, of course, determined by the connectivity of the world system and by the nature of Core–Periphery relations for the period in question. This means ecological degradation can be quite overarching due to the relations between regions of the world system and the global division of labor existing during that particular period. Coupled with this dynamics of capital accumulation—circumscribing and underlining the pace of ecological degradation—conflicts and wars further exacerbate the ecological degradation levels.

DEFORESTATION

Wood, with its many uses, is an important commodity in the reproduction of social life and the accumulation of capital. Over world history from at least 3000 B.C. onwards, forests have been intensively exploited to meet the needs of an evolving world system starting from such core centers as Mesopotamia and Harappa (Chew, 2001a; Perlin, 1991). As such, deforestation was the order of the day. More than 4500 years ago, we find the Mesopotamians and the Harappans deforesting their own hills and mountains, and conducting military campaigns and trade relations with their peripheries to seek a constant wood supply to reproduce their socioeconomic relations. By no means were the Harappans and Mesopotamians the exceptions. Kristiansen, analyzing early third millennium B.C. pollen profiles of the thy region in northwestern Denmark, has also alerted us to the extreme deforestation caused by extensive land use and animal husbandry practices (Kristiansen, 1998b). In fact, he has extended this deforestation level to most of northwestern Europe for this time sequence.

Such levels of deforestation have led to a social systemic collapses in Mesopotamia, Northwestern India, and Europe, and to realignments of communities and trading arrangements during the first Dark Age period between 2200 B.C.–1700 B.C. (Chew, 2001a; Kristiansen, 1998a). Approximately 500 years later, we find such ecologically degradative practices continuing in the eastern Mediterranean such as in Crete and Mycenaean Greece, and becoming acute during the next Dark Age from 1200 B.C.–700 B.C. The trend of deforestation was perpetuated further, especially during the Roman period (the Dark Age between A.D. 300–A.D. 900), and was followed later by core European powers such as Venice, Spain, Portugal, Holland, France, and England deforesting increasingly on a global basis. By no means was this degradative practice undertaken by only European powers. Deforestation of the landscape was also conducted by Imperial China and other early Southeast Asian polities from A.D. 500 onwards (Chew, 2001a). In the case of China, ecologically degradative shadows were cast over its peripheral areas such as Southeast Asia. This trend of global deforestation continues till our current era. We witness core powers such as Japan and the United States, not only intensively deforesting their own landscapes (in the case of the U.S.), but also certain peripheral areas in Southeast Asia, Latin America, parts of Africa and Russia to meet their own reproductive needs (Chew, 2001a; Dauvergne, 1997; Marchak, 1995; Tucker, 2000; WCFSD, 1999).

The intensity of deforestation seems to peak during long periods of economic expansion, and slow down during long phases of economic contraction as will be outlined later. This pacing parallels the identified periods of economic downturns and system collapses that are defined as Dark Ages of human history. It seems extreme deforestation occurs after a long period of economic expansion and reforestation whenever there is a slowdown in economic activity or a drop in human population in world history. In the long run, however, forest loss has outpaced reforestation. Specifically for southern Germany as indicated later, this has been the case. Since Neolithic times to the contemporary period, we have lost between seven and eight million square kilometers of closed forest and two to three million square kilometers of open woodland and shrub land. Thus, deforestation has a long history (Chew, 2001a; Williams, 2000). For the contemporary period, according to the World Commission on Forests and Sustainable Development (WCFSD), forests have virtually disappeared from around 25 countries, 18 others have lost more than 95 percent of their forests, and 11 around countries have lost 90 percent of their forests. Such losses on the world scale have led to decline in biodiversity and it is estimated that 12.5 percent of the world's 270,000 species of plants and about 75 percent of the world's mammals are threatened by decline in area forest (WCFSD, 1999). The biodiversity crisis is not a new biological phenomenon; it has occurred in the past, such as during the Dark Ages between A.D. 300–A.D. 900 (Chew, 2001a; Hughes, 1994).

Given the aforementioned, the present concerns about deforestation, and its outcomes identified on a global basis by the WCFSD have been enduring issues throughout world history (Chew, 2001a; Perlin, 1991; WCFSD, 1999). The casting of ecological degradative shadows over the whole world system as a consequence of Core–Periphery relations has also been a recurring thematic throughout world history (Chew, 2001a; Dauvergne, 1997). What is important to note is there seems to be cycles of reforestation and deforestation. In short, even at the level of ecology, "we have got rhythm" in the world system, to borrow a phrase from George Modelski (1999: 392). These long, depressive deforestation cycles last for about 500–600 years. For at least one region in southern Germany, preliminary indications of these long ecological cycles of deforestation can be seen of pollen count profiles (3000 B.C.–A.D. 1992) of deforested areas when we find extreme deforestation during the periods of the Dark Ages that have been periodized (see Fig. 1.1 and 1.2).[3]

The aforementioned discussion confirms our thesis that Dark Ages are both periods of ecological as well as socioeconomic stress. Figures

1.1 and 1.2 represent the long-range profiles of pollen count of two separate locations (Lake Constance and Lake Steisslingen) in southern Germany where the trends from the graphs reflect extreme periods of deforestation during the periods 2200 B.C.–1700 B.C.; 1200 B.C.– 700 B.C.; and A.D. 300–A.D. 900. Figure 1.2 further suggests that at least for the Lake Steisslingen region, there seems to be decreasing arboreal pollen over the long-term, and less and less recovery of the forest of this area. It is clear that with human settlement as early as 3000 B.C., deforestation was already there(Jacomet, 1990; Rosch, 1990). Human settlements have caused landscape changes such as deforestation.

For the later period the pollen count decreased between A.D. 300– A.D. 900 as indicated in Figures 1.1 and 1.2. This reduction was most likely the outcome of Roman conquest and occupation of southern Germany prior to A.D. 300 whereby imperial Rome extracted and deforested extensive areas within the Roman empire, and especially those outlying peripheral regions of the empire (Chew, 2001a). In the latter case, it is the outcome of resource extraction to meet core needs, thus engendering what I have termed ecological degradative shadows that are products of Core–Periphery relations in the world system (Chew, 1997, 2001a). Brown (2001) writing about the Dark Ages occurring between A.D. 300–A.D. 900 has noted such deforestation levels in northwestern Europe as a whole. Wary of such high

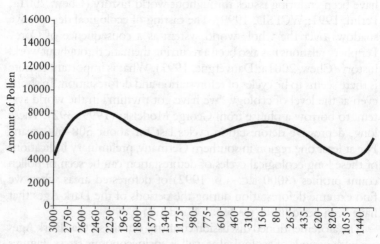

Figure 1.1: Pollen Count (Lake Constance)

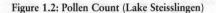
Figure 1.2: Pollen Count (Lake Steisslingen)

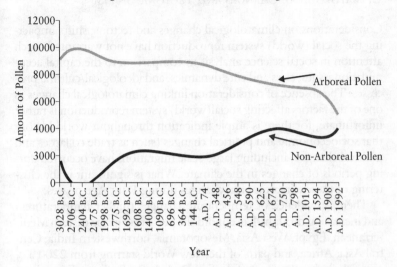

rates of forest loss, he has also speculated about the possibility of climate changes occurring as a result of this large-scale and long-term anthropogenic transformation of the landscape. Throughout world history, there is evidence of these types of degradative relationships. For the contemporary conditions, however, there exists extensive documentation (Chew, 2001a; Dauvergne, 1997; Marchak, 1995; WCFSD, 1999).

With deforestation there are also other consequences such as soil erosion There is ample evidence for as early as 2200 B.C., during the first Dark Ages (2200 B.C.–1700 B.C.) in Meospotamia and Harappa, that soil erosion as a consequence of deforestation had tremendous consequences for the agricultural economies of these early civilizations. It had led to severe economic stress on their social systems and coupled with climatological changes led to social systemic crisis for these civilizations (Chew, 1997, 2001a). Soil erosion was also a condition experienced by Minoan Crete and Mycenaean Greece from 1500 B.C. onwards culminating in their collapse during the Dark Age period 1200 B.C.–700 B.C. The occurrence of soil erosion during the decline of the Roman empire prior to the onset of the Dark Age (A.D. 300–A.D. 900) underlines the recurring nature of widespread soil erosion punctuating Dark Age periods. Even for our contemporary period, we find soil erosion as the order of the day as well (Chew, 1997, 2001a; McNeill, 2000; WCFSD, 1999).

CLIMATOLOGICAL CHANGES AND TECTONIC SHIFTS

Considerations on climatological changes and tectonic shifts impacting the social (world) system reproduction have not warranted much attention in social science analysis in comparison to the capital accumulation issues, class and elite dynamics, and ideological/cultural processes. The absence of consideration linking climatological changes as one of the factors affecting social (world) system reproduction is rather unfortunate, for there is ample indication throughout world history that socioeconomic and political changes (such as trade collapses and political changes) including large-scale migrations have occurred during periods of changes in the climate. What is significant is the clustering of these climatological changes during Dark Age phases.

There is evidence of temperature changes (higher temperatures) and increasing drought-like conditions persisting in the eastern Mediterranean, Egypt, West Asia, Mesopotamia, northwestern India, Central Asia, Africa, and parts of the New World starting from 2200 B.C. onwards during the onset of the first Dark Ages.[4] Such conditions have significant impact on social systems relying on irrigation fed agriculture, and on social and political stability.[5] During this period, besides southern Mesopotamia, we find regional abandonment and selected collapse of social and political systems of Egypt, Assyria, early Greece, Indus, Crete, Russia, and Palestine from 2200 B.C. onwards and another set of upheavals starting around the next Dark Ages from 1200 B.C. (Bell, 1971; Bottema, 1997; Chew, 2001a; Hassan, 1997; Krementski, 1997; Weiss and Bradley, 2001).

For ecological landscapes that are mostly semi-arid such as in southern Mesopotamia, a drop in rainfall would generate severe stress on agricultural production. These changes have been confirmed by evidence of decreased pollen yields, changes in volume of stream flow in the Tigris-Euphrates, dust spikes, and decrease in lake water levels, found in recent years (Weiss and Bradley, 2001). The Dead Sea area reported a 20 to 30 percent drop in precipitation from the earlier fall of 610 mm (Bar-Mathews et al., 1998, 1999; Bar-Mathews and Avalon, 1997). Pollen records from Lake Zeribar in West Asia suggest extreme drought (Bottema, 1997). The Lake Van cores document a dust spike around 2290 B.C.–2000 B.C., a decrease in lake levels and a rapid increase in aridity (Lemcke and Sturm, 1997). The Lake Van proxies provide a climate record for the Tigris-Euphrates headwaters region.

Given such climatological changes during the first Dark Ages between 2200 B.C.–1700 B.C., the agricultural sector in southern Mesopotamia was further stressed as increasing temperatures led to a rise in evapotranspiration. For irrigated agriculture which is the basis of southern Mesopotamian agricultural practices, this would mean a demand for more water. The enhanced application of irrigated water had a deleterious effect on agricultural lands with salinity problems which southern Mesopotamia was experiencing at that point. In northern Mesopotamia, such climatic conditions also impacted on towns such as Tell Brak, and Tell Leilan under Akkadian imperial rule, and shared the same fate as the other urbanized areas in the south (Weiss, 2000). Abandonment of towns and settlements in the Habur plains also followed.

During this period, in northwestern India, tectonic shifts occurred that diverted water courses. In turn, these diversions transformed some rivers into dry river-beds, further exacerbating the aridity, and thus severely impacting on socioeconomic conditions. The drying up of the *Sarasvati* river had tremendous implications for the Harappan urban complexes located on its river banks (Passehl, 2001). Agrawal and Sood (1982) noted tectonic shifts that diverted the course of the river Sutlej and the easterly rivers away from the Ghaggar, which over time died into a lake-like depression during this period. Thus, in northern and western Rajasthan, unstable river systems impacted socioeconomic life. Furthermore, tectonic disturbances also cut-off Lothal from its feeder river and eventually the port's access to the sea.

Temperature increases also impacted Egypt. During the first Dark Ages (2200 B.C.–1700 B.C.), climatological changes led to a reduced flow of the Nile, thus lowering its water levels, and inducing drought conditions that had systemic impact on the overall economy of Egypt and the surrounding lands (Bell, 1971; Hassan, 1997). The annual flooding of the Nile valley provides the rejuvenation of the agricultural landscape. On this basis, lower river levels would mean falling Nile flood levels. Flow in the Nile is a function of the amount of rain that falls on the Ethiopian Highlands, and the precipitation stored in the lakes of Lake Abhe, Lake Zway-Shala, and Lake Turkana. The rainfall on these highlands accounts for over 83 percent of the water of the Nile at Aswan. The seasonality of the rain is dependent on the Indian monsoon which arrives between June to August (Barrey and Chorley, 1992). Therefore, any changes in the monsoon would have had an impact on rainfall that ultimately lowered the flow of the Nile. Around 2200 B.C., a severe reduction in water level in the Lakes Abhe,

Zway-Shala, and Turkana was reported (Gasse, 2000; Johnson and Odade, 1996; Ricketts and Johnson, 1996). This led to a lower Nile flow and level that engendered aridity and drought conditions in Egypt (Bryson and Bryson, 1998; Hassan, 1986, 1997).

There were also reports of the invasion of dune sand in the valley near Memphis suggesting the increasing aridity of the landscape (Bell, 1971; Hassan, 1997). In Middle Egypt, sand dunes also invaded the flood plain. Lack of high floods from the Nile along with the dry climate led to severe pressure on the agricultural system as naturally irrigated areas for crop cultivation shrinked. Famine followed and has been confirmed by the ancient texts of Egypt (Hassan, 1971).

The above climatologically induced conditions led to reduced agricultural production which, in turn, had an impact on the Egyptian economy of the First Intermediate Period (Weiss, 2000). Flood failures occurred between 2180 B.C. and 2135 B.C., and again around 2005 B.C. and 1992 B.C. (Bell, 1975). Signs of famines emerged again around 1750 B.C., though they were not as severe as what occurred in 2200 B.C. (Bell, 1975).

In central Eurasia, preliminary data also confirmed marked changes in vegetation beginning around 2200 B.C. and lasting till around 1700 B.C. following increases in temperature (Heibert, 2000; Krementski, 1997). Pollen cores indicate a sharp decrease in tree pollen and an increase in steppe pollen. From 2200 B.C. to 2000 B.C., there was a severe reduction in forest area and an increase in steppification leading to an expansion in the steppe landscape from 1800 B.C. to 1700 B.C. Arid conditions also affected arable lands which caused severe pressure on animal husbandry of the steppe population. The lush feathergrass steppe that depicted the landscape near Kalmykia from 2500 B.C. to 2200 B.C. gave way to dry scrubby vegetation—wormwood steppe—and even desertification by 2200 B.C. to 1700 B.C. This changed ecological landscape led to outmigration of sedentary population from river valleys with increased time and exploitation of the steppe lands for animal feed.

Such climatological changes, tectonic shifts, and earthquakes recurred again around the next Dark Age from 1200 B.C to 700 B.C. impacting the Aegean with Crete experiencing such shifts as early as 1500 B.C. It has been argued that between 2800 B.C. and A.D. 400, a particularly active tectonic regime was in force in the southern Aegean (Manning, 1994). Such a pattern of geological conditions meant that volcanic eruptions and earthquakes around 1500 B.C. provided some of the circumstances for the demise of Crete (Chadwick, 1976; Marinatos, 1939; Warren, 1985). According to Chadwick, the earthquakes followed volcanic eruption on Thera, precipitated further the delimiting conditions for the Minoans (Chadwick, 1976). The volcanic ash not only killed vegetation but also destroyed the Minoan naval fleet. The loss of the latter undermined the Cretan naval supremacy, which for a long period had provided Minoan Crete the power to exercise its dominant position in this region of the world system.

For Mycenaean Greece, the natural environment by 1200 B.C. was severely stretched. Placed within such a context, the thesis of climatological change proposed by Rhys Carpenter (1968) for the demise of Mycenaean Greece needs to be considered. Basically, Carpenter's position is that with the shift in the tracks of the cyclonic storms that normally bring rain to Mycenaean Greece, a disruption in the rainfall pattern followed for the interior of the Greek mainland. This resulted in drought-like conditions during the 13th and 12th centuries B.C. The persistent drought was also accompanied by an increase in land temperature. As a consequence, the socioeconomic structure was impacted.

For Bryson et al. (1974) during this period (circa 13th century), drought conditions and increase in land temperature were also reported in other parts of the world system. The Anatolian plateau had a precipitation rate of 20–40 percent below normal and the temperature was 2.5–4 degrees centigrade above normal. The precipitation in Libya was 50 percent below normal and temperature was 1.5 degrees centigrade above normal. Finally, Bryson et al. (1974), also noted that settlements in northern Persia were abandoned due to drought. The precipitation was 50 percent below normal and temperature was 1.7–2.5 degrees centigrade above normal.

Besides climatological changes, earthquakes have also been attributed as causal factors for the decline of Mycenaean Greece. Earthquakes at Tiryns, Mycenae, the Argolid during the Late Helladic Period have been suggested for the decline of these two urbanized communities (Mylonas, 1996; Zanggar, 1993).

Similar climatological changes also happened during the Dark Ages that occurred between A.D. 300–A.D. 900. Temperature increases occurred in Europe, West Asia, China, and parts of the Americas (Broecker, 2001; Bryson and Padoch, 1980; DeMenocal, 2001; Weiss and Bradley, 2001). In fact, Broecker has suggested that this warming trend was a global phenomenon and lasted until A.D. 1200 (Broecker, 2001). Analysis of tree rings suggests such climatological shifts in

LIVERPOOL JOHN MOORES UNIVERSITY
LEARNING & INFORMATION SERVICES

Sweden as well.[7] Tree ring evidence from western Europe, Britain, and North America also revealed the drought-like conditions and slowed growth (Keys, 1999). This warming trend resulted in drought-like conditions being felt in the above geographic areas leading to some widespread famine, for example, in northern China and Korea around A.D. 530. Besides the socioeconomic tragedies experienced eg., trade route disruption, diseases, etc., political collapse of the classic Mayan culture and the Moche civilization of northern Peru also occurred. Some scholars have suggested that climatological changes might also be a contributing factor besides others such as overpopulation, deforestation, soil erosion, social warfare, etc., (Davis and Shaw, 2001; Weiss and Bradley, 2001).

In all, what I am suggesting is that during periods of so-called Dark Ages of world history, besides tremendous ecological damage—a consequence of a prior prolonged period of intensive and extensive socioeconomic expansion and concentration—it seems that climatological changes also were the order of the day. The latter, depending on the ecological landscape, impacted the reproduction of socioeconomic life. Mapping such interactions between climate changes, regime transition, and center–hinterland conflict provides insights into global transformations. Preliminary analyses such as those of Thompson and Chew have suggested a correlation between climate change and political–economic transitions for the period starting 2200 B.C. onwards for Egypt, Mesopotamia, and the Near East (Chew, 2002; Thompson, 2000). These preliminary studies show that interactions between climate changes, environmental deterioration, and socioeconomic and political transformations are a promising area of research.

SOCIOECONOMIC AND POLITICAL TRANSFORMATIONS DURING DARK AGES

As discussed in the previous sections, socioeconomic and political trends and patterns during the Dark Ages are reversals of what occur during the expansionary period. We note some general trends such as a fall in population levels for some areas, especially for highly urbanized communities. A decline or losses in certain material skills, decay in the cultural aspects of life, fall in living standards and thus wealth, political instability, loss of trading contacts and trade network collapses, and deurbanization, are other such trends.

If we examine the first identified Dark Age period (2200 B.C.–1700 B.C.) and its outcomes, political instability was one feature that highlighted political–economic events. In Egypt, the climatological changes during this period led to famines, and also brought about the dissipation of central authority. Drought conditions and lowered Nile flooding impacted the farmers' ability to pay taxes adversely. This resulted in poor revenue collection and distribution, leading to a decrease in the king's ability to deal with drought and famine or to pay for his army. As a result, the stability of the political regime was affected. The sum effects of this, in the realm of political stability as Bell has concluded, were shorter reigns (Bell, 1971). For example, between 2190 B.C.–2130 B.C., there were about 31 to 40 kings who came and went. Hassan (1997) covering a slightly different period, 2180 B.C.–2134 B.C., reported that around 18 pharaohs reigned in this short span. The collapse of the central monarchy of the old Kingdom around 2180 B.C. occurred within such dynamics.[8] Later in the period around 1700 B.C., short reigns also predominate (Bell, 1975). For example, between 1768 B.C. to 1740 B.C., there were 18 kings.

Political instability was also evident in the next Dark Age period between 1200 B.C.–700 B.C. Bell (1971) and Braudel (2001), for example, have noted that a second Dark Age began, around 1200 B.C., which was marked by the disappearance of the Hittite Empire of Anatolia, the end of Minoan Crete, and Mycenaean Greece, the decline of Egypt (Third Intermediary Period) and its empire with Babylonia and Assyria in decline around 1100 B.C.–1000 B.C. Collapse was widespread throughout the region.

During the third millennium Dark Age of 2200 B.C. Egypt witnessed, besides political instability, artistic degeneration and other reversals also occurred such as artistic degeneration and the scale of monumental building declined monument-building due to diminishing resources. The size and elaborateness of the pharaonic tombs decreased; the tombs of the kings became one chambered affairs with less ambitious layouts (Bovarski, 1998). Greece also encountered such similar trends in the later Dark Age period between 1200 B.C. to 700 B.C.: decline or loss in certain material skills, decay in the cultural aspects of life, fall in living standards and thus wealth, and loss of internal/external trading contacts (Snodgrass, 1971). For Greece, the archaeological evidence suggests socioeconomic patterns that are distinctively different from the style and level of sociocultural life prevailing prior to the onset of the Dark Age. The architecture and design of dwellings, and pottery and other objects recovered from excavated sites reflect ecological stress and scarcity of natural resources.

The above mentioned conditions directly affected sociocultural life in Greece during this Dark Age phase (1200 B.C.–700 B.C.). Pottery styles of this period were austere, unlike the decadent style of the prior era. The bulk of a pot was usually left plain in the natural color of the clay and the decorations covered at most a third of the surface area. The lack of intense firing suggests the scarcity of wood supplies as well. As recovery proceeds and the ecological balance is restored, we find the plain, rectilinear or curvilinear patterns in pottery designs giving way to images depicting animals and humans. These shifts indicate the loss and consequent gain in biodiversity during the onset of the Dark Ages.

Apart from pottery styles, there are remains which indicate a scarcity of natural resources, especially of metals. The use of obsidian and bones for blades and weapons underscores such scarcity, and suggests that trading routes and centers for sourcing the metals might have been disrupted or disappeared.

Ecological scarcity required a downscaling of material and cultural lifestyles. A reorganization of life along modest and rational lines is reflected in burial practices. The design of clothing and shoes were of the plainest kind. The downscaling of the civilization is exhibited further in the formation of decentralized communities and associated population losses. Whether this lifestyle trend is one that was actively sought as a consequence of ecological scarcity or occurred as an outcome of the depressive conditions of the Dark Age is difficult to gauge. What we are sure of is that as recovery proceeded—we begin to witness this by the mid-half of the 10th century B.C.—trading networks were re-established and communities were revived. Such an upswing was characterized by exuberance, materialistic consumption and accumulation. For during the Dark Age, material consumption declined, and most of the trading networks disappeared or were restricted only to the area of the Aegean Sea.

In the Mediterranean region extreme degradation of the ecological landscape precipitated socioeconomic and organizational changes in order to meet the resource scarcity, and also to reproduce some semblance of cultural and economic life of prior times. As a consequence, systemic reorganization occurred at various levels, from the way commodities are produced to clothing, fashions, and designs. Hierarchical social structures disappeared during the Dark Age as evident by burial practices, and were restored when recovery proceeded (Whitley, 1991). In Central and Eastern Europe, we also witness similar collapses of social hierarchy with communal burials replacing chiefly burials from 1250 B.C.–750 B.C. (Kristiansen, 1998a).

Another feature of the Dark Ages, the process of deurbanization, was witnessed during the first Dark Age period (2200 B.C–1700 B.C.). Cholistan in northwestern India experienced a drop in size in terms of settled areas from an average of 6.5 hectares in 3800 B.C.–3200 B.C. to 5.1 hectares by 1900 B.C.–1700 B.C., and finally to almost 50 percent less (2.6 hectares) by 1000 B.C. (Possehl, 2001). Elsewhere for the time period of 2200 B.C., similar signs of deteriorating conditions were also encountered in Anatolia with the abandonment of urban centers such as Troy II to Troy III-IV (Mellink, 1986; Wilkinson, 1990). Consequently, depopulation also resulted. Sedentary population settlements on the Anatolian plateau were also abandoned. To the west of Anatolia, Palestine also suffered from such crisis conditions. Walled towns were replaced by unwalled villages. There were signs of cave occupations and migratory movements. In some areas, settlements completely disappeared, and remaining settlement sites were reduced by more than half of what existed before 2200 B.C. (Harrison, 1997).

Across the Mediterranean from Palestine, the Aegean also experienced distress though not as sincerely. Between 2300 B.C.–1900 B.C., there was a loss of sedentary population. In central Eurasia also the case was similar. The changed ecological landscape led to outmigration of sedentary population from river valleys, leading to prolonged and increased exploitation of the steppe lands for animal feed. Denucleation occurred with establishment of smaller communities near oases. This spread occurred in Central Asia at Khorezm (south of the Aral Sea) and Margiana (Murghab delta) in Turkmenistan, Bactria, and western China. This process prompted by ecological degradation and environmental changes also occurred in Syria, Palestine, and Jordan. Outmigration from urban centers located on the coast to the interiors and establishment of smaller village type settlements resulted from these developments (McGovern, 1983).

On mainland Greece and Crete, this deurbanization process was repeated during the next Dark Ages from 1200 B.C. giving rise to small communities with lower population levels (Jameson et al, 1994; Watrous, 1994). Seen from the ecological point of view, this downscaling provided the necessary timing for ecological balance to be restored, and socioeconomic life to start afresh. In the case of Greece, from these small communities the Greek polis came to life and resulted in a flourish of political and economic life as soon as the social system recovered (Snodgrass, 1971). To this extent, the stressed ecological conditions that engendered deurbanization and the formation of small communities precipitated the rise of the polis and the Greek city states. We, therefore, need to realize that sometimes even scarcity of resources can have productive outcomes, which might not have occurred in bountiful conditions. The fact that the Dark Age lasted for over 500 years underscores the great extent of time required for ecological recovery and the immensity of the degradation that took place. What followed in the recovery phase, however, was a Dark Age-conditioned sociocultural and political lifestyle that formed the basis of western civilization as we know it today.

Beyond the core areas of the eastern Mediterranean littoral, the periphery of the system such as Central, Eastern, and Northern Europe had a different rhythm vis-a-vis economic expansion. Unlike the Near East, the Dark Ages from 1200 B.C. to 700 B.C. was a period of population increase, settlement expansion, agrarian intensification, and reorientation of trade and exchange for these regions (Chew, 2001a; Kristiansen, 1998a). With the collapse of the Near Eastern Mediterranean trade-networks, metal production boomed in Central and Eastern Europe, and the east–west exchange connection was strengthened, thus establishing a regional system (Urnfield) of trade exchanges and production. Regional system crisis emerged much later around 750 B.C., following centuries of intensive resource extraction, land exhaustion, and climatological changes when the climate became cooler and moister. Such differences in economic trajectories between the regions suggest that at this point in time (in terms of world system development) the synchronicity of relations and processes is not as linked to the extent that crisis in the core was felt throughout the periphery. Despite the lack of synchronicity, systemic change continued to occur. As we have stated above, for Central and Eastern Europe, regional system changes occurred at a later time after 1200 B.C., around 750 B.C., following centuries of landscape degradation.

Beyond this region, at the level of the world system, George Modelski and Bill Thompson have drawn some trends on urbanization and population levels since 4000 B.C. that complement the tendencies that we have identified for the Dark Ages (Modelski, 1999; Modelski and Thompson, 2001). Colin and Sarah McEvedy have also reported of slow population growth for the second Dark Age period

starting around A.D. 300–A.D. 1000, when growth of the global population was about only 15 percent in comparison to the prior period
which was about 100 percent (McEvedy and McEvedy, 1972). Returning to Modelski's data, what is fascinating about his periods of
dispersal (2300 B.C.–1200 B.C.; 100 B.C.–A.D. 980; and A.D. 1850/
1900–?) coincide fairly closely with the beginning of the Dark Ages
periods that world history has experienced and is/could be experiencing (Modelski and Thompson's third phase of dispersal starting about
A.D. 1850/1900—the latest phase—will be discussed in the next section of this chapter). For Modelski and Thompson, these periods of
dispersal follow periods of concentration which are phases of growth
of economic and political expansion. In this regard, my proposals on
the phases and nature of Dark Ages dovetail with their phases of dispersal. In addition, these phases of dispersal for Modelski and Thompson were also accompanied by large-scale migrations and hinterland incursions into the core zone (Modelski and Thompson, 1999).
Deteriorating environmental conditions and climatological changes
have been proposed as explanations for these movements and war-
ring activities (Brown, 2001; Modelski and Thompson, 2001). Besides the above, system-wide trade collapses during phases of dispersal
or Dark Ages has also been reported by Thompson for the first Dark
Age period, similar to what I have reported for Greece, the eastern
Mediterranean, and from southern Mesopotamia via the Persian Gulf
to the Indus (Chew, 2001a; Thompson, 2001).

THE COMING OF THE NEXT DARK AGE

From these preliminary investigations of long-term world system dynamics, there is indication that there is a long-term rhythm in the
world system. If such is the case, we need to further explore these
rhythmic motions that are long-term and large-scale. The recurring
nature of these Dark Ages over world history does suggest certain
tendencies that we might wish to consider in light of the ecological
crisis we face today. The indicators of ecological stress and the climatological changes do suggest that we might be approaching another
Dark Age, if we are not in it already.

We know about the changes that occurred in the ecological, socioeconomic, and political landscapes during past Dark Ages. The deforestation levels reach extreme levels as a consequence of the previous

phase of incessant growth of the world system. We are witnessing similar deforestation levels today. The WCFSD has warned against the ferocity of global deforestation and other organizations also have voiced similar concerns about the rate of deforestatoin (Chew, 2001a; Marchak, 1995; Tucker, 2000; WCFSD, 1999). Soil erosion, flooding, and endangering of species are often outcomes of deforestation and have occurred often in the past Dark Ages. The same are being signaled by scientists and environmentalists as dangers we are facing and will probably face in worse forms in the foreseeable future. Grimes (1999) and McNeill (2000) have documented various environmental degradative impacts of intensive and extensive resource extraction on atmospheric pollution on world scale for the contemporary period. McNeill (2000) maintains that atmospheric pollution that occurred as early as the end of the 1st Greek Dark Age, 2nd Roman Dark Age, and the medieval period—encountered as far away as Greenland (Hong et al., 1994).

According to the recent report on climatological changes by the Intergovernmental Panel on Climate Change (IPCC) and the United Nations Environment Programme (UNEP), anthropogenic induced climate change in terms of global temperature increases are expected for this decade and beyond. Such increases will have significant impact on socioeconomic life and water supply (IPCC, 2001; UNEP, 2002). Similar climate changes have been reported during earlier Dark Ages also, and we have noted the impact these changes have had for socio-economic and political landscape of the world system. In the *World Disasters Report* (1999) by the International Federation of Red Cross and Red Crescent, it was suggested that global warming and climate changes may have been responsible for the harsher natural disasters and flooding that we have been experiencing. The contemporary changes in temperature of the oceans (El Nino and La Nina phenomena), had also occurred in the past, and caused severe hardships for the communities inhabiting the bordering areas of the Pacific Ocean of the Americas (Fagan, 1999). Droughts triggered by El Nino have caused huge forest fires in Brazil and Peru. Besides the El Nino effects, for example, in 1998: typhoons and floods killed 500 and affected five million in the Philippines; floods killed 4,150 and affected 180 million people in China; killed 400 and affected 200,000 in Korea; killed 1,000 and affected 25,000 in Pakistan; killed 1,400 and affected almost 340,000 in India. Monsoons killed 1,300 and affected 31 million in Bangladesh, and killed 3,250 and affected 36 million in northern

India and Nepal. Two hurricanes killed a total of 14,000 persons and affected about seven million persons in the Caribbean and Central America. Economic costs alone are staggering. Losses were around $16 billion in Central America and the Caribbean; $2.5 billion in Argentina; $868 million in Korea; $223 million in Bangladesh; and $150 million in Romania.

Such contemporary ecological patterns tend to reflect the trends and tendencies of previous Dark Ages in terms of ecological degradation and climatological changes. In terms of the length of occurrence of Dark Ages, it seems that Dark Ages last for at least half-a-millennium.[9] In view of the above current trends in terms of climatological changes, biodiversity crisis, soil erosion, and deforestation levels perhaps we are heading into another Dark Age period. Table 1.1 is a tentative sketch of previous Dark Ages in terms of their length of occurrence.

Table 1.1: Tentative Periodization of Dark Ages

Dark Age A:	2200 B.C.–1700 B.C.
Dark Age B:	1200 B.C.–700 B.C.
Dark Age C:	A.D. 400/500–A.D. 900/1000
Dark Age D:	A.D. 1900/2000–?

My periodization of Dark Ages or ecological crisis is similar to the demarcation by Modelski and Thompson (2001). They have identified phases of concentration of the world economy in terms of economic expansion, population growth, and urbanization, etc., followed by phases of dispersion. Trade collapses, deurbanization, and fall in population levels characterize these phases. Furthermore, Modelski has also noted a phase of dispersal (deurbanization, trade collapses, etc.) in the modern era starting from A.D. 1850–1900, which is commensurate with the Dark Age D mentioned in Table 1.1 (Modelski, 1999).

This is just a preliminary attempt on my part to look for some ecological rhythm in the world system. We need to examine further these trends and tendencies using a more intensive examination of pollen profiles across time and space, and also careful scrutiny of the extent of Dark Age conditions across the zones of the world system in terms of systemic impact accompanied with a more precise periodization of these phases of ecological degradation.

A pertinent question is: what is the future of the world system, using the "Dark Age" framework, to understand the possible trajectory of global transformations and ecological recovery? If the past is any guide, the system will recover. Ecocentrically, Dark Ages should, in fact, be appreciated, for they are periods when the ecological balance is restored. We need, however, to note that the long duration for recovery, at least 500 years, indicates the immensity of the degradation that occurred in the previous Dark Ages. There is no reason to believe that under the current circumstances the length of the phase will be like the previous phases. In the previous Dark Age period, the world system was not as globalized and encompassing, and the system could expand in terms of search for natural resources and labor, thereby enabling previously degraded and exploited areas to recover. At this stage of the globalization process, our planet is fully encompassed. So, in case of an ecological collapse, there will be little leeway for the system to expand. Besides this, the level of connectivity of the world system in terms of production and reproduction processes is unprecedented today. This means that the collapse will be felt globally, unlike previous Dark Ages, whereby not all the peripheral areas were impacted by the collapse. What this leads to is that recovery will be much longer and that we will encounter an ecological landscape that is quite different from the one prior to collapse. The prior Dark Ages have also led to social, economic, and political changes.

The recurring nature of Dark Ages is troubling. It seems that over the course of world history, human communities continue to repeat the materialistic practices of the past, and thus engender ecological degradative outcomes. Coupled with these circumstances we find, over world history, movements to protect/conserve nature along with attempts at recycling (Chew, 2001a). The current efforts to protect the environment need to be considered in view of these long-term dynamics of a historical system with its set of repetitive socioenvironmental practices. To this extent, what impact do such current environmental actions play in light of the dynamics and structures of the historical system. The impact of such activities do reduce and temper the intensity of our degradative impact on nature, and as well, might help to reduce the length of a Dark Age period should it occur.

From a social evolutionary point of view and in view of the current state of globalization, should a Dark Age occur again, it might mean a transformation involving systemic changes that might not be viewed as progressive from a modernist point of view, i.e., unceasing accumulation and growth. We will probably encounter a sociocultural and political lifestyle reconfiguration conditioned by a Dark Age. Ecological sustainability might then become the basis of organization, not by choice but by necessity. If this is the case, production and exchange will need to be guided by entirely different rules, and possibly via "use value" instead of "exchange value". As a result, we might see a sociopolitical order quite different from the past. If this is the case, perhaps, this is the system transition that scholars have all been debating about over the years. In this sense, Dark Ages are interesting moments in world history!

NOTES

1. Revised version of paper presented to Plenary Panel, Conference on Globalization and the Environment: Prospects and Perils, American Sociological Association Annual Meetings, August 17, 2001, Anaheim, CA and published in *Global Society*, vol. 16, no. 4, 2002.
2. The dating of this first occurrence is based on the first crisis period of the Bronze Age world system that witnessed severe downturns in Egypt, Mesopotamia, West Asia, and the eastern parts of the Mediterranean.
3. Many thanks to Dan Sarabia, Oklahoma State University, for plotting Figure 1.2 and analytical support. Dr Matthias Gross, University of Bielefeld, also assisted in the analysis and interpretation. Thanks also to Dr J. Lechterbeck, Institut und Museum für Geologie und Paläontlogie, for the data for Figure 1.2, and Dr Manfred Rosch, Landesdenkmalamt Baden-Wurttemberg for Figure 1.1. See also, Rosch, 1990, 1996, and 1998.
4. By no means are these climate changes anthropogenic in origin (Weiss, 2000). The causes for these global climatic changes around 2200 B.C. of which West Asia is a subset, have been attributed to alterations in solar radiation, thermohaline alterations, or ocean tidal cycles with periodicities ranging from 1800 to 500 years. See, for example, Bentaleb. et al., 1997; Chew, 2001a; Enzel et al., 1999; Neumann and Parpola, 1987; Ratnagar, 1981; Weiss and Bradley, 2001.
5. For example, it has been estimated that a mere 1 degree centigrade rise may reduce annual rainfall by 30 millimeters in the Near East (Neumann and Parpola, 1987).
6. Wright (1968), Chadwick (1976), and Drews (1993) however, have challenged this thesis of climatological change affecting the socioeconomic structure of Mycenaean Greece in the later second millennium. Notwithstanding this, others such as Braudel (2001), Bryson et al. (1974), and Bryson and Padoch (1980), have indicated that the period of drought proposed by Carpenter (1968) appears to have prevailed during the time of Mycenaean decline, according to precipitation patterns examined.
7. I wish to thank Professor Bjorn Berglund, Department of Quaternary Geology, Lund University, Lund, Sweden for providing me with the dendroclimate charts.
8. Butzer (1997) has challenged this thesis that lowered Nile floods induced a demise of the Old Kingdom. Rather for Butzer (1997), the Old Kingdom collapse was a consequence of decentralization, dynastic weakness, a shift of wealth and power to several provincial centers during Dynasty six, the loss of royal power anchored in part on the trade monopoly with Syria being undercut by the Akkadian conquest of Byblos, and civil wars, etc.

9. By no means are all the Dark Ages identified. A new world Dark Age is supposed to have occurred between A.D. 1150 to A.D. 1300.

REFERENCES

Agrawal, D. P. and Sood, R. K. 1982. "Ecological Factors and the Harappan Civilization" in G. Possehl (ed.). *Harappan Civilization: A Contemporary Perspective*. New Delhi: Oxford University Press.

Bar-Mathews, M. and Avalon, A. 1997. "Late Quaternary Paleoclimate in the Eastern Mediterranean Region from Stable Isotope Analysis of Speleothems at Soreq Cave, Israel" in *Quaternary Research*, vol. 47, pp. 155–68.

Bar-Mathews, M. et al. 1998. "Middle to Late Holocene Paleoclimate in the Eastern Mediterranean Region" in A.S. Issar and N. Brown (eds). *Water, Environment and Society in Times of Climate Change*. Amsterdam: Kluwer.

———. 1999. "The Eastern Mediterranean Paleoclimate as a Reflection of Regional Events; Soreq Cave, Israel" in *Earth and Planetary Science Letters*, vol. 166, pp. 85–95.

Barry, R. and Chorley, R. 1992. *Atmosphere, Weather, and Climate*. New York: Routledge.

Bell, Barbara. 1971. "The Dark Ages in Ancient History I: The First Dark Age in Egypt" in *American Journal of Archaeology*, vol. 75, pp. 1–20.

———. 1975. "Climate and History of Egypt" in *American Journal of Archaeology*, vol. 79, pp. 223–79.

Bentaleb, I. et al. 1997. "Monsoon Regime Variations During the Late Holocene in Southwestern India" in H. Dalfes and G. Kukla (eds). *In Third Millennium* B.C. *Climate Change and Collapse*. Berlin: Springer Verlag.

Bintliff, J.J. 1982. "Climate Change, Archaeology and Quaternary Science in the Eastern Mediterranean Region" in A.F. Harding (ed.). *Climate Change in Later Prehistory*. Edinburgh: Edinburgh University Press.

Bottema, Sytze. 1997. "Third Millennium Climate in the Near East Based Upon Pollen Evidence" in H. Dalfes et al. (eds). *Third Millennium BC Climate Change and Old World Collapse*. Heidelberg: Springer Verlag.

Bovarski, Edward. 1998. "First Intermediate Period Private Tombs" in K. Bard (ed.). *Encyclopedia of Ancient Egypt*. New York: Routledge.

Braudel, Fernand. 2001. *Memory and the Mediterranean*. New York: Alfred Knopf.

Broecker, Walter S. 2001. "Was the Medieval Warm Period Global" in *Science*, vol. 291, February 23, pp. 1497–99.

Brown, Neville. 2001. *History and Climate Change*. London: Routledge.

Bryson, R.A. and Padoch, C. 1980. "On the Climate of History" in *Journal of Interdisciplinary History*, vol. 10, no. 4, pp. 583–97.

Bryson, R.A., H.H. Lamb and David L. Donley. 1974. "Drought and the Decline of Mycenae" in *Antiquity*, vol. XLVIII, no. 189. pp. 46–50.

Bryson, Robert and Reid Bryson. 1998. "Application of a Global Volcanicity Time Series on High Resolution Paleoclimatic Modeling of the Eastern Mediterranean" in A. Issar and N. Brown (ed.). *Water, Environment and Society in Times of Change*. Netherlands: Dordrecht.

Butzer, Karl W. 1997. *Sociopolitical Discontinuity in the Near East c. 2200 B.C.E.: Scenarios from Palestine and Egypt.* Berlin: J. Springler.

Carpenter, Rhys. 1968. *Discontinuity in Greek Civilization.* Cambridge: Cambridge University Press.

Chadwick, J. 1976. *The Mycenaean World.* New York: Cambridge University Press.

Chew, Sing C. 1997. "Accumulation, Deforestation, and World Ecological Degradation: 2500 B.C. to A.D. 1990" in *Advances in Human Ecology,* vol: 1. Westport CT.: Jai Press.

_____. 1999. "Ecological Relations and the Decline of Civilizations in the Bronze Age World System: Mesopotamia and Harappa: 2500 B.C.–1700 B.C." in W. Goldfrank, et al. *Ecology and the World System.* Greenwich CT: Greenwood Press.

_____. 2001a. *World Ecological Degradation: Accumulation, Urbanization, and Deforestation.* Lanham, MD: AltaMira Press/Rowman and Littlefield Publishers.

_____. 2001b. "Ecology in Command" in Sing C. Chew and David Knottnerus (eds). *Structure, Culture and History: Recent Issues in Social Theory.* Lanham, MD: Rowman and Littlefield.

_____. 2002. "From Harappa to Mesopotamia and Egypt to Mycenae: Dark Ages, Political-Economic Declines, and Environmental/Climatic Changes," paper presented at the Conference on Political Economy of World Systems, University of California, Riverside, May 3, 2002.

Childe, Gordon. 1942. *What Happened in History.* Harmondsworth: Penguin.

Dauvergne, Peter. 1997. *Shadows in the Forest: Japan and the Politics of Timber in Southeast Asia.* Cambridge, Mass.: MIT Press.

Davis, M. and Shaw, R. 2001. "Range Shifts and Adaptive Responses to Quaternary Climate Change" in *Science,* vol. 292, April 27, pp. 667–73.

DeMenocal, Peter B. 2001. "Cultural Response to Climate Change During the Late Holocene" in *Science,* vol. 292, April 27, pp. 667–72.

Desborough, V. R. 1972. *The Greek Dark Ages.* London: Ernest Benn.

Drews, Robert. 1993. *The End of the Bronze Age: Changes in Warfare and Catastrophe c. 1200 B.C.* New Jersey: Princeton University Press.

Enzel, Y. et al. 1999. "High Resolution Holocene Environmental Changes in the Thar Desert, Northwestern India" in *Science,* vol. 284, pp. 125–28.

Fagan, Brian. 1999. *Floods, Famines, and Emperors El Nino and the Fate of Civilizations.* New York: Basic Books.

Frank, Andre Gunder. 1993. "Bronze Age World System Cycles" in *Current Anthropology,* vol. 34, no. 4, pp. 383–429.

Gasse, F. 2000. "Hydrological Changes in the African Tropics Since the Last Glacial Maximum" in *Quaternary Science Review,* vol. 19, pp. 189–212.

Grimes, Peter. 1999. "The Horsemen and the Killing Fields: The Final Contradiction of Capitalism" in Walter Goldfrank (ed.) *Ecology and the World-System.* Westport, CT: Greenwood Press.

Harrison, Timothy. 1997. "Shifting Patterns of Settlement in the Highlands of Central Jordan During the Early Bronze Age" in *Bulletin of the American School of Oriental Research,* vol. 306, pp. 1–38.

Hassan, Fekri. 1986. "Holocene Lakes and Prehistoric Settlements of the Western Fayum" in *Journal of Archaeological Science,* vol. 13, pp. 483–501.

_____. 1997. "Nile Floods and Political Disorder in Early Egypt" in H. Dalfes et al. (eds). *Third Millennium BC Climate Change and Old World Collapse.* Heidelberg: Springer Verlag.

Hiebert, Fredrik. 2000. "Bronze Age Central Eurasian Cultures in their Steppe and Desert Environments" in G. Bawden and R. Reycraft (eds). *Environmental Disaster and the Archaeology of Human Response.* Albuquerque: University of New Mexico Press.

Hong S., Jean-Pierre Candolone, Clair C. Patterson, Claude F. Boutron. 1994. "Greenland Ice Evidence of Hemispheric Lead Pollution Two Millennia Ago by Greeks and Romans" in *Science,* vol. 265, pp. 1841–43.

Hughes, Donald. 1994. *Pans Travail.* Baltimore: Johns Hopkins University Press.

_____. **2001.** *Environmental History of the World.* London: Routledge.

IPCC (Intergovernmental Panel on Climate Change). 2001. *Climate Change 2001: Impacts, Adaptation, and Vulnerability,* Sixth Session, Geneva 2001.

Jacomet, Stefanie. 1990. "Verandarungen von Wirstschaff und Umwelt Wahrend des Spatneolithikums in Westlichen Bodenseegebieles" in Andre Bilamboz et al. (eds). Siedlungsar Chaologie im Alpenvorland II. Stuttgard: Konrad Theiss.

Jameson, Michael et al. 1994. *A Greek Countryside: The Southern Argolid from Prehistory to the Present Day.* Stanford: Stanford University Press.

Johnson, T. C. and Odade, E.O. (eds). 1996. *The Liminology, Climatology, and Paleoclimatology of the East African Lakes.* New York: Gordon and Breach.

Keys, David. 1999. *Catastrophe.* New York: Ballantyne Books.

Krementski, Constantin. 1997. "The Late Holocene Environmental and Climate Shift in Russia and Surrounding Lands" in H. Dalfes et al. (eds). *Third Millennium B.C. Climate Change and Old World Collapse.* Heidelberg: Springer Verlag.

Kristiansen, Kristian. 1993. *The Emergence of the European World System in the Bronze Age: Divergence, Convergence, and Social Evolution During the First and Second Millennia B.C. in Europe.* Sheffield Archaeological Monographs, no. 6.

_____. **1998a.** *Europe before History.* Cambridge: Cambridge University Press.

_____. **1998b.** "The Construction of a Bronze Age Landscape, Cosmology, Economy, and Social Organization in Thy, Northwestern Jutland" in Bernhard Hansel (ed.). *Mensch und Umwelt in der Bronzezeit Europas.* Kiel: Oetker-Voges Verlag.

Lemcke, G. and Sturm, M. 1997. "Trace Element Measurement as Proxy for the Reconstruction of Climatic Changes at Lake Van" in H. Dalfes et al. (eds). *Third Millennium B.C. Climate Change and Old World Collapse.* Heidelberg.: Springer Verlag.

Manning, Sturt W. 1994. "The Emergence of Divergence: Development and Decline in Bronze Age Crete and the Cyclades" in C. Mathers and S. Stoddatm (eds). *Development and Decline in the Mediterranean Bronze Age.* Sheffield: J.R. Collins.

Marchak, Pat. 1995. *Logging the Globe.* Vancouver: University of British Columbia Press.

Marinatos, S. 1939. "The Volcanic Eruption of Minoan Crete" in *Antiquity,* vol. 13, pp. 425–39.

McEvedy, Colin and Sarah McEvedy. 1972. *The Atlas of World History: The Dark Ages.* New York: Macmillan.

McGovern, P. 1983. "Central TransJordan in Late Bronze Age and Early Iron Ages: An Alternative Hypothesis of SocioEconomic Collapse" in A. Hadidi (ed.). *Studies in the History and Archaeology of Jordan.* London: Routledge and Kegan Paul.

McNeill, John. 2000. *Something New Under the Sun: An Environmental History in the Twentieth Century.* New York: W. W. Norton.

Mellink, Machfeld. 1986. "The Early Bronze Age in Western Anatolia: Aegean and Asiatic Correlations" in G. Cadogan (ed.). *End of the Early Bronze Age in the Aegean.* Leiden: Brill.

Modelski, George. 1999. "Ancient World Cities 4000-1000B.C.: Center/Hinterland in the World System" in *Global Society*, vol. 13, no. 4, pp. 383–92.

Modelski, George and Thompson, William. 1996. *Leading Sectors and World Powers*. Columbia: University of South Carolina Press.

_____. 1999. "The Evolutionary Pulse of the World System: Hinterland Incursion and Migrations: 4000 B.C. to A.D. 1500" in Nick Kardulias (ed.). *World System Theory in Practice*. Lanham, MD: Rowman and Littlefield.

_____. 2001. "Evolutionary Pulsations in the World System" in Sing C. Chew and David Knottnerus (eds). *Structure, Culture, and History*. Lanham, MD: Rowman and Littlefield.

Mylonas, George. 1996. *Mycenae and the Mycenaean Age*. Princeton: Princeton University press.

Neumann, J. and Parpola, S. 1987. "Climatic Change and 11–10th Century Eclipse of Assyria and Babylonia" in *Journal of Near Eastern Studies*, vol. 46, pp.161–82.

Perlin, John. 1991. *A Forest Journey: The Role of Wood in the Development of Civilization*. Cambridge, Mass.: Harvard University Press.

Possehl, Gregory. 2001. "The Drying Up of the Saravati" in G. Bawden and R. Reycraft (eds). *Environmental Disaster and the Archaeology of Human Response*. Albuquerque: University of New Mexico Press.

Ratnagar, Shereen. 1981. *Encounters: The Westerly Trade of the Harappan Civilization*. New Delhi: Oxford University Press.

Renfrew, Colin. 1979. *The Emergence of Civilization*. London: Collins.

Ricketts, R.C. and Johnson, T.C. 1996. "Climate Change in the Turkana Basin as Deduced from a 4000 Year Long Record" in *Earth and Planetary Science Letters*, vol. 142, pp. 7–17.

Rosch, Manfred. 1990. "Vegetationsgechichtliche Untersuchungen im Durchenbergried" in Andre Billamboz et al. (eds). *Siedlungsarchaologie im Alpenvorland II*. Stuttgart: Konrad Theiss.

_____. 1996. "New Approaches to Prehistoric Land-Use: Reconstruction in Southwestern Germany" in *Vegetation History and Archaeobotany*, vol. 5 no. 1, 2, pp. 45–57.

_____. 1998. "The History of Crops and Crop Weeds in Southwestern Germany from the Neolithic Period to Modern Times as shown by Archaeological Evidence" in *Vegetation History and Archaeobotany*, vol. 7, no. 2, pp. 65–78.

Shaffer, J. 1982. "Harappan Culture: A Reconsideration" in G. Possehl (ed.). *Harappan Civilization*. New Delhi: Oxford University Press.

Sheratt, Andrew. 1993. "What Would a Bronze Age World System Look Like? Relations between Temperate Europe and the Mediterranean in Later Prehistory" in *Journal of European Archaeology*, vol. 1, no. 2, pp. 1–37.

Snodgrass, A.M. 1971. *The Dark Age of Greece*. Edinburgh: University Press.

Thompson, William. 2000. "C-Waves, Center-Hinterland Contact and Regime Change in the Ancient Near East: Early Impacts of Globalization", paper presented in the International Studies Association Annual Meetings. Los Angeles.

_____. 2001. "Trade Pulsations, Collapse, and Reorientation in the Ancient World" paper presented in the International Studies Association Annual Meetings, Chicago, 2001.

Toynbee, A. J. 1939. *A Study of History: Vol. IV and V*. Oxford: Oxford University Press.

Tucker, Richard. 2000. *Insatiable Appetite: The United States and the Ecological Degradation of the Tropical World*. Berkeley: University of California Press.

UNEP (United Nations Environment Programme). 2002. *World Environment Outlook*. Nairobi: UNEP.

Warren, Peter M. 1985. "Minoan Palaces" in *Scientific American*, vol. 253, no. 1, pp. 94–103.

Watrous, Vance L. 1994. "Review of Aegean Prehistory III: Crete from Earliest Prehistory Through the Protopalatial Period" in *American Journal of Archaeology*, vol. 98, pp. 695–753.

WCFSD (World Commission on Forests and Sustainable Development). 1999. *Our Forests Our Future*. Cambridge: Cambridge University Press.

Weiss, H. 1982. "The Decline of Late Bronze Age Civilization as a Possible Response to Climate Change" in *Climate Change*, vol. 4, pp. 173–98.

————. 2000. "Beyond the Younger Drayas" in G. Bawden and R. Reycraft (eds). *Environmental Disaster and the Archaeology of Human Response*. Albuquerque: University of New Mexico Press.

Weiss, H. and Bradley, R. 2001. "Archaeology: What Drives Societal Collapse" in *Science*, vol. 291, no. 5504, pp. 609–10.

Whitley, James. 1991. *Style and Society in Dark Age Greece: The Changing Face of a Pre-Literate Society 1100–700 B.C.* Cambridge: Cambridge University Press.

Wilkinson, T.J. 1990. *Town and Country in Southeastern Anatolia*. Chicago: University of Chicago Press.

Williams, Michael. 2000. "Dark Ages and Dark Areas: Global Deforestation in the Deep Past" in *Journal of Historical Geography*, vol. 26, no. 1, pp. 28–46.

Wright, E.H. 1968. "Climatic Changes in Mycenean Greece" in *Antiquity*, vol. 42, pp. 123–27.

Zanggar, E. 1993. "Neolithic to Present Soil Erosion in Greece" in M. Bell and J. Boardman (eds). *Past and Present Soil Erosion*. Oxford: Oxford University Press.

2

CULTURES IN CONFLICT: WHO ARE WE?
WHO ARE THE OTHERS?[1]

Immanuel Wallerstein

Recognizing the power of raciology, which is used here as a short-hand term for a variety of essentializing and reductionist ways of thinking—that are both biological and cultural in character—is an essential part of confronting the continuing power of "race" to orchestrate our social, economic, cultural, and historical experiences (Gilroy, 2000).

Not so long ago, there was a Cold War. Everyone talked of it as an ideological battle. For some this was a war between the free world and the evil empire of communism; for others it was a war between the exploiting capitalist class and the exploited workers of the world. But almost everyone purported to believe that this was a life and death struggle over fundamental political values. One day, the Cold War ended. It was in fact rather sudden, and most unexpected. The European regimes that purported to be Marxist–Leninist almost all ceased to exist. The Asian countries with communist parties in power and Cuba continued to wear the same ideological clothing, it is true, but in general, the world seemed to accept that there was no more "Cold War," and by and large this was regarded with some relief. This new situation was greeted spectacularly by some as "the end of history," although most people seemed to think that history was continuing its ceaseless path. A new word, globalization, did become common currency to describe the marvellous new world about to begin or that had presumably already begun, and to which (in Mrs Thatcher's unforgettable prose)—there is no alternative. The very same moment of history saw the maturing of a strong new academic emphasis, one that had begun in the 1970s but seemed to reach an acme in the 1990s. It came to be known generically as cultural studies.

Culture was once a benign word. High culture was something of which to boast. No one cared to be described as uncultured. Culture meant restraint, cultivation, taste. But the new field of cultural studies harbored a more feisty mood. It was an academic upstart and announced in no uncertain terms that it was remedying a deep neglect in the structures of knowledge. Cultural studies was often associated with, allied with, the pursuit of something called multiculturalism. And multiculturalism was a political demand, a demand of groups that felt they were downtrodden, or ignored, or repressed. Meanwhile, in a different camp and from within the world establishment, there were voices using the concept of culture in quite a different way. They were telling us that the 21st century was going to be the century of a "clash of civilizations," and that we had to gird ourselves, politically (and implicitly militarily), to meet the challenge. What the proponents of multiculturalism took as a liberating prospect, the successful reassertion of non-Western cultures, the proponents of the clash of civilizations considered to be the prime menace.

What is going on here? And first of all, in what capacity do I speak of it? Am I speaking as an American in China—a citizen of the currently strongest state in the world system speaking to an audience of the most ancient civilization in the world? Or am I a pan-European addressing an audience of the non-Western world—a white among non-whites? Or am I a "modern worlder" addressing an audience at a university whose very name bespeaks modernity—a university of science and technology? Or am I simply an academic scholar among his peers—peers who happen to be working or studying in Hong Kong? Or am I a social scientist trying to cope with a concept whose primary locus is in the humanities—the concept of culture?

To be honest, I'm not sure which of these roles describes me, or describes me best, if any of them do. Nor am I sure which of these roles I wish to affect. We are far less in control of our biographies than we would like to think, and we can find it extraordinarily difficult to be "objective" in our analyses, if that means that we are required to shed our biographies in our scholarly work. Nor can any of us be classified so easily. Biographies are complex mixtures, and the weights of different locations in which we find ourselves are not necessarily easy to discern, by others or by ourselves. Nor do these weights remain constant over time. What I am today is not necessarily identical to what I was yesterday.

I think I come to you now as a social scientist who is attempting to understand the world in which we live, one who is deeply concerned about the trajectory of this world and who believes he has a moral duty to act within it and upon it. I think I am coming as a "modern worlder" who has nonetheless deep reservations about what the modern world has been and who is no longer sure at all that it has represented progress over earlier world-systems. I probably cannot escape being an American and a pan-European, and I see no good reason to try to do so. And, at my age, I certainly bear the sins as well as the virtues of a life as a scholar.

I am going to discuss about time, about universalism, and about particularism, and I am then going to use this discussion to answer the questions: who are the "we" and who are the "others" in our thoughts and in our politics. I must say that time, universalism, and particularism make sense only in the plural number, and I do not believe these words have any other meanings. There are multiple temporalities, multiple universalisms, and multiple particularisms. And a good deal of our confusion in discussing culture comes from suppressing this multiplicity in the analysis.

Let us start with temporalities. I opened my remarks by referring to the Cold War. The Cold War is usually dated as existing from 1945 to 1989. Actually André Fontaine insisted a long time ago that it began in 1917 (Fontaine, 1983). And starting it in 1917 changes the analysis considerably. But no matter. It is supposed to be over. Yet, when one listens to some voices in the United States, and some in China or Russia, it does not seem to be over for everyone. Such voices seem to take the ideological rhetoric of the Cold War as a continuing marker of how they define the current world reality. Perhaps we should not take them too seriously.

Proponents of realpolitik have always argued that ideology was merely rhetoric, meant to mask the raison d'état of the states, and that the ruling strata never paid too much attention to the ideology they officially espoused. Charles DeGaulle seemed to have little doubt that the Soviet Union was first and foremost the Russian empire and the U.S. the American empire, and he made his analyses and calculations on this basis. Was he wrong? When Richard Nixon went to China to meet Mao Zedong, was each subordinating ideology to raison d'état, or was each simply pursuing more long-range ideological objectives? Historians will no doubt continue to argue over this for centuries to come.

Today, the United States and China seem to share a common commitment to encouraging production for the world market. Yet each defines the roots of this commitment differently. American politicians and pundits persist in describing the U.S. as a country committed to free enterprise capitalism, while Chinese politicians and pundits persist in describing China as a country committed to socialism, now sometimes called market socialism. Are we as social scientists to take such self-descriptions at face value? And if not, how should be really describe the structures of each country?

Of course, one factor in these self-descriptions is the chronosophy[2] common to each country, or at least to its leaders and to most of its citizens. Each country is committed to a long-range optimism based on the assumption of linear progress. Each seems to be sure it is on the path to a more perfect society. These self-descriptions are, however, in some sense as much statements of the teleological objective towards which they are heading as analyses of the present. But there are other chronosophies which would give us different temporalities. And even within any chronosophy, there are other periodizations, which again give us different temporalities.

What is most important to remember is that we live in many of these social temporalities simultaneously. We can, for example, analyze the world in terms of the modern world system as an historical system, which would lead us to take as temporal boundaries the long 16th century to the present. And one of the many ways in which we could describe this system is the periodic shift of centricity, seeing it as having a succession of hegemonic powers, whose hegemony is always temporary. If we did this, we could talk of the rise of American hegemony burgeoning in the 1870s, reaching a peak in the period 1945–70, and now in the early stages of its decline. And we could of course ask the question, a frequently asked one indeed, as to who might be the successor hegemonic power. Some argue the case for Japan, and a few for China, and there are others who think that U.S. hegemony is still too much with us to think clearly about such an issue.

Or, still within the time boundaries of the modern world-system, we could see it as a pan-European project of world domination (the "expansion of Europe") and debate about when exactly this expansion peaked—in 1900, in 1945, in 1989?—and when did the pushback begin—when the Japanese defeated Russia in 1905, with the entry of the Chinese communists in Shanghai in 1949, with the Bandoeng Conference in 1955, or with the U.S. defeat in Vietnam in 1973? And then we could discuss the question whether this pushback is the signal of a structural crisis in the modern world-system, or (as some would have it) nothing but the end of a phase in a far longer historical process in which Asian global centrality had been temporarily displaced by a brief Western or European moment.

The multiple temporalities in which we live may cause us some analytic confusion, but they are far easier to think about and to handle than multiple universalisms. "Multiple universalisms" is of course an oxymoron. Universalism is supposed to mean the view that there exist laws or truths that apply to all persons, all groups, all historical social systems at all points in time and space. Hence it is unitary, unique, and unified. How can there be multiple versions of that which is one? Well, I could refer to some versions of Christian theology, which have long argued that there is a trinity in which God is both one and three, or to the Hindu idea that the Gods have many *avatars*. These are theological, not scientific, ideas but they do indicate a wisdom, the kind of wisdom science has often, to its peril, ignored, and often found validated at a later point in its own evolution.

But I do not wish to appeal to theological insights. It is quite clear that there are multiple universalisms both at the level of popular, community-based claims and also at the level of scholarly assertions. We can of course, speaking from within the framework of one of these claims, reject the others as patently false or at least badly worded, and this is regularly done. All nomothetic social science is based on precisely this procedure. There are many who would insist that the term "science" is reserved for those who, in any domain of knowledge, are working to build a unique universalism. I want to argue that not only unique universalism does not exist, nor could ever exist, but that science is the search for how multiple universalisms can best be navigated in a universe that is intrinsically uncertain, and therefore hopefully creative.[3] The modern world has been, for most of its history, a prisoner of Aristotle's doctrine of the excluded middle. Something is either A or not-A. There is no third possibility. But of course, quantum mechanics has gotten us used to the idea that things can be two different things at the same time, or at least can be measured in two quite different ways or can satisfy two different equations.

Light is a swarm of particles and a continuous wave as well. We do not have to choose, or rather we cannot. We face the same problem in social science. In the arena of public policy, groups regularly contend on the basis of different so-called basic values, or different priorities in values. We are in fact constantly faced with such issues in our personal lives. I read in the newspapers of the tragic situation of two European infants who are Siamese twins. The doctors say that, since the twins have only one heart and one lung, they can only be separated in such a way that one twin lives and the other dies. The doctors also say that, if they do not separate the twins, both will die within months. The parents say that they cannot allow one child to be killed in order that the other live. And the British courts are being asked to resolve juridically this moral dilemma, this difference in moral priorities.

Not all such choices are tragic. Not all of them require that we choose between competing rights to life. But the underlying issues are omnipresent, and we are all collectively being constantly asked to make historical choices. All the debates about outside intervention in the "internal affairs" of any country invoke on the one side claims about universal human rights and on the other side the right of countries not to be subordinate to the imperial and imperious imposition of the values of others on them. And it is this last debate which has been central to the modern world-system since its outset and which has come to the fore again in the last decade. The reality of the modern world-system, the capitalist world-economy, is that it is a hierarchical, unequal, polarizing system, whose political structure is that of an interstate system in which some states are manifestly stronger than others. In furtherance of the process of the endless accumulation of capital, stronger states are constantly imposing on weaker states their will, to the degree that they can. This is called imperialism, and is inherent in the structure of the world-system. Imperialism has always had, however, its moral defense. It has been justified on the basis of the "civilizing mission," the presumed moral necessity to force others to conform to the norms prescribed by universal values. It seems a curious coincidence that the values that are said to be universal are always those primarily observed by the imperial power. Resistance by the victims to such specious morality seems a self-evident virtue.

Yet, on the other hand, local despotisms have always thrived on their ability to maintain closed frontiers and to reject any and all "outside interference" with their nefarious doings. And we have become increasingly sensitive to the evils of non-intervention, given the enormity of the crimes that are sometimes committed under the cover of sovereignty. In this current era when so many governments and churches are apologizing for past misdeeds, we are constantly adjured to remember those, especially those who are seemingly powerful, who failed to protest (and perhaps thereby to prevent) the misdeeds of still others. From the Holocaust to Rwanda, the albatross of guilt is laid around our necks. But of course the guilt of non-intervention didn't start with the Holocaust. Before the Holocaust there was the Middle Passage of the Atlantic slave trade, and the countless slaughters of indigenous peoples, not to speak of the child labor which to this day pervades this globe. So, we cannot fail to confront these evaluations of the past and the present by pretending that this is an exercise of the political and not of the scientific world. It is after all a discussion of multiple universalisms, which we have all been sedulously avoiding. Since, however, there are many, many universalisms, should we give them all equal weight and place? This is another way of asking whether we should be totally relativistic. And the answer is surely not. Because if there are formulas of accommodation between many universalisms, it is also true that there are some universalisms which are truly incompatible with others. And we are thereby forced into a meta-debate: Is there a singular hierarchy of universalisms, some of which are reasonable and acceptable and others of which are deeply repugnant? And if the answer is yes, and I suspect it is, is this not simply another way of returning to the unique universalism we are trying to escape? In any case, to say there is a hierarchy of universalisms solves nothing since we still must decide on what basis we can judge which are the claims that we should firmly exclude.

There is no easy or immediate answer to such a question. The attempt to draw fuzzy lines instead is the only real alternative. It is our continuing quest for unifying the true and the good. The journey, rather than reaching some utopian arrival point, is the positive action. It is a moral action, but it is an intellectual one as well, one furthermore that can only be conducted plausibly by a truly worldwide collectivity of participants in the quest. Each will bring to the quest a different biography, a different experience with priorities, a different insight into the possible consequences of alternative paths. Each may restrain the worst impulses or the weakest judgment of the other. In practice, there are three major varieties of universalisms that have a hold on the modern mind. There are those which derive from the world religions (and of course there are many religions). There are those that derive from the secular Enlightenment ideals that have been central to modernity. And there are those which express the sense of the powerful that the basis of their power has been their righteous actions and that therefore imperial stretch is a virtue, not a vice.

We have learned once again in the last two decades not to underestimate the hold of religion on the minds of people and therefore on the politics of the world-system. Religions are universalist almost by definition. Even when they originate in very local situations, they almost always lay claim to being universal truth, applicable to all persons. Often, however, religious universalisms are thought to be more than merely applicable to all; they are seen as mandated for all. And even when the rhetoric is less compulsory in tone, almost all religions teach the uniqueness of their path to truth or to salvation. Some religions are more exclusionary than others, but all insist on the virtue of their particular path of doctrines and practices. The three most widespread religions in the world—Christianity, Islam, and Buddhism—are all proselytizing, the first two aggressively so. There is no doubt why they are the most widespread, or at least that might be the view of an non-committed observer.

So what do the religions of the world tell us? To love each other, to love everyone, and to love particularly those who share the faith or the practice. One cannot say that this is an unambiguous message. And the results of course, have been highly ambiguous. For while it is clear that religious authorities have regularly been a force for peace and tolerance, it is equally clear that they have regularly been a force for violence and intolerance. No doubt God moves in mysterious ways, but we simple humans may feel impelled to try to make sense of these ways and, dare I suggest it, to draw more coherent conclusions from our faiths and our sciences than mere fatalism. It was of course in revolt against the dominance of religions that Enlightenment humanism–scientism staked its claim to a truly universal universalism, one to which all persons had equal access via their rational insight and understanding of eternal verities, via their verification of these truths in ways that all could replicate. The problem here, as we know, is that when all persons exercised their insight and understanding they came up with different lists of truths. Of course, one could (and did) argue that this situation was temporary, to be resolved by rational debate. But in practice, this solution did not seem to eliminate the problem. And Enlightenment humanism–scientism was thereby forced to create a hierarchy of human beings, according to their degree of rationality. Some were clearly more rational than others, whether because of their education, their experience, or their natural intellectual gifts. These persons were specialists in knowledge. And it did seem to follow that a more rational world required the imposition by more rational persons of the practical implications of the eternal verities they had perceived. So, Enlightenment humanism–scientism entered the same ambiguous path as the world's religions. On the one hand, we were adjured to regard all humans as rational, and on the other hand we were adjured to respect the preeminence and political priority of those who were more rational. We were adjured to respect each other, to respect everyone, and to respect particularly those who shared our meritocratic skills and merited positions of advantage. Once again, a not unambiguous message.

Those who based their universalisms on the imperative of *might makes right* were at least more straightforward. Essentially, they told us that whatever is had to be and that polarizing hierarchies are and must be the result of unequal skills, wisdom, and moral virtue. This was theorized in the 19th century as somehow biological in origin. Biologically-based explanations have come into disfavor, ever since the Nazis took these theories to their logical conclusion. But never fear! It has been easy to replace these biological explanations with cultural ones. Those who have power and privilege are said to have it because they are heirs to a culture which provided them with skills, wisdom, and virtue. Do note the coming to the fore, in this context too, of the concept of culture.

What none of the three varieties of universalisms—the religious, the humanist-scientific, or the imperialist—have offered us however is a theory of multiple universalisms, or even a theory of a hierarchy of universalisms. For each it has seemed to be a competitive race to the top. This may explain why the 20th century, the most universalizing century in the history of humanity, was also the most brutal and the most destructive of human beings. When universalisms destroy or oppress, people take refuge in particularisms. It is an obvious defense, and most of the time a very necessary one. And it works, up to a point. Particularisms by definition deny universalisms. They say in effect, we are different and difference is a virtue. Your rules do not apply to us, or have negative effects on us, or are designed specifically to do us harm. We therefore amend them, or reject them outright, and our rejection has a status of at least moral equality with your assertion of the universalistic rules. It turns out, however, that there are multiple stances from which one can assert particularisms, and the cultural claims made in the name of the multiple particularisms can have quite different political meanings.

There are first of all the particularisms asserted by the current losers in the universalism races. The current losers are generically those to whom we refer as "minorities." A minority is not primarily a quantitative concept but one of social rank; it is those who are defined as different (in some specified way) from the group that is dominant—

dominant in the world-system, dominant in any institutional structure within the world-system such as the state-system, or the class
structure, or the meritocracy scales, or the constructed race–ethnic
hierarchies we find everywhere. Minorities do not necessarily begin
by proclaiming particularisms. They often try first to appeal to the
universalistic criteria of the winners, demanding equal rights. But they
quite frequently find that these criteria are then applied in such a way
that they lose anyway. And so they turn to particularisms with which
to confront the so-called majority.

The mechanism of these confrontational particularisms is quite familiar. It is to assert that the losers had, in fact, been ahead of the winners
on the universalistic criteria over the long-term, but that they had
been pushed temporarily behind by some act of illegitimate force,
and that the rank order is destined to be reversed once again. Or it is to
assert that the universalistic criteria are in reality particularistic criteria, no better (indeed worse) than the particularistic criteria of the
minority, and therefore the rank order is destined to be reversed. Or it
is to deny that any truly universalistic criteria can possibly exist, that
the rank order is always a matter of force, and that since the minorities
are a quantitative majority, the rank order is destined to be reversed.
Or it is to proclaim all these theses simultaneously. The emphasis in
this variety of particularism is always on "catching-up" to, and quite
often on "exceeding," the presently dominant group. It is seldom the
search for a new universalism, except one that may be achieved by the
total elimination of the currently dominant group.

There are then the particularisms of the declining middles. Social
science have said much about this. These groups may define themselves
in any way—class, race, ethnicity, language, religion. In the cease-
lessly polarizing pressures of the capitalist world-economy, there are
always clusters of people whose status in the prestige hierarchy and
whose standard of living is declining with reference to a recent past.
And such people are naturally anxious, resentful, and combative. Sometimes they may focus their angers on those responsible for this decline,
who will defend themselves on the basis of the inevitability of the
changes in terms of maximizing overall economic efficiency of production. But quite often, it is not easy to perceive what actions of the
powerful have led to the decline. And thus it is that those who are
suffering such declines come to scapegoat groups that seem even weaker
than they (but who are perceived, often incorrectly, to be improving
their status and income levels).

This is such a familiar story around the world, over the past centuries that it is scarcely worth spending time elaborating it. But it should be noted that in such situations we see fierce particularisms, often of a particularly nasty nature. And it follows that the groups who are then the target of these angers, these hatreds, respond by forging their own strong particularisms. Thus, we enter into a cycle of senseless violence, which can last a very long time, until the groups are exhausted, and the rest of the world too, and some kind of truce is imposed on the contending groups. In the process, scapegoating becomes the game of the third parties as well. They define the conflict as the result of eternal enmities. Frequently such claims are patently false assertions, but they do have the consequence of blaming both sets of victims— the original group that is declining because of the imperatives of capital accumulation and the still weaker group they are blaming for it— and minimize our ability to analyze the relevant causes of the fierce internecine combats. The cultural particularisms invoked in such situations are in no way a positive action, even if we can understand how they arose. In the end, we can only emerge from this vicious cycle by an appeal to relevant universalisms. There is a third variety of particularism, that of the persistently bottom groups, again however defined. That they are thought of, and think of themselves as particular, is of course basic to social definitions of identity. They are the pariahs of our system—Blacks, Roma, Harijan, Burakumin, Indios, Aborigines, Pygmies. The assertion of their particular identities has been in the 20th century, particularly the late-20th century, an essential element in their political mobilization to achieve minimal political, economic, and social rights. That they have overstated their arguments in some cases, that they have from time to time indulged in a counter-racism seems less relevant than the fact that, despite all their efforts, they have at best been only very moderately successful in emerging from the pariah category. The fact is that the social dice are still loaded against all these groups. And one of the major weapons used to keep them down is to assert the primacy of universalistic norms every time they demand compensatory intervention or assistance in overcoming the cumulative negative effect of centuries (if not more) of discriminatory treatment, what in the United States is called affirmative action. In all, however much the particularisms of the declining middles may have devastating social consequences, the particularisms of the persistently bottom groups tends to have positive consequences for all social strata, and not only for them. The greatest beneficiaries of affirmative action over the long run will be the so-called majorities.

There is a fourth variety of particularism with which we are all familiar. It is the particularism of the effete snobs, those who pride themselves on their "high culture" and denounce the vulgarity of the masses. Not that the masses are not vulgar.

The word vulgar after all comes from the Latin term for the "common people." In days of yore, the aristocracy defined their own behavior as high culture, and forbade the common people to engage in practices of high culture. For example, there were dress codes. But the modern world-system has created a superficial democratization of culture. We are all permitted to engage in these practices. And more and more people everywhere do.

The effete snobs are really that segment of the upper strata, sometimes especially found among those declining in wealth, who are determined to hold on to their cultural separation from the masses. This creates a curious game. As each cultural practice and artifact that is defined as "high" is copied and/or indulged in by the common people, it becomes redefined as vulgar. And the effete snobs rush to find new artifacts and practices. One of the places they find such practices is precisely in the protesting, antisystemic practices of the persistently bottom groups. This creates a constant strain, as everyone constantly reevaluates such artifacts and practices, amidst much confusion, frequent relabeling, and much struggle to appropriate the rights to them. A fifth kind of particularism is that of dominant elites. This is not quite the same as that of the effete snobs. For it does not garb itself as high culture but as basic cultural presuppositions, what I have called the geoculture, "the underside of geopolitics" (the title for second part of Wallerstein, 1991). This form of particularism hides itself behind the screen of universalism—in today's world, as the universalism of rationality. This form of particularism uses the denunciation of particularism as the most effective means of asserting its own primacy. The debates that result we have come to call in the United States the "culture wars"— again that word! These multiple varieties of particularisms of course are no more governed by the law of the excluded middle than are the multiple varieties of universalisms. We all move back and forth through all these varieties constantly, and espouse several of them at any given time and space. Nor are the political implications of each etched in stone. Their role is a function of the total social situation in which they occur and in which they are perceived. But we can of course evaluate these roles and we can support, ignore, or oppose them in terms of our own priorities in values.

If we look at the long historical evolution of the modern world system we see that the choices among temporalities, universalisms, and particularisms has been a central locus of our political struggles. One of the weapons the powerful have had, is to misdefine these debates, and thus to obscure them, in an imagery that argues that time and space are simply contexts within which we live rather than constructs that shape our lives. And universalism and particularism are defined as a critical antinomy which we can use to analyze all social action and between whose priority we all have to choose, and once and for all. This has been helpful to the winners and not at all to the losers, which is the most urgent reason why we must unthink this antinomy and make far more complex our appreciation of the options that are available to all of us.

Culture, too, is not just there. Its very definition is a battlefield, as I have argued elsewhere (Wallerstein, 1990). The uses of the concept of culture are furthermore manifold, as I have tried to show in this discussion. One of the most urgent tasks of cultural studies today is to take more emotional distance from culture, to regard the concept of culture itself, as well as the students of the concept, as an object of study. Equally, we need to deepen our understanding of the politics and the economics of culture. The sacred trinity of liberal ideology—the political, the economic, and the sociocultural—is one of the most oppressive weapons of the particularism of the dominant strata. It is probably the one that is most difficult and most necessary to unthink. I would, if I could, abolish all three adjectives from our vocabulary. But I do not think I can, yet, for one thing because I am not sure with what to replace them.

So, are cultures in conflict? Undoubtedly, but saying that does not tell us very much. We need to be aware that the historical system within which we live thrives by the effort to commodify everything. High culture has been commodified for at least two centuries, and the last half-a-century has seen a spectacular rise in the degree to which high culture is a profitable enterprise for all concerned—the manufacturers of cultural products and the artists whose products are packaged. In the last 20 years, we have seen how the culture of protest can be commodified as well. One doesn't assert one's identity, one pays to assert it, and one pays to observe others asserting it, and some people even sell us our identity (see Gilroy, 2000). One copyrights culture. These days, there is a struggle going on between the producers of music in the form of CDs who seek to sell these CDs and those who operate websites on the internet that enable consumers to download these CDs at no cost. But of course, the internet website expects to make its money from the advertisements that will be placed on its website. Virtually no one in this dispute speaks in favor of the true decommodification of cultural products. Is it the culture we pay to display the expression of our heritage or our souls or even our political demands or is it the internalization of values imposed on us for the profit of those who gain rent from the transmission of these displays? Or can we even distinguish the two? Not even folklore, traditionally defined as a non-commodity, escapes this deep involvement in the endless accumulation of capital.

Who then are we? Who are the others? It depends of course on which battle we are fighting. And is it local, national, or global? It also depends on our assessment of what is happening within our historical system. I have been arguing for some time now that our historical system, the capitalist world-economy, is in structural crisis. I have said that we are in the middle of a chaotic period, that a bifurcation is occurring, and that over the next 50 years, not only will our current system cease to exist but a new one will come into existence. Finally, I have argued that the nature of this new system is intrinsically unknowable in advance, but that nonetheless its nature will be fundamentally shaped by our actions in this era of transition in which "free will" seems to be at its optimal point. Finally, I have argued that the uncertain outcome may result in a historical system that is better, worse, or about the same morally as the present one, but that it is our moral and political duty to seek to make it better. I will not rehearse here the case I have made for the existence of such a structural crisis, nor for the chronosophy I am employing (Hopkins and Wallerstein, 1996; Wallerstein, 1998). Rather I want to outline the possible "we's" and the corresponding "others" in this crucial period of a struggle that is simultaneously political, economic, and cultural. Let me start by rejecting some possible "we's". I do not believe we are really living through, or should be living through a clash of civilizations, in which the Western world, the Islamic world, and an East Asian world find themselves arrayed against each other. Some people would like us to believe this, in order to weaken our hands in the real battles. But I see little real evidence of such a clash, outside the rhetoric of politicians and commentators. The multiple universalisms and particularisms that I have outlined exist within each of these presumed civilizational arenas, and in not significantly different proportions. Of course, the clash of civilizations is one formula for defining North–South conflicts. While I believe that North–South conflicts are a fundamental political reality of the contemporary world—how could they not be in a constantly polarizing world-system?—I do not draw the conclusion that virtue derives from geography, or that the spokespersons for each side at any moment reflect necessarily the interests of the larger group they purport to represent. There are too many cross-cutting interests at play, and too many tactical follies, for anyone to commit himself or herself unreservedly to one side or the other in the endless skirmishes. However, on the basic issue that there must be an end to the polarization and a drastic move towards equalizing the uses of the world's resources, I feel there cannot be any equivocation. It is for me a moral and political priority. Is then the "we" those delineated in the class struggle? Well, of course, but what exactly does that mean? We can draw a line between those who are living-off the surplus value produced by others and those who are not retaining all of the surplus value they are producing, and we can call this line that between the bourgeoisie and the proletariat, or some similar language. But in fact, of course, within each of these categories, there exists a complex, overlapping internal hierarchy. The existing system has not created two homogenized classes (much less one homogenized humanity), but a subtle skein of privilege and exploitation. That is why we have so many varieties of particularisms. Reducing this picture to two camps is no simple task, as none other than Karl Marx demonstrated in his classic political analysis, *The Eighteenth Brumaire*. If even Mao Zedong insisted that class struggle continued within a socialist society, we are made aware of how prudent we have to be in assigning "we-ness" on the basis of class.

Then there is the "we-ness" of nationhood. Nationalism has proved to be an extremely powerful appeal to solidarity in the last two centuries, and there is little sign that this appeal has disappeared from the horizon. We are all aware of the conflicts nationalism has bred between states. But I wish to remind about the conflicts that nationalism has bred within states. For nationalism is not a cost-free good. Look at Japan. In the post-Meiji period, nationalism became a strong weapon of constructing a modern state, one that was powerful, one that achieved its objectives in terms of advancing the relative status of Japan in the world system. It led ultimately to the seizure of Korea, the invasion of China, the conquest of Southeast Asia, and the attack on Pearl Harbor. Japan lost the Second World War, and suffered the atrocious price of Hiroshima. After the war, nationalism became itself an element of internal conflict within Japan. There are those who fear that any resuscitation of nationalist symbols might trigger a restoration of a militarist, aggressive, internally repressive regime. And there are those who feel that Japan alone is being denied its national(ist) identity, to the detriment of so-called traditional values.

Japan is not alone in this conflict about the utility of national(ist) identity. Both China and the United States are afflicted by the same latent (and not so latent) conflict. But so are a long list of states around the world. I draw from this the conclusion that invoking national identity is akin to risky surgical intervention. It may be essential for survival (or merely for improved health) in some situations, but beware the surgeon (political leader) whose hand slips or the side effects that no surgeon (political leader) could have prevented. If I, thus, reject civilization, class, and nation as easy, straightforward criteria of "we-ness" (not to speak of race, a totally malicious and invented criterion), with what are we left to navigate the difficult waters of a chaotic transition over the next 50 years from the historical system in which we live to some alternative system in which our descendants shall live? Nothing easy to define. Let us begin by asserting moral/political objectives. When a historical system is in crisis, one can move, it seems to me, in one of two basic directions. One can try to preserve the hierarchical structure of the existing world system, albeit in new forms and perhaps on new bases. Or one can try to reduce, if not altogether eliminate, the inequalities to the extent possible. And it will follow that most of us (but not all of us) will opt for one of the two alternatives in consequence of the degree of privilege we enjoy in the present system. It will follow that there could emerge two broad camps of persons, and that such camps could not be identified either by civilization, by nation, or even by current definitions of class status. The politics of the two camps is not hard to predict. The camp favoring hierarchies will enjoy the benefits of its current wealth, its power, therefore, to command intelligence and sophistication, not to speak of weaponry. Nonetheless, its strength, though manifest, is subject to one constraint, that of visibility. Since, by definition, this camp represents the numerical minority of the world's populations, it must attract others to support it by appealing to themes other than hierarchy. It must make its priorities less visible. This is not always easy, and to the extent it is achieved it can cause confusion and reduce solidarity among its core members. So it is not guaranteed victory.

Arrayed against it would be the camp of the numerical majority. But this is a highly divided camp, divided by the multiple particularisms and even by the multiple universalisms. The formula that can overcome this disunity has already been proclaimed. It is the formula of the rainbow coalition. But this is far easier said than done. Advantage of each participant in such a formula is middle-run, and short-run considerations force themselves upon all of us with great regularity. We seldom have the discipline, or even the resources, with which to ignore short-run advantage. We live after all in the short-run as individuals. It is only collectively that we live in the middle-run, and can place such an alternate temporality into our schema of priorities. And when one thinks of creating not a national rainbow coalition but a global one, we realize what a formidable political task this is, and how little time there is to forge such a coalition. How then does one go about trying to do this? In part, this is a political task that has to be pursued simultaneously at the local, the national, the regional, and the global levels. It is one in which one has to concentrate, if one is to succeed in pulling together a meaningful coalition, on the middle-run question of the kind of replacement system we wish to construct while not ignoring the short-run problem of alleviating the miseries under the existing system. I feel it is not my function to go further in outlining a political strategy. Rather I wish to concentrate on the intellectual contributions that social science can make in this era of transition. I think the first thing we can do is to unthink the social science categories bequeathed to us by the existing world system and that have so hobbled us in our analyses not only of current reality but of the possible alternatives to it we might construct. Recognizing the existence of multiple temporalities, multiple universalisms, multiple particularisms is a first step. But of course we need to do far more than simply acknowledge their existence. We have to begin to figure out how they fit together, and what is the optimal mix, and in what situations. This is an agenda for major reconstruction of our knowledge systems. I have not discussed about the "two cultures"—that presumed fundamental epistemological split between the humanities and the sciences. This split, reproduced within social science as the Methodenstreit between idiographic and nomothetic methodologies, is in fact a recent invention. It is no more than 200 to 250 years old, and is itself a prime creation of the modern world-system. It is also deeply irrational, since science is a cultural phenomenon, a prisoner of its cultural context, while the humanities have no language that is not scientific, or they could not communicate coherently their message to anyone (Wallerstein, 1999: Part II). One thing we all need to do is to read far more widely. Reading is a part of the process of theoretical discovery, of uncovering the clues and the links that lay buried in the mass of deposited knowledge products. We need to point our students towards reflection on fundamental epistemological issues. We must cease fearing either philosophy or science, since in the end they are the same thing, and we can only do either by doing both, or by recognizing that they are a single enterprise. In the process, we shall become fully aware of the multiple universalisms that govern our universe, and begin for the first time to be substantively rational, that is to reach a consensus, however interim, on the priorities of values and of truths in a universe where we must constantly make choices, and therefore be creative.

If social scientists, in fact, scholars of all fields, can succeed in thus reconstructing their enterprise, and that is a very big if, we shall have contributed massively to the historical choices that all of us are necessarily making in this era of transition. This will not be the end of history, either. But it will allow us to proceed on a better foot. There is said to be a Qing dynasty saying: People fear the rulers; the rulers fear the foreign devils; the foreign devils fear the people. Of course, the Qing already had experience with the modern world-system. But we, the people, we are also the foreign devils. In the end there are no others, or at least no others that we cannot control if collectively we set our minds to it, discuss it, weigh alternatives, and choose, creatively. In a socially constructed world, it is we who construct the world.

NOTES

1. Y.K. Pao Distinguished Chair Lecture, Center for Cultural Studies, Hong Kong University of Science and Technology, September 20, 2000.
2. On the concept of chronosophy, see Pomian, 1979. Pomian uses the term in contrast to chronometry and chronology, saying "it speaks of time; it makes time the object of a discourse or rather of discourse in general" (pp. 568–69).
3. See Prigogine, 1997. It should be noted that the original title in French, *La fin des Certitudes*, uses the plural for certainty.

REFERENCES

Fontaine, André. 1983. *Histoire De La Guerre Froide*. Two Volumes. Paris: Fayard.

Gilroy, Paul. 2000. *Against Race: Imagining Political Cultural Beyond the Color Lines*. Cambridge: Harvard University Press.

Hopkins, Terence K. and Wallerstein, Immanuel. 1996. *The Age of Transition: Trajectory of the World System, 1945–2025*. London: Zed Books.

Pomian, Kryzysztof. 1979. "The Secular Evolution of the Concept of Cycles" in *Review*, vol. 2, no. 4, pp. 568–69.

Prigogine, Ilya. 1997. *The End of Certainty*. New York: Free Press.

Wallerstein, Immanuel. 1990. "Culture as the Battleground of the Modern World System" in *Theory, Culture and Society*, vol. 7, pp. 31–56.

_____. 1991. *Geopolitics and Geoculture: Essays on the Changing World System*. Cambridge: Cambridge University Press.

_____. 1998. *Utopistics: Or Historical Choices of the Twenty-First Century*. New York: New Press.

_____. 1999. *The End of the World As We Know It: Social Sciences for the Twenty-First Century*. Minneapolis: University of Minnesota.

3

ALTRUISM AND THE PROSPECTS FOR
A COMMON HUMANITY

Jay Weinstein and Elvira del Pozo

According to an ancient Hindu myth, when *Brahma* created the universe, he placed human beings on millions of planets throughout the cosmos. However, these planets were located so far apart from each other that it was impossible for humans of one world to meet or even communicate with those of another. Then the spiritual evolution of humanity began. It was deemed that when the inhabitants of one world had evolved to a level of morality so advanced that they could not pollute others, the technologies that enable space/time travel would be discovered and contact would be made. Thus, when the end of the current cycle of birth, death, and rebirth reaches its conclusion, humanity will at last realize its potential as a single soul within the Great Soul.

Like all good myths, the truth of this one lies in the real choices it presents to people willing to look beyond the literal, imaginative story. A situation parallel to that portrayed in the myth now faces the 6.5 billion human beings who inhabit the earth. We are rapidly becoming one, for better and for worse.

Many names have been given to this process; and because names create realities, it matters very much which one we use. Some, beginning with the sociologist Harold Innes and his student Marshall McLuhan, see it as a movement towards a *global village*. Architect and futurist Buckminster Fuller referred to the *Spaceship Earth*. Now current in many quarters is the term globalization. Some, with good reason, speak of *capitalist imperialism*. Others say Modernization, Westernization, Postmodernization, or Internationalization. Sociologist George Ritzer has influenced many with his evocative term,

McDonaldization. However, for the purposes of this discussion, we have chosen to call the process *coming to species consciousness*. This concept helps one avoid some of the unwanted connotations that "globalization" and the other terms carry, and it causes one to view the process in light of the *Brahmin* creation myth.

HIGHLIGHTS IN THE HISTORY OF THE IDEA

The idea of species consciousness has been expressed in many different cultures and historical eras beyond the ancient Hindu version. One of its most powerful statements is found in the *Ethics*, written in 1677 by the Dutch-born philosopher Baruch (Benedict de) Spinoza. According to Spinoza, underlying all of the diversity that characterizes various nations and ethnicities of the world, there is a fundamental "harmony." He believed that this harmony could be understood if we think clearly about the nature of humanity, and that it would be realized if and when people act reasonably toward one another. "Nothing can be in more harmony with the nature of any given thing than other individuals of the same species," Spinoza wrote. "Therefore, for man in the preservation of his being and the enjoyment of the rational life there is nothing more useful than his fellow-man who is led by reason" (*Ethics*, Part IV, Appendix: proposition IX).

THE POSSIBILITY OF SPECIES CONSCIOUSNESS

Spinoza and those who embrace his viewpoint believe that a species consciousness is possible; in fact, they assume that it is inherent in human nature. They also realize, however, that it is not automatic. For there are many forces arrayed against it, including habit, superstition, and prevailing public opinion, that must be overcome before we can understand ourselves "under the form of eternity."[1] This is an important point to remember as we consider the possible outcomes of the rapid sociocultural changes now underway. That is, if we are going to achieve species consciousness, something must be done: a program must be created and implemented to bring it about.

Spinoza chose to emphasize a program that involved a turn towards what he called "reason." This concept suggests that if one thinks about the human condition in a clear and orderly way it becomes apparent that every individual person is part of a larger, effective whole.

To paraphrase the words of the poet John Donne: *No one is an island. No one stands alone.*

Unfortunately, from a contemporary standpoint, "reason" is an outmoded term that now can mean just about anything one chooses. For example, it can be argued that it is reasonable for a person or group to commit genocide, provided that the deed is planned clearly and systematically (logically).[2] Today, the program that will help us realize our common humanity must give directives that are far more specific than "be rational," even if we do understand what Spinoza really meant in his arguments against irrational philosophies and theologies.[3]

The German philosopher Immanuel Kant (who lived during the era of the American and French Revolutions) was not the first writer to attempt to improve upon Spinoza's program, but he is certainly among the best remembered and most widely read. Kant believed that there exist certain moral standards—rules of right and wrong— that allow people to understand themselves "under the form of eternity." These rules are absolute, or "categorical," in that they are valid everywhere and always. In addition, such rules are expressed in the form of a command, as an "imperative," because one cannot avoid acting in the way(s) they stipulate and still be considered an ethical person. In his *Foundation for the Metaphysic of Morals* (1838; 1961: 581–82), Kant notes that an:

> [I]mperative is Categorical [when] it concerns not the matter of action, or its intended result, but its form and the principle of which it is itself a result; and what is essentially good in it consists in the mental disposition, let the consequence be what it may. This imperative may be called that of Morality.

In recognizing the importance of eternal, moral rules in the movement toward a species consciousness, Kant goes beyond the assertion that "reason" is all that is required to understand and achieve a common humanity. For one thing, because our actions must be rule governed, the movement is viewed as normative and thus requires learning. It may be true that the potential to understand ourselves as part of a physical and spiritual whole is inborn, or at least intuitive, and that even the youngest children can grasp the idea. However, by the time most people reach maturity, they have either forgotten or have "unlearned" it—or, it is possible, they never understood it at all.

In any case, Kant implied, people need to learn, and to learn how to act in accord with, the categorical imperatives. This normative aspect also allows for the possibility that people can think and behave in a manner that appears "rational" and at the same time act immorally: for example, when orderly, clear thinking nevertheless goes against or ignores a key imperative. Finally, when the importance of imperatives is considered, it is obvious that the possibility of achieving species consciousness is just that, a possibility, not something that is inevitable. In brief, reason is necessary, but it must be guided by the "rules of the game."

ENTER ALTRUISM

So, we might ask, did Kant have any particular moral imperative(s) in mind when he connected them to the quest for a common humanity? The answer is "yes," he had a very important one in mind. In fact, in keeping with his view that such moral norms are universal and eternal, he drew upon what we now know to be a cultural universal: a norm that is part of the morality of every human society ever studied.[4] Because it is so common, it has been expressed in many different ways. Most people in the English speaking world know it as the Golden Rule: "do unto others as you would have others do unto you." Kant put it this way (as translated from the original German): "Act only on that maxim whereby you can at the same time will that it should become a universal law." In other words, see to it that anything that you might do could and should be done by everyone else in the world (see Hill, 1993).

Because of Kant's influence in academic circles, his ideas—including his categorical imperative—were studied carefully by his contemporaries; and they have continued to influence social thinkers to this day. Two of his contemporaries in France, Henri Saint-Simon (the older) and August Comte (the younger), worked on developing moral philosophy in what is now a familiar direction. For in Revolutionary France, Kant's work along with other sources, especially the writings of Adam Smith and his students (known collectively as the "Scottish moralist" philosophers), became the foundation for a new field that Comte called *Sociology*.

Saint-Simon and Comte investigated many important topics, such as the possibility of studying human relationships according to the scientific method (another idea that can be traced to Kant). Often overlooked in their innovations, however, is their interest in the kind of behavior specified in the Golden Rule, Kant's imperative, and in similar moral norms. From a sociological perspective, such behavior is *prosocial*, for the collective good. This can be contrasted with behavior that is *selfish*, for the good of the self. Comte coined the terms whereby we still refer to these contrasting modes of action: *altruism* and *egoism*. Using Comte's word, then, the Golden Rule and the categorical imperative counsel *altruism*. Thus the essential connection was made between altruism on one hand, and the movement toward species consciousness, on the other, a connection of which the French founders of sociology were well aware:

> Comte considered altruism and egoism to be two distinct motives within the individual. He did not deny the existence of self-serving motives, even for helping; the impulse to seek self-benefit and self-gratification he called *egoism*. But Comte believed that some social behavior was an expression of an unselfish desire to 'live for others.' It was this second type of motivation to benefit others that he called *altruism* (Comte, 1851; 1875; quoted in Batson, 1991: 5).

Well before the words "altruism" and "egoism" were coined, people had asked the obvious question, are the two actually mutually exclusive? Is it possible for some acts to be both prosocial and selfish?[5] Those who are familiar with Adam Smith's *invisible hand* know that a good, strong case can be made that they are not mutually exclusive. In fact, for Smith and the many people whom he has influenced, under certain conditions egoistical behavior is the best way to benefit others. Conversely, it seems that often the best way to benefit the self is to act for the benefit of others.

These ideas are not new. Moreover, they and the philosophies and worldviews based upon them are accepted widely and staunchly defended by many very intelligent and influential people, and with good reason. As our lives, our nations, and the world continue to change at an ever-accelerating pace, it will become increasingly important to reflect on the possibility that under some circumstances altruism and egoism can be mutually reinforcing. However, it is equally important to understand that the argument that egoism leads to the common good is often used as a justification for selfish behavior.

The circumstances described by Smith in his *Wealth of Nations* relate specifically to economic conditions; and the common good that is presumed to be the outcome of selfish behavior is only an economic good. Unless we believe that economic benefits are the only kind that really count, the argument in *Wealth of Nations* cannot be generalized.

Moreover, Smith himself said much the same in his far broader exploration of moral outcomes in his earlier book, *Theory of Moral Sentiments* (which argues against selfishness as unethical).

Even more relevant is the fact that the economic conditions that Smith believed would allow selfishness to eventuate in collective benefits do not exist, never existed, and cannot exist. When we consider these conditions, it is clear that the truth of the proposition that selfishness is prosocial, lies in the realm of pure mathematics, not social science. The conditions are that an infinite number of independent producers, each of whom produces an infinitesimally small part of a total output of a commodity in such a way that no producer's product can be distinguished from that of another producer. These commodities are then purchased by an infinite number of consumers, each acting on its own behalf with no relationship to any other consumer or producer and purchasing an infinitesimally small portion of the total output. Moreover, this must occur with no interference whatever by government, the church, or any other institution. Under these conditions, if producers and consumers all act to maximize their own personal benefits, all will benefit optimally.

Yet, we might ask, what happens if the number of producers and consumers is relatively small? What if some producers put more commodities on the market than others? What if producers cooperate with one another, if consumers act in concert, or if governments do act to favor some producers, some consumers, or both? What if governments are consumers? In other words, what happens in reality? With such questions in mind, one can be confident that those who argue against doing good for others because, they claim, selfishness will lead to a better result usually have another agenda.

Part of the problem with viewing altruism and egoism as exact opposites is semantic. That is, we now know that better definitions of the terms are needed so as to avoid confusion. Recently, James Ozinga (1999), a political scientist in the US, has offered at least a partial solution to the problem. According to him, "altruism is behavior benefiting someone else at a cost to oneself." Egoism, which Ozinga equates with selfishness, is thus "behavior that benefits oneself at some cost to others." These definitions are not entirely satisfactory, in part because some ambiguity still remains; but they do stress an important point: Benefits often (but, as Ozinga suggests, not always) entail costs as well. Although it does oversimplify most real life situations, this pair of definitions does indicate that altruism and egoism *can be* mutually exclusive: either I benefit you or I do not. We return to the question of definitions later.

ANALYZING SPECIES CONSCIOUSNESS

As we are using the term here, *species consciousness* is borrowed from the writings of Karl Marx, who spoke of class-consciousness. It is based on the distinction between a class—or other group—*in itself* versus one *for itself*. A group in itself is one whose members share common characteristics, locale, conditions of life, etc., that set it off from other groups. A group for itself is a group in itself whose members also share a common understanding that theirs is a distinct group, with distinct interests, and capable of acting in its own behalf. According to Marx, the working class can act collectively in its struggle for justice only when it has become a class for itself (which he referred to as the "proletariat") that has achieved true class-consciousness.

It is essential to Marx's theory that a class/group for-itself has a clearly identifiable other. Marx put it more strongly: an enemy is required against which the class/group can identify itself. According to this theory, understanding the other and understanding the collective self are mutually reinforcing processes. The more a self-conscious group can know about the other, its characteristics, interests, and goals, the higher the degree of its consciousness and understanding of its own interests.

Who, then, is to play the role of the other when we speak of humanity as a group for itself? That is, if all people are to think of themselves as one, who or what remains to provide the all-important contrast? As Marx himself—and many other social philosophers and scientists—prophesied, that role is to be played by *nature*. This cannot of course be the antagonistic conquer-or-be-conquered image of nature that characterized Marx and other 19th century intellectuals. For we now understand our ecosystems much better than they did. We now realize that nature cannot and should not be conquered; for humanity is part of nature. Along with the movement toward species consciousness, we have learned a critical lesson (hopefully not too late): nature is to be followed, respected as a teacher, and cooperated with. We know this to be true, but—among the ironies associated with our current plight—it is a lesson that cannot be applied effectively until we can think as a common humanity.

At times, Marx or Marxists seem to be arguing that the evolution of the workers in a capitalist society from a class in-itself to a class that is a conscious, active agent of revolutionary social change is somehow inevitable.[6] However, history has proved otherwise. Working-class movements, especially the modern labor movement that has been inspired considerably by Marx's ideas and actions, have had a substantial impact on the world in which we live. Yet, capitalism is still alive and well; in fact, it may be more powerful and have a greater geographic reach than ever. With this in mind, if humanity today can be considered a group in itself, and if humanity is moving toward species consciousness, it is entirely possible that the end will never be achieved. It can even happen that things regress in such a way that the net movement during certain periods may be *away* from unity. This suggests that active steps must be taken or, as noted, a program needs to be developed and implemented to ensure (as much as such things can be ensured) that we maintain the proper course.

SUMMARY OF THE HISTORY OF THE IDEA

The concept of a common humanity with a consciousness of itself is very old and widely discussed. In fact, for many centuries in Western and Eastern philosophy, the idea was believed to be self-evident to anyone who could reason properly. Ultimately, such beliefs were dismissed as too vague and/or ambiguous. However, in several instances, such as in Immanuel Kant's writings on morality, philosophers attempted to make the quest for a common humanity more specific. In the early 19th century, Kant in particular proposed in his moral imperative a certain kind of thought and action that would be an effective means to achieve the goal of species consciousness. At about the same time, Auguste Comte, founder of the discipline of sociology, coined the term to refer to such thought and action that is used to this day: *altruism*. In this way, the links between a common humanity, species consciousness, reason, moral imperatives, and altruism were forged.

In Karl Marx's revolutionary program to create a common humanity, one finds the key principle of a group in-itself. This indicates that group-consciousness, including in this context species-consciousness, is the product of common life conditions plus a shared understanding by members of the group (species) that they have common interests—that the well-being of each depends on the well-being of all. Also necessary is a common other against which the group (species) can identify itself. In the case of the human species, in particular, this other is *nature*, with which humanity as a whole can and must cooperate in order to survive and prosper. Because, it appears, the achievement of species consciousness is neither automatic nor inevitable, the need for a program to guide the quest is once more apparent. In the following section, we discuss such a program.

APPLIED SOCIOLOGY AND THE QUEST FOR A COMMON HUMANITY

Thus far, we have discussed some aspects of species consciousness and the related concept of a common humanity. Our exploration has also briefly touched on several related ideas, including Kant's imperative, Comte's altruism, and Marx's theory of social change. This has helped to lay the foundation for addressing four key questions that do (or ought to) concern people today. These are:

1. What is the alternative to species consciousness, and what would the consequences be if people did *not* pursue it?
2. Is altruism real or is it just a dream of philosophers?
3. What is the relationship between altruism and the quest for a common humanity?
4. Assuming that such a quest is possible and desirable, what needs to be done?

First we consider the first three questions together, then we continue with a few additional thoughts on each as we attempt to answer the fourth question.

THE ALTERNATIVES

Short of an enormous and unforeseen catastrophe, there appears to be nothing that can stop the increasing connectedness occurring between and among people in all parts of the world. Promoted by powerful technologies and institutions such as the Internet, satellite television, radio, and telephones, the spread of English as a common world language, common currencies such as the Euro and the Dollar, and the growth, consolidation, and ever-expanding reach of multinational corporations, McLuhan's "global village" is, or is on the verge of becoming, a reality. Yet, if "village" is the proper metaphor, it is hardly a village at peace.

The social, economic, and political inequalities that exist between and within the village's "neighborhoods" range from substantial to enormous and from enormous to (there is no other way to put it) obscene. Some residents own two or more cars that cost tens of thousands of dollars each, whereas others cannot even afford an ox cart. Many political and religious "leaders" of the village are benefiting mightily, some as never before, by preaching hatred and intolerance of one's neighbors. God's name is routinely invoked to justify all manner of murder and mayhem. In some neighborhoods, residents are on the verge of starvation, while in others food is thrown away by the ton.

The emerging political system of the village is highly undemocratic. It is, rather, an autocracy in which those individuals, groups, and geographic regions currently wielding the most power have shaped the system in a way that will keep them in power well into the foreseeable future. Free markets and sovereign consumers do not characterize the village's emerging economy, as its defenders would like us to believe. Nor is the economy the socialistic system once embraced by capitalism's critics, which operates according to the principle of "from each according to his abilities and to each according to his needs." Instead, it has thus far proved to be simply a more extended and more coordinated version of the system of huge monopolistic corporations that first emerged in the early 20th century.[7] As the global village has taken shape, these corporations have achieved unparalleled political influence. It has also become increasingly clear that they are indifferent to the goods and services they actually produce. For their main business is to maximize profits by underpaying and, when desirable, laying-off workers and by cajoling, tricking, or forcing consumers to buy more and more things that are less and less important.

The glamorous and seemingly unstoppable spread of the Internet, cell phones, the dollar, and corporate economics has an another, often unpleasant side that residents of the more affluent neighborhoods tend to overlook. Along the same channels that bring innovations such as satellite TV to the far corners of the village, great fear and anxiety flow about the loss of traditional, local beliefs and practices.

In response to such fears, the less privileged residents seek solace in what they believe to be the past (even if it is a largely mythical past). Old languages, art, and music are revived from the brink of extinction; and ethnic power and "cleansing" movements arise to challenge the cultural homogenization overtaking the village. Religious fundamentalism is embraced in increasing numbers by adherents of the village's major faiths: Christianity, Islam, Judaism, Hinduism, and in smaller sects and denominations as well, in response to the forces of secularization. Nationalism, and its frequent companion militarism, experiences a significant revival in an attempt to counter the reach of multinational institutions. These are not aberrations or mysterious contradictions. Rather, the current growth and popularity of such movements, and the potential of social conflict that they entail, are as much a part of the global village as e-mail or MTV. As Benjamin Barber notes in his widely read work on this phenomenon, "the two axial principles of our age—tribalism and globalism—clash at every point except one: they may both be threatening to democracy."[8]

In the absence of species consciousness, there is no reason to believe that current trends will cease or even slow down. To the contrary, a global village that is not a village for-itself is bound to be a village in continual conflict and strife: autocratic politics, monopolistic economics, exploitation, religious intolerance, inter-ethnic violence, and militarism. Of course, these are hardly new problems; but they are serious and dangerous in a new way when they occur in humanity's one and only village, with no other place to go and no one other than ourselves to whom we can turn for help. That is why the need for all people to see themselves as one has never been more urgent.

IS ALTRUISM REAL?

We have noted that an intimate relationship exists between altruism and the quest for a common humanity. The next several pages focus on the phenomenon of altruism and the large body of research literature that has been produced on the subject, especially literature that discusses the extent to which people are and/or can be altruistic.

Just as Comte argued that both altruism and egoism are inherent in the human condition, current academic research on the subject tends to assume that our behavior is based on multiple motives, two of which are selfishness and unselfishness. Some studies view such motives as mutually reinforcing and others see them as mutually exclusive. In any case, there is no doubt that altruism is a highly disputed phenomenon. Yet, most explanations are useful, at least to the extent that they help understand what is meant by the possibility or impossibility of altruism.

Scholars refer to altruism by using terms such as *sharing, loving, cooperating, helping*, and *comforting*. Some authors are stricter than

others in their definitions, and carefully address the subtle but meaningful distinctions of these apparently related terms. For instance, some
people believe that *helping* is more connected to charitable activities
than it is to altruism. Some scholars claim that there is no such thing
as other-directed behavior. Others maintain that there can be other-
directed behavior but that it is not independent of one's interests in
oneself. Whereas other scholars argue that human beings often do act
to benefit others, independent of one's self-interest. This last perspective,
which is the one most relevant to assessing the prospects for the development of a species consciousness, is also the most controversial.

In the last few decades, social scientists have evolved in their thinking about altruism. Earlier, this work was characterized by a skeptical
viewpoint that assumed that if one pays close attention, what might
appear as altruistic behavior on the surface is actually motivated by
egoism. Although today there is a greater tendency to accept altruism
as part of human nature,[9] uncertainty surrounding this topic continues, and many social scientists still believe that all normal behavior is
concerned with the pursuit of individual self-interest. The research is
extensive in the sense that it is of interest to philosophers, social/be-
havioral scientists, and most recently to ethnologists, geneticists, sociobiologists, and other natural scientists. Therefore, to address the
question of whether or not altruism is possible, one must consider
how it is viewed from these various perspectives and disciplines.

Here we briefly summarize some of the most recent research on
altruism according to the broad classifications of disciplines, although
it is difficult and in some instances, unfair to create clear and neat
distinctions between the different fields.[10] For example, psychologists
and sociologists have focused on motives and intentions, with psychologists more interested in the benefits or costs to the actor and
sociologists emphasizing the costs to the actor that involve other-
directed sentiments. In contrast, sociobiologists, economists, and evolutionary theorists tend not to consider motives at all. This is because
sociobiologists and economists employ a cost–benefit analysis in explaining altruistic behavior, and evolutionary theorists emphasize consequences to the actor and the recipient but without reference to any
thought or awareness.

Research in several fields leaves many unanswered questions about
the reality of altruism. The ambiguity is, in part, the result of differences among disciplinary perspectives from which the problem is
viewed. Some studies focus on motivation, others do not even see

motives as necessary; some studies are concerned with the behavior of individuals, whereas others look to the group level, etc. Another factor that cannot be ignored is an ideological tendency to dismiss apparently altruistic acts as mere manifestations of selfishness. Those who take this position tend to credit themselves as "realists." Yet, on reflection, it seems obvious that no facts or logical arguments will persuade such people that altruism can sometimes be realistic. Thus, they actually have little to contribute to serious research on the subject.

Despite this ambiguity and the disciplinary and ideological obstacles, it is obvious that the phenomenon of altruism is currently of interest to a wide range of scholars in many fields. Moreover, as our knowledge about altruism, egoism, and their sources and consequences increases, it becomes increasingly clear that our behavior toward others is intimately connected to our self-preservation—as individuals, as groups, and as a species. Sociologists and others are still far from solving all of the riddles that are associated with altruism, but a significant movement among those interested in it is taking shape around the connection between pro-social behavior and perceptions of a common humanity. With this in mind, we now turn to the work of one of the leaders of this movement.

ALTRUISM AND PERCEPTIONS OF A COMMON HUMANITY

A significant contribution to the literature on altruism is the work of political psychologist Kristen Monroe. In *The Heart of Altruism: Perceptions of a Common Humanity*, Monroe defines altruism as "behavior intended to benefit another, even when this risks possible sacrifice to the welfare of the actor" (Monroe, 1996: 6). Monroe examines the possible influences that encourage altruism and highlights the importance of separating this discussion from a rational choice perspective. As a staunch advocate of the plausibility of altruism as part of human nature, Monroe succinctly argues against the limitations provided by rational choice theorists. (As noted above, the key to their argument is that egoism is normal behavior, even in the presence of other-directed acts.)

Monroe's work is based on an indepth study of individuals whose behavior can be placed along a continuum from altruistic to egoistic and which includes several points in between. As in Fogelman's work, the individuals assumed to be the most altruistic are rescuers of Jews during the Holocaust. In addition to the rescuers, along the continuum from more to less altruistic are heroes, philanthropists, and entrepreneurs. For Monroe, entrepreneurs display the least altruistic behavior. Using these categories, she contrasts research findings with theoretical assumptions based on both rational choice and altruistic theories. Her conclusion is that rational choice theories cannot account for the behavior of altruists.

Monroe originally believed that the roots of altruism might be traced to factors such as parental modeling, education, and religion; but her findings did not support this. Rather, she discovered that what sets the more altruistic subjects apart from the others is a shared general perspective, a "cognitive orientation." She concluded that the perspective itself, and not the specific factors, consistently accounted for altruism.

For Monroe, the altruistic perspective is best understood in philosophical and psychological terms, although she uses principles from other social sciences as well. In fact, it is quite complex and consists of several components: cognition and cognitive processes, expectations, worldviews, empathy, and views of self. Following is a brief description of each of these components.

- Cognition is the process by which individuals make sense of the world. It consists of being aware of something and making a judgment about it. It also accounts for cultural norms. It allows one to interpret how altruists see themselves, as members of a group or as individuals.
- Expectations imply what the altruist expects will occur under certain circumstances. These include opinions, beliefs, and stereotypes of what helping means.
- Worldviews consist of people's ideas about the world and themselves, for example, how they think about themselves as individuals and as members of groups.
- Empathy is the result of a cognitive and affective response toward someone *else's* feelings.
- Finally, views of self are related to one's identity perception and whether or not it is consistent with behavior.

Based on these components, the most altruistic subjects—especially the rescuers—consistently saw themselves as members of a shared humanity. They thought of themselves as ordinary people who had not done anything praiseworthy by saving other people's lives. They exhibited a universalistic worldview, in which being part of the human community was more important than being part of a just world or believing in the inherent goodness of people. They understood what is meant to be in need, and therefore felt that they had no choice in their actions.

Monroe's concept of common humanity reinforces the findings of other research on altruism. For instance, Sorokin noted how his "good neighbors" had a similar attitude toward the whole world and humanity. Similarly, Oliner and Oliner (1988: 84) referred to a kind of cognition or inclusiveness as "a predisposition to regard all people (universally) as equals and to apply similar standards of right and wrong to them without regard to social status or ethnicity." Fogelman, too, discussed the importance of "awareness" or the process of transformation that a bystander goes through before becoming a rescuer. Such awareness signifies that others are in need and that all should be treated equally. In a broader sense, Monroe's research draws on Kant's categorical imperative, Comte's altruism, and Marx's theories of social change, as discussed earlier.

Monroe's concept at first proved difficult to test empirically. For each of her key components include several intricate, multi-leveled variables. However, her more recent research (Monroe, 2001) suggests further ways to analyze the altruistic perspective, in the context of rescue behavior and other uncalculated, spontaneous acts. Although this is highly analytical work, rooted in psychological, linguistic, and psychoanalytic theories, it does provide a clearer understanding of the interconnections among altruism, morality, and our sense of selves. In particular, she has discovered that "morality is driven not by ratiocination or religion but by identity and perceptions of self in relation to others" (Monroe, 2001: 491). That is, the human need for consistency and self-esteem, and our desire to be treated by others as we treat them, result in a "universal entitlement." This is an entitlement to extend universal rights to others (compare with Kant's categorical imperative); and, according to Monroe, it is what drives people to be moral actors.

ELEMENTS OF THE PROGRAM

If it is both desirable and possible for people, everywhere, to become more altruistic, then the next step is to advance the program meant to achieve this goal, the program begun by Spinoza, Kant, Comte, and

Marx. We have noted how researchers in several disciplines are interested in the phenomenon of altruism. However, the field that has the potential to make one of the most important contributions to the *practical* aspects of this research is "applied sociology." There are two main reasons for this. First, the field, although labeled "sociology," is highly interdisciplinary and thus includes insights and principles from psychology, social philosophy, biology, anthropology, and political science.[11] Second, sociology was founded by Comte and his contemporaries as an applied field and with the explicit mission of promoting altruistic thought, behavior, and institutions.

Many "mainstream" sociologists have, of course, taken the field in different directions. Yet, the original interest in altruism and related phenomena has been kept alive, at least at the margins of the discipline and especially among those involved in sociological practice. So, we may ask, is there in applied sociology a program that links the research of Oliner and Oliner, Fogelman, Monroe, Harvey Sarner, and the others with moral imperatives, altruism, species consciousness, and the human prospect? Our answer to this question is a cautious "yes." Although a complete and perfect program is yet to be created, applied sociology today is well on its way to developing a commonly accepted set of ethical dimensions and/or moral imperatives that feature altruism.[12] In fact, a framework for this task has already been established.

The framework to which we refer was first proposed by the sociologist, Pitirim A. Sorokin (1880–1968), whose work was mentioned earlier. Sorokin was the first Chair of the Department of Sociology at Harvard University, and he served as President of the American Sociological Association in 1964. Among the key concepts introduced by him are *sensate* and *ideational* culture types, *creative altruism*, and *integralism*. Since Sorokin's death, several studies have supplemented his approach, some with explicit reference to him but, because his contributions were generally ignored, most lacking such citations.[13] Among the works that do cite him are those of Kristen Monroe, especially in relation to her discovery of the important cognitive orientation, perception of a common humanity.

CREATIVE ALTRUISM: A SUMMARY

We focus here on Sorokin's work at the Research Center in Creative Altruism at the Harvard University to examine his concept of creative altruism and to indicate how it can be used by applied sociologists today. Also relevant are Sorokin's contributions as viewed by his biographer, Barry V. Johnston, who stated that, by the end of his long and productive career, Sorokin had arrived at an integrated theory of social action and reform (Johnston, 1995: 127–28). He states:

> [Sorokin's paradigm] frames a universe of discourse, produces an ontological and epistemological consensus on the nature of social reality and knowledge; sets malleable boundaries for doing sociology; and emphasizes the application of knowledge to practical problems of existence (Johnston, 1998: 17).

Guided by these principles, applied sociologists are currently in a position to influence the movement toward a species consciousness by practicing what Sorokin preached. That is, the study of creative altruism and the methodologies to put it into practice are key steps in developing a program for our global village that works (see Weinstein, 2000a: 6).

Following the founding of the Research Center for Creative Altruism at Harvard University in the late 1940s, Sorokin explored the principles of a social science based on an integral philosophy and a new applied science, which he called *amitology* (see Sorokin, 1954a; 1954b). His integral philosophy, or integralism, is presented as the solution to problems associated with the most recent stage of a long historical cycle. This cycle is comprised of three alternating *types* of cultures: the *sensate*, the dominant type in the contemporary Western world; the *ideational*, characterized by spirituality and altruism; and the *idealistic*, a transitional stage that occurs between the other two. These are described and illustrated extensively in his comprehensive four-volume study, *Social and Cultural Dynamics* (Sorokin, 1962; also see Johnston, 1995: 143–49). Sorokin believed that the present stage, which he further defined as *cynical* or *late sensate*, is on the verge of decline and that a new, *idealistic* stage might be emerging (if it could be helped along).

According to Sorokin, each type of culture is characterized by a particular way of knowing about reality. The sensate stage is characterized by a core belief that truth is based on the senses alone. This is opposed to both the truth of reason and a supersensory truth, which permeate the idealistic and ideational types of cultures. By the rule of "logico-meaningful" affinity, whereby specific cultural traits reflect the master values, the sensate stage is dominated by materialism, greed, and egoism.

With the help of philanthropist Eli Lilly and others, Sorokin founded the Center to combat the exclusive role played by sensate beliefs and practices in contemporary society. In their place, he sought to promote behavior based on altruistic values and *integralism*, which combines all three ways of knowing reality (the sensory, the rational, and the super-rational). This combination is the hallmark of idealistic culture. To Sorokin, the time had come to do something about transforming society through the application of integralism, to act in a reconstructive way (Johnston, 1995: 127, 128, 240).

As Johnston (1995: 204) observes, however, "the research of the Center failed to start a significant mass movement or to institutionalize the study of altruism in the social sciences." The sociological community showed little interest in altruism, integralism, or the reconstruction of society. In fact Sorokin's work, especially the earlier volumes of *Dynamics,* was criticized as metaphysical. Johnston (1995: 174) suggests the reason for this negative reaction:

> Sorokin's methods simply will not sustain his arguments with the precision he desires...what he has produced in *Dynamics* and the works that follow is a broad and valuable philosophy of history. It is a start, not a science...

As Johnston also points out, the critics failed to see that in the fourth volume of *Dynamics,* Sorokin had arrived at integralism, a theory of social reform. It appears that by then the intellectual community was no longer interested. Nevertheless, many sociologists now believe that the time has come to continue the work that began with Sorokin's explorations. Clearly, given the nature of today's social problems and the challenges of the global village, it might be wise at least to consider what Sorokin called "positive types of social phenomena." For, as he argued, too much of social science has focused on negative types:

> A scientific study of positive types of social phenomena is a necessary antidote to that of negative types of our cultural, social and personal world. The moral effect alone fully justifies a further investigation of persons and groups of good will and good deeds (Sorokin, 1950: 87).

AMITOLOGICAL PRINCIPLES

The active part of Sorokin's program was the development of *amitology*, the applied aspect of integralism. Sorokin defines amitology in *The*

Ways and Power of Love (1954b) as: "The applied science or art of developing friendship, mutual aid and love in individual and intergroup relations." If the goals of amitology are to be achieved, Sorokin noted, not only is it necessary to investigate altruistic phenomena, but altruistic acts must be practiced by ordinary people involved in common social settings. Sorokin wrote in *Altruistic Love* (Sorokin, 1950: 10), referring to the altruistic activities of "good-neighbors":

> Great altruists alone cannot supply even the very minimum of love and mutual help necessary for any surviving society…it is furnished by thousands and millions of our plain "good-neighbors." Each giving a modest contribution of love, in their totality they produce an enormous amount of "love energy". Without this moral foundation of the deeds of the "good-neighbors" no society can be satisfactory.

At the Center, Sorokin produced his major works on altruism, from which we can draw some of his definitions.[14] In *Reconstruction* (Sorokin, 1948), he defines altruism as the action that produces and maintains the physical and/or psychological good of others. It is formed by love and empathy, and in its extreme form may require the free sacrifice of self for another. In *Altruistic Love* (Sorokin, 1950), he characterizes "good neighbors" along these lines:

> A quest for sympathy, understanding, and encouragement—the desire to find a co-sympathizer in either despair or loneliness—is just as strong in human beings as the need for food or clothing.

These comments obviously point to the importance of altruistic phenomena. However, if such ideas are to aid in our quest for a "global village at peace," we must first teach and learn about their underlying values and positive effects. Our schools and colleges must develop and offer courses that focus on the teachings of altruism. Then, on this informed basis, we might try to modify our culture and social institutions by acting through the concerted actions of individuals united as groups.

This and the preceding section have reviewed some of the literature on altruism principally to stress the importance of learning and teaching about it, and the ways in which we might approach practicing it in the real world. Of course, many people are already altruistically inclined; but the philosophy and techniques of altruism are, rarely if ever, part of our formal education. Even more serious is the fact that most people, even those who study sociology, have not had the opportunity to reflect on the phenomenon. One gets the impression that when people hear about altruism, they either disregard it as unimportant, or they believe that it is unattainable.[15]

Taken as a whole, the research literature on the subject strongly indicates that various *degrees* of altruism exist; and much human behavior can be explored along the diverse range encompassed by the concept and phenomenon. This, in turn, suggests the need to invent more effective techniques for ennobling human beings, and, through these perfected techniques and increased knowledge, it will become possible to develop strategies for planned social change (Sorokin, 1948: 234). Finally, in order for our techniques and plans to be truly effective, we must show not only that they are important to pursue, but also that they work. Although we have seen that much research and related work remain to be done, considering the centrality of the concept of altruism in the social science tradition and the current state of affairs in the world, it seems well worth the effort.

DEGREES OF ALTRUISM IN THE WORK OF SOROKIN AND MONROE

The observation by Sorokin and Monroe that there are degrees of altruistic behavior—that might be measured along a continuum—is tied to a contrast between the "rational" actors of classical economic theory and altruists. Monroe has pointed out that rational choice theories, that equate seemingly altruistic behavior with acts pursued solely for extrinsic rewards, cannot account for altruism. Not all normal human behavior consists of the pursuit of individual self-interest. You will recall that, based on her research, the factor that best explains altruism is a cognitive orientation, one that is not considered in rational choice or related theories: the perception of a common humanity:

> While there are clear cognitive influences on altruism, the influence does not take the form traditionally suggested in the literature. Instead, the relevant cognitive component centered more on altruist's world views and canonical expectations about what constitutes normal behavior and on their *perceptions of a shared humanity* (Monroe, 1996: 197, emphasis ours).

Monroe's ideas about what it means to perceive a shared or common humanity should sound a familiar note by now. A worldview is:

important to the extent to which it provides a sense of connectedness to others ... a perception of self at one with all mankind ... a different way of seeing things. It is not any mystical blending of the self with another; rather it is a very simple but deeply felt recognition that we all share certain characteristics and are entitled to certain rights, merely by virtue of our common humanity. It constitutes a powerful statement about what it means to be a common humanity (p. 206).

In directly addressing the question of degrees of altruism, Monroe (1996: 7) observes that "the world is not divided into altruists and non-altruists." Rather, pure self-interested behavior and pure altruism are the two poles of continuum, and normal behavior generally occurs at some point between them. Some people "engage in quasi-altruistic behavior, in other words, without being altruists." And, in her analysis, quasi-altruistic behavior is normal behavior, which exhibits some but not all of the defining characteristics of altruism. Based on a series of intense, indepth interviews with several ordinary people and "good-neighbors," she delineated three broad categories of quasi-altruistic motivation: (*a*) spontaneity; (*b*) lack of choice; and (*c*) the constancy and universality of the altruistic bond (Monroe, 1996: 234).

Similarly, Sorokin (1950: 39) found that "...the majority of 'good-neighbors' have a similar attitude toward the whole world and humanity." He states:

They are not notable altruists; but all in all they are seemingly above the average in their altruistic activities and "good-neighborliness." Most of them do not look heroic in their good deeds. Their altruism is plain and fairly ordinary. It is however, real...their plain good deeds make the moral foundation of any society (Sorokin, 1950: 7–10).

These findings bear on recent and future research in sociology and other fields. For example, we might narrow our focus to the study of particular degrees of altruism (from no altruism to pure altruism) and various behavioral patterns (spontaneity, lack of choice, constancy, and universality) along Monroe's continuum. Also, we might concentrate on specific social contexts. Thus, on the high end of the scale of Monroe's altruism, we might study heroes. Or, on the low end, we may prefer to focus on the type of persons who we are more likely to encounter in our day-to-day interactions.

CONCLUSION: ALTRUISM AND THE GLOBAL VILLAGE

Popular culture and perspectives like rational choice theory would have us believe that altruism as something dangerous, impossible or, at best, of little practical value. Yet, a considerable amount of research in several fields has demonstrated that it is real. In fact, the theories of Sorokin, Monroe, and others have suggested that altruism can mitigate if not solve many of the social problems encountered today, including such controversial issues as religious and ethnic intolerance, welfare, aging, family crisis, health care, drug addiction, homelessness, and abortion. More than a century after Comte's death and decades after Sorokin's, the study of altruism is now beginning to make inroads into our educational system, while people everywhere are beginning to take altruism seriously as a behavioral option to "rational selfishness."

Sociology in general and applied sociology in particular has a major role to play in these changes. For there is obviously a close connection between pro-social behavior and the belief that all humans have common needs and interests. Moreover, the existence of a common humanity is a core belief among sociologists. Indeed the sociological enterprise is premised on the view that as a species humanity is essentially one, but that socialization and other sociocultural forces create profound differences among us. Those who teach sociology have nothing to teach if it isn't this: Whereas there are degrees of altruism, the idea of "degrees" of humanity, from less to more, higher to lower, etc., has no scientific basis.

In this light, all of us, experts and laypersons alike, would benefit substantially from further study of Monroe's observation that perspective promotes altruism. The perception that a common humanity exists and the type of thinking related to this perception can lead to altruistic behavior. This is an especially important task because intolerance, homelessness, and many other of today's social problems are caused or intensified by egocentric, self-interested behavior, and the perception held by some people that others are less than human. Many problems can be solved if we follow Kant's categorical imperative. We know that people in situations of conflict often do forget that we are all human. They tend to deal with others in terms of stereotypes or as enemies. The failure to recognize our common humanity does stand in the way of effective resolution of a large proportion of the problems faced in today's society.

The mission to insert into our practical work the imperative that others are no less human than ourselves is both timely and potentially effective. And it may be an important step toward improving human relations before it is really too late. Of course, as is true of other well-intended programs, this is much easier said than done. In this case, there are several obstacles to putting these sound—but not especially novel— ideas into practice. One is the tenacity of egoistical models in the social sciences and in culture generally, and the consequent failure to grant altruism a serious role in human affairs. Strong opposition to altruism exists in beliefs such as those outlined above. That is, in our type of culture altruism is understood to be deviant behavior:

> "Good neighbors" and saints are deviants who rise above the level of moral conduct demanded by the official law. Their actions are "superlegal." Some of these superlegal actions do not conflict with the official law; others result in conflict between the good-neighbors and saints on the one hand, and the official law and government on the other (Sorokin, 1950: 208).

Sorokin believed that the more altruistic a person is, the more likely he or she is to come in conflict with society's prevailing norms. He also thought that altruistic people are more likely to come in conflict with others who, for one reason or another, feel uncomfortable about altruistic behavior. Thus, learning about altruism also entails trying to understand why altruism is viewed as a threat:

> Can there be a pure and lofty altruism, not generating collision and conflict...tentatively, the answer is that there is such a way, but that it requires among other conditions, an extension of our "in-group" feelings to all humanity; and this extension must be real, manifested not only in our speech reactions but in our entire behavior...Jesus rightly said that he brought not only peace but also the sword. So does any unselfish person or deed! (Sorokin, 1950: 83–84).

As we gain a better understanding of why some people are more altruistic than others and what shapes altruistic acts may take, stereotypes will cease to limit our ability to resolve many of today's problems such as sexism or ethnic conflict. Learning about "good neighbors" as deviants may reveal much about the moral values and ethical boundaries of ordinary people. By insisting that we are all human beings, all part of one world, we may be able to be more effective actors. We would then be prepared to meet the challenges of this late sensate era and, at last, to realize the promise sensed by the first sociological students of altruism, especially Comte. That is, the promise of what Sorokin called "the ennoblement of human personality." He states:

> The practice of kindness and love is one of the best therapies for many mental disorders; for the elimination of sorrow, loneliness and unhappiness; for the mitigation of hatred and other antisocial tendencies, and, above all, for the ennoblement of human personality, for release in man of his creative forces, and for the attainment of union with God and peace with oneself, others, and the universe (Sorokin, 1948: 225).

NOTES

1. Spinoza's idea of "species consciousness" is also expressed in his argument that the physical unity of humanity is reflected in its unitary mind, "under the form of eternity." "The mind does not conceive anything under the form of eternity, except in so far as it conceives its own body under the form of eternity" (*Ethics*, Part V, proposition XXIX).

2. The sociologists Max Weber and Karl Mannheim, among others, attempted to rescue the related concept of "rationality" by distinguishing between (*a*) acts (or thoughts) that are rational in relation to a specific task; and (*b*) those that are rational in relation to a widely accepted system of values. In this way, the clear and orderly pursuit of genocide might be considered rational in the first sense but irrational in the second, because genocide is widely viewed as immoral. It has now become clear that the situation is more complex than that, and there are many levels of rationality. For example, the group pursuing what some would label "genocide" might believe that it is protecting itself from an imminent and evil threat. Thus, in relation to that group's value system, so-called genocide is actually self-preservation and a rational means to achieve peace and security. The rest of the world might believe that it is irrational, but that just increases the complexity of our judgments.

3. Spinoza was hardly the first philosopher to argue that the unitary nature of humanity is obvious to anyone who thinks clearly about the matter. Socrates, the founder of Western philosophy, defined "ignorance" as the inability to conceive of (and act towards) others as one does of (towards) oneself (see Ozinga, 1999, especially p. xvi).

4. The question of what constitutes cultural universals and, if they exist, what they are is one of the most hotly debated issues in social science. For background on this debate, see Brown (1991).

5. The Dutch-born physician Bernard de Mandeville provided one of the earliest and best-argued cases in favor of the altruistic effects of egoism, throughout his work but especially in his famous *Fable of the Bees*. See Schneider (1987).

6. It is unlikely that Marx really thought that the achievement of class-consciousness by workers was automatic. If this were the case, then the Communist Party, of which Marx was a founder, would not have been necessary; nor would the Party's main function—to lead the workers to victory in class struggle—need to be performed.

7. One of the most recent and most complete studies of the emergence of corporate power is Derber (2000).

8. Several sociologists and other observers have written about the dialectic of globalization, in which cosmopolitan innovations *and* local reactions to them are viewed as parts of a whole. The basic premise is that modernity does not replace tradition; instead it displaces tradition. In this way, rather than disappearing, traditional values and practices move over, so to speak, to make room for modern ways. As a result of such coexistence there is bound to be conflict, action/reaction. An early statement of this view is in Weinstein and McNulty (1980). Also see Weinstein (1997: Chapter 14). Benjamin Barber (1995) has popularized this perspective in his contrast between "Jihad versus McWorld."

9. See Piliavin and Charng's review of the literature on altruism since the early 1980s (Piliavin and Charng, 1990).

10. Dividing this research by discipline, at least initially, allows one to seek a clear synthesis within and between the various approaches, especially in the areas of psychology, sociology, and evolutionary biology. See the additional bibliography following the Reference section, for other examples of the variety of disciplinary orientations.

11. As is true of other practice-oriented fields, the main purpose of applied sociology is not to advance the knowledge base of the discipline (although this often happens). Rather, it is to solve practical problems for clients. But practical problems (for example, how to better organize a state-wide childcare program) are just problems and do not come with labels such as "sociological," or "political." Thus, it is generally necessary for the applied sociologist to draw on knowledge from other fields, within a broad sociological framework.

12. To many academic social scientists this might seem a rather strange, if not unappealing, project. For it assumes that we can and should agree about the kinds of social relations we would like to create or avoid in the global village. On reflection, however, these concerns make us uncomfortable only when viewed from a largely outmoded "value free" perspective in which such partisanship is to be avoided— not sought out. For today's sociological practitioner, the search for the right and the wrong ways to conduct human affairs is no more unusual than the physician's attempt to define health and illness.

13. Among the works of special relevance to our discussion are: Hutchinson (1993), Macaulay (1970), Midlarsky and Kahana (1994), Oliner and Oliner (1988), Paul, Miller, and Paul (1993), Penner (1995), Piliavin and Charng (1990), Rushton (1980), Wildavsky (1993), and Wispé (1978).

14. August Comte, who coined the term "altruism" in the 1850s, believed that some social behavior was an expression of an "unselfish desire to live for others" (Batson, 1991).

15. We have noted that "altruism and apposite concepts have been viewed as 'soft' and marginal to the main thrust of social scientific research" (Weinstein, 2000b).

REFERENCES

Batson, C. Daniel. 1991. *The Altruism Question: Toward a Social Psychological Answer.* Hillsdale, NJ: Lawerence Erlbaum Associates.

Barber, Benjamin R. 1995. *Jihad vs McWorld*. New York: Times Books.

Ben-David, Joseph. 1971. *The Scientist's Role in Society*. Englewood Cliffs, NJ: Prentice-Hall.

Brown, Donald. 1991. *Human Universals*. Philadelphia: Temple University Press.

Comte, I. Auguste. [1851] 1875. *System of Positive Philosophy* (Vol. 1). London: Longmans, Green & Co.

Derber, Charles. 2000. *Corporation Nation: How Corporations are Taking Over Our Lives and What We Can Do About It*. New York: St. Martins Griffin.

Fogelman, Eva. 1994. *Conscience and Courage*. New York: Anchor Books.

Hill, Thomas E., Jr. 1993. "Beneficence and Self-Love: A Kantian Perspective" in Ellen Frankel Paul, Fred D. Miller Jr., and Jeffrey Paul (ed). *Altruism*. Cambridge: Cambridge University Press.

Hsu, Francis L.K. (ed.). 1983. *Rugged Individualism Reconsidered: Essays in Psychological Anthropology*.

_____. 1990. *Psychological Anthropology: Approaches to Culture and Personality*. Homewood, IL: Dorsey Press.

Hutchinson, Elizabeth (ed.). 1993. *Social Service Review*, vol. 67, no. 3. Special Issue: *Altruism*. Chicago: University of Chicago Press.

Johnston, Barry V. 1995. *Pitirim A. Sorokin: An Intellectual Biography*. Lawrence Kansas: University Press of Kansas.

_____. 1998. "Pitirim A. Sorokin and Sociological Theory for the Twenty-First Century" in *Michigan Sociological Review*, vol. 12, (Fall): 1–23.

Kant, Immanuel. 1838 [1961]. "Foundation for the Metaphysic of Morals" in W. Kaufman (ed.). *Philosophical Classics: Bacon to Kant*. Englewood Cliffs, NJ: Prentice-Hall.

Macaulay, Jacqueline. 1970. *Altruism and Helping Behavior: Social Psychological Studies of Some Antecedants and Consequences*. New York: Academic Press.

Midlarsky, Elizabeth and Eva Kahana. 1994. *Altruism in Later Life*. Thousand Oaks, CA.: Sage Publications.

Monroe, Kristen Renwick. 1996. *The Heart of Altruism: Perceptions of a Common Humanity*. Princeton, NJ.: Princeton University Press.

_____. 2001. "Morality and a Sense of Self: The Importance of Identity and Categorization for Moral Action" in *American Journal of Political Science*, vol. 45, no. 3: 491–507.

Monroe, Kristen Renwick, M.C. Barton, and U. Klingermann (eds). 1990. "Altruism and the Theory of Rational Action: Rescuers of Jews in Nazi Europe" in *Ethics* (October): 103–22.

Oliner, Samuei P., and Pearl M. Oliner. 1988. *The Altruistic Personality: Rescuers of Jews in Nazi Europe*. New York: Free Press.

Ozinga, James R. 1999. *Altruism*. Westport, Conn.: Praeger.

Paul, Ellen Frankel, Fred D. Miller Jr., and Jeffrey Paul (eds). 1993. *Altruism*. Cambridge: Cambridge University Press.

Penner, Paul S. 1995. *Altruistic Behavior: An Inquiry into Motivation*. Amsterdam and Atlanta: Ropi B. V.

Piliavin, Jane Allyn and Hong-Wen Charng. 1990. "Altruism: A Review of Recent Theory and Research" in W. Richard Scott and Judith Blake (eds). *Annual Review of Sociology*, vol. 16: 27–65.

Rushton, J. Philippe. 1980. *Altruism, Socialization, and Society*. Englewood Cliffs, NJ: Prentice-Hall.

Sarner, Harvey. 1997. *Rescue in Albania: One Hundred Percent of Jews in Albania Rescued from Holocaust*. Cathedral City, CA.: Brunswick.

Schneider, Louis. 1968. "Pitirim A. Sorokin: Social Science in the 'Grand Manner'" in *Social Science Quarterly* (June): 142–51.

————. 1987. *Paradox and Society*. Edited with a foreword by Jay Weinstein. New Brumswick, NJ: Transaction Books.

Schroeder, David A., Louis A. Penner, John F. Dovidio, and Jane A. Piliavin. 1995. *The Psychology of Helping and Altruism: Problems and Puzzles*. New York: McGraw-Hill.

Sorokin, Pitirim A. 1941. *Crisis of Our Age*. New York: Dutton. Bedminster Press.

————. 1948. *The Reconstruction of Humanity*. Boston: Beacon Press.

————. 1950. *Altruistic Love: A Study of American "Good Neighbors" and Christian Saints*. Boston: Beacon Press.

————. 1954a. *Forms and Techniques of Altruistic and Spiritual Growth: A Symposium*. Boston: Beacon Press.

————. 1954b. *The Ways and Power of Love*. Boston: Beacon Press.

————. 1962 [1937–41]. *Social and Cultural Dynamics*, vol. 4. New York:

Spinoza, Baruch (Benedict de). 1677. *Ethics*. Translated from the Latin by R.H.M. Elwes (1883). *MTSU Philosophy WebWorks*, Hypertext Edition © 1997.

Weinstein, Jay. 1981. *Sociology/Technology: Foundations of Postacademic Social Science*. New Brunswick, NJ: Transaction Books.

————. 1997. *Social and Cultural Change: Social Science for a Dynamic World*. Boston: Allyn and Bacon.

————. 2000a. "Creative Altruism: A Classical Theoretical Framework for Contemporary Applied Sociology" presented at a meeting of the North Central Sociological Association, Pittsburgh, PA, 2000.

————. 2000b. "Creative Altruism: Restoring Sorokin's Applied Sociology." *Journal of Applied Sociology* 17, 1: 86–117.

Weinstein, Jay and Michael McNulty. 1980. "The Interpenetration of Traditional and Modern Structures: A Spatial Perspective" in *Studies in Comparative International Development*, vol. XV, no. 2 (Summer): 36–48.

Wildavsky, Aaron. 1993. "On the Social Construction of Distinction: Risk, Rape, Public Goods, and Altruism" in Michael Hechter, Lynn Nadel, and Richard E. Michod (eds). *The Origin of Values*. New York: de Gruyter.

Wispé, Lauren, (ed.). 1978. *Altruism, Sympathy, and Helping: Psychological and Sociological Principles*. New York: Academic Press.

4

GLOBALIZATION, ALTRUISM, AND SOCIOLOGY OF HUMANITY

Samir Dasgupta

We have perhaps talked too much, and for much too long, about globalization.

From the late 1970s and the early 1980s, some prime incidents unfolded in the world's sociopolitical and economic sphere. Fall of the Soviet Union, the subsequent termination of the Cold War, demolition of the Berlin Wall, and the Asian Crisis are some major events which accelerated the expansion of globalization at the beginning of the new millennium. This may be called as the "burst of globalization." But theorists sharing a deep sense of concern about social reality are suffering from a crisis of intellectual and humanitarian stimulation.

In the unending debates about globalization, people often take extreme, dichotomous views. It is indeed tough to place the debates on a continuum.

Contemporary segmented realities suggest that the spirit of "we-ness" and the process of globalization as such, represent a myth. It is perhaps a tragedy that a spirit so much endowed with the promise of reconstructing the world, instead expresses symptoms of uncertainty, dissonance, fundamentalism, threat, exclusion, and identity crisis. It demands rethinking the globalization discourse. Social scientists and altruists are divided over how globalization promotes homogeneity, integration, and co-existence on one hand, and disparity, dejection, differences, dissonance, and unevenness on the other.

There is, expectedly, no single definition of globalization. Indeed, some argue that its significance has been much exaggerated, but as the ever-increasing numbers of books and articles discussing different aspects of globalization indicate, it appears to be an idea whose time has come, in sociology in particular, and in the social sciences in general. As Waters (1995) suggests, it may be "the concept of the 1990s."

Globalization has irrevocably changed the spirit of human interaction and integration. The world is shrinking and time dominates over space, transforming interactional heterogeneity into global homogeneity. Philosophically speaking, globalization is a concept depicting the creation of one world, cultural integration, world market, power extension from the "metropolis" to the "satellites," and global communication. So the argument goes, globalization will result in a borderless world where economic disparity, cultural stagnation and political meanness are put aside in an emerging pact of a shared universal humanity.

However, the reality of *real-time* communication and borderless community has also brought to the surface the widening gap and even disparity that co-exists in the same spatial proximity. This may be called *other globalization* which is gloomy and anxiety-ridden for the vast numbers of the "excluded" populace in our world.

The widening gap between the rich and the poor and rampant commercialization and commodification of social life undermine the social integration in the Third World countries and also threaten the moral, ethical and economic fabric of those societies. As a result anxiety over the loss of cultural, social and economic identity and the weakening of ethnic and communal solidarity and social harmony seems widespread.

Globalization can be analyzed as the unfolding resolution of the contradiction between ever increasing capital and its national, political, and social formations. It also indicates the sequential shifts of the zone of capital accumulation from the local, regional, state, national, and to the global levels. It certainly signifies the triumph of capitalism, and thus, globalization has been termed as the second bourgeois revolution (Teeple, 2000). Chossudovsky (2001) writes, "The globalization of poverty in the late 20th century is unprecedented in world history.... This poverty is not, however, the consequence of a 'scarcity' of human and material resources. Rather it is the result of a system of global oversupply predicted on unemployment and the worldwide minimization of labour costs" (p. 26). This so-called bourgeois revolution has in several places caused economic genocide, destruction of national economy, price dollarization, and global hunger on one hand and fear of social identity, humane existence, survival uncertainty, mental exclusion, fundamentalism, terrorism, ethnic disintegration and global–local clash on the other.

This crisis can be attributed to the crisis of human values. It is undeniable that there is a set of common values that humanity has shared over centuries and it is the *only* gateway to the ideal globalization discourse. By and large humanity has always been in favor of accepting the necessity and significance of global dialogue and rejection of force. Promotion of understanding in the cultural, economic, and political arena and the strengthening of the foundations of freedom, rationality, and human rights have always been recognized as pursuable goals at a global level. Indeed, if humanity devotes all its efforts to institutionalizing dialogue, conflict resolution through discourse and understanding, it will leave an invaluable legacy for the benefit of future generations. "The west and the rest" dichotomy makes our world not compressed but divided. The horror of contrast between winners and losers, between "lions" and "foxes" at all levels of human existence feeds a pervasive mood of uncertainty that creates a situation of "either–or" mentality and exclusion–inclusion fear psychosis.

Naomi Klein (2002) states with anguish, "Globalization is now on trial because on the other side of all these virtual fences are real people, shut out of schools, hospitals, workplaces, their own farms, homes and communities. Mass privatization and deregulation have bred armies of locked-out people, whose services are no longer needed, whose life styles are written off as 'backward', whose basic needs go unmet" (p. iii). These fenced-out people remain and grow even more helpless and powerless. Factors like spatial and country origin, illiteracy, ill-health, morbidity, life-chances of millions of identity crisis and the threat of exclusion by the global winners, decide the Third World citizens today.

It may be argued that globalization gives an erroneous impression about the extension of capitalism to the remotest corners of our globe. That it is nothing, but an innovative process of capitalist exploitation ("managerial" or "flexible capitalism") in the guise of humanity and a sense of liberalism. The newly introduced "free market" gospel thus resists the ethics of globalization, which ultimately impedes the goals of a common humanity. For this reason, globalization may be assumed as a fragile and incomplete project, which suffers from reality–illusion dilemma.

This illusion–reality dilemma creates negative consequence for globalization. Global economic institutions can enhance the quality of life and can foster a balanced economic growth, a claim which stands in contrast to the reality.

The philosophy behind the globalization process should be non-commercial and should be concerned with love, compassion, and altruism. Our world today demands a humane process of globalization.

The initiators of globalization have failed to move to a world vision of inclusion, of participation, of humanizing the differences, discrimination and dissonance. Commonalties, which would unite the people of "the rest" might have been possible if they were not dejected and excluded. The globalizers have created a global gloom where we can see a dichotomy of "revolutions of rising expectations" and "revolutions of rising frustrations."

We are not born fundamentalists or born terrorists. The threat of global exclusion creates such an identity crisis of humanity. Let me cite an illustration:

> On July 20, 2000, on the shores of Lake Tiberias, two young families were enjoying a summer day, strangers to each other. A young boy decided to swim in the waters of a lake that touches three countries. A few minutes into joyful swim, panic or fatigue overwhelmed him, and he gasped for air. From the shore, the first two notices were a young man, father of the other young family. Instinctively, he dove into the waters and within minutes he rescued the young boy, who managed with a bit of help to regain the shore and the safety of the sands. Unfortunately, the young man who saved the boy was physically overcome and drowned. What history recorded of that day on Lake Tiberias is that the young boy who was saved was of the Jewish faith and the young father who helped him was of the Muslim faith. Under the new paradigm, one father had saved the life of a young boy who was not his own, as any parent would do, no matter when, no matter where, even at the cost of his own life (cited from Picco, 2001).

Today, the human ethics like longing and striving for peace, justice, partnership, and truth, appear as misnomers in global conduct. What is clear is that the global–local dichotomy is giving birth to an uncertain globalization where there is no room for humanity. In inner spaces of our world, we witness the tragic events of the division of humanity. Globalization as a humanity threatening phenomenon has come to possess our habitat. One of my friends, Abbas Mehdi, also a contributor to this volume, suffered from the sad demise of his dearest little sister. She became a victim of militarization in recent Iraq. I am taking the liberty of citing from his heartbreaking message about the event. I call this globalization gloom.

> This is what Iraq's liberation looks like to me right now: a woman bleeding to death on a public highway, unable to get help because coalition forces have blocked the road while looking for insurgents. A

large room in a hospital, where corpses are laid at random on a dirty floor, some of them uncovered, with nothing to identify them, a scene of horror for those trying to find the bodies of their loved ones.

The woman is my younger sister. She was involved in a car accident on the road between Najaf and Baghdad, traveling home after visiting my parents. When she finally reached the hospital in Baghdad after being stuck on the road for more than six hours, no one could do much for her, and no one was able to get in touch with her family. The hospital was overwhelmed and disorganized, and telephone lines were down.

My parents didn't find out what had happened to their daughter until two days after her death. When my other sisters finally got to the hospital, the staff didn't even know exactly where her body was. They were directed to a large room full of corpses.

'Do you remember when we lost our luggage in Jordan?' one of my sisters asks me. 'It was like that. The bodies were lying all over the floor like lost baggage.'

'I have been working for regime change in Iraq, hoping that Saddam Hussein would fall from power and that peace, democracy and stability would come to my country. Yet I opposed last year's invasion. I feared what the cost might be for the Iraqi people of being subjected to yet another war, weakened as they were by the last Gulf War and the war with Iran, and by protracted economic sanctions. Now that scenario has played itself out and come home to me personally in a way that I never expected, fearful though I was for Iraq and for my family.... As I talk with friends and relations who have gathered for my sister's burial, what I hear most plainly is hopelessness. Hopelessness, frustration and resignation....

'She was lucky,' one person says bitterly. 'It is as if we are all dead already,' someone else says. Yet another is grateful that he has no money—that is why the thieves have left him alone, he says....

My eldest sister tells of waiting in a long line to buy cooking gas. There was a quarrel, voices were raised, the American soldiers panicked and started to fire their guns, and the result was that six people died before her eyes. When I spoke to my younger sister in Baghdad last year, I could often hear the sound of gunfire in the background.

The Iraqi people I speak to are very frightened by the danger and random deaths they see all around them, at home, at work, in the street. They are also worn down by the hardships of their everyday lives. In this oil-rich nation, people wait in line for 5 to 10 hours for gas. The supply of electricity is still erratic, and clean water isn't always available. The main reaction of many Americans to the Iraq war and its aftermath may simply be confusion, but for me, and the people of Iraq, it has meant suffering, destruction, and pain. In fact, the latest war has been hugely costly to everyone concerned, to Iraq, to the United

States and to the rest of the world, in material and nonmaterial ways. No one is safe there now, not U.N. staff, or Paul Bremer, or Paul Wolfowitz. Even when the president of the United States visited Baghdad, he arrived in a darkened plane, in utmost secrecy, and stayed for only a few hours. My sister would not have died from her injuries if she had not been in a country that is unbearably unstable, to the point of anarchy. In this situation, no one is a winner, and no one feels liberated.

This specific case is enough to predict the destiny of the deprived majorities. This globalization hypocrisy and its effect on "the rest" of the world indicate that we are living in a sorry period. In India, Gujarat witnessed one of the deadliest communal riots in our recent memory. Insurgency and secessionism as the expressions of ethnopolitical upsurge, took roots in Punjab, Kashmir, Nagaland and Manipur, in Tripura, in Assam, Meghalaya and Arunachal states. In the era of globalization the Indian State is under growing pressure, like demands for new states, multi-level government, regionalization of the political forces, secessionist movement, violence, insurgency and terrorism in the Northeast, caste/class/agrarian violence, growing influence of Hindutva, attacks on the minorities, environmental hazards, Indo–Pakistan conflict, Indo–Bangladesh border problems, nuclearization of South Asia, and so many such risk factors. At the global level, severe famine in Somalia, economic genocide in Rwanda, corruption and economic and political turmoil in Bangladesh, debt burden in Brazil, Argentina and Bolivia, economic disintegration in Peru, are some examples of globalization deconstruction.

Do these indicators express the true spirit of globalization mission? How are the meanings of global humanity and altruism to be seen today? In the era of globalization, social scientists are trying to analyze the ideal meaning of altruism which they argue mainly stems from the perception of human rationality.

Rational choice theorists believe that decisions are based on rational thought. For the most part, rational decisions are made with the intention of receiving some type of benefit or reward. However, people sometimes make decisions that have no obvious remuneration. From a rational choice theorists' perspective, altruism provides an explanation for decisions in which the rationale is not quite clear. Because selfish acts and decisions with apparent self-benefit clearly demonstrate rational thought, altruism can be thought of as the rationale for selfless decisions.

The altruists divide altruism into two categories: "goods altruism" and "participation altruism." Goods altruism is the idea that we want other people to have things. Therefore, we do charity and support government decisions that benefit others. Sometimes we gain satisfaction from participating in an activity for non-selfish reasons; an emotion derived from participation altruism. When altruism blends with human rationality and emotion, the globalization process can become a harmonious process. But when it lacks this element, harmony does not remain uniform.

GLOBAL VILLAGE: HARMONY WITHOUT UNIFORMITY

We had a pot, made of clay, filled in water. We could see our faces in that water. Once the pot had broken and our faces disappeared. This is the destiny of heated global influence. The water denotes our socioeconomic and sociocultural elements or resources and our faces represent our deep-rooted traditional identities and values. The question arises: is our existence or identity is at stake because of being a party to globalization? Does globalization intend to reshape and remake us as the new men of new civilization? Once Rabindranath Tagore aptly remarked, "India has received all and accepted all."

No one could deny the relevance of humane values to the concept of development. Development must be "by" and "for" people, as they are the initiators and beneficiaries. If someone views technoeconomic foundation as the only prime mover in the development process, he would not do justice. The process of capital accumulation depends mostly on the quality of natural resources and techno-wealth, which could accelerate the pace of human need and demand. The development of any country identifies the development of collective personalities and self-identities. But the globalization circle has created such an orbit where the faces of humanity merged with the rationality of irrationality. This is the root source of crisis of globalization.

GLOBAL DISPARITY

Misery and deprivation is rampant in our world. It presents a "picture of horror and dejection for majority of people who were born to face a slow and agonizing death". (Dadayan, 1988). The *New Times* (1983) reports that in the Third World there are: starving—over 500 million; life expectancy under 60—1.7 billion; lacking medical care—1.5 billion; living in extreme poverty—over 1 billion; unemployed and underemployed—more than 500 million; annual per capita income under $150—800 million; illiterate adults—814 million; children having no access to school education and unable to attend school—over 200 billion. J. Tinbergen (1976: 21) notes, "we have a situation where, in the Third World, millions of people toil under a broiling sun from morning till dusk for miserable rewards and premature death without even discovering the reasons why."

The statistics reveals that since the 1960s (when globalization started gaining strength) income disparity among countries had increased worldwide. It is evident from the various World Development Reports that the wealthy countries have experienced a steady growth in their share of the world GNP, while the poorest countries have experienced with a tragic decline in their share of world GNP. Between 1960 and 1991, the richest fifth of all nations had its share of world income rise from 70 percent to 85 percent, while the poorest fifth of all nations had its share fall from 2.3 percent to 1.4 percent (UNDP, 1994).

Using the Weberian model of capitalist development we could evaluate the logic behind globalization (see Figure 4.1).

DEBT BURDEN

Debt burdens have increased the ever growing gap between the developed and the Third World countries. According to the World Bank, the debt of developing countries rose by 8 percent to just over $2 trillion in 1995. The Third World debt has grown from $9 billion in 1955 to $572 billion in 1980, and $2177 billion in 1996. Its debt service—including interest and principal—is close to $245 billion in 1998 (Gelinas, 1998). Debt is increasing in percentage of GNP as well. The overall Third World debt to GNP ratio reached 27 percent in 1980 and 38 percent in 1994. For sub-Saharan Africa, it has reached up to 79 percent. For countries like Madagascar, Coted'Ivoire, and Zambia, it is over 200 percent. Nicaragua is overburdened with around 801 percent. In case of Congo, it is 454 percent and for Mozambique it is 450 percent. Practically the debt burden in the Third World countries has reached 2 trillion dollars: entire countries have been destabilized as a consequence of the collapse of national currencies often

Figure 4.1: Relation between Economy and Globalization

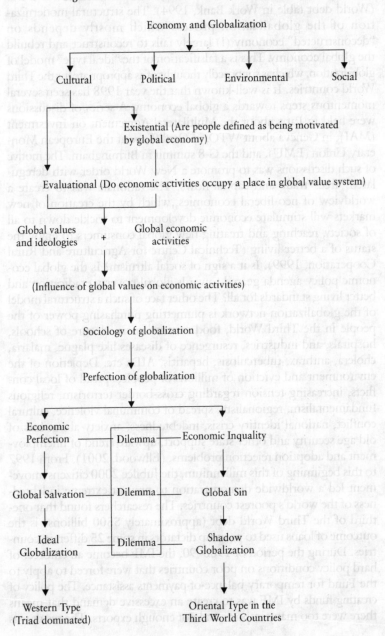

resulting in the outbreak of social strife, ethnic conflicts and civil war (World debt table in Work Bank, 1994). The structural modernization of the globalization process which mostly depends on "deconstructed" economy (!) largely fails to reconstruct and rebuild the global economy. This is a falsification of the "ideal type" model of globalization, which is supposedly thought of as appropriate for the Third World countries. It is well-known that the year 1998 has seen several momentous steps towards a global economy. A series of discussions were held in Paris about the Multilateral Agreement on Investment (MAI), in Geneva about WTO, in Cardiff about the European Monetary Union (EMU), and the G-8 summit in Birmingham. The motive of such discussions was to promote a New World order with deregulated "free" trade and capital-flows. The rationale was to create a worldview of neo-liberal economies, which by the creation of new markets will stimulate economic development to trickle down to all of society, reaching and treating new global consumers to enjoy the status of a better living (Technical Centre for Agriculture and Rural Cooperation, 1999). Is it a sign of social altruism? Is the global economic policy agenda geared towards global poverty eradication and better living standards for all? The other face of such a structural model of the globalization network is plumetting purchasing power of the people in the Third World, food security crisis, closure of schools, hospitals, and industries, resurgence of diseases like plague, malaria, cholera, anthrax, tuberculosis, hepatitis, AIDs etc. Depletion of the environment and eviction of millions of people, spread of local conflicts, increasing tension regarding cross-border terrorism, religious fundamentalism, regionalism, spread of communal violence, cultural conflict, national identity crisis, indebtedness, anxiety about loss of old age security and other state support, upward trend of unemployment and adoption rejection problems. (Ellwood, 2001). From 1997 to this beginning of this millennium, the Jubilee 2000 citizens' movement led a worldwide demonstration to prevent extreme indebtedness of the world's poorest countries. The researchers found that one-third of the Third World debt (approximately $500 billions) is the outcome of loans used to prop-up dictators in some 25 different countries. During the period of 1980–90, the IMF become an enforcer of hard policy conditions on poor countries that were forced to apply to the Fund for temporary balance-of-payments assistance. The policy of creating funds by IMF was to create an excessive demand that means there were too many imports and not enough exports. The result was the devaluation of the currency and cutting of government expenditure. This retards the economy, and rate and intensity of domestic demand that results in "fewer imports, along with more, and cheaper, exports". Then IMF intends to eliminate the balance-of-payments. "Countries were more or less forced to adopt these austerity measures if they wanted to get the IMF seal of approval" (Ellwood, 2001: 46). The 1980s were a "lost decade" for much of the Third World. Growth stagnated and debt doubled to almost $1,500 billion by the end of the decade. By 1999, it was nearly $3,000 billion. The foreign debts of developing countries are more than two trillion US dollars and still growing. The result is a debt of over $400 for every man, woman and child in the developing world—where average income in the poorest countries is less than a dollar a day. All these aspects of globalization of poverty (Chossudovsky, 2001) are turning our society into an anomic state, where marginality along with the offshoots of global–local and winners–losers dichotomy, are the forces behind the support for anti-globalization protest movements. Chakravarthi Raghavan in a lecture (1998) rightly pointed out:

> For we are living in dangerous time, with the entire post-war edifice of multilaterlism and cooperation crumbling. The danger today arises on the economic front, and has already spilled over into political and social arena; at the root is the attempt to repeat history, with active neo-mercantilism of the powerful countries lurking behind the rhetoric of neo-liberalism and globalization.

In the age of global consumerism and exploitation it is very difficult to imagine democratic globalization with a sense of humane feeling and altruism. Re-imagination may only be possible if the process of globalization starts anew from the below.

GLOBALIZATION AND INDIAN PHILOSOPHY

Indian society is old, largely tradition bound, and has covered a span of around 5,000 years since the period of its first known civilization (Dube, 1990). Indian society has been an example of religious and ethnic coexistence all along. The synthesis is yet to be the issue of debate. Once Cramb aptly remarked that, India is not only the Italy of Asia ... it is not only the land of romance, art and beauty ... India is religion. Most of the major religions of the world—Hinduism, Islam,

Christianity, Buddhism, Jainism—are found here with their numerous cults, doctrines, and ideals and ideas. In a word, India has always followed a pattern of cultural pluralism.

The Indus Valley Civilization, known to be the dawn of Indian civilization was also multi-ethnic in character. Hinduism draws largely on Brahmanical texts, such as the Vedas, the Upanishads and the *Bhagavadgita*. The normative principles of Hinduism are based on beliefs, ideals, and logic of permissiveness, liberalism, being and becoming, creation and destruction, hedonism, utilitarianism and spiritual transcendence (Singh, 1973).

Vedic thought in India expresses that man is throughout a bundle of *Kama* (desire). Possession of desires gives him second birth but their absence make him one with *Brahma*. *Brahma* is one, and represents our globe. The concept of globalization is inherent in the Hindu philosophy. Globalism is very much related to sublimation and the blend represents the true nature of *Karma* (deed) which ultimately leads to *moksha* (salvation). So altruism is the basic tenet of the *Bhagavadgita*— it is their *dharma* (religion) which makes him *Punyabana* (virtuous). The altruistic philosophy began to take a liberal shape with the ties of interaction between Indo-Aryans and the earlier inhabitants. With the sense of widening the canvas of altruism, Indian society was divided into four groups on the basis of macro division of labor—the *Brahmins* (priests/twice born), the *Kshatriya* (the warriors and the aristocrats), *Vaishya* (cultivators) and the *Shudra* (the servants). This initially liberal division of labor ultimately rendered Indian society hierarchic and segregated. This unpredictable outcome of the division of labor created a special "social category" called caste. A "clean" or "pure" caste began to dominate over the unclean or impure category. The question of purity and pollution began to disturb the sedate life of Indian society. The polarization of humanity was created with the definitive motive of making politicization of humanity. Ultimately, the divine sense of altruism was converted into rational sense of either *purchasable* or *consumer altruism*. The system or process of "divide and rule" got underway. But the core of Indian philosophy talks about divinity and salvation, about holy and sacred tradition, about global harmony and cosmic rhythm, about spiritual transcendence and morality irrespective of space, time, labor, and human qualities. In traditional Indian society the issue of todays' modernism i.e., space–time linkage or space over time concept was conceived by the philosophers. Hindu philosophy didn't preach syndicated Hinduism or Hindu nationalism, rather, it always advocated the doctrine of divinity, eternity, and universalism. Let me quote from the chapter of invocation of the *Bhagavadgita*, which denotes the philosophy of today's globalism. *"Him we salute … salute to that supreme one who is bodied forth in Brahma."* The globalization agenda, if not overshadowed by vested interests of capital accumulation, can become noble and egalitarian. If it were altruistic and humane, as the *Bhagavadgita* tells, *"the right is to work only; but never to the fruits thereof"*, then the defoliation and disparity would not dominate our global economic scenario.

Three characters of *Prakriti* (nature) are *Sattva* (equilibrium), *Rajasa* (attraction) and *Tamasa* (inertia) in Indian Vedantic philosophy, which binds men of our world with *Guna*. This global tie of humane bondage leads to infinite altruism. An altruistic man should be *"He who is everywhere unattached, not pleased at receiving good, nor vexed at evil, his wisdom is fixed"* (*The Bhagavadgita*, Chapter 2). The concept of "species consciousness" (see Weinstein and Pozo in this volume) derived from the oneness of mind, wisdom of self-realization, love for the global kinsmen, path of knowledge and path of work for the active. The anti-concept of "species-consciousness" is hypocrisy: *"He, who restraining the organs of action, sits resolving in the mind, thoughts regarding objects of sense, he, of deluded understanding, is called a hypocrite"* (*The Bhagavadgita*, Passage 6, Way of Action). Thus, *Brahma*, created mankind together with the motive of "good-consciousness": *"By this shall ye multiply…."* Thus the multiplication i.e., the global men represent a unit of our "super organic" surrounding. The globalization process itself signifies the work of *Yajna*, i.e., sacrifice which is of following types: *a*) *Deba-Yajna* (offering sacrifice); *b*) *Brahma-Yajna* (transmission and acquisition of knowledge); *c*) *Pitr-Yajna* (offering liberation); *d*) *Nr. Yajna* (the feeding of the hungry); and *e*) *Bhuta Yajna* (the feeding of the animals). This highly philosophic altruistic version of the *Gita*, can become the guiding light for the process of globalization. The real altruism in our philosophy means, *"do thou always perform actions which are obligatory, without attachment, by performing action without attachment, one attains to the highest."*

In modern society, crisis and disparity arise mainly because of uneven distribution of wealth, comfort, and assistance. Our philosophy tells that only he, who looks with equal regard upon well-wishers, friends, foes, neutrals, the hateful, the relatives, the neighbors and the righteous and the unrighteous, attains "universal self." The center of global village is nothing but the universal self. It would be the "ideal type" model of a global village, if all living beings of the globe could derive their sense of power from the same center. The Indian philosophical system visualized globalization since its inception during the vedic ages: *"I see Thee boundless form on every side with manifold arms, stomachs, mouths, and eyes; neither the end nor the middle, nor also the beginning of Thee do I see, O Lord of the Universe, O Universal Form ... I cannot distinguish East from the West, nor the North from the South."*

I have mentioned earlier about the epistemological break-up in Indian Vedantic philosophy. The nature of true altruism for better living lies in the seed of *Sattvika* i.e., knowledge related to sincere desire, having no demand of result or fruit. But practicing *Rajasika* (motive of gaining honor and ostentation) and *Tamasika* (motive of ruining other to gain something) knowledge should not be the prominent forces in our notion of altruistic globalization.

The tradition began to change with the emergence of British rule in India. From the end of 17th century right up to the beginning of the 18th, India had been wading through a bewildering welter of cultural, social, political, and economic ideals and ideas. Politically overthrown by the British, India came under the sway of an exotic civilization. However, the hypnotic spell of a foreign civilization began to recede slowly but steadily with the mighty reform movements during the 18th and the 19th centuries.

The first phase of reform movements called for changes in the culture and values of the Indian society and the second meant for synthesis of new cultural and valuational ideals and ideas with the traditional forms. Both the reformers accepted the ideal-typical cultural context of Indian society. The social thought, which lies embedded in reform movement, was the issue of unity in diversity: assimilation, transmission and transformation of soul from "I" to "we." The "we"-ness is the only indicator of humanitarian philosophy of Indian society. Social thinkers, poets, patriots and prophets, and reformers, all were believers of a humanized globalization—globalization in terms of human interaction, in terms of emotional closeness, spiritual transcendentalism, and human values.

Rabindranath Tagore, the great poet and social thinker believes that we have to come down from our towers and share our soul with the helpless. Here the individual self blends with the global selves. Otherwise the concept of the globalization of economy would be turned into "globalization of poverty." Table 4.1 illustrates the extent of poverty at a global level.

Table 4.1: Country-wise Percentage of Population Living below Poverty Line

Country	Percentage of population living below poverty line (1998)
Brazil	17.4
Vietnam	50.9
Zambia	86.0
Peru	49.0
Mexico	10.1
Pakistan	34.0
Bangladesh	35.6
Indonesia	15.1
India	35.0

Source: *World Development Report*, 2001.

The estimates in Table 4.1 do not include people living in insular pockets of poverty, therefore do not give the whole picture. It is estimated that, about 80 percent of the rural population in India is living below subsistence level i.e., below 2400 calories. 'The Structural Adjustment Programme initiated by the WTO and the IMF, more or less failed to achieve its target of removing global economic disparity. It is evident from the report of UN Development Program (1994), that the earnings of five richest countries of the world from the global market increased from 70 percent to 85 percent whereas the earning of the poor countries decreased to 1.4 percent from 2.3 percent. Besides, the victims of the absolute poverty and hopelessness in most of the Third World countries, now beget a new concept like "inequalization" instead of globalization. The disparity is so acute that free-ride aid and free-riding behavior cannot even be thought of. Side by side, a three fold increase in trade dependency occurred over a 45 year period (1950–95), with no sign of slowing down. In the year 1995 the "Tri-polar concentration" has accelerated the speed of globalization process. But stimulated by the aid system, indebtedness has also been globalized. The financial and economic dependence of the underdeveloped countries has several dimensions: "massive modern technology transfers," which have made the undeveloped economies dependent on a know-how they cannot pay for, and thus, are unable to increase productivity on their own. The latter acts as a mode of reinforcement for the former, pursued by the IMF and the World Bank's structural adjustment program, leading to great indebtedness of the underdeveloped countries. The Third World with no control over the mechanisms of the globalization of capital and market is becoming highly marginalized and depressed. A new political class emerges, which acts as a true intermediary for the aidocracy. Another important dimension is use of military aid, which is used to repress the progressive social movements. The development ideology when viewed as a virtuous deed or a moral obligation called the seventh seal (Gelinas, 1998).

The above mentioned seals have sealed the humane rationale of globalization policy and prospects, because the Third World debt has increased from $9 billion in 1955 to $572 billion in 1980 and $2,177 billion in 1996. The formation of OECD from OEEC in 1961 brought together all the industrialized capitalist countries. In 1977 there were about 190 sovereign, economically and geo-politically interdependent countries in the world. Twenty-nine OECD countries are on the top of the ladder, the middle section consists of 23 countries and the rest i.e., 126 underdeveloped countries are on the last steps of the development ladder. The last step consists of four categories of underdeveloped countries like high income petroleum exporting countries, developing countries, maldeveloped countries (India belongs to this category with per capita GNP of around $340) and least developed countries (*World Development Indicators*, 1997; *Human Development Report*, 1997). Development assistance as defined by the agreement is "the granting of resources to developing countries as donations or preferential credit, such as long-term loans at interest rates at least 25 percent below the market value." But the computation of interest rate and market rate results profit for the donors. The net financial transfers from the Third World to the developed countries (1983–95) totaled approximately $300 billion (World Bank, World Debt Tables, 1995).

Besides, ODA and other loan giving agencies like multi-lateral and bilateral aid-givers (amount of loan given to the beneficiaries—$70 billion per year), "take aid" scheme (amount of loan given in 1991 was $50 billion which increased to $159 billion by 1995) and NGOs (only 9 percent of the total loan given by all aid agencies for the global development). The Third World therefore still suffers from the disease of socioeconomic and sociopolitical malnutrition. The prime reasons for such underdevelopment are excessive population increase, missing institutions, lack of capital formation, lack of entrepreneurship, debt burden, vicious circle of poverty, hunger and malnutrition and different endowment conditions (Siebert, 1999). Precisely, the context of underdevelopment focuses on, *a*) financial dependence; *b*) overseas oriented economic system; *c*) national economic dislocation; and *d*) subordination of elite to foreign interests and influence of category classification (Gelinas, 1998). If we recall hymns from the *Bhagavadgita* i.e., love for the global kinsmen or *Sattvika* attitude i.e., *"sincere desire having no demand of result or fruit"*—the disparity would be removed and globalization of humanity would dominate over globalization. Rabindranath Tagore, once said, "Thou powerful country! Don't lead us to the path of competition—lead ourselves to the arena of cooperation."

ALTRUISM AND SOCIOLOGY OF HUMANITY

Indian civilization has a long tradition of philosophical and meta-physical speculation. Indian society would have been fractured and disintegrated had it not been for the traditions of religion of human-ity, the doctrine of *Atma* (self), and *Karma* (duty). The Indian social thinkers have analyzed these epistemological connotations. Sitting on a small rock of *Kanyakumari*, at the southern tip of India, Swami Vivekananda, the great thinker meditation not upon God but upon India. Engrossed in deep meditation he felt that India would rise only through a renewal and restoration of that highest spiritual conscious-ness and altruistic humanity. Inspite of chronic underdevelopment India is alive in her religion and culture. Vivekananda felt that India's only deficiency was poverty and she must have to learn from the world how to remove it. So Vivekananda advocated the necessity of learn-ing western science and technology. Romain Rolland said that just as, at the call of Jesus, the dead Lazarus came to life, so also, at Vivekananda's call, a moribund India was infused with new life. So far my view is concerned the 1893 was the year of inception of the concept of globalization. On Monday, September 11, 1893, the Par-liament of Religions as an adjunct of the World's Columbian Exposi-tions, held in Chicago to celebrate the four hundredth anniversary of the discovery of America by Christopher Columbus with the mission to bring the countries of the world into a more friendly relationship. Vivekananda in his "Chicago Address" quoted a few lines from a hymn to "Sisters and Brothers in America": "As the different streams having their sources in different places all mingle their water in the sea, so O Lord, the different paths which men take through different tenden-cies, various though they appear, crooked or straight, all lead to Thee." His "calling" was the true calling of globalization in the spiritual and humane sense: "Sectarianism, bigotry and its horrible descendant, fanaticism have long possessed this beautiful earth. They have filled the earth with violence, drenched it often and often with human blood, destroyed civilization and sent whole nations to despair. Had it not been for there horrible demons, human society would be far more advanced than it is now. But their time is come; and I fervently hope that the bell that tolled this morning in honour of this convention may be the death-knell of all fanaticism, of all persecutions with the sword or with the pen and of all uncharitable feelings. ..." (Chicago Address, 11 September, 1893). Doesn't this message symbolize the true form of altruism and the essence of sociology of humanity? The Third World has always been assigned a marginal place in the international economic order and the prescriptions for advancement were either half-hearted or completely misguided. Although advances have been made for some, the pressing issues of global inequality and poverty remain. The implementation of actually existing development has involved environmental destruction, exploitation, state oppression, and impoverishment (Kiely, 1998). Indian philosophy teaches that a man ought to live in this world like a lotus leaf, which grows in water but is never moistened by water; so a man ought to live in the world—his heart for fellow men and hands for duty. This philosophy of altruism can lead to the "ideal type" of a global village.

Here lies the philosophical crisis of the globalization process. What is theory, especially social or sociological theory? It is merely the abstraction—the expression of thinking of one's self—expression of transcendental condition. When it blends with reality the issue of applied theory comes into fore. And all the theories in sociology mostly stem from the humane attributes. It takes different shapes, forms, and approaches only because of one's perception and sense of vision. So theory is just a travelling of one's mind, vision, and angular axis, a coming up of different thoughts through various conditions and circumstances to the same goal i.e., to crate a better, humane world. "It is the same light coming through glasses of different colours and there little variations are necessary for adaptations." (Chicago address, 1893). So the Positivistic approach, Structural–Functional approach, Conflict approach, Interactionist approaches, Phenomenological school, Structuration theory, Modernism and Postmodernism have emerged. The deductions or inferences of most of the schools (may be pragmatic, may be empirical, may be abstract, may be applied) are humanistic and act as an effective force in liberalization of the human spirit. But the debate between realism and idealism continues. The exponents of the philosophy of science however, tend to renounce metaphysics, with which the Indian philosophers were mostly concerned. Herbert Fiegl (1967) defends the scientific status of such metaphysical problems as the relationship between consciousness and the brain. Some believe it as the construction of scientific ontology. The rapid development of experimental science in the 18th and the early 19th centuries was pregnant with the empirical methods of research. In the 1830s, positivism came out with a demand to oust idealistic philosophers from science and subjected idealism and religion to sharp criticism regarding them both as products of the mythological stage in the development of human spirit (Naletov, 1984). Comte considered it immaterial whether men's personified abstractions were later turned into souls or fluids and, thus, rejected metaphysics as going outside the limits of science. So he discarded metaphysics as an expression of mysticism, idealism or dialectics. The Vienna circle launched a struggle against metaphysics and (Schlick, 1925; Ludwig Wittgenstein, 1949) demanded verification of the metaphysical proof. But Carnap (1971) viewed that universal laws appear to be senseless from the philosophy of verification principle. His inductive logic (also called "logical empiricism") led him "beyond its limits right into the arms of metaphysics (Naletov, 1984). Carnap (1971) regards metaphysics not as knowledge but rather as poetry with illusion of knowledge. But logical empiricism sometimes confines our thinking into the cage of narrow methodology to study man and society. Man is always vain, fickle, unique, and marvelous. A theory of science could not search for any general injunctions. Man can only be studied in terms of spiritual and practical activity. Here metaphysics blends with idealism and considers everything to be a function of reason and regards "being" in terms of man's mindset. Thus, mental images of man produce his practical activity. This might be called epistemological realism (Trigg, 1980). Sociology of humanity emerged from such an epistemological realism or solipsism. Still a bipolar approach is in operation to study man in society: a) scientific; and b) anti-scientific. But my view is that the scientific method of studying man in the era of globalization fails to achieve its humane target. But the anti-scientific approach which we call philosophic, (real base of scientism!), could develop a view of studying man as the representative of the global human race. The practitioners of such a philosophy are the humanists. Though a section of the sociologists views the doctrine of humanism as pseudo-study of man's real life or, the study of eternal and timeless values or a set of wishes or normative demands of the individual. But the doctrine of globalization policy, which creates global malady now, demands humanistic assessment because scientism of globalization fails to achieve the need and demand of man's real life. Here scientism blends with aid-trading. Therefore how to guarantee protection of man's personal dignity, how to protect, human rights, how to develop man's potentialities and capacities, and how to make life without destructive wars, hunger, famine, poverty and disease—all demand altruistic and humane theory. Peter L. Berger (1963: 188–89) states, "... there is a peculiar human value in the sociologists responsibility for evaluating his findings, as far as he is psychologically able, without regard to his own prejudices, likes or dislikes, hopes or fears ... but it is especially different to exercise in a discipline that touches so clearly on the human passions." Under the pressure of scientific realism sociology's data are cut so from the "living marrow of human life" (Berger, 1963) that the basic and inherent sensitivity of humanism has lost its significance. Understanding of the humanistic place of sociology, as Berger (1963) views, implies an openness of mind and a catholicity of vision. The emergence of Renaissance was the starter of such a humanistic philosophy in sociology. It is the theory, which tells about freedom. Edward Shils (1961) thought of man as possessing with cognitive, aesthetic and moral capacities. Man is not a machine. He is soft and tender. He has sense of reasoning, emotion, moral choice, aesthetic orientation, and creativity, and a sublime soul. The time has come again to build theory on the humanistic perspective because late modernism demands the analysis of self-interpretation of man. Shils (1961: 620–23) said:

> sociology is humanistic because it attempts to understand whatever man does, in categories that acknowledge his humanity; his need for cognitive orientation; his capacity for rational judgement and action, for affectionate attachment, for aesthetic expression and response, for moral decision.... Sociology is a continuation and elaboration of the permanent and necessary effort of man to understand himself and his species.

The humanistic sociological study now goes beyond the individual and is directing to the "Trans-individual and Trans-historical" network. Experimental sociology and scientism only attempts to cast the result and procedure of this collective self-interpretation. Here lies the importance of applied sociological research. The bottom-line of applied sociological research is not only to explore generalization in technical manipulation of data; it is like going beyond a melting pot. Applied sociological research speaks of man's self-interpretation, assimilation, and self-transmission and thus it helps the progress of humanity.

> Every step forward faces a new danger. Every new virtue that renders if possible can all too readily become a vice that will undo it ... love can turn to tyranny and then to hatred the sense of nationality can become a monstrous exclusiveness ... Sociological analysis ... is part of this movement. Without this movement, there would be no sociological analysis (Shils, 1961: 620–23).

In India, sociology of humanity has its roots in the writings of our ancient sages, Vedantic philosophy, Brahmanical texts, and social thinkers. They had attempted to study human being only in terms of love, interaction and goodness of human quality, which is always divine and transcendental. Sree Ramkrishna, a pious saint said, "attainment of highest ideal of humanity is the attainment of divinity." Plato contended that cognition leads to love and love affects both morality and knowledge creativity. "Love does no wrong to God or man and suffers no wrong from God or man. For love does not suffer from violence, if it suffers, since violence does not touch love; and everyone becomes a poet when love touches him" (Plato's symposium). Plotinus (A.D. 205–70) the neo-Platonic philosopher has talked about three types of love; *a*) A God or divine love; *b*) A demon, or human love; and *c*) A passion or animal love. The divine–human–animal co-existence may create risky altruism but their synthesis may be a calling of postmodern Renaissance. The philosophical tradition in India posits the identity of man in a totality i.e., entire cosmos. Thus universal love and compassion are based on metaphysics (it is difficult to denounce) which is the only basis of modern applied sociology. The oriental wisdom is defined not only by freedom from the egoism of the senses and comprehensiveness and sense of proportion of goals and values, but also by universal *altruism* and comparison (Mukerjee, 1960). *The Bhagavadgita*, the sacred text of Hindus, written around the beginning of the last millennium, develops a global religion of charity in terms of *Sarva-avatara* (Universal incarnation), *Sarva bhute daya* (Universal compassion), and *Sarva Mukti* (Universal salvation). It is also evident from Indian philosophic texts that the charity, benevolence and compassion are the true identities of altruism and humanism, which are not only the expressions of metaphysics but lead to reality.

Bertrand Russell said, "I mean sympathy as an emotion not as a theoretical principle." This altruistic metaphysics or metaphysical altruism changes its form and character from time to time and sociologists get maximum benefit from the changed version to build up new socio-logical theory. Comte's positivism is such a changed or metamorphosed version of metaphysics. Western philosophy mainly depends on the Kantian theme of justice and equality. The post-Kantian thought in-troduced a cultural and economic determinism. The most prominent followers of this school of thought are Marx and, Hegel. In India, the ethics were founded on the pure metaphysics of the:

> in dwelling of God in man fosters infinite charity and compassion for all sentient beings, and is equalitarian, buoyant and dynamic. In her non-theistic ethical systems it is introspection that establishes an in-ward continuity of self and the universe as a whole including more than man and generates reverence for man absolutely every common man (Mukerjee, 1960: 172).

Historically, with this view, the Bhakti movement (egalitarian in its core) character the impetus of building theory of altruism in India. And Comte's dictum of altruism has acted as fuel to light sociological theory of altruism in the academic sphere in India. The kernel of *Mahayana* moral idealism is! "Can there be bliss when all that lives must suffer? Shalt thou be saved and hear the whole world cry"! A true world-picture can be assessed in terms of scientific methodology or empirical verification, proof, and principle. But it is more impor-tant to study the modern world picture in terms of humanity, love, interaction and moral values. Wisdom, erasing the boundaries of self is the true sense of altruism and humanism which global late modern society demands. The issue of universalism and impersonalism of wis-dom and emotion is conducive to the promotion of the world commu-nity of today. Global co-operation rests far less on laws, conventions, treaties, institutions and aid-giver organizations, and far more on sym-pathies, habits, and aspirations (Mukerjee, 1960). Indian sociologists recognize the philosophy of social sciences as expressions of universal values, insight, experiences, and practices of man. The goal is to mould and shape *one community*, *one culture* and *one world*. The Indian concept of *Metaphysical Triad* i.e., Man–Selftranscendence–Universe (Mukerjee, 1960), and makes the universal person and global community viable and builds a sociology with a sociological Triad: Personality–Transcendence–Social universe. Cooley named it "growth of the larger mind." The "triad" or the concept of the growth of the larger mind advocates the hidden philosophy of applied sociology. Because "Man is not simply an organism bounded by an epidermis ... he is also an essence beyond the boundaries of skin and person" (Shils, 1961: 10–11). Thus metaphysical thinking lies embedded in applied sociological research and denotes the true spirit of altruism and humanity. But Benoy Kumar Sarkar (1916), an Indian Sociologist, was in favor of positivism. In Comte's judgement, humanity has been marching towards a stage in which positive knowledge or scientific experience is dominant" (Sarkar, 1916). In his essay, "Asiatic Positivism" (1916: 73) Sarkar states: "if the term [Positivism] be applied to any inculcation of humanitarian principles or social duties and the like, every religion is surely positivistic and every human being is a positivist." Inspite of such a bi-polar debate between metaphysics and positivism, Indian sociology tells the theory of humanism. To remove global malady, to use globalization for better living standards and a brighter tomorrow for the deprived, the ability to understand and transmit "species consciousness" must be inculcated. Amartya Sen in a recent interview (*The Times of India*, December 2, 2001) expressed his discontent about the political situation in the world. He said, "The narrow categorization of civilization ... is a hazard to the human rights movement" Weinstein's version (in this volume) gives us a new dimension in this regard: "Learning about good neighbours as deviants may reveal much about the moral values and ethical boundaries of ordinary people. By insisting that we are all human beings, all part of one world, we may be able to be more effective actors". But the Hindu–Muslim riots in 1940, or the cross-border terrorism in Kashmir does not depict such a bright picture of humanism. The rioters or the terrorists stop being workers or capitalists (Sen, 2001) and ultimately they are unable to set their home in order. "What do the religions of the world tell us? To love each other, to love everyone.... Religions authorities have regularly been a force for peace and tolerance, it is equally clear that they have regularly been a force for violence and intolerance. No doubt God moves in mysterious ways, but we simple humans may feel impelled to try to make reuse of there days and, dare I suggest it, to draw conclusions from our faiths and our sciences than mere fatalism" (Immanuel Wallerstein, in this volume). Adopting global policy of benign altruism can only solve the problem of such religious dualism between peace and violence and between tolerance and aggressiveness. If sociological theories were used for such a social cause, the blend of theory with action would contribute to social progress in the world context.

CONCLUDING REMARKS

The co-operation, transcendental interaction, coexistence and synthesis of aid and love can lead to a true globalization. Second, the policymakers, planners, and initiators should have it in mind that aid should not go with trade, but with universal love. Third, we should start with what the people in the Third World countries have, not with what they lack. There is a famous Chinese proverb, which comes to my mind:

Give a man a fish and you feed him for a day,
Teach a man to fish and you feed him for life.

Now my question to the policymakers, aid-givers and sociologists is: what is the true sense of altruism? To provide aid to the Third World or to create livelihood capacities? The challenge of globalization is now facing such a strange interlude, and the right answer will decide the future of globalization. After all, in this global age, only a truly global ethics can be of real value, and with hunger, starvation and anxiety-ridden survival and economic uncertainty, it cannot be the discourse of humanity. The globalization with such global–local dichotomy and threat of exclusion is nothing but a deviant globalization.

NOTE

1. Paper presented in the Seminar of Society for Applied Sociology (SAS) in Sacramento, California, in 2002.

REFERENCES

Albrow, Martin. 1990. "Introduction" in Martin Albrow and Elizabeth King (eds). *Globalisation, Knowledge and Society: Readings from International Sociology*. London: Sage.
Allen, Tim and Thomas, Alan (ed.). 2000. *Poverty and Development into the 21st Century*. London: Oxford University Press.
Annon, Kofi A. 2001. "Foreword" in Giandomenico Picco (ed.). *Crossing the Divide*. New Jersey: School of Diplomacy and International Relations, Seton Hall University.
Bardis, Panos, D. *The Measurement of Love in Social Science*. Kansas, USA.
Berger, Peter, L. 1963. *Invitation to Sociology: A Humanistic Perspective*. England: Penguin Books.

Bhattacharyya, Swapan Kumar. 1990. *Indian Sociology: The Role of Benoy Kumar Sarkar*. Burdwan: University of Burdwan.

Carnap, Rudolf. 1971. "A Basic System of Inductive Logic" in R. Carnap and R. Jeffrey (eds). *Studies in Inductive Logic and Probability*. Berkeley: Univ. of California Press.

Chossudovsky, Michel. 2001. *The Globalisation of Poverty*. Goa: Other India Press.

Comte, Auguste. 1855. *The Positive Philosophy of Auguste Comte* (H. Martineau's translation). New York: Blanchard.

Dadayan, V. 1988. *The Orbits of the Global Economy*. Moscow: Progress Publisher.

Dasgupta, Samir and Roychoudhury, Jayanta. 1980. "Origin and Development of Sociology in India—A Brief Review" in *The Calcutta Review*, vol. 5, nos. 3 & 4.

Dube, S.C. 1990. *Indian Society*. New Delhi: National Book Trust.

Ellwood, Wayne. 2001. *The No-Nonsense Guide to Globalization*. London: Oxford University Press in association with Verso.

Fedoseyev, P.N. 1988. "Man in Today's World" in I.S. Kulikova and V.V. Mshvenieradze (eds). The *Philosophical Conception of Man*. Moscow: Progress Publishers.

Fiegl, Herbert. 1967. *The "Mental" and the "Physical."* Minneapolis: University of Minnesota Press.

Gelinas, Jacques, B. 1998. *Freedom From Debt*. Dhaka: The University Press Limited.

Giddens, A. 1990. *The Consequences of Modernity*. Oxford: Blackwell, Oxford.

Huizer, Gerrit. 2003. *Globalization From Above and From Below: A Dialectical Process*. Inhoud.

Kiely Ray, 1998. *Introduction: Globalisation, (Post) Modernity and the Third World* in Ray Kiely and Phil Marfleet (eds). *Globalisation and the Third World*. London and New York: Routledge.

Klein, Naomi. 2002. *Fences and Windows: Dispatches from the Front Lines of the Globalization Debate*. Canada: Knopf.

Mcluhan, Marshall. 1964. *Understanding Media*. London: Routledge.

Marx Karl and F. Engels. 1848. *The Communist Manifesto*. Moscow: Progress Publisher.

Mukerjee, Radhakamal. 1960. *The Philosophy of Social Sciences*. London: Macmillan & Co. Ltd.

Naletov, Igor. 1984. *Alternatives to Positivism*. Moscow: Progress Publishers.

Picco, Giandomenico, (ed). 2001. *Crossing the Divide*. School of Diplomacy and International Relations, Seton Hall University, New Jersey.

Roger, Trigg. 1980. *Reality at Risk: A Defence of Realism in Philosophy and the Sciences*. N.J.: Barnes & Noble Books.

Sandler, Todd. 1997. *Global Challenges*. Cambridge: Cambridge University Press.

Sarkar, Benoy Kumar. 1916. *Chinese Religion Through Hindu Eyes: A Study in the Tendencies of the Asiatic Mentality*. Sanghai: The Commercial Press Limited. Reprinted in 1976 from New Delhi: Oriental Books Reprint Corporations.

Schlick, Moritz. 1925. *Allgemeine Erkenntnislehre*. Berlin: Springer.

Sen, Amartya. 2001. *Poverty and Famines*. New Delhi: Oxford University Press.

Sengupta, Chandan. 2001. "Conceptualising Globalisation" in *Economic and Political Weekly*, Aug 18, 2001.

Shils, E. 1961. "The Calling of Sociology" in Talcott Parsons et al. (eds). 1961. *Theories of Society*. New York: The Free Press of Glencoe.

Siebert, Horst. 1999. *The World Economy*. London and New York: Routledge.

Singh, Yogendra. 1973. *Modernization of Indian Tradition*. New Delhi: Thompson Press (India) Ltd.

Singh, Yogendra. 1986. *Indian Sociology: Social Conditioning and Emerging Concerns.* New Delhi: Vistaar.

Sklair, Leslie. 1991. *Sociology of the Global System.* Harvester Wheatsheaf Hemel Hemptead.

———. 1999. "Competing Conceptions of Globalizations" in *Journal of World-Systems Research*, vol. 5, no. 2.

Swami Vivekananda. 2001. *Chicago Address.* Kolkata: Advaita Ashrama Publications Department.

Tagore, Rabindranath: *History of India.* Kolkata Viswa Bharati. *The Bhagavadgita.*

Teeple, Gary. 2000. *Globalization and the Decline of Social Reform into the Twenty-First Century.* Aurora Ontario: Garamond Press.

Tinbergen, Jan. 1976. *Reshaping the International Order.* (A Report to the Club of Rome). New York: E.P. Dutton & Co., Inc.

UNDP (United Nations Development Programme). 1994. *Human Development Report.* New York: United Nations.

Unnithan, T.K.N. 1982. "A New Sociology for India" in P.K.B. Nayar (ed.). *Sociology in India.* Delhi: B.R. Publishing Corporation.

Walia, Nona and Amartya Sen. 2001. "A Nobel Cause" in *Times of India:* December 2, 2001.

Wallerstein, Immanuel. 2000. *Cultures in Conflict?* Y.K. Pao Distinguished Chair Lecture, Hongkong, September 20, 2000.

Waters, M. 1995. *Globalization.* London: Routledge, 1995.

Weber, Max. *The Protestant Ethic and the Spirit of Capitalism.* Charles Scribner's Sons, New York, 1958.

Wittgenstein, Ludwig. 1949. *Tractatus Logico-Philosophicus.* London: Routledge and Kegan Paul.

World Bank. 1994. *World Bank Report.* Oxford: Oxford University Press.

World Development Report. 2000, 2001. *Attacking Poverty.* Oxford University Press.

World Development Report. 1992. *Development and the Environment.* Oxford University Press.

5

GLOBALIZATION, MULTINATIONAL CORPORATIONS, AND WHITE-COLLAR CRIME: CASES AND CONSEQUENCES FOR TRANSITIONAL ECONOMIES[1]

Verghese Chirayath and Ernest De Zolt

INTRODUCTION

This chapter examines adverse consequences for transitional economies in their interaction with multinational corporations. Using case studies, it highlights how globalization results in further opportunities for the expansion of global capitalism, with false promises to developing nations. While lucrative financial terms, weak environmental regulations, and low wage labor attract multinationals, they rarely contribute to the economic self-sufficiency objectives of the developing nations. Instead, transitional economies serve as a platform for corporate criminality.

Market pressures on multinationals to cultivate global dominance coupled with economic pressures on developing nations to participate more fully in the world economy lead to white-collar crime. While the preferred methodology for examining white-collar crime is the analysis of aggregate data, this chapter, by default, utilizes a case analysis design. Aggregate white-collar crime data sources are unavailable or incomplete as they apply to transitional economies. Therefore, the data from three white-collar crime cases: Infant Formula in the Third World, Union Carbide in Bhopal, India, and Enron near Mumbai, India, are evaluated against three theoretical assumptions that examine the impact of globalization on criminal corporate behavior.

1. The transnational encouragement of the hypermobility of capital, the unending search for cheap labor, and the immobility of

domestic labor, lead to the misuse and abuse of power by corporations. Globalization leads to expansionism rather than genuine economic development.

2. Corporate criminal behavior is learned, as is conventional corporate behavior through formal channels of corporate socialization and through the selective association with competitors. This learning includes not only techniques of committing crime but the values associated with their rationalization.

3. The commission of white-collar crime occurs through either the internalization of criminal corporate goals or the use of deviant means in accomplishing conventional goals.

To the extent that multinational corporations adhere to these assumptions, increase in the frequency of white-collar crime are expected. Less developed countries must rely on their own regulatory agencies and indirectly on regulations of the home country of the multinational corporation to minimize adverse social and economic effects resulting from the presence of multinationals.

THEORETICAL FOUNDATIONS

WHITE-COLLAR CRIME

The theoretical conceptualization of white-collar crime, by Edwin Sutherland, as "a crime committed by a person of respectability and high social status in the course of his occupation" has met with philosophical and legal challenges over *content* and *form* since its inception in 1939. James Coleman's (2001) review of the literature notes that Sutherland's original definition of white-collar crime has undergone multiple revisions. In 1970, the definition of white-collar crime was amended to include any successful acquisition of property through trickery (Edelhertz, 1970). While intending to extend the scope and surveillance of white-collar crime through nonphysical acts of deception for profit regardless of the severity of the criminal act or the social standing of the perpetrator, the reverse occurred. White-collar crime was redefined downward to include many common acts of street crime that de-emphasized its unique occurrence.

In the mid-to-late 1970s and early 1980s, the definition of white-collar crime shifted once again, this time to an emphasis on elite deviance.

See Clinard and Quinney (1973); Clinard and Yeager (1980); Schrager and Short, (1978); and Simon and Eitzen (1982). The problems associated with defining white-collar crime under the category of elite deviance are twofold: (*a*) definitions of deviance usually rely upon community standards of interpretation; and (*b*) as a result, many forms of criminality are overlooked or dismissed. When this occurs, formerly defined acts of white-collar crime get redefined as normal business practice. More recently, white-collar crime has undergone a retrospective definition that applies Edwin Sutherland's idea of a public violation of trust (see Friedrichs, 1996; Shapiro, 1990) occurring within a prestigious occupational setting (Green, 1990).

While definitional changes to the *content* of white-collar crime have occurred, changes to the *form* of white-collar crime have also been documented. Discrimination, sexual harassment, political violence, environmental crime, bribery, and corruption are emerging as conceptual forms of white-collar crime. We argue in this chapter that when the socialization practices of multinational corporations combine with the economic needs of transitional economies many of the aforementioned forms of white-collar crimes take place.

TRANSITIONAL ECONOMIES AND MULTINATIONAL CORPORATIONS

While definitions of white-collar crime continue to emerge, multinational corporations are continuing to extend their influence over the world economy. As Immanuel Wallerstein's (1984) theory of global stratification suggests, over the past 450 years the nations of the world have been linked as a result of colonization, a global division of labor, and the increasing role of multinational corporations. For Wallerstein, the Core of world systems theory consists of more developed, technologically sophisticated nations that control the global economy and of Periphery nations that supply raw materials and labor to the Core nations. The transfer of these resources occurs on terms set by the latter.

Semi-periphery nations, defined here as transitional economies, in turn, engage periphery nations through "colonial" dependency strategies not unlike those through which core nations engage semi-periphery nations. This hierarchical arrangement leads to a global division of labor where workers from semi-periphery and periphery nations contribute to the production process with unequal results. Given the dependence of semi-periphery and periphery nations on core nations for access into global markets, it is not surprising to understand the significant advantage owned by core nations and their multinational corporations (Amin, 1974; Emmanuel, 1972; Frank, 1966, 1967, 1980). The increased dependence on core nations and their multinational corporations minimizes the opportunity of semi-periphery and periphery nations to compete economically with core nations (see, Table 5.1).

Table 5.1: Twenty Largest U.S. Multinational Corporations in 1980

Company	Foreign Revenue ($)	Total Revenue ($)	Foreign Operations (%)
1. Exxon	56,999	79,107	72
2. Mobile	27,401	45,477	60
3. Texaco	26,023	38,350	68
4. Ford Motor	19,106	43,514	44
5. Standard Oil (C)	17,490	29,948	58
6. General Motors	16,751	66,311	25
7. IBM	12,244	22,863	54
8. ITT	11,579	21,996	53
9. Gulf Oil	11,102	23,910	46
10. Englehard Minerals	9,790	18,102	54
11. Citcorp	7,287	10,904	67
12. General Electric	4,997	22,980	22
13. Bank America	4,728	9,450	50
14. Conoco	4,709	13,030	36
15. Dow Chemical	4,672	9,255	51
16. Occidental Petro	4,573	9,638	47
17. Chase Manhattan	3,786	6,079	62
18. Standard Oil (IN)	3,725	18,930	20
19. El du Pont de Nemours	3,357	12,572	27
20. Xerox	3,316	7,027	47

Source: *Forbes*, July 7, 1980, p. 102.

Limited domestic economic opportunities in semi-periphery and in periphery nations and their transitional economies leave few options than to rely on multinational corporations in order to compete in the global market. A cursory review of the literature on transitional economies illustrates this fact. In general, the overreliance on small and medium-sized businesses to rebuild formerly state-managed economies is less than ideal, and time-consuming (Anderson and Pomfret, 2001; Bartlett, 2001; Smallbone, Welter, Isakova, and Slomanski, 2001; Woodward, 2001). Moreover, simultaneous political reform strategies need to be undertaken to provide sound economic re-tooling, regardless of emphasis on either small or medium-sized businesses or multinationals (Garrod, 2000; Rana, 1995; Rutkowski, 1996; and

Wai-chung, 2000). Not lost on the revitalization of a nation's political economy is the cost of "doing business," that is, ethical economic development through corporate citizenship (Anderson and Pomfret, 2000; Jones and Kato, 1996; and Tisdell, 2001). The concern for semi-periphery and periphery nations is how to develop a universal structure of corporate citizenship and ethics without causing adverse economic consequences for host nations (Leisinger, 1996; Mokhiber and Weissman, 2001; and Sexty, 1998).

Notwithstanding the inequality and stratification of semi-periphery and periphery nations brought about by the multinationals, the internal class relations in these nations reinforce global inequality by keeping domestic wages and corporate taxes low and domestic labor opportunities limited (Kerbo, 2000). Multinational corporate involvement exacerbates income disparity between the poorest and wealthiest 20 percent of household incomes. The lowest income quintile in countries such as Bangladesh and India consume twice as much of the national income as in the United States for the same quintile because of social policies reflecting the adverse influence of multinationals (see, Table 5.2).

Nations with transitional economies do not stand alone resolving contradictions between ethical behavior and economic growth. Multinational corporations struggle with their own contradictions over the ethical versus the prudent in the pursuit of profit maximization. Clinard and Yeager (1980: 92) caution multinationals that they "...operate in countries where bribery, sexual harassment, racial discrimination, and a lack of concern for the environment are neither illegal nor unethical or unusual." Multinational corporations need to balance profit maximization, corporate citizenship, and regulatory compliance in resolving the competing interests of their shareholders with those of host nations.

THE ORGANIZATION AND WHITE-COLLAR CRIME: DEVIANT GOALS, DEVIANT MEANS, AND DOMINANT COALITIONS

The sociological literature on organizations informs the topic of white-collar crime through its discussion of deviant goals, deviant means, and dominant coalitions. Whether a corporation, as an entity, engages in criminal organizational goal setting or an individual corporate actor engages in deviant means in the pursuit of legitimate organizational goals, the motivation is likely to be found in the organizational culture (see Aldrich, 1999; Boatright, 1999; Hall, 2002; and Ott, 1989).

Table 5.2: Cross-National Comparison of Income Inequality within Nations
(percentage of total household incomes in the mid-1990s)

Country	Poorest 20%	Top 20%
Bangladesh	9.4	37.9
India	9.2	39.3
Kenya	3.4	62.1
Zambia	3.9	50.4
Indonesia	8.4	43.1
Philippines	5.9	49.6
El Salvador	3.7	54.4
Egypt	8.7	41.1
Thailand	5.0	52.7
Peru	4.9	50.4
Costa Rica	4.0	51.8
Brazil	2.5	64.2
Panama	2.0	60.1
Mexico	4.1	65.3
Chile	3.5	60.1
China	5.5	47.5
Malaysia	4.6	53.7
Vietnam	7.8	44.0
Venezuela	4.3	51.8
Spain	7.5	40.3
Ireland	6.7	42.9
Italy	7.6	38.9
United Kingdom	7.1	39.8
Netherlands	8.0	37.9
France	7.2	40.1
West Germany	9.0	32.1
United States	4.8	45.1

Source: World Bank (1999: 198–99).

The difficulty in examining a cause and effect relationship between organizational culture and white-collar crime is due to the existence of multiple normative standards in most organizations. Multiple normative standards are constructed through varying patterns of differential association that lead to the emergence of dominant coalitions, groups with competing views on organizational goal setting (Thompson, 1967). While organizations direct individual efforts toward the fulfillment of stated organizational goals, individuals do not always conform to organizational efforts. As a result, individuals and/or coalitions sometimes commit organizational resources to existing goals in a manner consistent with white-collar criminal activity (Sherman, 1974).

METHODOLOGY

In the absence of aggregate white-collar crime data, this chapter examines white-collar crime in transitional economies through a critical analysis of three cases. Taken together, the cases are not representative, but illustrative of the interactions between transitional economies and multinational corporations. Each case is examined according to its setting, deviant activity, corporate defense strategy, response to deviant corporate activity, outcomes of the case, role of regulating agencies, and the likelihood of repetition of deviant acts (see, Table 5.3). Moreover, each case is examined in relation to our three theoretical assumptions. What follows are three case narratives which are amplified in Table 5.4.

CASE NARRATIVES

THE INFANT FORMULA CASE

In the Infant Formula case, 33 multinational corporations show fit to extend the sale of infant formula through aggressive marketing and sales in developing nations. They did this with the knowledge that many of the parents, if not most of them, would have to use impure contaminated water in making infant formula for their children, or to "stretch" formula with more water. The corporations were also aware of the risks involved in serving infant formula that had been mixed with contaminated water (diarrhea and death) but chose to go ahead with their pursuit of additional market share and profits. For these reasons, the case matches both our first and third assumptions (Ermann and Clements II, 1984).

THE UNION CARBIDE/BHOPAL CASE

The Union Carbide accident in Bhopal represents many of the issues and controversies of what takes place when multinationals operate in developing nations. Bhopal continues to count its dead and injured even after 18 years and Union Carbide has had to trim its global operations due in part to its history of accidents. Use of local labor by the company resulted in what is now referred to as the "trained incapacity" of

Table 5.3: White-Collar Crime in Transitional Economies: Three Cases

	Infant Formula in Third World	Union Carbide in Bhopal, India	Enron in the United States and India
Setting	Throughout the Third World.	Bhopal, India.	Houston, Texas and Maharashtra State, India.
Deviant Activity	At least 33 multinational corporations, including Nestle and three U.S. companies; American Home Products, Abbott Laboratories, and Bristol Myers, engaged in unethical marketing practices, including distribution of free formula samples and exploitation of the idea that formula feeding was "modern" in countries lacking the infrastructure, especially safe drinking water, required for formula feeding. Many children died as a result of mixing the formula with unsafe drinking water.	As part of the cost-cutting measures, the Union Carbide workforce in Bhopal had been cut in half between 1980–84. Training had been reduced from six months to 15 days. The use of local labor, insufficiently trained in emergency management, for a sophisticated pesticide production process resulted in inadequate response to an accidental leak of approximately 40 tons of methylisocyanate (MIC), a highly toxic, flammable chemical used in making pesticides. When this chemical reacted with water, a violent chemical reaction occurred, resulting in the deaths of at least 2500 people in December, 1984.	Enron overestimated its earnings by $583 million in five years, and kept large amounts of debt off their balance sheets through business partnerships and the formation of dummy companies. The company forced its employees to purchase Enron stock for their retirement even as the value of the stock plummeted. Top company executives cashed in their Enron stocks, which sold at $90 a share in August 2000, before bankruptcy was declared in December 2001. A review of options exercised and sold by Enron executives in 2001 indicate that top officials collected about $117 million. Enron paid Arthur Anderson to be both its auditors and consultants, creating a conflict of interest. Enron's close contacts with Vice President Cheney were instrumental in establishing a $2.8 billion gas-fired power plant named Dhabol Power Company outside Bombay, India despite violent protests.
Corporate Defense Strategy	Nestle first denied that a problem existed. Corporate explanations of what happened focused on an interrelated set of social changes, urbanization, imitation of life-styles in industrialized countries, company marketing techniques that stressed the need for modern women to work outside the house thereby requiring infant formula and mother–child separation.	It was Union Carbide's position that the Indian Government invited them to locate in India as a way to help a poor, developing nation attain self-sufficiency in food production, and to save foreign exchange currency by using local labor. Union Carbide blamed their Indian counterparts for the disaster for lack of oversight of production and storage facilities.	Enron blamed Arthur Anderson for deceiving them. The firing of Arthur Anderson as Enron's auditor may well have been another defense strategy; Enron's chairman repeatedly stated that he was unaware of the activities of errant employees and what wrongs they may have committed without company approval. Enron attempted to sell itself to a much smaller competitor, Dynegy. However, Dynegy pulled out of the proposed merger because of its perception that the purchase may well have diffused Enron's wrongdoing. The Dhabol project was defended

	Infant Formula in Third World	Union Carbide in Bhopal, India	Enron in the United States and India
Response to Wrong Corporate Activity	Many consumer groups including OXFAM (of Oxford University), the Interfaith Center in Corporate Responsibility (ICCR) and the Infant Formula Action Coalition (INFACT) advocated for an infant formula boycott. They made infant formula an attractive issue and addressed numerous religious groups to raise their awareness and knowledge of the harm cause by the use of infant formula. ICCR charged the companies that sold infant formula with aggressive marketing tactics, which caused women to change from breast-feeding to bottle-feeding.	The Indian Government imposed fines on those seen as responsible for the disaster and paid out monetary settlements to victims. Victims have complained that the settlements are inadequate. Numerous groups in Bhopal, formed to document Union Carbide's unsafe practices in plants elsewhere in the world pointed out: • a 25,000 gallon spill of propylene oxide, a cancer causing chemical in the Canada River in West Virginia • the exposure to mercury of 402 employees in Indonesia who now suffer from kidney diseases • the poisoning of 998 people in California who ate watermelon that had been contaminated with Union Carbide's Temic pesticide	by Enron as meeting India's quest for power despite strong opposition in India. The legal charges against Enron carry possible prison sentences. The false statements made in relation to the sale of securities and construction of dummy corporations explicitly for the purpose of camouflaging the financial situation of the company carry penalties of up to 10 years in prison. Enron is the target of more than a dozen investigations by the Securities and Exchange Commission, the Justice Department, and Congressional Committees.
Outcomes of the Case	Nestle eventually agreed to halt distribution of free samples and to advocate breast feeding of infants, a practice long endorsed and encouraged by the World Health Organization. The United Nations passed a resolution specifying appropriate infant formula making practices. U.S. firms have changed their marketing policies and some developing nations have passed legislation to limit the distribution of infant formula.	Death estimates range from 2,500 and 250,000 to much higher recent estimates, that include the 10,000 deaths resulting from long-term complications. In 1984, Union Carbide employed over 55,000 people in 137 countries. By contrast, today the company employs 13,000 people in 20 countries.	Enron's bankruptcy has left over 5,600 people without jobs. By the time the company filed for bankruptcy, the value of its stock had fallen $0.29 a share. Enron proposes to give its creditors a proposal to restructure itself as OpCo Energy Company by "bundling" its power plants, electric utilities, natural gas pipelines, and oil and gas exploration assets. U.S. banks loaned one billion dollars to Enron and face a potential loss of 400 million dollars in unsecured loans. The outcomes in India remain uncertain at best. As India's largest power facility Dhabol's failure is bound to have nationwide repercussions. Three Indian banks funded Dhabol to the tune of $1.4 billion. These banks alone are expected to lose $208 million in interest income over the next year.

(Table 5.3 Contd.)

(Table 5.3 Contd.)

	Infant Formula in Third World	Union Carbide in Bhopal, India	Enron in the United States and India
Role of Regulating Agencies	Despite a largely successful boycott, no regulatory organization had jurisdiction over this case.	While the Indian Government has tried to represent the families of victims in this case there is widespread dissatisfaction with such representation and with Union Carbide due to the meager monetary settlements and health prognosis of victims.	Several congressional committees are investigating Enron, each with a different focus including: employee retirement plans; Enron's relationship with its auditor, Arthur Anderson; the destruction of Enron-related documents and securities fraud and the impact of Enron's collapse on investors and capital markets, and Enron's use of offshore entities. Enron is also being investigated by the Securities Exchange Commission and the Justice Department. On a broader scale, the lack of transparency in financial dealings of many corporations may create similar problems. More regulation of accounting practices is needed.
Likelihood of Repetition	Uncertain. While the infant formula boycott was successful in terminating unethical methods of distributing infant formula, there is no guarantee that another mobilization of activists would resume in the event of similar practices by well-to-do corporations in developing nations.	High Probability: Multinationals generate increasing levels of their profits from their operation in developing nations. Since they do so at the explicit invitation of local governments it is likely that accidents such as the one in Bhopal will reoccur since developing nations lack infrastructure to respond to accidents, have high rates of illiteracy and seek out collaboration with corporations that have the technology and resources to locate in developing nations.	High probability: This case illustrates an increasingly probable outcome when multinational corporations operate in developing nations. It also illustrates the indirect dependency of developing countries on the regulatory procedures in the developed countries. While the reorganization of Enron as OpCO Energy Company may result in closer scrutiny of the new organization, the reorganizers will have to convince creditors that their plan is viable and must assist Enron in recovering some of the $60–100 billion that Enron is owed.

those very same workers. Capital mobility, cheap labor, and weaker environmental regulations facilitated Union Carbide's decision to locate in India and what learning (and lack thereof) took place precipitated the accident. Union Carbide's willingness to reduce training for Bhopal employees was additional evidence as to the complexity of the corporation in what has been called the worst industrial accident of the 20th century. All three assumptions of our chapter are supported by this case.

THE ENRON/DHABOL CASE

The Enron bankruptcy and its consequences at the Dhabol Power Plant outside Mumbai is yet another prominent case of a multinational corporation and its affiliation with a subsidiary in a developing nation. Enron initially owned 85 percent of the Dhabol Power Plant that was later reduced to 65 percent ownership. Beyond massive job losses, both in India and in the United States, the decision of Enron to file for bankruptcy has left Dhabol "high and dry." Both Indian and United States investments in the project were made with the assumption that a two billion eight-hundred thousand dollar, gas-fired power plant would pay handsome dividends. Enron's actions may result in further debts for the Indian Government without many prospects for

Table 5.4: Comparison of Case Study Adherence to Theoretical Assumptions

		Assumption #1	Assumption #2	Assumption #3
Case Studies	Bristol-Meyers, Nestle, and Infant Formula			+
	Union Carbide's Bhopal Accident	+	+	+
	Enron's Venture in the Dhabol Power Company	+		+

1. The transnational encouragement of the hyper-mobility of capital, the unending search for cheap foreign labor, and the immobility of domestic labor, leads to the misuse and abuse of power by the corporate state. Globalization leads to expansionism rather than genuine economic development.
2. Corporate criminal behavior is learned, as is conventional corporate behavior through formal channels of corporate socialization and through the selective association with competitors. This learning includes not only techniques of committing crime but the values associated with their rationalization.
3. The commission of corporate crime occurs though the internalization of criminal corporate goals or through the use of deviant means in accomplishing conventional goals.

the power that was originally projected from the Indian subsidiary. No doubt Dhabol internalized Enron's rosy projections for power generation in the future much to its dismay. Assumptions 1 and 3 of our chapter are supported by this case.

Summary

Multinational corporations have both benefits and drawbacks for transitional economies. Chief among the benefits are the promotion of higher employment, greater access to international markets, and the mobilization of capital for productive purposes that might have gone to other less fruitful purposes. Among the most frequently heard criticisms are the misapplication of host country resources, the exploitation of host country wealth for the benefit of citizens of other nations, and the diversion of local savings from investment by host-country nationals (Ferrante, 2000).

The three cases in this chapter deal with multinational corporations and their questionable operations in developing nations. In the first case (Infant Formula) we see a situation in which public pressure actually changed the behavior of a multinational corporation. In the second case (Union Carbide) we see a situation in which the Indian Government facilitated Union Carbide's willingness to produce pesticides ostensibly to make India self-sufficient in food production. In the third case (Enron/Dhabol) we see a corporation in which Indian ownership of Dhabol was insignificant in comparison to the United States multinational arrangements.

Global stratification and corporate power is illustrated in these cases which demonstrate serious drawbacks for developing nations in their encounters with multinationals. Core nations are in the business of using raw materials from developing nations for their own benefit at the expense of host nations. Multinational expansion in developing nations is inevitable as new markets beckon and new governments face the serious challenges of unemployment, illiteracy, poor health, and the other social and economic conditions of the Third World. Multinationals, however, may also succumb to the three factors most commonly associated with organizational misconduct: that is, competitive pressures, resource scarcity, and regulatory failure. How these factors are resolved in specific nations will determine the extent of benefits to developing nations and multinationals.

IMPLICATIONS

Transitional economies are characterized by weak regulatory climates. Often, in order to attract multinationals these economies have to further weaken either the regulations or their enforcement. While such alternatives may pose internal dilemmas for transitional economies, they pose additional incentives for multinationals to look elsewhere, where no such obstacles exist.

The second dilemma for transitional economies lies in ownership of projects linked to multinationals. While many developing nations have a goal of majority ownership (51 percent), multinationals may be unwilling to take such risks.

The third dilemma for transitional economies is the necessity of a guarantee of project completion. Multinationals require socioeconomic and political stability as a prerequisite for initiating a project; nevertheless, they may leave the host nation "holding the bag," should they pull out before completion.

NOTE

1. Paper presented at the First Annual International Conference on Business Ethics and Transitional Economies. Celakovice, Czech Republic.

REFERENCES

Aldrich, Howard. 1999. *Organizations Evolving*. London: Sage Publications.

Amin, Samir. 1974. *Accumulation on a World Scale*. New York: Monthly Review Press.

Anderson, K. and R. Pomfret. 2000. "Challenges Facing Small and Medium-Sized Enterprises in the Kyrgyz Republic, 1996–97." MOCT–MOST, vol. 11, pp. 205–19.

Bartlett, W. 2001. "SME Development Policies in Different Stages of Transition." MOCT–MOST, vol. 11, pp. 197–204.

Boatright, John. 1999. *Ethics and the Conduct of Business*. Englewood Cliffs: Prentice-Hall Inc.

Clinard, Marshall B. and Peter C. Yeager. 1980. *Corporate Crime*. Glencoe, IL: The Free Press.

Clinard, Marshall B. and Richard Quinney. 1973. *Criminal Behavior Systems*. Second Edition. New York: Holt, Rinehart and Winston.

Coleman, James William. 2001. *The Criminal Elite: Understanding White-Collar Crime*. California: Worth Publishing.

Earnhart, D. 2000. "Environmental Crime and Punishment in the Czech Republic: Penalties against Firms and Employees" in *Journal of Comparative Economics*, vol. 28, pp. 379–99.

Edelhertz, Herbert. 1970. *The Nature, Impact, and Prosecution of White Collar Crime*. Washington D.C.: U.S. Government Printing Office.

Emmanuel, Arghiri. 1972. *Unequal Exchange: A Study of the Imperialism of Trade*. New York: Monthly Review Press.

Ermann, David M. and William H. Clements II. 1984. "From the Interfaith Center on Corporate Responsibility" in *Social Problems*, vol. 32, pp. 185–86. Republished in David Ermann and Richard Lundmann. 1987. *Corporate and Governmental Deviance: Problems of Organizational Behavior in Contemporary Society*. New York: Oxford University Press.

Ermann, David M., and Richard J. Lundman. 1987. *Corporate and Governmental Deviance: Problems of Organizational Behavior in Contemporary Society*. New York: Oxford University Press.

Ferrante, Joan. 2000. *Sociology of the United States in a Global Community*. New York: Wadswarth Publishing.

Frank, Andre Gundar. 1966. *The Development of Underdevelopment*. New York: Monthly Review Press.

_____. 1967. *Capitalism and Underdevelopment in Latin America*. New York: Monthly Review Press.

_____. 1980. *Crisis in the Third World*. New York: Holmes & Meier.

Friedrichs, David O. 1996. *Trusted Criminals: White Collar Crime in Contemporary Society*. Belmont, Calif.: Wadsworth.

Garrod, N. 2000. "Environmental contingencies and sustainable modes of corporate governance" in *Journal of Accounting and Public Policy*, vol. 19, pp. 237–61.

Green, Gary S. 1990. *Occupational Crime*. Chicago: Nelson-Hall.

Hall, Richard, H. 2002. *Organizations: Structures, Process, and Outcomes*. New Jersey: Prentice-Hall Inc.

Jones, D.C. and T. Kato. 1996. "The Determinants of Chief Executive Compensation in Transitional Economies: Evidence from Bulgaria" in *Labour Economics*, vol. 3, pp. 319–36.

Kerbo, Harold, R. 2000. *Social Stratification and Inequality: Class Conflict in Historical, Comparative, and Global Perspective*. Boston, MA: McGraw-Hill.

Leisinger, K.M. 1996. "Multinational Corporations, Governance Deficits, and Corruption: Discussing a Complex Issue from the Perspective of Business Ethics." Proceedings of the 9th Annual Conference of the European Business Ethics Network "Working Across Cultures" (Frankfurt).

Mokhiber, R. and R. Weissman. 2001. "Corporations Behaving Badly: The Ten Worst Corporations of 2001" in *Multinational Monitor*, vol. 22, no. 12.

Ott, Steven, J. 1989. *The Organizational Culture Perspective*. California: Brooks/Cole Publishing.

Rana, P.B. 1995. "Reform Strategies in Transitional Economies: Lessons from Asia" in *World Development*, vol. 23, no. 7, pp. 1157–69.

Rutkowski, M. 1996. "Labour Market Policies in Transition Economies" MOCT–MOST, vol. 1, pp. 19–38.

Schrager, Laura Shill and James F. Short Jr. 1978. "Toward a Sociology of Organizational Crime" in *Social Problems*, vol. 25, April. pp. 407–19.

Shapiro Susan. 1990. "Collaring the Crime, Not the Criminal: Reconsidering the Concept of White Collar Crime" in *American Sociological Review*, vol. 55, June. 407–19.

Sherman, Lawrence, W. 1974. "Deviant Organizations" in M. David Ermann and Richard D. Lundman (eds). 1987. *Corporate and Governmental Deviance*. New York: Oxford University Press.

Sexty, R.W. 1998. "Teaching Business Ethics in Transitional Economies: Avoiding Ethical Missionary" in *Journal of Business Ethics*, vol. 17, pp. 1311–17.

Simon, David R. and D. Stanley Eitzen. 1982. *Elite Deviance*. Boston: Allyn and Bacon.

Smallbone, D., F. Welter, N. Isakova and A. Slomanski. 2001. "The Contribution of Small and Medium Enterprises to Economic Development in Ukraine and Belarus: Some Policy Perspectives". MOCT–MOST, vol. 11, pp. 253–73.

Srivastava, Paul. 1992. *Bhopal: Anatomy of Crisis*. London: Chapman Publishers.

Tisdell, C. 2001. "Transitional Economies and Economic Globalisation: Social and Environmental Consequences" in *International Journal of Social Economics*, vol. 28, no. 5/6/7, pp. 577–90.

Thompson, James. D. 1967. *Organizations in Action*. New York: McGraw-Hill.

Wai-chung Yeung, H. 2000. "Local Politics and Foreign Ventures in China's Transitional Economy: The Political Economy of Singaporean Investments in China" in *Political Geography*, vol. 19, pp. 809–40.

Wallerstein, Immanuel. 1984. *The Politics of the World Economy: The State, the Movements and the Civilizations*. New York: Cambridge University Press.

Woodward, R. 2001. "SME Support in Post-Communist Countries: Moving from Individual to Cooperative Approaches (Reflections on the Polish Case)" MOCT–MOST, vol. 11, pp. 275–94.

6

EMPOWERMENT VERSUS DEVELOPMENT: THE EFFECTS OF WOMEN'S EMPOWERMENT AND ECONOMIC DEVELOPMENT ON CHILDREN'S NUTRITIONAL WELL-BEING

Robyn Bateman Driskell

INTRODUCTION

There exists evidence that children's nutritional well-being, as reflected by degree of underweight, wasting, and stunting, shows improvement with economic development. From this perspective all members of a society are ultimately benefited when the economy grows, principally because economic growth leads to increase in wages, which in turn is spent on a greater quantity and variety of food. However, because of women's centrality in providing for children, some analysts argue that the empowerment of women has a more powerful influence on children's well-being than economic development. Under certain circumstances, women's empowerment may be dependent on development, making the effects of economic development on children contingent on whether it improves the lives of women. Using data from the World Bank, these hypotheses are evaluated in this chapter. The results yield some significant relationships with both the empowerment variables and development variables. According to the variables used in this research, women's empowerment is slightly more significant than economic development on children's nutritional well-being.

Children's nutritional well-being remains a significant problem in developing countries, as malnutrition is a global issue. Some economists argue that countries do develop their way out of problems such as malnutrition (see, Mellor, 1989), while other scholars assert that the empowerment of women is a more effective means of improving children's nutritional status (see, Blumberg, 1988). This chapter examines the issues of women's empowerment and economic development as they affect children's nutritional health. One side of the debate regards women's empowerment as one of the most important and determining influences on children's nutritional intake (Abbi et al., 1988; Behrman and Wolfe, 1987 and Bennett, 1988). It is argued that, because of women's centrality in providing for children, the empowerment of women has a more powerful influence on children's welfare than the trickle down effect of economic development generated benefits (Christian et al., 1988). Under certain circumstances, empowerment may be dependent on economic development (Gate, 2001), making the effects of economic development on children's nutritional well-being contingent on whether or not it improves the lives of women. A woman's socioeconomic condition is a vital determinant of the food intake, health, and growth of her children (Rogers and Youssef, 1988). In most cultures, women are providers of food as well as caretakers of children. They grow food or earn the money to buy it, they prepare it, and they mediate its distribution among household members. Women's ability to create income and to control resource allocation directly affects the nutritional status of their children throughout the children's growth (Antrobus, 2001; Rogers and Youssef, 1988).

The other side of the debate as mentioned earlier, argues that economic development is needed within a nation to improve nutritional well-being of children. Evidence exists that children's nutritional well-being, as reflected by degree of underweight, wasting, and stunting, improves with economic development. This perspective implies that all members of a society necessarily and ultimately gain as the economy grows. As the wages tend to increase at all levels, the food availability and variety/quality improves, positively affecting the health status of children. (For instance see, Akin et al., 1985; Baulch and Hoddinott, 2000; Chase-Dunn, 1975; Firebaugh, 1992; and Firebaugh and Beck, 1994).

This chapter presents both sides of the debate: Empowerment versus development. First, the arguments of women's empowerment and economic development are reviewed as they affect the nutritional well-being of children. Then, using data from the World Bank, a statistical analysis is conducted to determine significant effects of women's empowerment and economic development on children's nutritional health. It is expected that the empowerment of women will have a stronger effect on children's nutritional well-being than will economic development. The first section discusses the empowerment of women, the role of the mother, and her influence on the child's nutritional well-being. The second section discusses the effects of economic development on children's nutritional well-being. Finally, the two perspectives are compared, based on the available data.

EMPOWERMENT

The existing body of literature on the debate paradigm about women's empowerment discusses the efforts of empowerment and, occasionally, theoretical and conceptual issues. The components of the empowerment paradigm are present in the literature but have not yet been formulated into a consistent framework (Endeley, 2001; Sharma, 2000). Empowerment is easy to define in its absence: powerlessness, real or imagined; learned helplessness; alienation; and loss of a sense of control over one's life, can be said to be the characteristics. In many instances, political powerlessness and empowerment are linked, while other concepts discuss it in terms of psychological phenomena. Some researchers consider empowerment to be a macro-level process for increasing collective power (Sharma, 2000; Uchudi, 2001), while others describe it as a micro-level process in which feelings of increased power develop without a corresponding change in structural arrangements (Milgram, 2001). Where the relationship among empowerment, power, and powerlessness are considered in the empowerment literature, they are conceptualized as phenomena reflecting access to and use of resources (Endeley, 2001; Gate, 2001; Love, 1991; and Torre, 1986).

Torre (1986: 18) defines empowerment as a "social process enabling people, individually or in groups, to become strong enough to participate within, share in the control of, and influence, the social structure in which they live." One possible outcome of the process of empowerment is re-establishment of the balance of power lost when structural conditions result in the manifestation of anomie or alienation, through social change. The process of empowerment reflects an alternative way of conceptualizing power. Within the context of empowerment, power is used to help others rather than to dominate or coerce them (Endeley, 2001; Gate, 2001; and Love, 1991).

Some scholars tend to equate empowerment with the process of sharing power with or delegating power to subordinates. This implies that there is essentially no conceptual difference between power and empowerment—that empowerment is simply a type of authority relationship in which the superordinate actor delegates decision-making power (Bennett, 1988; Blumberg, 1988). Consequently, empowerment is also defined relationally (a leader shares or delegates his/her power with subordinates) or motivationally (an individual is led to believe he/she has control through enhancement of his/her personal efficacy) (Sharma, 2000). In this context, empowerment is conceptualized as a process that enables feelings of self-efficacy or personal power (Hunt and Kasynathan, 2001; Love, 1991; and Torre, 1986). Women's empowerment increases as their economic power, income, education, literacy, and labor force participation increases.

Women's relative economic power is conceptualized in terms of degrees of control of key economic resources: income, property, food, and other means of production (Pinstrup-Andersen and Caicedo, 1978). Greater the women's relative economic power, the greater their control over their own lives (Bennett, 1988). Women's economic power affects control over fertility patterns, life options, decisions about marriage and divorce, and overall household authority. When a woman's relative economic leverage increases, her input into household decision-making increases. Although women's relative economic power has risen slightly over the past few decades, it tends to fall more rapidly than it rises. Decline in a woman's base of independently controlled economic resources often precedes rapid decreases in her relative power position in household decisions (Blumberg, 1988).

When it comes to input into household decision-making, the extent to which a woman derives income from the market economy proves very important. Earning women tend to spend it primarily on items for daily household consumption or for their children's support (Lomperis, 1991). While household income may rise, nutritional levels fall as women became very dependent on their husbands for household expenditure (Blumberg, 1988).

Control of income by women affects the entire gamut of outcomes from food availability for the children in a particular family to how much food is grown in a particular country (Pinstrup-Andersen and Caicedo, 1978). The mainstream approach and techniques to economic development often ignore the possibility that the family has an internal economy differentiated primarily along the axes of gender. Negative effects of economic development programs extend from the well-being of the women's families to the well-being of particular development projects, to the well-being of entire regions (Chase-Dunn, 1975; Firebaugh, 1992; Firebaugh and Beck, 1994). Blumberg (1988) emphasizes the importance of control over income as a major determinant of empowerment issues ranging from control of one's body to the degree of marital power.

One key step in understanding women's role in the determination of child health and nutritional status may be a careful investigation of the process of resource allocation within the household. The more income a woman receives, the more decision-making power she has (Rogers and Youssef, 1988). Research shows that household income is not always pooled and that men and women often have separate, culturally designated obligations to meet different sets of needs within and beyond the conjugal family. In particular, it has been observed that women are often responsible for providing all or at least part of the resources needed to support their children (Bennett, 1988; Levin et al., 1999). Child health is generally related to the level and distribution of wealth, or permanent income in the household (Thomas et al., 1990).

At the micro level of the family, empowerment comes from who earns, controls, and spends the money (Bennett, 1988; Pinstrup-Andersen and Caicedo, 1978; Rogers and Youssef, 1988). Research indicates that at every level of income: (*a*) women retain a smaller portion of income for personal expenditures; and (*b*) spend more on family and children's well-being and basic human needs than do men. Women's earnings are essential for family survival (Blumberg, 1988) and woman's increased income can have an effect on her status and power and on her children's nutritional health (Levin et al., 1999).

The micro level economics and micro-finance services to women is often considered a major strategy for empowering women (Hunt and Kasynathan, 2001; Milgram, 2001). The micro-finance or credit is intended to raise household income and women's spending power as she has leverage of new financial and knowledge-based resources (Young and Alderman, 1997). Micro-finance services allow for access to financial services which enhance both the women and children's quality of life and well-being (Milgram, 2001; Renken, 2001).

For the purposes of this chapter, a broad and general definition of empowerment of women will be used. Empowerment is described as having power or authority to make decisions about the family. An empowered woman is one who has the ability to delegate responsibilities, exercise options, give permission, resolve matters within the family and has access to valuable resources. Empowerment can be gained through various means including educational attainment, labor force participation, and gaining control over her income. The main hypothesis concerning the empowerment of women is that, with increased power for women (including the various types of power and the variety of means to gain power), children's nutritional well-being is enhanced. An important variable that influences the empowerment of women certainly includes educational attainment.

EDUCATION

In many societies, education improves women's status and increases their power within the society, although the increases in status and power may be minimal. Educational attainment is often linked with increased nutritional knowledge (Abbi et al., 1988; Behrman and Wolfe, 1987; Caldwell, 1979; Christian et al., 1988; Cleland, 1990; Das Gupta, 1990; Thomas et al., 1990). The mother's level of schooling may play an important role in determining the household's level of nutrition and health (Desai, 2000; Sahn and Alderman, 1997). Education may be a far more determining factor to women's access to health care than governmental strategies (Ojanuga and Gilbert, 1992). The World Bank (1993) and others have suggested that increasing the education of women may be an important means for improving nutrition and health in developing countries (Abbi et al., 1988; Behrman and Wolfe, 1987; Caldwell, 1979; Christian et al., 1988; Cleland, 1990; Das Gupta, 1990; and Thomas et al., 1990). Accordingly, the level of education can be one of many determinants of the nutritional well-being of children.

In many research studies, even after controlling for income, education is found to have a significantly positive effect on child health status (Behrman and Wolfe, 1987; Christian et al., 1988; Thomas et al., 1990). Education increases the efficiency of parents in the determination of their children's health. It is often argued that education provides women with the ability to understand and adopt new methods of child care (Christian et al., 1988).

Health is affected by consumption of nutrients, by water and sanitation conditions, by health-related inputs such as medical care utilization, and by the mother's schooling and age. A mother's schooling is included in the research because it is widely hypothesized that her education and experience affect household productivity and household nutrition levels (Behrman and Wolfe, 1987; Desai, 2000). In most societies, it is the mother who is most directly involved in the care of young children, and women's education is therefore more likely to have a direct effect on survival (Abbi et al., 1988; Caldwell, 1979; Cleland, 1990; and Das Gupta, 1990). In many cases, education may succeed in ending traditional and unhealthy practices (Hobcraft et al., 1984).

Abbi et al. (1988) analyze the effects of mothers' knowledge of nutrition on children's nutritional status, while controlling for the effects of the socioeconomic characteristics of the family. Unless the mothers' economic status improves simultaneously with increased nutrition knowledge, the mothers may not be able to practice what they know. Along with education, only literacy may also have an effect on children's nutritional well-being. Research increasingly suggest that literacy helps increase economic production and that the higher the level of a woman's literacy skills, the better her family is nourished (Charlton, 1984; Lomperis, 1991). Research indicates a positive relationship between the mother's literacy status and the nutritional status of her children by weight for age, height for age, and weight for height (Christian et al., 1988; Thomas et al., 1990). A higher percentage of the children of the literate mothers were of normal status or had a mild grade of malnutrition than the percentage of the children of illiterate mothers; a smaller proportion of the children of the literate mothers were moderately or severely malnourished than of those of illiterate mothers (Alderman and Garcia, 1994; Christian et al., 1988). While the level of education for mothers is seen as affecting the nutritional well-being of their children, it is certainly not the only factor. Participation in the labor force also tends to increase women's empowerment and, in turn, to improve the overall nutritional well-being of the children.

EMPLOYMENT

Another factor influencing women's empowerment is employment or labor-force participation. There are two sides to the issue of working mothers. One side asserts that labor force participation among women increases their status and empowers them, increasing the overall family income, and ultimately benefiting the whole family, including the nutritional health of the children (Bennett, 1988; Rogers and Youssef, 1988). Work outside the home is likely to be associated with modernity and higher family income, both of which increases the nutritional well-being of children and overall survival (Hobcraft et al., 1984). Working women usually have greater access to resources and greater economic power within society. Women participating in the labor force have the ability and power to purchase items necessary for their children's nutritional health (Matthews and Power, 2002). Accordingly, the work status of the mother can be an important determinant of her children's health.

The opposing side on this issue argues that working outside the home may prevent mothers from properly caring for their children and thus negatively affect the children's health. Labor force participation among women may have a substantial effect on children through lack of proper feedings early on in life (Hobcraft et al., 1984). Research indicates that the children of working mothers have lower nutritional status than those of mothers who do not work outside the home (Rogers and Youssef, 1988). These studies have not controlled either for the family's income level or for other important variables such as the presence of an employed male and land-tenure status (Bennett, 1988).

Bennett (1988) maintains that the available literature does not provide clear evidence that the children of working mothers have lower nutritional status than those of mothers who do not work outside the home. In its most basic form, this uncertainty raises the question of whether women's income producing work (which is increasingly recognized as crucial to the survival of poor families) results in an improvement or a deterioration in the health and nutritional status of their children (Bennett, 1988; Blumberg, 1988; Pinstrup-Andersen and Caicedo, 1978).

Economic power, income, education, literacy, and employment all affect the empowerment of women. Research has shown ways in which education and employment are important variables in the empowerment of women, yet these variable can also be linked to a country's level of economic development. It is thought that with higher levels of economic development, higher levels of educational attainment and labor force participation will be found within the nation (Preston, 1975). Now, we turn our attention to examine the effects of economic development on the nutritional well-being of children.

ECONOMIC DEVELOPMENT

Evidence exists that children's nutritional well-being, as reflected by degree of underweight, wasting, and stunting, improves with economic development (Uchudi, 2001). From this perspective, all members of a society ultimately benefit when the economy grows, primarily because economic growth leads to increased wages, which in turn are spent on a greater quantity and variety of food (Caldwell et al., 1975; Chase-Dunn, 1975; Firebaugh and Beck, 1994; Mellor, 1988; Preston, 1975). Although the literature both supports and denies these hypotheses, economic development theories assert that nutrition improves with economic development (Caldwell et al., 1975; Chase-Dunn, 1975; Firebaugh and Beck, 1994; Mellor, 1988; Preston, 1975). Factors of diet, technology, and income influence a child's nutritional intake (Chase-Dunn and Hall, 1993; Firebaugh, 1992).

Malnutrition continues to be one of the most serious global problems of human health and welfare in many developing countries. Malnutrition is caused by a variety of food supply and demand-related factors, as well as by factors determining nutrient utilization in the human body (Akin et al., 1985; Evers and McIntosh, 1977; and Smil, 1989). The single most important factor affecting malnutrition is low incomes among certain groups of the population (Gage, 1997; Hobcraft et al., 1984; Pinstrup-Andersen and Caicedo, 1978; and Uchudi, 2001). A family's nutritional well-being is expected to improve with increased wages and higher income (Bennett, 1988; Rogers and Youssef, 1988; and Uchudi, 2001).

The problem of nutritional deficiencies is one of unequal distribution of available nutrients rather than absolute scarcity (Akin et al., 1985; and Smil, 1989). According to research, considerable improvements in human nutrition can be made, even in the absence of an expansion in overall food supply (Hoddinott and Kinsey, 2001), by allowing a larger proportion of income growth to be obtained by nutritionally deficient income groups (Firebaugh and Beck, 1994; Preston, 1975). Policies aimed at the expansion of food supplies without a simultaneous increase in the incomes of nutrient-deficient consumer groups entail large nutritional waste, and for that reason, are relatively ineffective. The most effective approach appears to be simultaneous increase in the purchasing power of deficient groups and in the food supply (Pinstrup-Andersen and Caicedo, 1978). Economic development alone will not solve problems of malnutrition. In many cases, those suffering from malnutrition are not the ones who benefit from economic development within a country (Endeley, 2001). Income distribution and food supply policies have been discussed exclusively from the point of view of one potential goal: improving human nutrition (Pinstrup-Andersen and Caicedo, 1978).

This chapter focuses on economic development because it is probably the best single indicator of living standards in a country. There is no reason to expect a direct influence of economic development on malnutrition; economic development simply measures the rate of entry of new goods and services into the household and business sectors (Firebaugh, 1992; Mellor, 1988). Its influence is indirect: A higher economic development implies and facilitates, though it does not necessarily entail, larger real consumption of items affecting health, such as food, housing, medical and public health services, education, leisure, and health-related research (Preston, 1975). There is a movement away from economic determinism in nutrition analysis. Malnutrition and mortality have become increasingly dissociated from levels of economic growth because of a diffusion of medical and health technologies, facilities and personnel that occurs with economic development (Bradshaw et al., 1993; Preston, 1975; and Young and Alderman, 1997).

Research examines the influence of a country's level of income on mortality as it works endogenously through such factors as nutrition, medical and public health services, and literacy. Income, food, and literacy unquestionably placed limits on levels of life expectancy attained in the 1930s, as they do today (Christian et al., 1988; Das Gupta, 1990; and Preston, 1975). Factors exogenous to a country's current level of economic development are identified as being responsible for an increase in life expectancy and nutritional well-being (Bennett, 1988; Caldwell et al., 1975; Gage, 1997).

In conclusion, the review of the literature indicates the effects of women's status and economic development on children's nutritional health in developing countries. Women play an essential role in the nutritional intake of children. Some analysts argue that the empowerment of women has a more powerful influence on children's welfare than the economic development of a country (Abbi et al., 1988; Behrman and Wolfe, 1987; Caldwell, 1979; Christian et al., 1988; Cleland, 1990; Das Gupta, 1990; Thomas et al., 1990). Others argue that, with economic development in the developing countries, children's nutrition improves (Caldwell et al., 1975; Chase-Dunn, 1975; Firebaugh and Beck, 1994; Mellor, 1988; Preston, 1975).

The present chapter tests competing hypotheses regarding the impact of economic development and women's empowerment. A number of recent research studies examine the effects of economic development on the well-being of children, focusing principally on mortality and life-expectancy as outcomes (Firebaugh, 1992; Firebaugh and Beck,

1994). At least one study considered nutrition as an effect, using "calories consumed per capita" (Bradshaw et al., 1993). However, as Evers and McIntosh (1977) have demonstrated, this variable measures the amount of calories available in a particular country divided by that country's population. It measures neither purchase nor actual intake or energy from food. Thus, this indicator suffers from invalidity. The present study utilizes indicators of adequacy of physical growth in children (weight and height of children compared to standards for age and sex) (see Evers and McIntosh, 1977). Using these indicators, this research fills a gap in the existing literature and provides a much needed source on the nutritional well-being of children as related to the empowerment of women and economic development.

METHODS

SAMPLE AND DATA

Countries included in the analysis are those for which data are available for measuring women's empowerment, economic development, and children's nutritional status. Data are available from the World Bank (1993). While the number of countries used to test the hypothesis is less than 70, recent tests of dependency theory hypotheses that utilize the World Bank data have comparably small samples (see, Chase-Dunn and Hall, 1993; Firebaugh, 1992). The countries covered in the analysis include those for which data are available for one or more of the dependent variables and the independent variables. These include: Mozambique, Mali, Sierra Leone, Malawi, Ethiopia, Niger, Mauritania, Burundi, Cambodia, Bhutan, Yemen, Senegal, Bangladesh, Madagascar, Sudan, Tanzania, Nigeria, Uganda, Bolivia, Pakistan, Laos, Camaroon, Togo, India, Ghana, Cote d'Ivorire, Haiti, Zaire, Peru, Morocco, Congo, Kenya, Honduras, Algeria, Indonesia, Guatemala, Egypt, Nicaragua, Myanmar, Turkey, Zimbabwe, Botswana, Brazil, Ecuador, Vietnam, Papua New Guinea, Dominican Republic, Philippines, Tunesia, Iran, Syria, Paraguay, Columbia, Venezuela, China, Sri Lanka, Thailand, Panama, Mauritius, Chile, Uruguay, Costa Rica, Jamaica, Kuwait, and the United States. The countries listed are similar to those countries included in previous research (see, Firebaugh, 1992; Chase-Dunn and Hall, 1993).

VARIABLES

The dependent variables that describe children's nutritional well-being consist of the percentage of children who are of moderate to severe underweight category (0–4 years), severe underweight (0–4 years), moderate to severe wasting (12–23 months), and moderate to severe stunting (24–59 months). Data for such variables are not routinely collected by many countries, however, they are available for the 1980–85 period.

Underweight is defined as low weight for age; data are available for children of age 0–4 years. Moderate and severe underweight is below minus two standard deviations from median weight for age of reference population. Severe underweight is below minus three standard deviations from median weight for age of reference population.

Stunting is defined as low height-for-age; data are available for children of age 24–59 months. Moderate and severe stunting is below minus two standard deviations from median height for age of reference population.

Wasting is defined as low weight-for-height; data are available for children of age 12–23 months. Moderate to severe stunting or wasting means, respectively, height-for-age or weight-for-height more than two standard deviations below the median of the National Center for Health Statistics (NCHS) reference population. Stunting is interpreted as measuring chronic malnutrition and wasting as measuring acute or short-term malnutrition, whether the cause is inadequate food intake, or infectious disease, or both. Mild or moderate malnutrition is not considered a disease, but all degrees of malnutrition increase the risk of death in children.

The independent variable which represents economic development is the *energy consumption per capita* (kg of oil equivalent). Investigators such as Chase-Dunn (1975), Bollen (1983), and Timberlake (1984) have previously used energy consumption per capita as the indicator of economic development. The advantages of using this measure include its conceptual connection to economic development, its high correlation with gross national product per capita, and its low correlation with various indicators of women's empowerment.

The independent variables representing empowerment are the primary education enrollment ratio and female labor force participation as a percentage of the total. *Primary enrollment ratios* express the percentage of the total number of children in the particular age group enrolled in each educational level. School enrollment serves as a proxy for women's empowerment. Education data refer to a variety of years, generally not more than two years distant from those specified; however, figures for females sometimes refer to a year earlier than that for overall totals. Primary school enrollment data are estimates of children of all ages enrolled in primary school. Figures are expressed as the ratio of pupils to the population of school-age children. Although many countries consider primary school age to be 6 to 11 years, other do not. For some countries with universal primary education, the gross enrollment ratios may exceed 100 percent because some pupils are younger or older than the country's standard primary school age. *Female labor force participation* is defined as the percentage of women within the specific country who are actively employed and participating in the paid labor force. Data may understate the number of employed women because of persons who have irregular, casual, or unstructured jobs and report themselves as not working. Female labor force participation serves as a proxy for women's empowerment.

Several additional indicators of economic development and women's empowerment were examined, yet due to the high collinearity of these variables, the results were unstable. With certain combinations, the signs and direction of relationships changed. Factor analyzing (principal components) the economic development and then women's empowerment variables together was attempted; yet collinearity problems still existed. Due to these various problems, several variables were dropped. Therefore only one independent variable represents the economic development and two variables represent the empowerment of women.[1]

FINDINGS

Table 6.1 gives the OLS regression model results of the four measures of children's nutritional well-being on selected independent variables for the year 1980.

As shown in the Table 6.1, the findings support the hypotheses for both economic development and women's empowerment. For the purposes of this chapter, economic development is represented by the energy consumption per capita. The empowerment variable is represented by the primary education enrollment ratio and the percent of female labor force participation. These findings show that the greater

Table 6.1: Regressions of Four Measures of Children's Nutritional Well-Being on Selected Independent Variables, 1980

	Model 1 moderate/severe underweight		Model 2 severe underweight		Model 3 wasting		Model 4 stunting	
	B (SE)	beta	B (SE)	beta	B (SE)	beta	B (SE)	beta
Energy	-.003* (.001)	-.290	-.001 (.001)	-.204	-.001 (.001)	-.217	-.006** (.001)	-.486
Enrollment	-.171** (.060)	-.341	-.062** (.029)	-.340	-.078** (.030)	-.342	-.076 (.072)	-.140
Labor Force	.176 (.144)	.144	-.078 (.064)	-.091	.128 (.075)	.224	.115 (.181)	.083
Adj. Rsq.	.245**		.136*		.206**		.232**	
N=	57		38		49		47	

* significant at the .05 level
** significant at the .01 level
Energy= Energy consumption per capita
Enrollment= Primary education enrollment ratio
Labor Force= The percentage of female labor force participation

the economic development of a country and the higher the level of women's empowerment, the less likely children will suffer from moderately/severe underweight, severe underweight, wasting, and stunting. Although, the empowerment of women has a stronger effect on the nutritional well-being of children than the energy consumption per capita of a country.

While the data used to test the hypotheses are the best available, they do have some limitations that must be acknowledged. Due to the cross-sectional nature of the data, the analysis does not represent a cause–effect relationship. Cross-sectional data are limited in that they are based on a single point in time and therefore lack historical complexities and variations. Since both the independent and dependent variables are measured at nearly the same time period, one cannot assume that the independent variables occurred prior to the dependent variable. Therefore, the findings of this study suggest that independent and dependent variables are correlated with each other, without reference to temporality.[2]

Model 1 presents the OLS results examining the dependent variable of percentage of children suffering from moderate to severe underweight. In Model 1, energy consumption per capita has a significant effect at 0.05 level on the percent of children suffering from moderate to severe underweight. Primary education enrollment ratio is significant at the 0.01 level and has a greater effect on moderate to severe underweight than the energy consumption. The negative relationship indicates the higher the energy consumption per capita, the fewer children suffering from moderate to severe underweight; and as the primary education enrollment ratio increases, the number of children suffering from moderate to severe underweight decreases. Previous studies show contradictory results of the effects of female labor force participation. According to Model 1, as the percentage of female labor force participation increases, so does moderate to severe underweight, however, this is not significant. Twenty-four percentage of the variance is explained in the Model with the dependent variable of moderate to severe underweight.

Model 2 test the effects on the percentage of children suffering from severe underweight (0–4 years). As energy consumption increases and as the percent of female labor force participation increases, the percentage of children suffering from severe underweight decreases, although the relationship is not significant in this model. As primary education enrollment ratio increases, the percentage of children suffering from severe underweight significantly decreases. Unlike Model 1, the percent of female labor force participation in Model 2 indicates an inverse relationship with the percentage of children suffering from severe underweight.

Model 3 examines the percentage of children suffering from moderate to severe wasting (12–23 months) as the dependent variable. The energy consumption per capita has an inverse relationship but is not significant. The primary education enrollment ratio has a significant effect on wasting. As the primary education enrollment ratio increases, wasting decreases. Similar to the findings in Model 1, as the percent of female labor force participation increases, the percent of children suffering from wasting increases.

Finally, Model 4 considers the percentage of children suffering from moderate to severe stunting (24–59 months) as the dependent variable. The negative association between the dependent and independent variables energy consumption and primary education enrollment still exists. As energy consumption per capita increases, the percentage of children suffering from moderate to severe stunting significantly decreases. Unlike Model 1, 2, and 3, this model makes a stronger case for the effects of economic development.

Table 6.2 shows the regression results of the four models measuring children's nutritional well-being in the year 1985.

The 1985 findings in Table 6.2 continue to support both the hypotheses for economic development and women's empowerment, although a stronger case can be made for the women's empowerment hypothesis according to these results in Model 1, 2, and 3. The 1985 results are quite similar to the 1980 findings, although the model's fit improves.

In Model 1 of Table 6.2, the relationship between the dependent variable of moderate to severe underweight and the independent variables of energy consumption and primary education enrollment continues to be significant in 1985. Enrollment has a stronger effect on moderate to severe underweight and is significant at the 0.001 level. Same as Model 1 in the 1980s results, when the percentage of female labor force participation decreases, so does the percentage of children suffering from moderate to severe underweight and the effects insignificant.

In Model 2, the effect on the percentage of children suffering from severe underweight is quite similar to the 1980 Model 2 results from Table 6.1. All of the independent variables have a negative relationship, while the primary education enrollment is significant. The significance

Table 6.2: Regressions of Four Measures of Children's Nutritional Well-Being on Selected Independent Variables, 1985

	Model 1 moderate/severe underweight		Model 2 severe underweight		Model 3 wasting		Model 4 stunting	
	B (SE)	beta	B (SE)	beta	B (SE)	beta	B (SE)	beta
Energy	-.004* (.001)	-.314	-.001 (.001)	-.193	-.001 (.001)	-.210	-.007** (.002)	-.481
Enrollment	-.218** (.061)	-.341	-.097** (.029)	-.501	-.092** (.032)	-.391	-.114 (.073)	-.202
Labor Force	.085 (.154)	.064	-.048 (.067)	-.106	.078 (.083)	.125	.070 (.195)	.046
Adj.Rsq.	.328**		.289**		.221**		.290**	
N=	53		34		47		46	

* significant at the 0.05 level
** significant at the 0.01 level
Energy= Energy consumption per capita
Enrollment= Primary education enrollment ratio
Labor Force= The percentage of female labor force participation

level of primary education enrollment has increased to the 0.001 level in 1985.

The third regression model of the 1985 data examines the percentage of children suffering from moderate to severe wasting. As in 1980, the relationship of energy consumption per capita and primary education enrollment is negative, whereas the percentage of female labor force participation relationship is positive. The primary education enrollment variable has a significant negative effect on wasting.

Finally, Model 4 considers stunting. The findings show that energy consumption has a significant relationship on stunting again in 1985, making a stronger argument for the effects of economic development on children's stunting than women's empowerment in this Model.

CONCLUSIONS

The results of the regression analysis support both the women's empowerment and economic development hypotheses. As the primary education enrollment ratio and the energy consumption per capita increased in 1980 and 1985, children's nutritional well-being, as reflected by degree of underweight, wasting, and stunting improved. The primary education enrollment ratio of females represented the empowerment of women and yielded the most significant results in both 1980 and 1985. The primary education enrollment ratio of females has a significant relationship with the dependent variable of moderate to severe underweight, and wasting in 1980 and 1985. In each of these cases, the primary education enrollment ratio effect on the dependent variable is significantly stronger than the energy consumption per capita effect on children's nutritional well-being. The energy consumption per capita represents the economic development variable and also yields significant results. Energy consumption has a significant relationship with moderate to severe underweight (Model 1) and stunting (Model 4) in 1980 and 1985. The percentage of female labor force participation is not significant in either 1980 or 1985. This research has shown that the empowerment of women has a more powerful influence on children's welfare than the economic development.

Since research is an ongoing process, further study and analysis of women's empowerment and economic development is necessary. To complement existing women's empowerment research, further research is needed to address issues related to women's labor force participation. It is important to note that there are several characteristics specific to women that affect labor force participation and earnings (e.g., marital status, children present in the home, etc.). Further research is also necessary to address the effectiveness of policies and programs constructed to initiate economic development in developing countries. Finally, it is suggested that a more detailed and focused investigation should be conducted using methodologies such as case studies, focus groups, and other approaches that give a more individualized perspective to capture the finer nuances associated with children's nutritional well-being and women's empowerment.

Several practical applications are derived from this study. Policy implications stemming from the results concern the role of women's empowerment on the nutritional health of their children. Programs and policies in less developed nations need to target women and develop strategies for improving their status and power. An obvious target area includes improvement in human-capital resources and educational attainment of women. Economic development programs that pour money for economic development of a nation without controlling the direction or flow of the money will most likely not improve the nutritional health of children. Social service agencies and policy makers should be aware of the needs of women and children. Services for these populations need to be provided to and focus on regions that have high rates of malnutrition, high proportions of female-headed households, less educated populations, and high unemployment rates. Herein lies the impact of this study's findings. This research provides evidence—from two different time periods—that children's nutritional well-being is associated with the empowerment of women.

NOTES

1. Because data on nutritional status in essence were available for a single time period, a longitudinal analysis was precluded. However, independent variables such as women's education attainments are measured at earlier points in time, permitting a "quasi-longitudinal analysis." Neither heteroscedasticity nor multivariate outliers were detected; therefore, no countries were dropped from the analysis. Ordinary least squares regression models were used to test the hypotheses. The data for malnutrition in children are available for many peripheral and semi-periphery countries and for few countries of the core. Data for a number of differing years are available for both the indicators of development and empowerment. Thus, a number of

models were tested with varying degrees of lag between the time period for the nutrition indicators and the various independent variables.
2. Considerable effort has been made to standardize the data; nevertheless, statistical methods, coverage, practices, and definitions differ widely among countries. In addition, the statistical systems in many developing economies are still weak, and this affects the availability and reliability of the data. Moreover, cross-country and cross-time comparisons always involve complex technical problems that cannot be fully and unequivocally resolved. The data are drawn from sources thought to be most authoritative, but many of them are subject to considerable margins of error. Because not all data are updated, some figures, especially those relating to current periods, may be extrapolated. Several estimates are derived from models based on assumptions about recent trends and prevailing conditions. Issues related to the reliability of demographic indicators are reviewed in the U.N. *World Population Trends and Policies*. Readers are urged to take these limitations into account in interpreting the indicators, particularly when making comparisons across economies.

REFERENCES

Abbi, Rita, Parul Christian, Sunder Gujaral, and Tara Gopaldas. 1988. "Mothers' Nutrition Knowledge and Child Nutritional Status in India" in *Food and Nutrition Bulletin*, vol. 10, pp. 51–54.

Akin, John S., Charles C. Griffin, David K. Guilkey, and Barry M. Popkin. 1985. *The Demand for Primary Health Services in the Third World*. New York: Rowman and Allnheld.

Alderman, Harold and Marito Garcia. 1994. "Food Security and Health Security: Explaining the Levels of Nutritional Status in Pakistan" in *Economic Development and Cultural Change*, vol. 42, no. 3, pp. 485–507.

Antrobus, Peggy. 2001. "Women and Children's Well-Being in the Age of Globalization: A Focus on St. Vincent and the Grenadines and Small Island Developing States" in *Development*, vol. 44, no. 2, pp. 53–57.

Baulch, Bob and John Hoddinott. 2000. "Economic Mobility and Poverty Dynamics in Developing Countries" in *The Journal of Development Studies*, vol. 36, no. 6, pp. 1–24.

Behrman, Jere R., and Barbara L. Wolfe. 1987. "How Does Mother's Schooling Affect Family Health, Nutrition, Medical Care Usage, and Household Sanitation?" in *Journal of Econometrics*, vol. 36, pp. 185–204.

Bennett, Lynn. 1988. "The Role of Women in Income Production and Intra-Household Allocation of Resources as a Determinant of Child Nutrition and Health" in *Food and Nutrition Bulletin*, vol. 10, pp. 16–26.

Blumberg, Rae Lesser. 1988. "Income Under Female Versus Male Control" in *Journal of Family Issues*, vol. 9, pp. 51–84.

Bollen, Kenneth. 1983. "World System Position, Dependency, and Democracy: The Cross-National Evidence" in *American Sociological Review*, vol. 48, pp. 468–79.

Bradshaw, York, Rita Noonan, Laura Gash, and Claudia Buchmann Sershen. 1993. "Borrowing Against The Future: Children And Third World Indebtedness" in *Social Forces*, vol. 71, pp. 629–56.

Caldwell, John C. 1979. "Education as a Factor in Mortality Decline: An Examination of Nigerian Data" in *Population Studies*, vol. 33, pp. 395–413.

Caldwell, John C., N.O. Addo, A. Igun, S.K. Gaisie, and P.O. Olusanya (eds). 1975. *Population Growth and Socioeconomic Change in West Africa*. New York: Columbia University Press.

Charlton, Sue Ellen M. 1984. *Women in Third World Development*. Boulder, CO: Westview Press.

Chase-Dunn, Christopher. 1975. "The Effects of International Economic Dependence on Development and Inequality" in *American Sociological Review*, vol. 40, pp. 720–38.

Chase-Dunn, Christopher, and Thomas D. Hall. 1993. "Comparing World Systems: Concepts And Working Hypotheses" in *Social Forces*, vol. 71, pp. 851–86.

Christian, Parul, Rita Abbi, Sunder Gujaral, and Tara Gopaldas. 1988. "The Role Of Maternal Literacy And Nutrition Knowledge In Determining Children's Nutritional Status" in *Food and Nutrition Bulletin*, vol. 10, pp. 35–40.

Cleland, John. 1990. "Maternal Education and Child Survival: Further Evidence and Explanation" in John C. Caldwell, S. Findley, P. Caldwell, G. Santow, W. Cosford, J. Braid, and D. Groers-Freeman (eds). *What We Know About Health Transition: The Cultural, Social, and Behavioral Determinants of Health*. Canberra: Australian National University.

Das Gupta, Monica. 1990. "Death Clustering, Mother's Education and the Determinants of Child Mortality in Rural Punjab, India" in John C. Caldwell, S. Findley, P. Caldwell, G. Santow, W. Cosford, J. Braid, and D. Groers-Freeman (eds). *What We Know About Health Transition: The cultural, social, and behavioral determinants of health*. Canberra: Australian National University, pp. 441–61.

Desai, Sonalde. 2000. "Maternal Education and Child Health: A Feminist Dilemma" in *Feminist Studies*, vol. 26, no. 2, pp. 425–46.

Endeley, Joyce B. 2001. "Conceptualizing Women's Empowerment in Societies in Cameroon: How Does Money Fit In?" in *Gender and Development*, vol. 9, no. 1, pp. 34–41.

Evers, Susan and Wm. Alex McIntosh. 1977. "Social Indicators of Human Nutrition: Measures of Nutritional Status" in *Social Indicators Research*, vol. 4, pp. 185–205.

Firebaugh, Glenn. 1992. "Growth Effects of Foreign and Domestic Investment" in *American Journal of Sociology*, vol. 98, pp. 105–30.

Firebaugh, Glenn and Frank D. Beck. 1994. "Does Economic Growth Benefit the Masses?" in *American Sociological Review*, vol. 59, pp. 631–53.

Gage, Anastasia J. 1997. "Familial and Socioeconomic Influences on Children's Well-Being: An Examination of Preschool Children in Kenya" in *Social Science and Medicine*, vol. 45, no. 12, pp. 1811–28.

Gate, Smita. 2001. "Empowerment of Women in Watershed Management: Guraiya Panchayat, Madhya Pradesh" in *Indian Journal of Gender Studies*, vol. 8, no. 2, pp. 247–56.

Hoddinott, John and Bill Kinsey. 2001. "Child Growth in the Time of Drought" in *Oxford Bulletin of Economics and Statistics*, vol. 63, no. 4, pp. 409–36.

Hobcraft, J.N., J.W. McDonald, and S.O. Rutstein. 1984. "Socio-Economic Factors in Infant and Child Mortality: A Cross-National Comparison" in *Population Studies*, vol. 38, pp. 193–223.

Hunt, Juliet and Nalini Kasynathan. 2001. "Pathways to Empowerment? Reflections on Microfinance and Transformation in Gender Relations in South Asia" in *Gender and Development*, vol. 9, no. 1, pp. 42–52.

Levin, Carol E., Marie T. Ruel, Saul S. Morris, Daniel G. Maxwell, Margaret Armar-Klemesu, and Clement Ahiadeke. 1999. "Working Women in an Urban Setting: Traders, Vendors, and Food Security in Accra" in *World Development*, vol. 27, no. 11, pp. 1977–91.

Lomperis, Ana Maria Turner. 1991. "Teaching Mothers to Read: Evidence from Colombia on the Key Role of Maternal Education in Preschool Child Nutritional Health" in *Journal of Developing Areas*, vol. 26, no. 1, pp. 25–52.

Love, Gayle. 1991. "Empowerment Processes in Shelters for Battered Women", Unpublished Ph.D. dissertation, University of Texas, Texas.

Matthews, Sharon and Chris Power. 2002. "Socio-Economic Gradients in Psychological Distress: A Focus on Women, Social Roles and Work-Home Characteristics" in *Social Science and Medicine*, vol. 54, no. 5, pp. 799–810.

Mellor, John W. 1989. "Global Food Balances and Food Security" in *World Development*, vol. 16, pp. 997–1011.

Milgram, B. Lynne. 2001. "Operationalizing Microfinance: Women and Craftwork in Ifugao, Upland Philippines" in *Human Organization*, vol. 60, no. 3, pp. 212–24.

Ojanuga, Durrenda Nash and Cathy Gilbert. 1992. "Women's Access to Health Care in Developing Countries" in *Social Science and Medicine*, vol. 35, no. 4, pp. 613–17.

Pinstrup-Andersen, Per, and Elizabeth Caicedo. 1978. "The Potential Impact of Changes in Income Distribution on Food Demand and Human Nutrition" in *American Journal of Agricultural Economics*, vol. 60(August), pp. 402–415.

Preston, Samuel H. 1975. "The Changing Relation between Mortality and Level of Economic Development" in *Population Studies*, vol. 29, pp. 231–48.

Renken, Lynn. 2001. "Microfinance in Pakistan: Perpetuation of Power or a Viable Avenue for Empowerment?" in Weiss, Anita M., and Giani, S. Zulfiqar (eds). 2001. *Power and Civil Society in Pakistan*. Oxford, UK: Oxford University Press, pp. 248–74.

Rogers, Beatrice Lorge and Nadia Youssef. 1988. "The Importance of Women's Involvement in Economic Activities in the Improvement of Child Nutrition and Health" in *Food and Nutrition Bulletin*, vol. 10, pp. 33–41.

Sahn, David E. and Harold Alderman. 1997. "On the Determinants of Nutrition in Mozambique: The Importance of Age-Specific Effects" in *World Development*, vol. 25, no. 4, pp. 577–88.

Sharma, S.L. 2000. "Empowerment without Antagonism: A Case for Reformulation of Women's Empowerment Approach" in *Sociological Bulletin*, vol. 49, no. 1, pp. 19–39.

Smil, Vaclav. 1989. "Diet and Western Mortality" in *Population and Development Review*, vol. 15, pp. 399–414.

Thomas, Duncan, John Strauss, and Maria-Helen Henriques. 1990. "How Does Mother's Education Affect Child Height?" in *The Journal of Human Resources*, vol. 26, pp. 183–211.

Timberlake, Michael. 1984. "Dependence and Government Repression" in *American Sociological Review*, vol. 49, pp. 141–46.

Torre, Dorothy Ann. 1986. "Empowerment: Structured Conceptualization and Instrument Development." Unpublished Ph.D. dissertation, UMI Dissertation Information Service; UMI # 8607315.

Uchudi, Joseph Masudi. 2001. "Covariates of Child Mortality in Mali: Does the Health-Seeking Behaviour of the Mother Matter?" in *Journal of Biosocial Science*, vol. 33, no. 1, pp. 33–54.

World Bank. 1993. *World Development Report*. Washington, DC: World Bank.

Young, Gay and Heather Alderman. 1997. "The Organization of Labor Resources in Juarez Families: A Focus on Working Women's Households During Economic Restructuring" in *The International Journal of Sociology and Social Policy*, vol. 17, no. 11–12, pp. 97–115.

7

GLOBALIZATION AND DISPARITY: A REAPPRAISAL

Samir Dasgupta and Kaushik Chattopadhyay

The concept of globalization is becoming a fad word, fast turning into a shibboleth, a magic incantation, a passkey meant to unlock the gates to all present and future mysteries. We are all being globalized. Despite the rapid burst of words about globalization, there is controversy about its conceptualization, paradigmatic orientation, meaning generation, and meaning negotiation. In a word, globalization implies a shift—of polity, economy, culture, and technology. It is the unfolding resolution of the contradiction between ever expanding capital and its national political and social formations. If we assume the impact of globalization on the Third World countries, it appears sometimes as a misnomer, sometimes as utopia, and sometimes very inspiring and bright.

Large-scale deprivation, uncertainty and exploitation have also been the product of globalization for the Third World countries. This chapter focuses on the global disparity between the developed and Third World nations, and delves into the questions of its origin, dimensions, and related issues. Table 7.1 brings out the disparity between the two.

Table 7.1: Ratio of Per-capita Product

Year/Period	Developed Western Countries		Underdeveloped Countries
1770	1.2	:	1
Turn of the 19th	$ 190		$ 150
Century	(per capita income)		(per capita income)
1850	Per capita income increased by 50 to 70 percent		
At the beginning of the World War I	11.3	:	1
2000	14 +	:	1

Source: *New Times*, 1983, no.12; also in Dadayan, 1988.

The reason for this stark disparity most probably was the appearance of managerial capitalism and colonialism, which created the disparity and the divided selves. The process of exploitation of the people by the capitalists has changed its image from time to time. Marx (1848) on the exploitation by the colonists wrote maintained that the discovery of gold and silver in America, the extirpation, enslavement and entombment in mines of the aboriginal population, the beginning of the conquest and looting of the East Indies, the turning of Africa into a warren for the commercial hunting of black skins, signalized the rosy dawn of the era of capitalist production. A Soviet social scientist, N.P. Shmelyov writes that the treasure gained from beyond Europe by means of robbery, enslavement of the people of America, Asia and Africa, murder, treachery and subordination flowed into the metropolises where it was turned into capital. And the capital comes dripping from head to foot, from every pore, with blood and dirt (Marx, 1848). The contracts between wealth and poverty in the developing countries are sharper than in their developed counterparts. In 1983 (the concept of "shadow globalization" gained popularity around the 1960s, Switzerland had a per capita GDP 4.3 times that of Greece ($13,338 and $3,558 respectively), the per capita GDP of the UAE was no less than 187 times that of Bangladesh ($23,546 and $126 respectively). The 15 "richest" countries in the capitalist world included seven developing states ... there are 55 countries in the group where the per capita GDP exceeds $1500,55 between $150 and $1500 and 50 with less than $500 of which the group of 38 least developed countries have a GDP equivalent to $20.1 per capita which is 50 times less than the developed capitalist countries and 52 times less than the United States. Statistics reveal that since 1960, income disparity among countries had increased worldwide. It is evident from the *Human Development Report* (1999) that the wealthy countries have experienced a steady growth in their share of the world GNP, while the poorest countries have experienced a tragic decline in their share in the same. Between 1960 and 1991, the richest fifth of all nations had its share of world income rise from 70 percent to 85 percent, while the poorest fifth of all nations had its share fall from 2.3 percent to 1.4 percent (UN Development Programme, 1994). This trend towards greater disparity gives indication of continuing into this millennium as well (Sandler, 1997). This chronic disparity indicates the dilemma whether globalization policy would be able to reduce the tension of conflict arising from global inequality; or, inequality itself would become the prime mover towards economic equality, social integration and crisis reduction.

The Tables 7.2 and 7.3 express the structural issues involved:

Table 7.2: Worldwide Income Inequality Increase, 1989

Cohort of Nations (%)	(%) share of world GNP	(%) share of world trade	(%) share of world investment	(%) share of world savings
Richest 20	82.7	81.23	80.56	80.51
Fourth 20	11.7	13.94	12.65	13.39
Third 20	2.3	2.53	2.95	2.59
Second 20	1.9	1.35	2.62	2.53
Poorest 20	1.4	0.95	1.25	0.98

Source: UNDP (1992).

Table 7.3: Worldwide Income Disparity, 1960–91

Year	Poorest 20% of nations*	Richest 20% of nations	Richest to Poorest ratio	Gini coefficient
1960	2.3	70.2	30 to 1	0.69
1970	2.3	73.9	32 to 1	0.71
1980	1.7	76.3	45 to 1	0.79
1989	1.4	82.7	59 to 1	0.87
1991	1.4	84.7	61 to 1	–

Source: UNDP (1992, 1994).
*Percentage of World GNP.

With globalization, the rate of global disparity is increasing steadily. The poorest 40 percent (cohort of nations) nations are suffering from underdevelopment. The income disparity between top 20 percent richest countries and lowest 20 percent poor countries shows a distinct mark of horror and dejection. The ratio of GNP between these two type of nations i.e., 61:1 is not even alarming but deadening too.

But the heads of the global village are preaching the depressed people through economic, cultural and political satellites that they can minimize increasing inequality and would arrest the greatest threats to mankind with globalization. But their promises contradict the grim reality. An ideal global village with a single roof for all is aimed at, but the reality stands for confusion. Will increasing world inequality worsen or alleviate global conflicts? Furthermore, will increased inequality make these conflicts easier or more difficult to address in the future? (Sandler, 1997). The people in the Third World countries are now in confusion whether they would be the beneficiaries of the global challenge or they would be the worsen victims of increased global inequality. The "free-rider-aid, a new type of foreign aid," a section of the development experts assume, may replace "traditionally tied and untied foreign-aid of the post-World War-II period" and the corresponding behavior patterns on the part of the poor may limit greater worldwide inequality. However, this might be only an utopia because the condition of global disparity itself tends to limit the impact of free-ride aid and free riding behavior as the accelerating inputs of globalization process. It is evident from the report of the UNDP (1996) that the wealthiest 1 percent people owned 36 percent of the world's financial assets in 1990.

By the early 1990s, there were around 37,000 Trans National Corporations (TNCs) controlling over 200,000 foreign affiliates worldwide, generating sales of more than $4.8 trillion (UNCTAD, 1994: 86). Today, the TNCs are enjoying an enviable 50 percent share of the world's largest selling economic units. Their influence on world economy is rampant now and is snowballing day by day. For example, the combined sales of the world's largest 350 TNCs totaled nearly one-third of the combined GNPs of the "advanced" capitalist countries (*New Internationalist,* 1993: 18). Moreover, the leading 600 TNCs are responsible for one-fifth of the world's total industrial and agricultural production. Thus, for these institutions, globalization of the world economy means the free movement of capital "across national boundaries" (Ohmae, 1991). So, in the prevailing condition we cannot think of a single, independent, indigenous economy, as financial capital in the global network is highly mobile and is playing a key role in determining the fate of the Third World economies.

Foreign investment has clearly been a major factor in stimulating economic growth and development in recent times. In 1996, Hirst and Thompson had estimated that in the early 1900s around 28 percent of the world's population received 91 percent of global Direct Foreign Investment (DFI) and the rest 72 percent of the population received 8 percent of global DFI (pp. 67–68). These figures are based at the level of nation states rather than the people in nation states. In the real world, not all people within a country will benefit from investment—indeed, many of the major recipients of DFI (First as well as the Third World) have high rates of unemployment. These figures ultimately depicted the pattern of the diversification of Third World. Thus, it is evident that economic ties are strengthening in global era but the global hierarchies still exist and are actually intensifying (cited in Kiely, 1998b: 49). The US President Truman argued that there was a need for the countries of the modern world to solve the problem of the underdeveloped areas. "More than half of the people of the world are living in conditions approaching misery. Their food is inadequate, they are victims of disease. Their economic life is primitive and stagnant. Their poverty is a handicap and a threat both to them and to more prosperous areas" (cited in Escobar, 1995: 3). Truman's version, for the first time in world history, gave birth to a concept of "underdeveloped" areas in juxtaposition with the "developed" ones. That there was a yawning gap between the poor and the rich had now been explicitly recognized. In spite of the efforts initiated to minimize it beginning with Truman, the gap has been mounting steadily, especialy since the early 1990s. In the 1990s, the richest country was richer by eight times than the poorest one, which increased to 36 times in the 1980s (Freeman, 1991: 155). The UNDP Human Development Report (1992), determined that from 1960 to 1989 those countries with the richest 20 percent of world's population saw their share of global output (income) rise from 70.2 percent to 82.7 percent while the share of those with the poorest 20 percent shrank from 2.3 to 1.4 percent. The ratio of incomes of rich to poor income earners therefore increased from 30:1 to 59:1 in this period (New Internationalist, 1996: 19). Hirst and Thompson (1995) showed that in the ambiguous International system, problems for the relatively poorer countries is not imperial domination but sheer neglect and exclusion. Joseph Stiglitz (2002) has analyzed the evolution of the structural adjustment policies, the effects that they have on the economies of the Third World and the interests they serve. He says that despite repeated promises of poverty reduction made over the last decade of the 20th century, the actual number of people living in poverty has actually increased by almost 100 million. This occurred at the same time that the total world income actually increased by an average of 2.5 percent annually. In his analysis of how the structural adjustment or the globalization program has damaged the economies of the developing world, including even Russia, he lays much of the blame on the IMF's insistence on rapid privatization and capital market deregulation. Stiglitz also says, "Perhaps the most serious concern with privatization, as it has often been practised, is corruption," which he jokingly calls "Briberization."

GLOBALIZATION: A MISNOMER?

The term globalization is now a subject of intensive analysis. Many countries initially skeptical towards it are accepting the inputs of globalization either as a forced inception due to political and economic constraints or as a matter of continuing process of development. The triad of the United States, Europe and Japan, backed by the IMF and the World Bank, are significantly successful in spreading their policies and ideology to the developing as well as the developed countries. It has bi-polar realities: *a*) creating a global situation of open market it has created high hopes and aspiration among the developing countries to emulate the Western countries and the global nucleus; and *b*) creating an unbridgeable disparity between the Periphery and the Core. The two opposite contending forces of globalization process i.e., relentless and compulsive pursuit of economic growth and the maladies of global disparity, have created a dilemma for the Third World countries. And the crisis is very acute in the case of India.

In India, globalization with its economic liberalism and reformation have failed to create a very sunny impact. The annual rate of industrial growth in India was 13 percent in 1995–96 which decreased to 2.3 percent only in the year 2001–2002. The annual growth rate of GDP in the year 1993–94 was 7.1 percent which reduced to 5.1 percent by the year 1997–2001. With the acceptance of globalization in India, restrictions on impact of foreign commodities is being removed. Its not unlikely that this and masses are attracted to these would affect the growth of indigenous industrial development negatively.

The World Development Report (2000–2001) accepts the view of poverty as encompassing not only low income and consumption but also low achievement in education, health, nutrition and other areas of human development. By definition, poverty now includes powerlessness and voicelessness and vulnerability and fear. These dimensions of human deprivation emerged forcefully from the voices of the poor who were studied as a background for the *World Development Report* 2000–2001. The study systematically sought the views of more than 60,000 poor men and women living in 60 poor countries. The basic outcome of the study revealed: (*a*) Increasing education leads to better health outcomes; (*b*) Improving health increases income earning potential; (*c*) Providing safety nets allows poor people to engage in higher risk, higher return activities; (*d*) Estimated the discrimination against women, ethnic minorities and other disadvantaged groups and concluding that gross underutilization of the precious human resource endowment is the immediate determinant of human deprivation; and (e) Lack of equal opportunities for all emanate from such conditions.

And the sole cause of such a disparity is the trans-national triadic capitalism. Historically speaking, the features of the current stage of capitalism has taken its shape on and from the post-war period. The dualism of the national monopoly capitalism leads to the marginalization (Bruno, 1998) of the current trans-national triadic capitalism. The Table 7.4 reveals the causal effect of such a trans-national triadic capitalism.

Table 7.4: Causal Effects of Trans-national Triadic Capitalism

Production Mode	Institution	Market forms
Primordial community	Village community	Local
Feudal	Regional authority	Regional
Capitalist / socialist	Nation state	National
Triadic capitalist	Transnational	Global

The current usage of globalization is perceived by the poor countries as a means used by the initiators of globalization to accumulate capital. But the latter speak of globalization as a means to control market and available resources so as to increment worldwide profits, to reduce poverty of the Third World countries, and to generate a cohesion between rich and weaker parts of the globe without the constraints of bureaucratic red tapism. But reality has another version to show. A strong voice of protest against globalization has risen from more or less all parts of the globe. This "anti globalization" slogan has a strong base of reality. A senior administrator for Porter Novelli (cited in Hunter and Yates, 2002: 323) writes,

A friend of mine told me a story very soon after the genocide in Rwanda. He was there as a military representative accompanying an NGO tour of the area. The situation was awful. There was also no infrastructure to get to the people in need. And so there were United Nations convoys that just could not get through. This delegation literally sat there on the road for hours going nowhere. By the time they finally reached their destination, they discovered that Coke had already been there for two weeks distributing what they needed. What a fascinating thing— Coke got there before the UN. It shows you just how powerful the global market is and this brand in particular. I suppose if Microsoft needs to be there, they'll be there too.

So, one may argue that globalization remains, in both source and character, American. The social scientists are now considering McDonalization or Americanization as a synonym of globalization. For example, McDonald serves fast food to 20 millions people worldwide each day, Coca-Cola serves billions of people worldwide everyday, MTV reaches half-a-billion people per year etc.

ROLE OF ALTERNATIVE DEVELOPMENT FORA

A section of the development specialists holds the view that the motive of spreading global net is partially being performed and activized by the non-governmental agencies (NGOs). The increased interest and funding of NGOs are generally thought to have a much greater capacity to reach down to the local, grassroots level: Many bilateral and multilateral aid programs now seek to claim their political neutrality and altruism by linking with NGOs to spend huge amount of resources on their behalf. In the mid-1990s, for example, the US amazed observers by asserting that it intended to channel half its aid through NGOs (Todaro, 1977). It is very interesting to note that many organizations calling themselves NGOs are in fact largely funded by governments or from official state resources. For example, Norwegian Church Aid (NCA) is mostly funded by the Norwegian state. The Indian government ministries have established a number of Japanese NGOs. Zimbabwe follows the same path. The NGOs generally call them either as philanthropic organization or as humanitarian agencies. One can raise the question; do NGOs act as agents of the globalization initiators? Do NGOs maintain a parallel form of private development agency? Do NGOs help create the prevalent global mindset about the distressed people in the Third World?

NGOs are working on environmental protection, health condition, famine and hunger, the protection of human rights and lobbying within and outside the country. In some countries of the Third World, their development action sometimes go beyond the limits determined by the state/country development rate. So their actions and development promotion are more functional than the structural globalization. They have direct access to the distressed rural and tribal people, they run localized projects of development and, thus, are widening the canvas of their actions and activities steadily—their voice is sometimes very much accountable to policymakers and they advocate at both the national and international levels. They have a history of metamorphosis. They are now moving on to the promotion of small-scale self-reliance and to a "third generation strategy" for sustainable development, involving "facilitating development by other organizations" (Korten, 1990). The development experts have pointed out that the impact of development NGOs is highly localized and often transitory. It is now being called as the initiator of local developmentalism. The number of NGOs with consultative status with the United Nations Economic and Social Council (ECOSOC) has increased from about 200 in 1950 to 1,500 in 1995. Since the late 1980s, over 4,000 development NGOs based on OECD countries have been spreading out six billion annually for relief and developmental work.

It is estimated that there are now over 200,000 grassroots NGOs in Asia, Africa, and Latin America. Lester Salamon quotes, "A veritable associational revolution now seems underway at the global way that may constitute as significant a social and political development of the latter twentieth century as the rise of the nation-state was of the nineteenth century" (Edwards and Hulme, 1995: 3).

Edwards and Hulme (1995) comment that in the new policy agenda which combines market economies and liberal democratic politics, NGOs are simultaneously viewed as market based actors and placed in a central position as components of civil society. At present, NGOs are influential social forces and they play a major role in stimulating public awareness. They frequently act as "watch dogs" (Yearley, 1996) and sometimes seek publicity to shame those governments and companies which are perceived to be "bad performers." But the reality tells another story. Poverty is viewed by the globalizers as a product of "errors" which could be "corrected" (Amin, 1997). But global malady, particularly in the Third World countries, opened the door for a new vision. Their disillusionment with the global development project created an alternative forum i.e., the other voices of the planet representing growing network of NGOs that now challenge developmentalism. (McMichael, 1994). This shift in thinking expressed by NGOs is not simply of scale—from global to local—but also of subsistence. So this alternative forum is seen as highly acceptable to the deprived majorities in the Third World countries. But side by side, being funded by the developed countries, the NGOs in the guise of alternative fora, attempt to spread the message of globalization awareness. It is very interesting to note that the NGOs today generate enormous amount of "hype" helped by governments and funding agencies for empowering the poor, but in practice they are more accountable to their donors than to their beneficiaries and ultimately they are not likely to go for radical social change. And their aidocracy often echoes the interest of the donors. "The Development set is bright and noble/our thoughts are deep and our vision global/Although we move with the better classes/our thoughts are always with the masses ..." (Goggins, "The Development Set" Africa, 1978). But the real aidocracy means: (*a*) do not harm; (*b*) cooperation is an external support to an internal dynamism; and (*c*) effort with what they have, not with what they lack.

GLOBALISM WITHOUT EGALITARIANISM

The term "globalization" has come to be emotionally charged in public discourse and has become a buzzword now. In fact, the hallmark of globalization is the emergence of a single social system—the process hastened by a worldwide network of economic, political and social relationships—able to produce a unique social order. The spread of Buddhism from Benaras, Christianity from Jerusalem and Islam from Mecca can be identified as historic events in this regard. The 15th century maritime expeditions can be considered as the beginning of coming together of the peoples of this world. Later, colonialism as a new age of inter-civilizational communication, played an instrumental role in fostering "proto-globalization," long before the global revolution in the field of information technology. Many of the practices which attended the growth and development of East India company, as "the first transnational," duly accompany the aspirates of globalism—the destruction of indigenous industry, the ruin of self-reliance, uprooting and forced migrations of whole populations.

Present day globalization, as we see it or as we feel it, is a collection of processes in which economic, political, cultural and other ties are made between different countries. This interdependence contributed towards forming a new pattern for our daily lives. Now a days, internet and fax machines are connecting people who were once secluded, job availability for a person is widening, cross-border monetary transaction has increased manifold, trade patterns are altering quickly and aftermaths of any event today is not confined within the national boundary, considerably affecting other countries too. The economic action patterns of local actors and institutions are moulded by external agencies, which epitomize the global changes in this regard, taking place around us. Our local banks, supermarkets and other stores are often units of a larger chain or network. The goods on display in the shelves of the departmental stores carry the mark of paradigmatic global changes in the fields of production and distribution systems. Thus, the home-trading systems in different countries are connecting different people with a single global marketing system. The new management system is successfully converting the old division of labor into a completely different one since the 1970s, and accelerating the world capitalist economy thereby.

Globalization intensifies human interaction involving travel, trade, and migration, as said by the Head of International Newsgathering, CNN, "I've been to North Korea nine times, nine times to Iraq, 40 times to China, Somalia and Bosnia, 10 times to Cuba. And I'm leaving this weekend to go to Belgrade. Yeah, I'm a frequent traveller" (Hunter and Yates, 2002: 333). An executive from AT&T, Vice-President of Strategic Marketing and Research Trends, Coca-Cola, and the Vice-President for International Programs, World Vision, also share the same experience. Thus, we can say that globalization has undoubtedly created an opening in global travelling, but for the people living at the base of the social pyramid it is still unaffordable. Actually, interdependence (among rich and poor nations) is the cliché of the contemporary world, an expression that creates an agreeable illusion of equality, though between profoundly unequal countries, it means dominance and subordination of the weaker one. This is yet another attempt to rewrite history, and we have seen and heard a great deal of it since the official "death" of socialism.

ARE THE RICH GETTING RICHER AND THE POOR GETTING POORER?

At this juncture our prime interest is to assess that how the footloose investment by the TNCs is posing a threat to the economic sovereignty of the Third World countries. The development of a qualitative shift in world economy is being caused by the rapid growth of the TNCs. They have already changed the concentrating tendency of capital. In this respect, financial capital enjoys an edge over the industrial one since it does not have to bear any fixed, locational costs. This process is lessening the ability of the nation states to control their national currency and encouraging trading on the basis of regional economic alliances, e.g., we have seen—Austria, Belgium, Denmark, Finland, Holland, Portugal, France, Germany, Greece, Ireland, Italy, Luxembourg, Spain, Sweden, Turkey and the UK—the 16 members of the European Union (EU) were striving all through the 1990s to establish "a united economy with common economic, security, and judicial policies." In 1999, 11 of them had successfully achieved a single European currency called the "Euro." As a consequence, weaker economies (such as Italy) suddenly have a currency that is tantamount to the currency of stronger economies (such as Germany). And the trade barriers among these countries have been removed giving rise to financial transactions. Although not as formal as the EU, others regional economic alliances are emerging in Asia, North America, South and Central America, Southern Africa, and East Africa. Hence it is clear that some regional economic and trading ties of their own type are being formed within a single global system, which is superior to the nation state. The phenomenon can be aptly summed up as regionalism within globalism. It can be further illustrated and visualized as some bowls kept on a large plate. But through imposing some restrictions on the movement of capital and labor, the nation state still now continues to be the core unit of analysis in this *deja vu* phase of capitalism.

After the World War II, the direct colonial domination became extinct. The traditional "rest," handicapped by poverty, malnutrition, and hunger aspired for a better life and started to daydream about development (which they thought, can be achieved primarily through economic growth)—thus succumbing to the modernized West. From the late 1960s, companies operating in the West and Japan confronted a profit squeeze due to increase in their labor costs, which in turn was a result of trade unions winning higher wages for their workers. In order to secure their profit the companies then started searching for a region to relocate their business where trade unions are weak and cheap labor is easily procurable. The Third World, because of its high unemployment rate and staggering economic condition (the International Labour Organization figures for 1972 estimated that 39 percent of the population of the Third World was "destitute" and 67 percent was described as seriously poor), was just the ticket they were looking for. Moreover, the vast unexplored markets of the Third World also beckoned the developed and they readily felt the need of a quick circulation of finished products. Impelled by the thought, they started shifting their production units in different regions of the Third World.

As a result, the newly industrializing countries of East Asia—South Korea, Taiwan, Hong Kong and Singapore—had emerged (Frank, 1981). In one decade (1980–90) the volume of cross-border transactions in equities grew from $120 billion a year to $1.4 trillion and international bank lending stock rate from $324 billion to $7.5 trillion (Hoogvelt, 1997).

The increase in cross-border monetary transactions yielded unfavorable conditions for the advanced capitalist states. Relocation of industrial capital in low-cost areas was followed by a subsequent rise in unemployment in these countries (Peet, 1986). In the post-World War II era, they, particularly the US, have passed through two different types of economic growth. The time-period of 30 years (1945–75) was a golden age for the American middle-class people; because then it was easy for a high school graduate to secure a blue-collar job or even a white-collar job for himself (Farley, 1996). The emergence of newly industrializing countries and the increasing availability of low-cost labor decreased the real wage for the workers of high-income nations. It pushed the middle-class towards tough competition and gradually they were habituated to stand in long, serpentine queues in front of the unemployment office (Bluestone and Harrison, 1982; Farley, 1996; Levy, 1998; Newman, 1993). The whole thing in effect; put a stoppage on the growth and development of the middle-class, increased poverty and a new term "underclass" was coined to describe those people disconnected from the economic mainstream.

Though the investment of mobile capital helped to expedite employment in the Third World yet the overall result was not desirable. The cheap labor of the Periphery has promoted industrialization welcoming the "super-exploitation" for them that aided in capital accumulation. This availability of low-cost labor became the foremost reason

Figure 7.1: Class Structure and Economic Development

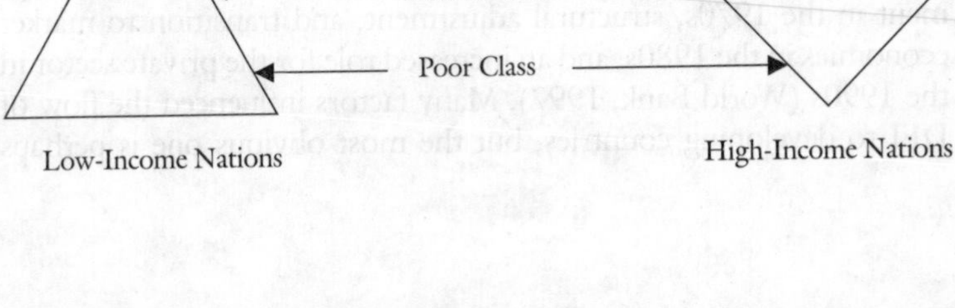

Elite Class

Middle Class

Poor Class

Low-Income Nations   High-Income Nations

of attraction of foreign investment that indicated the commencement of privatization of state-owned enterprises. Increasingly, agencies monitoring and promoting the process marked special areas as Export Processing Zones (EPZs) in the periphery countries. By 1992, more than 80 countries of the Third World had privatized some 6,800 previously state-run enterprises, mostly monopoly suppliers of essential public services like water, electricity, and telecommunications (Hoogvelt, 1997). The General Agreement on Trade and Tariff (GATT) and the newly established World Trade Organization (WTO) has further hastened this process of privatization assisting to set up a truly global economy. TNCs through the World Bank and the International Monetary Fund (IMF) are influencing Government policies in the Third World countries. In 1991, Structural Adjustment Programme (SAP), *inter alia*, required open market for foreigners and lesser reliance on public sector units in India. As such, the moves of globalization, privatization, and liberalization are being carried out, eventually leading to widespread amendments in the laws, acts, and rules and regulations of the Third World countries. To illustrate: a few favorable provisions for TNCs are to include: (*a*) permission of setting up 100 percent wholly owned subsidiaries in some cases; (*b*) automatic approval of 51 percent investment in equity capital; (*c*) permission to use foreign trademark; (*d*) formation of monopolies through mergers and acquisitions; (*e*) utilization of forestry minerals and mines for their industries; (*f*) giving land to them for farming and processing of agricultural produce; and (*h*) permission to enter into the national sector (Agarwal, 1999: 84).

Foreign investment has clearly been a major factor in stimulating economic growth and development in recent times. The contribution that TNCs can make as agents of growth, structural change, and international integration has made DFI a coveted tool of economic development (Bhattacharya and Palaha, 1996). Direct Foreign Investment in developing countries has a long history. It has fluctuated over time, as investors have responded to changes in the environment for investment including government policies towards DFIs and the broader economic policy framework. Hence, trends in DFI have reflected changes in policy stances by developing countries from import substitution in the 1950s and 1960s, through natural resource-led development in the 1970s, structural adjustment, and transition to market economies in the 1980s, and an increased role for the private sector in the 1990s (World Bank, 1997). Many factors influenced the flow of DFI to developing countries, but the most obvious one is perhaps their own willingness to allow it. DFI may actually be harmful to the recipient country if the economy is highly protected and if foreign investment takes place behind high tariff walls. This type of investment is generally referred to as "tariff pumping," whose priority objective is to take advantage of the protected markets in the host country (Sebastian, 1994). During the period 1991–93, the developing countries as a whole got around 31 percent of the total global stock of DFI. This investment was highly concentrated in particular regions. The distribution was—Africa received 1.7 percent of the world total; Latin America and the Caribbean got 9.8 percent; West Asia 0.8 percent; East, South and South-East Asia 18.8 percent (UNCTAD, 1995). In 1996, Hirst and Thompson have estimated that in the early 1900s, around 28 percent of the world's population received 91 percent of global DFI and so around 72 percent of the population received 8 percent of global DFI (pp. 67–68). These figures are based at the level of nation states rather than people in the nation states. In the real world, not all people within a country will benefit from investment— indeed, many of the major recipients of DFI (First as well as the Third World) have high rates of unemployment. These figures ultimately depicted the pattern of the diversification of Third World. Thus, it is evident that economic ties are strengthening in global era but the global hierarchies still exist and are actually intensifying (pp. 49–55, cited in Kiely, 1998a: 49).

The TNCs invest in the Third World far a variety of reasons— utilization of lucrative domestic market, availability of cheap raw materials and cheap labor and last but not the least—to avoid the stringent state regulation of the First World. Needless to say that it is easy to motivate, through advertising, the consumers of the Third World than those of the First World to purchase a particular commodity and the TNCs surely have the ability to spend more on campaigning than the local companies (Jenkins, 1988), which even enabled some TNCs to promote the sale of "inappropriate products"—like selling an air-cooler to an Eskimo! From 1970 onwards Nestle was accused of promoting the sale of powdered milk for babies in areas where potential customers did not have access to safe, potable water which led to serious health hazards and even proved fatal for children (Muller, 1982).

But the underdeveloped Third World societies have no way to innovate new paths of development. They await the impact of industrial transformation. These societies therefore have to tread similar paths to those already followed by the industrialized countries, reproducing the "achievements of industrial society" (Giddens, 1982). The fate of these undeveloped and developing societies, therefore, is determined by the fate of developed nations and vice versa. For instance, in 1997, the Asian economy stagnated all of a sudden and then declined. The Asian stock markets experienced the worst condition in the middle of 1998 when the US stock market also plummeted, falling over 1000 points between July and September. In late 1998, when the Asian economies came round, the US stock market, was also reactivated and energized. This is a reminder of the fact that we live in an inter-connected world (Bradshaw, 2001: 4).

IS GLOBAL POLITY FEASIBLE?

The astounding technological advancements in the field of telecom-munication have created an interconnected and consolidated world economy wiping off the national boundaries. Even though there are thousands of ethnic and cultural divisions throughout the world, many countries share the language of money. A noteworthy feature of today's world is that economic unification and political disintegration are occurring simultaneously. Since 1989, the total count of countries of the world has increased than before. Countries are dividing up along ethnic, cultural and religious lines, with different groups calling for self-rule based on one or more characteristics (Naisbitt, 1994). In between 1991 and 1993, 25 new countries have been added to the Atlas. The erstwhile USSR and some countries of the Eastern Europe have under-gone political fragmentation due to internal conflicts aroused by differ-ent ethnic, religious, cultural, economical and political issues. John Naisbitt foresees that there will be reoccurrence of this incident in near future.

> I feel confident that the EU, which seeks to go beyond trade and bind countries politically—moving toward a common foreign policy and defense, as well as a common currency—is doomed to failure. There are many who disagree with me—vociferously. But that is because they do not understand that although people want to come together to trade more freely, they want to be independent politically and culturally. There will be no real union of Europe (1994:10).

Hence it can be said that economic unity is rather easier to achieve than political unity. The political conflicts rose in different parts of the world in different times depending on various issues are symbolizing a "distant thunder" for the human civilization. It is hard to believe that during 1990s only, the political struggle in former Yugoslavia killed about a quarter million people! "The movements for sovereignty" have already achieved a global status—as in US, 140,000 native Hawaiians are fighting for a separate nation; the Zapatista National Liberation Army is engaged in a warfare with the Mexican Government for the autonomy of the province of Chiapas (Golden, 1995). The new Parliament in Scotland marked the beginning of political disunion in UK Hence, to be precise, the differences in culture, ethnicity, nationality, religion an economic privilege hinder political consolidation.

Another important factor that affects the political life and indirectly retards the process of political consolidation is the innate feature of labor movement, i.e., the eternal conflict between the workers and the economic and political authorities. Daniel Bell suggested in his *The Coming of Post-Industrialized Society* (1974) that post-industrial society has superseded industrialism which resulted in a hedonistic cultural environment typical of advanced capitalist societies and incompatible with the dominance of rationality required by the economic system and in the backdrop of it the general health of labor movements has become more and more important. The labor movement that engaged in industrializing countries in the 19th century was an important part of democratization (Collier, 1999). In that time, labor movements were organized not only for wage-hike and improvement of working conditions, but also for public protests and campaigning for their nominees in the elections, which ultimately expanded their democratic practices. The significant issues for workers were tax-funded pensions, disability payments, unemployment benefits, and public education systems. Thus, for the expansion of welfare rights, this type of labor movement was instrumental (Tilly, 1995).

However, today the changing face of global geography of industrial output distributes factory jobs in areas away from the preliminary industrial settings, and pushes the workforce-composition of the wealthy countries towards the service sector. Interestingly, service workers have always shown greater reluctance in joining unions than the laborers of industries. It explains why the percentage of US workers belonging to unions has suffered a sharp fall. On the other hand, the bargaining power of the laborers, backed by the threats of work stoppage, has been markedly reduced both in direct and indirect way due to greater global mobility of investment—now it is comparatively easy for investors to channel their investment into some other business, and not surprisingly, even on the other side of our planet. Hence in direct sense, the global movement of capital has put the investors in an advantageous position—workers will not find new jobs nearly as readily as investors will find something else to do with their money.

On the other hand, the unchecked growth of service sector is stratifying the workers on the basis of their economic and social status. Consequently, their motive is being diversified and hence the possibility of organizing a unified social movement is waning. Therefore, the success rates of the labor movements in rich countries have experienced a downfall from what it was in the 19th and 20th centuries. Standing on the threshold of the 21st century if we start listing the cause responsible for delimiting the governments' duties and capabilities we will find the principal factors are eagerness to go private, the global extension of the range of communication as well as economic activities and lastly the dwindled regulatory capability. National states have failed to satisfy what the workers' movement has traditionally demanded from them to do. Nowadays, if workers of a country with minimum wage laws, occupational safety rules and anti-pollution legislation bargain with investors; the latter will simply transfer his business to some other countries where these restrictions do not apply at all.

Whether the workers will be able to guarantee the same rights in this new arrangement of power as they did in a few national states in the 19th and early 20th centuries, is a pertinent question of this era. And another equally important question is that—does the weakening of labor movement, which along with other forms of social activism played a major role in democratizing many national states, signals a general decay of democracy?

The abject condition of labor movement in the US, disintegration of former Yugoslavia and emergence of four new republics (recognized by UN) or reunion of West and East Germany through the destruction of the Berlin Wall—these are all local events having global influences although occurring within specific political territories. In practice, national politics is always territorially limited. Global politics—in which we could discern the flavor of globalization—has international relation and political culture as its two major ingredients. However, state always tries to solve the problems occurred within its political perimeter and to maintain its sovereignty. Globalization is a process that defies boundaries and hence the above-mentioned activities of state impede it. Naturally, the question that strikes in our mind is—then how it is possible to form a global polity?

Among all the incidents in the course of political history of the world, the formation of organized nation state provides the most effective means to establish sovereignty over political territories, but nation state still has territorial limitations. Still now, new countries come into existence on the basis of ethnicity, which hampers the formation of global polity on the basis of humanity. Globalization threatens this limited sovereignty. Some commentators like Waters (1995: 122–23) claim that complete political globalization is achievable because territories are now being defied and annihilated by transcendent cultural items that are transmissible by symbolic media. The spread of liberal democracy and of post-materialist values is not a *sui generis* development in each society where they take place but are carried from one society to another. Those who doubt on the effectiveness of culture might prefer to compare the bloody and fierce revolution that established nation states from the 17th to the 19th century with the "bloodless coups and velvet revolutions" that have taken place in the final stage of 20th century. These suggest that the future of complete political globalization is a true possibility. If this is possible, then my prime question is—who will be the head of this global polity or who will be responsible for global governance?

TECHNOLOGY: IS IT A BOON OR A BANE?

Man has won a dominant position on earth by his command of technology. All other animals are forced to adapt to the natural conditions however hostile they are. In sharp contrast, man alone changes the very shape of his world according to his need. He moves things about and transforms them to create an environment hospitable for him. He has thus passed through different stages of civilization and has now reached the threshold of a global age.

Technology, being a basic trait of all human societies, involves extension, permutation and combination of the fundamental artifacts—radio, telephone, television, record-and-playback-machine and computer etc.—which help us to delve into this global age more and more. Now, one regional activity influences another and vice versa. New innovations and remodeling of the previous ones are doing away with the old systems and making us habituated with a new "Web Lifestyle", which has some substantial advantages: better access to information, new ways of thinking, advanced modes of communication, new research techniques, new pattern of high-yielding production systems, new business and employment opportunities, increase in life-expectancy, new worlds of convenience... the list can go on.

But technology is not always liberating. The proposed Cyberspace Electronic Security Act will heighten the restrictions on freedom and lack of privacy in the US. The law would enable the police and other law enforcers to check private computers for secret information (O' Harrow, 1999). The Justice Department claims that implementation of such a law is becoming more and more necessary because computers are now being increasingly used for a variety of crimes. Relevance of such enactment has increased by leaps and bounds after the destruction of the WTC by terrorist groups on the September 11, 2001.

The "Web Lifestyle" fathered by the technological innovations in the postmodern society, is not equally available for everybody. A statistics reveals that only one-fourth of the US families with incomes below $30,000 have home computers while 80 percent of those with incomes exceeding $100,000 possess it. Access to the Internet is 20 times greater in families with incomes of $75,000 and above than those having lower incomes; and the former category is nine times more likely to own personal computers than the latter (Sack, 2000). The disparity between the "haves" and the "have nots," is even more pronounced and exposed when we take a broader view. In a comparative study, we find that the US and other developed countries have almost 18.5 times the number of personal computers and about 86.5 times the number of Internet connections than what the middle-income countries do. The number of personal computers and Internet users are so nominal in low-income countries that they are "statistically negligible".

Possibly, in today's world there is no other inequality as great as technological inequality—even the simple technologies that are in frequent use in the lives of the peoples of the developed countries are yet-to-be-realized dreams for the poor countries. It sounds unbelievable that almost two-third of the world's population has never made a telephone call, use of computers seems to be a far more distant reality. India, the largest democratic country on this planet, has a meagre five million-telephone connection for a population of a billion. (World Bank, 1998).

Almost all the Third World countries are socially, economically, and technologically nearly homologous. As a number of infertile women

Table 7.5: Technological Inequality, 1996–97

	Personal Computers per 1,000 Persons	Internet Hosts per 10,000 Persons
High-Income Countries		
Finland	182.10	653.60
Germany	233.20	106.70
Japan	128.00	75.80
Switzerland	408.50	208.00
United States	362.40	442.10
Middle-Income Countries		
Algeria	3.40	0.01
Brazil	18.40	4.20
Mexico	29.00	3.70
Russia	23.70	5.50
South Africa	37.70	30.70
Low-Income Countries		
China	3.00	0.21
Ivory Coast	1.40	0.17
India	1.50	0.05
Kenya	1.50	0.16
Uganda	0.50	0.01

Source: World Bank, 1998.
Note: Data on personal computers in low-income countries are estimates; few low-income countries have date on personal computer use.

in the Third World cannot have children by alternative means singularly due to economic reasons. The picture is markedly different when the First World countries are taken into account. Recent developments in genetics has put mankind in a demigod position enabling him to create new lives in the laboratory and, thus, to totally change the biological and cultural basis of the family. Hitherto, "*in vitro* (in glass) fertilization" (and "embryo transplantation") is offered only to married women but if this restriction (which seems to be rather anachronistic keeping in mind the increasing occurrences of non-marital relationships) is withdrawn, this technological marvel will lead us to "deliberate fatherless motherhood," which is historically unknown (Beck, 1992: 206). Its consequences can be easily predicted—sperm banks will be set up, abolishing social fatherhood. May be, packed sperms will be available in the global market bearing labels like "comes from UK" "comes from USA" etc. and people will run after it! If motherhood of virgins through sperm purchasing becomes socially sanctioned then the unavoidable questions are—who will be responsible for the

quality control of these embryos and what will be the ethnic identity
of these children in that social environment?

CULTURE: LOCALLY GLOBAL, ·OR GLOBALLY LOCAL?

The colossal use of the word globalization helps it to achieve a global
status, in which culture positions itself at the center. In practice, culture is a set of tangible and intangible elements including beliefs values, norms, material objects, rituals, technologies, *et al.*, that shape
and add meaning to the daily lives of a particular group of people. It
plays a pivotal role in any society since it designs the pattern of social
action without which the members of a society would be unable to
understand each other at all. Through interactions among people,
social action changes its form and thus culture is also changed. Earlier, colonialism, trade, migration, missionary activities, technological
changes (particularly, the advancement of production and communication system) incorporation of tribals into states and large-scale systems of exchange were the principal factors behind cultural diffusion
that resulted in cultural imperialism or globalization of culture (Eriksen,
1995: 278).

Presently, for the modern communication system, space can no
longer be said to create a clear buffer between cultures. Newspaper,
radio, TV and the last of all—the Internet has linked up different
cultures, making broad avenues for cultural exchange or cultural fusion to proceed which fathers new cultural forms, ideas and objects.
"Tradition and old assumptions about community based on geographic
location are rubbing up against the realities of a networked, changing
world. The strain is accompanied by violent conflict in some places
(like Serbia and Indonesia), social repression in other places (like Af-
ghanistan), and denunciation of globalization virtually everywhere"
(Healey, 2001a: 141).

Due to the spread of global culture today, many societies are facing
cultural lags. The reason is that the material culture diffuses and changes
quite quickly than its non-material counterpart (Ogburn, 1964).
Present day TNCs and other foreign agencies, by means of state-of-
the-art technology, introduce us to the new, newer and newest "materials" or "cultural products" which we are yet to think of. And that is
not all. Through their advertisements they claim that if you do not
buy their products you will lose something—they try to hammer this

idea into our (consumers') minds, side by side, "intellectuals and cultural elites" function "as both the commentators and practitioners of cultural globalization" (Yan, 2002: 35). Though, in non-material aspect of culture, their influence is limited and so is less impressive than that of the TNCs in the material field.

The values, beliefs, ideas, ethics, and artifacts of the occidental culture sneak into the territory of the orient through different media and thereby produce cultural hybridization. Socialization, a life-long process by which one adopts the non-material elements of a particular culture and familiarizes himself with its material components, plays an important role in permanent coalescence of many cultures. Children are socialized into a set of subcultural ambiences rather than a single cultural environment. Interactively, socialization helps children to adopt their culture. It is noteworthy that during the adoption "they are also re-inventing or creating new meaning for aspects of it" (Corsaro, 1997: 18). Adolescence culture distinguishably influences the larger one. The youths are the main vectors of the global culture. They are the most loyal and zealous customers of the alien culture too. For them Coke, Pop CDs, denims, the ingredients of the imported culture, are "prestige commodities"—the rate of acceptance being very high. In addition to that, abundant portrayal of violence and sex in TV has degraded their normal behavior pattern. Hence the mushrooming youth cultures—representatives of the globe at the globules—are starkly different from the traditional ones that were once prevalent there. So, the younger members of the society are not only subjected to the process of socialization but also are forming their own culture which is often based on blind aping of the Western one.

At the same time a good number of youths, mostly in the Third World countries, rear a negative version about the global high-hatting of the US in different issues. So, beneath the external flow of global culture there is also an undercurrent of political nationalism among the youths, which invokes a sense of patriotism and self-identity in their minds under certain circumstances.

Earlier, we have mentioned that media acts as vehicles of "Web Lifestyle." Actually there exists some forms of an authority which—in order to secure their interests—advocates the global spread of a particular culture. And to achieve this, they are actively trying to take-over the control of the world media and manipulate it according to their need—which in short can be termed as "media imperialism" (Giddens, 1989: 559). However to explain the thing, practical examples will prove more effective rather than theoretical jargons.

A multitude of the Periphery, who were almost untouched by the widespread western consumerist culture even a decade back, are now going to be acquainted with it. These people were not under the direct influence of the cable TV network. Hence they were not so much exposed to the global cultural trends and the culture that they maintained was almost pristine. But now foreign investment is being permitted in the print media, these people will soon succumb to the West—culturally. In India, the previous ban on foreign investment in print media, imposed by Nehru's cabinet in 1955, has been lifted and 26 percent DFI in newspapers and 74 percent in specialized magazines has been granted initially (June 25, 2002). Actually, the Indian Government was pressurized by the foreign politics (read US and UK) and the TNCs to take the decision. From their previous experience of investment in the electronic media, the TNCs have realized that until they could control the press they will not be totally successful in motivating people to buy their products and capturing the vast and unexplored markets of the Third World thereby. Hence the decision will prove fruitful for them in monetary terms and side by side it will also speed up the cultural hybridization that is taking place around the globe. Moreover, a logical speculation suggests that in the near future the "de-Indianization" of the "still-new-Indian" media will multiply the percentage of DFI. Chomsky bestows two responsibilities on media as the democracy-keeper of the society—first, it "must report the news fairly, completely, and without bias, and second, it "must function as a watchdog for the public against abuses of power"— which are sure to be shirked under the aegis of foreign participation (Cogswell, 1996: 69). The anticipation will not be irrational that the press will be a mere campaigner of the TNCs in the coming days, "transmit biased information instead of news, and do their masters' bidding without even being asked" (Cogswell, 1996: 82). To put it simply, they will be engaged in publishing the recent news about the Hollywood chartbusters, gossips of Bollywood and advertisements for Coke, Ford, McDonald and other corporate houses etc., rather than depicting the misery of the native people.

Earlier, we have hinted at the ramified media-network and showed how it imports alien culture and thus alters the interpretations of the cultural elements. The process leads towards cultural "creolization." However we should not forget the other function of the media, that is, providing its investors with better access to information of even the farthest corner of the world. Mass media, in the Chomskian view, is just a "public relation industry for the rich and powerful" (Cogswell, 1996: 69). Its pertinent now to discuss the term cultural creolization. According to Eriksen, cultural "creolization" or "hybridization" refers to the intermingling and mutual influencing of two or several bodies of cultural flow (or "tradition")" (1995: 284). In his book on postmodernism, Powell presents us with its true picture—"all the world's culture, rituals, races, data banks, myths and musical motifs are intermixing like a smorgasbord in an earthquake" (1998: 2). We further clarify it by culling the example of contemporary style of the world music, which is a meeting place of different cultural influences.

The postmodern world music has a kaleidoscopic flavor. It has tinges of different regional music in it. By just switching on the TV one can hear a music band is singing:

> a blend of Irish love song, Indian raga, heavy-metal anthem, Mongolian Buddhist chant—and all to the tune of peyote drums, gamelans, didgeridoos, panpipes, nose flutes, alpenhorns, sitars and tambourines. And all these sounds may be produced not by the original instrument but electronically, to a danceable reggae or hip-hop beat, and broadcast worldwide via satellite to millions of viewers (Powell, 1998: 1).

In essence, the postmodern artists like the ancient explorers, simply dive into the unknown and strive to showcase it through their creations. I can cite example of Indipop singer Daler Mehndi for a better elucidation. He sings Punjabi folk numbers punched with preludes and interludes on the piano, guitar, keyboard or saxophone, and uses beats on octapad, thumba, bongo or congo and makes an international business on this hodge-podge. And one thing to note, he does not need to pay any royalty for this. However it must be admitted that he has bestowed a global status to a local culture. But in doing so, he did make some compromises. He did commodify and commercialize the original folk music deliberately, which denotes a sheer loss of originality and authenticity.

Again, in sharp contrast, we have seen Uday Shankar enthrals the audience in Europe and America with his dance-shows in 1940s. These shows were mainly based on Hindu mythological stories, which were generously applauded. At present, Tagore and his works are immensely popular in the western countries. I can also mention the name of the *sitar*—maestro Ravi Shankar who has contributed considerably in globalizing the Indian classical music. Today American students are crowding his music schools in the US. All these facts indicate a single thing, that is, the local culture also has the capability to influence the influential global culture or to say it differently, and the local culture can get globalized. Such reciprocal influences are the basic traits of cultural hybridization.

In the postmodern era when occidental consumerist culture strangulates the rural culture; pop, rap and the hegemony of the Hollywood reaches the remotest nook of the world and jeopardizes the cultural heritages there—even then some local cultures are fighting valiantly to safeguard their own identity and sovereignty allowing some minor changes and thus positioning the wolves as the final fortress before the onslaught of "Americanization." A proposition by Levi-Strauss, every culture must give out its "creative potential" by choosing the perfect equilibrium between "isolation" and "contact" with surroundings, further supports it. Thus, local culture but local customs assimilate some features of extraneous culture and conventional lifestyle continues to be very much active. In the last decade for instance, urban peoples of India, China (and other Third World countries) accepted some characteristics of western culture-entrepreneurship, individualism and consumerism. But the rural people of these countries even now are very much less enthusiastic in this regard.

Today western culture seeps more and more into the far-flung and the remote places on the earth, which poses a threat to all the local cultures, resulting in a slow and gradual change in them, and some weaker culture may pale out in this process. As we write in English although it is not our vernacular, to air our thoughts globally. However, hitherto, local culture advocates its identify in its own way. Depending on Healey's position, the reasons behind the co-existence of local and global culture can be pointed out as given later:

First, culture creates a sense of "we-feeling" through standardized behavior among the people of a territorial community. Their connection with others, from different geographic locations, of "similar interests and concerns," which creates a "shared meaning" about life, does not hamper their links with those from the same geographic location.

Second, local culture is "surprisingly resilient and durable" to survive under pressure. Actually values, norms, customs and other non-material components of culture remains so deeply embedded in their minds that it is tough for a global culture to eradicate there.

Third, global culture has to rely on local culture to reach the local people, that is, because global messages are most effective when they are put via local languages. For instance, Christian church services in

Africa have endeared local customs, dance, music and languages. Hence the global culture, till now, is incomplete without the local, which means the co-existence of the first and the second, at least at present.

Fourth, we have stated earlier that children are socialized into a mosaic of cultures. Therefore, we have an innate inclination towards cultural diversity and so it will be ridiculous to think that peoples around the globe will accept a "single global super-culture."

Finally, there are many people who value the old customs and ideas that contain "deep personal meanings." They refuse cultural homogenization by cultivating the traditional things.

ETHNICITY: A JOURNEY FROM CHAOS TO COSMOS, IS IT?

It has been recognized that in the modern world, at least till date, the local cultures have not been totally engulfed by the global one—they make their presence felt quite distinctly. Their existence actually indicates thriving of the different cultural groups over the globe. If we take approximately that a particular culture is practiced by a particular group of people who are racially identical, then logically speaking, the existence of such cultural groups in turn signifies that of the different ethnic groups. The protesters will surely raise the question—is it justified saying that a particular race is related to a particular culture, always? And in this regard they may also cite the example of the high-earning blacks of the US that belong to a culture completely different from their low-earning brothers. But one should remember that through the course of history, the others have influenced each and every race (and its culture). Hence the very idea of "one-race-one-culture" has been hampered again and again since there were continuous incorporations from the foreign cultures to a racial culture. Migration, colonization and (at present) the functioning of mass-media has supported it greatly. If each of the races could be made to survive independently, without the tiniest bit of external influence—then surely each race will create its own culture. As for example, due to the initially limited spread of the Islam religion and its hyper-orthodoxy, the Islamic culture is relatively free from alien influences and so has retained its original and primitive form in all respects.

Previously, we have said that local cultures are being threatened by the global culture. Consequently, the latter replaces the former and gets localized. Hence, there exists an antagonistic relationship between them, which results in cultural conflicts. In a broader perspective, we can describe this as the inter-relation between the practitioners of the local culture and those of the global one. In essence, the concept of ethnic group is intertwined with culture since the genesis of an ethnic group follows from the loyalty of a particular group of people to a special culture. Although Max Weber (1968: 389) and Herbert Blumer (1987: 193) mentioned a few more points in this respect—"real or putative common ancestry," "subjective belief in their common descent because of similarities in physical type," "kinship" etc. So, in defining an ethnic group the racial factor is obviously a criterion but that does not equalize an ethnic group with a racial one.

Now, we are acquainted with the intense relation between the ethnic group and culture. However, the question remains that—if there exist a few groups of people, each one pertaining to a particular culture, can we call these groups as ethnic groups? The answer is "no." In fact, two culturally different groups are never identified as ethnic groups. The reason is that until the members of different cultural groups interact with each other their fidelity to their culture remains untested. But if the groups come in even a minimum contact of each other, it causes to germinate the idea of "our culture" and "their culture" in the minds of the group members. As Cohen pointed out in his *The Symbolic Construction of Community*—"People become aware of their culture when they stand at its boundaries: when they encounter other cultures, or when they become aware of other ways of doing things, or merely of contradictions to their own culture" (1985). Interrelation among various cultural groups often leads to the high hating of the practitioners of the relatively stronger culture on those of the weaker one and thus resists cultural assimilation. This is what we term as ethnocentrism—cultural superciliousness. Here the main ethnic responses are food preferences, table manners, toilet habits, health practices, patterns of sexual behavior, religion, common beliefs etc.

"Ethnicity is a product of conquest, colonization, and immigration. That is, ethnicity implies dislocation from one's original country, region, or nation, that is, homeland" (Oommen, 2002: 16). The connection between *ethnie* and nation is an intentional human creation by rising political classes striving to dislodge the feudal autarchy. Thus from the last decades of 18th country deliberate attempts were made across the world (and particularly, in Europe) to rear a national consciousness in favor of the nation state—the modern form of political organization (Waters, 1995: 133–39). Since the 1960s, "cultural identity and uniqueness" became legal political resources in large parts of the world. For a nation state to exist, its leaders must legalize a particular power structure and advertise the ability of the nation to fulfil the needs of its population. In most cases, an effective nationalism enjoys an inherent relationship with an ethnic, ideology emphasizing on "shared descent" and "state apparatus." A nationalist ideology may be defined in ethnic perspective, which involves right to its own state depending on ethnic groups. So, clearly nationalism and ethnicity are inseparably related, but there are many ethnic groups, which are not nations, and there are aplenty of such nations, which are not mono-ethnic, which justifies that polyethnic countries or nations are not formed on ethnic principles. Actually, most of the countries of the world are inhabited multiethnically but are dominated monoethnically; the French in France, the English in Great Britain and so on (Eriksen, 1995: 249–77). From the above discussion, two things are clear. First, when an ethnie demands its legitimacy within a definite boundary and acquires it, then it becomes a nation. And when this nation attains political jurisdiction then it is converted into a state. Second, all the modern nations are culturally hybridized. And this existence of multiple cultural centers within the states bears the testimony of its multiethnic characteristic.

Polyethnicity is at the heart of the Indian state. Being heterogeneous in nature it comprises of numerous social and ethnic groups. What is essential to manage such a state-machinery is "to go back to the constitutional imperative of respecting each social and ethnic group and providing them sufficient space to evolve a polity of 'unity in diversity'" (Pinto, 2000: 196). But this is not happening. Ethnocentrism has assumed such an alarming shape here that the national elite forces to impose Hindu national culture on the ethnic groups ranked lower in the caste hierarchy. These groups are judged as inferior, primitive and under developed and their cultural heritages and belittled by comparing them with that of the majoritarian culture. Naturally, the elite is an anathema to these groups, who suppress and oppress their culture manipulating the state apparatus. Consequently, there is dissatisfaction and anguish among these groups against this cultural invasion, which may erupt, into an Armageddon that may irreversible change the social, political and ethnic structure of the country.

If we extend our vision beyond our national boundaries, we could see the object condition of the African countries (Somalia, Sudan, Rwanda, Liberia)—poverty, ethnic conflict, political disintegration and the result is a flooding population of "international refugees" (IR) and "internally displaced persons" (IDP). The latter, 16 million or 60 percent of the total IDPs of the world, are the victims of the ethnopolitical conflict during late 1980s and early 1990s, while the former totaled about six million out of the total regional population of 600 million (Darnton, 1994a: A2). And that is not all, the international trend in this regard is also alarming—IR court has soared to 23 millions (1994) from 10.5 millions (1984) in just 10 years (Darnton, 1994b: A2). However, there is an active endeavor to curb this menace. In 1993 the US navy uninvitedly landed in Somalia to keep a vigil on the ongoing civil war in the absence of a proper government. This trend is a step towards "revival of colonialism" as opined by Paul Johnson, an US historian (1993: 22).

The concept of globalization has added a new dimension in the discourse of ethnicity. Globalization can be viewed as a tool called deterritorializer or international connector or rather specifically, an ethnic pluralizer, which frees ethnicity from all specific perimeters or political bounding. Paradoxical though it may sound, yet globalization can be defined as a differentiating and simultaneously integrating process. On one hand it pluralizes the world by globalizing the cultural tenets, absorbing ethnic minorities and encouraging the spread of the "universal culture" backed by the western modernity, thereby enervating the so-called "putative nexus" between nation and state. But on the other, it also fuels the political "disruption of confederations of nations" like the Czechoslovakia, UK, USSR, etc. However, there is one thing of interest. The neonate countries are also territorially surrounded and hence the critics and cynics can justifiably doubt on the de-territorializing capabilities of globalization. From another viewpoint, globalization pushes center towards periphery and vice versa. To illustrate, we say, an *ethnie* is positioned in the Periphery where it has little power but when it emerges as a nation it has greater power and thus is said to have moved towards the "centre of the polity." The reverse may happen, to exemplify, if a dominating ethnic group in a polyethnic nation looses its dominance and monopoly then it is moved from a state of higher power and authority (center) to a lower one (periphery).

Hence the global picture of ethnicity is all about mixing, merging and often about securing an identity of its own. It is longer an impediment to love and marriage. And probably a menu of a ethnic restaurant makes you feel the thing better—it combines delicacies and cuisines that are offspring of different ethnic and cultural centers. The establishment of "ethnic theme parks" in Japan, (one of the rare most specimens of the "ideal type"—"one-nation, one-state") where one can find "The German Happiness kingdom," "Canadian World", "Venice of Japan," "Holland village" etc., further corroborates the view discussed so far (*Economist*, Jan, 22–28, 1994). To sum up all the things, globalization is an effective weapon to develop multicultural (and hence necessarily multiethnic) societies.

GLOBALIZATION: INEQUALITY EXPOSED

From the late 1980s or the early 1990s some important incidents started to happen in the world's sociopolitical and economic fields. Fall of the USSR, which signaled the official "death" of state socialism, and the subsequent termination of the "Cold War"; demolition of Berlin Wall; the "Asian Crisis," are some major examples in this regard which facilitated the "rejuvenation" of globalization at the fag end of the 20th century. This, actually re-established the occidental influence upon the world in all senses which resulted into a variety of phenomena—formation of new global market network; gradual decay of government sectors and rapid uprising of private sectors; mushrooming of MNCs and NGOs, formation of WTO etc. as power centers; rise of G-7, G-10, G-22, OECD *et al.*, as regional blocks and policy co-ordination groups; invention of latest communication techniques (internet, cellular phone, fax etc); germination of value-based human rights; the scourge of AIDS on the human civilization—each possessing its own importance in respective domains.

All these things, as I mentioned earlier, symbolized a lot of changes in world-politics, culture and economics—among them "de-territorializaiton" and reduction of controlling power of the nation states are noteworthy. Through these alterations the global politics drastically remodelled itself and advanced toward its present state to a great extent. However, there has been a good deal of debate among the theorists on the merits and demerits of these changes and the following "outburst of globalization." Side by side, those who are from the pro-globalization group, strove hard to project and publicize the positive aspects of globalization and indeed, their efforts did not end in smoke. They claimed "that the world has moved permanently into a new and promising era; that the growing density of market relations allows more stable as well as faster growth (and) that single set of policies—liberalization of markets for goods and finances small govt. and fiscal discipline—is best for capturing the benefits of globalization" (Wade, 2000). Hence it will be justified to describe globalization in terms of neo-liberal economic policies instead of a mere economic liberalism. Logically, a question that occurs to our minds is that whether these "neo-liberal economic policies" will protect the interest of the common people (and the poor)? We find the answer in a White Paper, published by the UK Government, *Making Globalization Work for the Poor* (2000) where it has been stated that "globalization creates unprecedented new opportunities for sustainable development and poverty reduction." Surely an exaggerated and intentionally hyper-optimized view to secure their own interests. But the Paper, however, indirectly admits that globalization poses a great threat to employment, livelihoods, and environment, and hence jeopardizes the human security in general. Small the message may look like; but, rationally thinking, not too small to ignore.

In our daily lives, we mostly encounter such incidents, which support the latter version. To corroborate this argument, we choose India as an example. Her external debt is mounting by leaps and bounds day by day in this so-called "utopian age of globalization." The adjoining table statistically proves it.

Table 7.6: India's External Debt and Debt Servicing

Year	Total External Debt (US dollars Million)	Debt-GDP Ratio	Debt Servicing as % of Current Receipts
1990–91	83.80	30.4	35.3
1991–92	85.28	41.0	30.2
1992–93	90.02	39.8	28.6
1993–94	92.69	35.9	26.9
1994–95	99.01	32.7	27.5
1995–96	92.20	28.7	24.3
1996–97	91.38	26.0	25.4
1997–98	92.88	23.8	18.3

Source: *Economic Survey,* New Delhi, Ministry of Finance, GOI.

Hence in today's India, each child is born-indebted for which he or she is not liable at all. The other countries of the periphery are in a more or less similar position, which enables the First World countries—the big daddies of global politics—to exploit them, to impose economic policies on them for the lure of filthy lucre. This, at one hand, magnifies the importance and influence of the TNCs and on the other, hikes the prices of the essential food items e.g., grains, vegetables, sugar, edible oil, seeds and increases poverty thereby. S.P. Gupta estimates that poverty ratio in India has rocketed to 39 percent in 1993–94 from the previous 35.5 percent in 1990–91 (1995). One thing to note that, the ratio has shot up greatly after 1991, since the implementation of New Economic Policies towards enhanced global orientation. Things are quite similar in Argentina too.

The autonomy of culture is a much-debated issue in the discussion on cultural globalization or the "cultural direction" of global changes. Some commentators like Waters has given culture the paramount importance while explaining globalization. They opine that basically, globalization is a cultural phenomenon. Waters defined globalization as the "culturization of social life" further adding that actually culture is the central theme of globalization, not politics or not even economics, that can convey its "message" most elegantly. The process of globalization is characteristically distinguished through values, ethics, choices, tastes etc., rather than through economic and political matters. Waters has also proposed a theorem to portray the roles of culture in globalization: "material exchanges localize; political exchanges internationalize; and symbolic exchanges globalise" (1995: 9). The resulting globalized culture is untidy (what its supporters euphemistically call "diversity" is being unabashedly and unabatedly maintained and multiplied by the media) rather than being compact and well–organized—it has interconnections among its different units but the whole the thing in effect is not "unified" or centralized.

Globalization is certainly converting the world into a single-global village, but has failed to weed out the inequalities in society in various aspects of life-politics, economics engineering, medical science, and others (we have repeatedly emphasized on these topics and discussed them at length in the previous segments of our writing). Inequality snowballs within and across societies and is mainly propped against ethnicity or racism, gender bias etc. But as globalization consolidates its position in today's world, economic inequality and polarization have become two unavoidable concomitants of it. The UNDP's report on globalization presents a perfect word-picture of this situation—"Globalization expands the opportunities for unprecedented human advance for some but shrinks those opportunities for others and erodes human security. It is integrating economy, culture and governance but fragmenting societies. Driven by commercial market forces, globalization in this era seeks to promote economic efficiency, generate growth and yield profits. But it misses out on the goals of equity, poverty eradication and enhanced human security (UNDP, 1999: 43–44). To sum up it all, the rich are getting richer and the poor poorer. Mr. Gus Speth—Chief, UN's Development Program—foresees that economic inequality is going to take an "inhuman" state in the coming days.

To catch the real image of the economic inequality of modern world, one should throw one's eyes on the appalling condition of the children—particularly in the Third World countries where they are the "most exploited group" all those lovely, innocent faces, often they become the worst suffers.

Zillions of people live below the poverty line in the Third World countries—they are not able to manage a square meal everyday. Chronic hunger, malnutrition, "chillpenury," starvation, ill-health and indebtedness are the general features of their daily life. Consequently, and very naturally they treat their children as income sources for the family. The poor little fellows, stripped of education, games and all the love, laughter and enjoyment of childhood, work for nominal wages to supplement the family income. Often they became easy targets of the smugglers and anti-socials, and are pushed to drug trafficking and prostitution (UNICEF, 1995). They are exploited inhumanly. Due to lack of nutritious food and excessive work most of them die in prematured ages.

Figure 7.2: Child Death Rates by Country's Economic Status, 1996

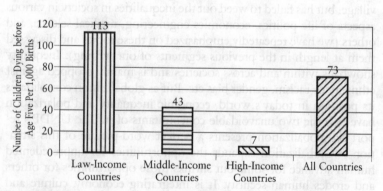

Source: World Bank, 1998.

Figure 7.2 shows a comparison of child mortality rates in high, middle and low-income countries. The disparity is evident and is a burning proof of the economic inequality of modern times. And that's not all—when thousands of people in the underdeveloped countries die of starvation each year then America throws their excess agricultural produces in sea sack by sack, one after another (we call ourselves civilized, do not we?)! Can anything be more inhumane than that?

Globalization rears a powerful ideology that is based on neo-liberal economic policies. It targets to establish a so-called "utopian," self-regulated market economy. We, however, would feel rather comfortable to replace the word "self-regulated" by "US regulated" since, to us, globalization and Americanization are two different faces of the same coin.

Inequality is at the heart of globalization. The process of globalization is itself multiplying economic, technological, political, cultural and above all social inequality. Still today, the Europeans and the Americans consider the culture of the Third World countries as outdated, inferior, and primitive. They are economically strong, armed with nuclear weapons and they are the major powers of world politics today. Socially, all the Third World countries are hitherto riddled with illiteracy and superstitions. Vast areas of sub-Saharan Africa, East and South Asia, Latin America and West Asia are educationally backward. In India, Pakistan, Bangladesh, Congo and Nigeria, there are a total of about 50 million children who are deprived of primary education. Hence in true sense, globalization is still confined within the concept of western supremacy and eastern slavery. And for those underdeveloped countries of the Third World, globalization is the other name of US imperialism. This globalization has no altruistic viewpoint, as it is market-centered. The process practices autarchy, exclusivism or single-handedness instead of a radical universalism, based on democracy and equality that can be achieved through a united struggle. This is perhaps the germination of the pulse bit of globalization protest movement.

References

Amin, Samir. 1997. *Capitalism in the Age of Globalization*. London: Sage.

Agarwal, H.N. 1999. "Multinationals in India—Indispensable Global Corporates : An Exposition" in P.P. Arya and B.B. Tandon (eds). *Multinationals versus Swadeshi Today : A Policy Framework for Economic Nationalism*. New Delhi: Deep and Deep Publications, pp. 76–87.

LIVERPOOL JOHN MOORES UNIVERSITY
LEARNING & INFORMATION SERVICES

Allen, J. 1995. "Crossing Borders: Footloose Multinationals?" in J. Allen and C. Hamnett (eds). *A Shrinking World? Global Unevenness and Inequality*. Oxford: Oxford University Press, pp. 55–102.

Beck, Ulrich. 1992. *Risk Society: Towards a New Modernity*. London: Sage Publications.

Bell, D. 1974. *The Coming of Post-Industrial Society*. New York: Basic Books.

———. 1976. *The Cultural Contradictions of Capitalism*. New York: Basic Books.

Bhattacharya, B. and Palaha, Satinder. 1996. *Policy Impediments to Trade and FDI in India*. New Delhi: Wheeler Publishing House.

Bluestone, B. and B. Harrison. 1982. *The Deindustrialization of America*. New York: Basic Books.

Blumer, H. 1987. "Ethnicity and the Welfare State" in *International Social Science Journal*, USA.

Bradshaw, Y., and Wallace, M. 1996. *Global Inequalities*. Thousand Oaks: Pine Forge Press.

Bradshaw, Y.W. 2001. "A Global View of Society: How Can Sociology Help Us Understanding Global Trends?" in York W. Bradshaw, Joseph F. Healey and Rebecca Smith (eds). *Sociology for a New Century*. London: Pine Forge Press, pp. 1–34.

Bruno, Amoreso. 1998. *On Globalization: Capitalism in the 21st Century*. London: Macmillan.

Cogswell, David. 1996. *Chomsky : For Beginners*. Hyderabad: Orient Longman Limited.

Cohen, Anthony, P. 1985. *The Symbolic Construction of Community*. Routledge: London.

Collier, R.B. 1999. *Paths Toward Democracy: The Working Class and Elites in Western Europe and South America*. Cambridge: Cambridge University Press.

Corsaro, W. 1997. *The Sociology of Childhood*. Thousand Oaks, CA: Pine Forge Press.

Dadayan, V. 1988. *The Orbits of the Global Economy*. Moscow: Progress Publishers.

Darnton, John. 1994a. "Crisis-torn Africa Becomes Continent of Refugees" *The New York Times*. May 23, p. A2.

———. 1994b. "U.N Faces Refugee Crisis that Never Ends" *The New York Times*. August 8, p. A1.

———. 1993. *Ethnicity and Nationalism: Anthropological Perspectives*. London: Pluto Press.

Edwards, M. and Hulme, D. (eds). 1995. *Non-governmental Organisations: Performance and Accountability: Beyond the Magic Bullet*. London/West Hartford: Earthscan/Kumarian.

Eriksen, T.H. 1995. *Small Places, Large Issues: An Introduction to Social and Cultural Anthropology*. London: Pluto Press.

Escobar, A. 1995. *Encountering Development*, University Press. Princeton: Princeton.

Farley, R. 1996. *The New American Reality*. New York: Russell Sage Foundation.

Featherstone, M. (ed.). 1990. *Global Culture: Nationalism, Globalization and Modernity*. London: Sage.

Frank, A.G. 1981. *Crisis in the Third World*. London: Heinemann.

Freeman, A. 1991. "The Economic Background and Consequences of the Gulf War" in H. Bresneeth and N. Yuval-Davis (eds). *The Gulf War and the New World Order*. London. Zed Books, pp. 153–65.

Giddens, A. 1982. *Sociology: A Brief But Critical Introduction*. London: Macmillan.

Giddens, A. 1985. *The Nation-State and Violence.* Cambridge: Polity Press.

———. 1989. *Sociology.* Cambridge: Polity Press.

———. 1990. *Consequences of Modernity.* Cambridge: Polity Press.

Golden, T. 1995. "In Mexico, Both Army and Rebels Say They are in Control" *New York,* February 24, p. A3.

Gupta, S. P. 1995. "Recent Economic Reforms and its Impact on Poor" a Paper presented at the National Conference on Poverty and Employment, New Delhi, March 27–29.

Hall, S. 1992. "The Question of Cultural Identity" in S.Hall, D. Held and T. McGrew (eds). *Modernity and Its Futures.* Cambridge: Polity, pp. 274–316.

Harvey, D. 1989. *The Conditions of Post Modernity.* Oxford: Blackwell.

Healey, Joseph F. 2001a. "Culture and Society: Can Local Culture Coexist with Global Culture" in York W. Bradshaw, Joseph F. Healey, and Rebecca Smith (eds). *Sociology for a New Century.* London: Pine Forge Press, pp. 117–47.

———. 2001b. "Inequality: Are the Rich Getting Richer and the Poor Getting Poorer?" in York W. Bradshaw, Joseph F. Healey, and Rebecca Smith (eds). *Sociology for a New Century.* London: Pine Forge Press, pp. 161–96.

Hirst, P. and Thompson, G. 1995. "Globalization and the Future of the Nation-State" in *Economy and Society,* vol. 24, no. 3, pp. 408–42.

Hoogvelt, Ankie. 1997. *Globalization and the Post-Colonial World: The New Political Economy of Development.* London: Macmillan Press.

Hunter, J.D and Yates, J. 2002. "In the Vanguard Globalization: The World of American Globalizers" in Peter L. Berger and Samuel P. Huntington (eds). *Many Globalizations: Cultural Diversity in the Contemporary World.* New York: Oxford University Press.

Jenkins, R. 1987. *Transnational Corporations and Uneven Development.* London: Methuen.

———. 1988. "Transnational Corporations and Third World Consumption: Implications of Competitive Strategies" in *Word Development,* vol. 16, pp. 1363–70.

Johnson, Paul. 1993. "Colonialism's Back—and Not a Moment Too Soon" in *The New York Times Magazine,* April 18, p. 22.

Kellner, D. 1995. *Media Culture.* London: Routledge.

Kiely, Ray. 1998a. "The Crisis of Global Development" in Ray Kiely and Phil Marfleet (eds). *Globalisation and the Third World.* London: Routledge, pp. 23–43.

———. 1998b. "Transnational Companies, Global Capital and the Third World" in Ray Kiely and Phil Marfleet (eds). *Globalisation and the Third World.* London: Routledge, pp. 45–66.

Kitching, G. 1982. *Development and Underdevelopment in Historical Perspective.* London: Methuen.

Korten, D. 1990. *Getting to the Twenty-First Century: Voluntary Action and the Global Agenda.* West Hardford CT: Kumarian Press.

Levy, F. 1998. *The New Dollars and Dreams: American Incomes and Economic Change.* New York: Russell Sage Foundation.

McMichael, Philip. 1994. *Development and Social Change: A Global Perspective.* California: Pine Forge Press.

Muller, M. 1982. *The Health of Nations.* London: Pinter.

Naisbitt, J. 1994. *Global Paradox.* New York: Morrow.

New Internationalist. 1993. "The New Globalism: The Facts," *The New Globalism,* August, pp. 18–99.

New Internationalist. 1996. 'Green Economics: The Facts," *Seeds of Change*, April, pp. 18–19.

Newman, K. 1993. *Declining Fortunes: The Withering of the American Dream*. New York: Harper Collins.

O'Harrow, R., Jr. 1999. "Justice Department Pushes for Power to Unlock PC Security Systems" in *New York Times*, August 20, p. A1.

Ogburn, W.E. 1964. *On Culture and Social Change*. Chicago: University of Chicago Press.

Ohmae, K. 1991. *The Borderless World*. London: Fontana.

Oommen, T.K. 2002. *Pluralism, Equality and Identity*. New Delhi: Oxford University Press.

Peet, R. 1986. 'Industrial Devolution and the Crisis of International Capitalism" in *Antipode*, vol. 18, pp. 78–95.

Pinto, Ambrose. 2000. "Basic Conflict of 'We' and 'They' between Social and Ethnic Groups" in I. Ahmad, P.S. Ghosh and H. Reifeld (eds). *Pluralism and Equality: Values in Indian Society and Politics*. New Delhi: Sage Publications.

Powell, Jim. 1998. *Postmodernism: for Beginners*. Hyderabad: Orient Longman Limited.

Sack, K. 2000. 'Core Denounces Disparities in Minority Access to Computers" *New York Times*. April 4, p. A12.

Sandler, Todd. 1997. *Global Challenges*. Cambridge: Cambridge University Press.

Sebastian, Morris. 1994. "Prospects for FDI and Multinational Activity in the 90s" in *Economic and Political Weekly*, vol. XXIX, no. 19, May 7.

Stiglitz, Joseph. 2002. *Globalization and Its Discontent*. New Delhi: Penguin Books.

Tilly, C. 1995. "Globalization Threatens Labour's Rights" in *International Labour and Working-Class History*, vol. 47, pp. 1–23.

Tinbergen, Jan. (1976): Reshaping the International Order (A Report to the Club of Rome), E.P. Dutton & Co., Inc. New York.

Todaro, M. 1977. *Economic Development*. Harlow: Longman.

UNCTAD. 1994. *World Investment Report*. New York: United Nations.

_____. 1995. *World Investment Report—Preliminary*. New York: United Nations.

UNDP (United Nations Development Programme). 1992–99. *Human Development Report(s)*. New York: Oxford University Press.

UNICEF. 1995. *The State of the World's Children*. New York: Oxford University Press.

Wade, Robert. 2000. "Wheels within Wheels: Rethinking the Asian crisis and the Asian Model" in *Annual Review of Political Science*, vol. 3, pp. 85–115.

Wallerstein, Immanuel. 1974. *The Modern World System: Capitalist Agriculture and the Origins of the European World-economy in the Sixteenth Century*. London: Academic Press.

Waters, Malcolm. 1995. *Globalization*. London: Routledge.

Weber, Max. 1968. "Economy and Society" in G. Rath and C. Wittich (eds). *An Outline of Interpretative Sociology*, vol. I. New York: Bedminister press.

World Bank. 1997. *The Role of FDI Developing Countries*. I.E.C.

_____. 1998. *World Development Report*. Oxford: Oxford University Press.

World Trade Organization. 1995. *Regionalism and the World Trading System*. Geneva.

Yan, Yunxiang. 2002. "Managed Globalization: State Power and Cultural Transition in China" in Peter L. Berger and Samuel P. Huntington (eds). *Many Globalizations: Cultural Diversity in the Contemporary World*. New York: Oxford University Press, pp. 19–47.

Yearley, Steven. 1996. Sociology, Environmentalism, Globalization. London: Sage.

8

GLOBALIZATION AND THE ARAB WORLD:
A SOCIOECONOMIC PERSPECTIVE

Abbas Mehdi

INTRODUCTION

During the 1960s and 1970s, the Arab nations were able to adapt to the times, and consequently were able to enjoy some of the fastest growing economies in the world. Since the late 1980s, however, economic growth performance has been dismal. Unemployment has risen and become widespread. Real wages have declined, and a large section of the population are approaching poverty levels. Coupled with an increase in population, the present scenario is truly worrying. The threats and opportunities presented by globalization are particularly acute for the Arab world, especially as it realizes these mounting difficulties and moves away from dependence on finite natural resources. A commonly held viewpoint is that globalization will come to the rescue of failing Arab economies, which have been suffering from reduced oil revenues since 1985. The thinking is that economic growth will be a cure-all, and that participation in the global economy is the best chance for the Arab World towards realizing the potential of their rapid population growth over the last 30 years.

It would be wise, however, for us to take a more measured look at the effects of globalization on the Arab countries, especially taking into account those nations' changing patterns of migration, the role of their public sectors, and the complexities of their labor markets. We should ask the following questions: Why has the actual experience of Arab countries with globalization—contrary to theoretical expectations—been negative rather than positive? Why has globalization led to economic decline rather than growth? Also, are these failures simply a matter of shortsighted domestic policies, or do the flaws indeed lie within the framework of the new global economy?

We will see that the answers to these questions lead us to the following conclusion: Integration into the world economy is not only desirable for the Arab nations, it is essential, especially if widespread economic and social chaos is to be avoided.

GLOBALIZATION: A BACKGROUND

The last few decades of the 20th century brought momentous political, economic, and social changes that continue to redefine the fundamental concepts of political, economic, and social development. Countries around the globe have seen a period of profound economic and social transition in recent years, and the 21st century is likely to amplify and accelerate these transitions. Rapid changes in the world economy have encouraged global and regional integration and have required governments to rethink economic development strategies, and to establish new institutions and partnerships through which they can build economically viable and socially equitable societies.

One of the distinguishing features of globalization is the powerful apparatus of communication, which presents an image of a world unified by new technology and products. Although the world's people and continents have always been connected through exchanges of goods, literature, and ideas, the communications revolution has made those connections exponentially more rapid and far-reaching than ever before.

In the late 20th century, "globalization" replaced "development" as the topic of serious discourse amongst political and corporate elites. Although there was a universal paradigm of what it meant to "develop," each nation had its own version of development that corresponded to its own cultural and natural resource endowments and political structure. But globalization has funneled these various paradigms of development onto a single and single-minded path. Nations today are driven by globalization towards the liberalization of trade and capital markets, toward an increasing internationalization of production and distribution strategies, and toward technological change. Globalization encourages nations to rapidly dismantle barriers to the international trade of goods and services and the mobility of capital.

Of course, globalization has profound implications for developing countries. It creates incredible opportunities—bigger trade markets, larger private capital inflows, and improved access to technology, just to name a few. But new opportunities are accompanied by new challenges, tough challenges, in economic management. Walking the path of globalization requires adopting and maintaining liberal trade and investment methods, challenges many nations are finding it hard to meet.

As a result of the differing relationships between globalization's benefits and its obstacles, the term has acquired considerable emotive force. Some view it as a process that is beneficial—a key to the future world of positive economic development that is both inevitable and irreversible. Others regard the term with hostility, fearfully believing that globalization increases inequality within and between nations, and that it threatens employment and living standards and thwarts social progress (McMichael, 2000). But, for better or for worse, globalization can't be halted or ignored. The powerful forces that drive globalization are linked to technological advances in transportation and communication, advances that have a life of their own and are largely independent of government policies.

Hence, participation in globalization may not be optional. National economies have lost much of their distinct claims to domestic developments and products, and domestic economic management strategies have become ineffective to the point of irrelevance. Internationalization is, in this view, seen as a tide sweeping over borders in which technology and irresistible market forces are irreversibly transforming the globe system. Transnational corporations and global governance organizations, such as the World Bank and the IMF, enforce the conformity of all nations, no matter their location or preferences.

There is a great deal of difference, however, between this extreme and unforgiving definition of globalization, which requires an international economy that "subsumes and subordinates national-level processes," and a more nuanced view, which emphasizes the role of national-level policies and actors, and grants control ultimately not to inexorable economic forces but to politics. With this more flexible vision of globalization, we can see current changes in "a longer historical perspective ...distinct but not unprecedented," and as not necessarily involving either the emergence of or movement toward an economic system different from what we have known (Abu-Lughod, 1989).

William Tabb (1997) argued that it is important to see that the stricter of the two globalization theses is based on a myth, has profound political implications which are defeatist, and is not based on a sound analysis of what is a more complex and contestable set of processes.

Also, Joseph A. Schumpeter (1962) observed half-a-century ago that modern capitalist economies are not static but marked by dynamic processes that pose continuous challenges to those who manage or govern them. Capitalism has always been a global system, even if the particular ways the world economy affects workers in particular places changes over time. Economic historians ask us to see the present in such a perspective. It is not necessarily the case that during the last two decades the pace of world economic integration has increased; it has simply taken a new form under the liberalized regime of free trade and capital flow.

Even if we adopt the more sensible definition of globalization, however, we must still admit to some negative social consequences of the new trends (UNDP, 2002). These include increased inequality both within and between countries, increased poverty, increased vulnerability to social risks such as unemployment and crime, and increased chances of individuals, communities, countries and entire regions being altogether excluded from the benefits enjoyed by the rest of the world (Deacon, 2000). Globalization may also have damaged the capacity of governments to act in socially compensatory ways. In the past, countries were in the habit of implementing and benefiting from their own national policies. Even the more open economies felt that they could manage their own destinies (Deacon, 2000). However, a nation's destiny today is no longer solely in its own hands.

Not surprisingly, globalization is often blamed for employment problems throughout the world. In 1980, nearly 70 percent of the world's labor force was sheltered from international competition by trade barriers, capital controls, and planned trade. But by 2000, fewer than 10 percent of workers were living in countries insulated from world markets.

And yet, while public perceptions often blame globalization for increasing unemployment, there is increasing skepticism about such a causal link amongst academic circles. Neither trade nor capital flows, it is argued, provide a significant explanation for the problems in employment and wage-dispersion. Industrialized nations' imports of manufactured goods from developing and transitional economies represent less than 4 percent of the GDP of the countries belonging to the Organization for Economic Cooperation and Development (OECD), while exports to these countries are a major source of counter-cyclical demand. The cumulative net transfer of capital to these countries represents only 2 percent of the total capital stock of the industrialized economies. The growing academic opinion however, is that problems lie less in globalization than in long-standing structural problems in labor and product markets, technology, and macroeconomic policy.

This gap between public perception and expert opinion is a striking feature of the debate today. But whatever the final judgment may be, we have to recognize that the coincidence of globalization with unemployment represents an example of political, rather than economic, causation. Perceptions of global structural adjustments, whether they are founded in truth or not, are generating political and social tensions that will drive the debate about globalization well into the next century.

THE POLITICAL, ECONOMIC, AND SOCIAL STRUCTURE OF THE ARAB WORLD

Before we can examine the effects of globalization on the Arab world, we must first familiarize ourselves with its political, economic, and social structures. The Arab people, who are distributed over 22 countries, largely share a common religion, language, and culture. The population of Arab countries totaled about 284 million in 2000, and has grown rapidly in the past 30 years. With the current growth rate of 2.7 percent (or 10 million people annually, compared with a global growth rate averaged at 1.7 percent), demographic projections show that the Arab populations will reach 459 million in 2020 (UNDP, 2002).

Population distribution in the Arab nations is highly concentrated along river valleys and seacoast areas; hence, there is great diversity between these countries in terms of population size. For instance, Egypt has about 67 million people, Sudan has 31 million, Algeria and Morocco both have about 30 million, while Bahrain's population is only 640,000. The populations of Qatar, Kuwait and the United Arab Emirates are similarly small, with 560,000, 1.91 million, and 2.61 million respectively (UNDP, 2002).

Arab nations also differ greatly in terms of natural resource endowment (particularly oil). Thus, the classification of Arab countries into oil economies (Algeria, Iraq, Bahrain, Kuwait, Oman, Qatar, and Saudi Arabia, and United Arab emirates) and non-oil economies (Egypt, Jordan, Morocco, Syria, Tunisia, Mauritania, Sudan, and Yemen, Comoros, Somalia, Palestine, Djibouti) is important for our analysis of the region.

The GDP growth of these two groups of nations is, not surprisingly, quite different as well. Between 1991 and 1995, the GDP growth for oil-producers was 0.11 percent, and 1.25 for non-oil-producers (Alonso-Gamo, 1997). In 1988, the six oil-producing countries of the Gulf Corporate Council (GCC), which includes Bahrain, Kuwait, Oman, Qatar, and Saudi Arabia, and the United Arab Emirates saw a GDP growth of 46 percent, despite their population share of only 11 percent (Ali and Elbadawi, 2000).

These figures show how closely the fortunes of Arab countries are tied to the oil market. When oil prices are high, so are the government revenues and the private sector incomes. When the oil market is in recession, government debt accumulates and both government and private industries cut jobs. During the Oil Boom (primarily in the 1960s and 1970s), economic growth of Arab countries was among the highest in the world; unemployment was virtually non-existent, and development was rapid, and social payoffs were enormous. Primary school enrollment shot up from 61 percent in 1965 to 98 percent in 1991, and adult literacy improved from 34 to 53 percent during 1970 to 1990. Poverty went down too; by 1990, only 5 percent of the Arab world lived on less than $1 a day—the global benchmark for absolute poverty—compared with 14.7 percent in East Asia and 28.8 percent in Latin America (World Bank, 1995).

The drop in oil prices in 1982 and their subsequent collapse in 1986 marked the end of the Oil Boom era, and the results were, and still are devastating. The unemployment rate went up about 20 percent in Algeria, Yemen, Lebanon and Jordan, and 15 percent in Egypt, Tunisia, and Morocco. By comparison, East Asian unemployment rate was about 3 percent and in Europe about 8 percent (World Bank, 1995). Since 1986, the real per capita incomes in Arab nations have declined by 2 percent annually—more than in any developing nation. The situation in oil-producing countries was even worse, with a 4 percent annual loss in real per capita incomes between 1980 and 1991 (World Bank, 1995). Currently, the unemployment rates in Arab nations are among the highest in the world, averaging 20 percent non-oil producing economies. Unemployment among the young is even more prevalent, averaging more than twice national averages (Keller and Nabli, 2002).

With the high population growth rate in the Arab nations, the labor force will grow at a similarly high rate of 3 percent (highest in the world). By 2030, the Arab workforce population is forecast to be a full 62 percent of the total population, or around 318 million. These figures show a major challenge for the economy, requiring at least a 6 percent annual economic growth in order to absorb the population increase. Even now, though, the economies cannot keep up with the sizes of their workforces. According to the World Employment Report (1998), only 37 percent of employable workers were participating in the labor force in Egypt, 29 percent in Jordan, 32 percent in Saudi Arabia, and 37 percent in Kuwait (UNDP, 2002).

The supply of indigenous labor in oil-producing economies is unusually small, not only because of the small populations of those countries, but also because of the general absence of women from the workforce and the increased number of students in higher education. The combination of rapid economic development and a limited supply of indigenous labor in oil-producing countries between 1970 and 1985 have resulted in a considerable dependence on migrant labor, mainly from non-oil-producing countries. The migrant labor force constitutes 35 percent of the labor force on average, and as much as 80 percent in some countries (World Bank, 1995).

Several Arab nations, such as Jordan, Iraq, Syria, and Lebanon, both import and export labor. An example of this phenomenon is Jordan, where as a result of the departure of large numbers of workers to oil-producing countries (where rewards for their services were higher than those they could get at home), vacancies were created that could not be filled by the remaining Jordanian workforce. This shortage, then, attracts workers from other non-oil-producing countries, who migrate and replace the deported indigenous population. Before the Gulf war in 1991, about half of Jordan's entire labor force worked in the Gulf, and a similar number of foreign workers were employed in Jordan; they amounted to 20 percent of Jordan's GDP. Similarly, about two million, or 10 percent, of the Egyptian workforce worked in oil-producing countries, and they amounted to about 6 percent of the GDP in Egypt (World Bank, 1995). Between 1970 and 1985, this arrangement worked very well for both oil-producing and non-oil-producing countries. It met the needs of both groups by supplying human capital to one group and monetary capital to the other. This dynamic regional workforce was quite effective in channeling Arab prosperity.

One long-lasting outcome of the Oil Boom period was the overexpansion of the public sector. In the mid-1980s, for example, the fraction of the national workforce employed by the public sector was 44 percent in Bahrain, 88 percent in Kuwait, 61 percent in Oman, 54 percent in Saudi Arabia and about 75 percent in the United Arab Emirates (World Bank, 1995). The result, though, was the creation of a public sector that now greatly exceeds the needs of the domestic economy.

The inefficiency of the public sector in Arab economies has long-term implications for public welfare. Although, public sector jobs pay relatively less than the private sector jobs, they are still preferred because of flexible hours (allowing employees to hold multiple jobs), shorter hours, and non-wage benefits such as pensions. An added difficulty is the expectations the Oil Boom raised in the populations of oil-producing nations. Everyone naturally wants to acquire a share of the wealth. Those with entrepreneurial skills—a minority in any society—will find their opportunities in private business ventures. A much larger group, however, seeks a secure job with the government. Thus, the labor market suffers from a shortage of skilled workers and an excess of public sector laborers.

Despite the similarities of public sector problems in the Arab World, the public sectors in oil economies suffer most, from poor employment practices and a segmented labor force. In Kuwait, for example, 95 percent of public sector employees are Kuwaitis, while 95 percent of private sector employees are expatriates.

GLOBALIZATION AND THE ARAB WORLD

Considering, then, the political, economic and social structures we have discussed above with regards to Arab nations, let us return to those questions posed at the beginning of this chapter: Why has the actual experience of Arab countries with globalization been negative rather than positive? Why has globalization led to economic decline rather than growth? Do these failures stem from Arab nations' domestic policies and infrastructure, or are the results of the framework of global economy itself?

To be sure, the present institutional arrangements within Arab countries make it difficult for their economies to achieve high rates of growth. Indeed, we can to a considerable degree blame the poor economic performance of Arab economies on poor socioeconomic and political policies and structures. We can furthermore find a variety of evidence to support these statements:

UNFAVORABLE GROSS DOMESTIC PRODUCT

The combined GDP of all Arab countries was $531.2 billion in 1999—
less than that of Spain, for instance, whose GDP was $595.5 billion
(UNDP, 1999).

THE FAILURES OF THE PUBLIC SECTOR

There are some elements that define a motivated and progressive society, such as a motivation to achieve, a vision of opportunities, a sense of
discipline, and a committed work ethic. These qualities are strained in
the oil-producing countries as a result of decades of socialization into
oil generated revenues. Oil revenues allowed for provision of free education, employment guarantees in the public sector, and non-competitive
jobs for a large segment of a sizeable work force. The strain of these
elements has created a culture of dependency and contributes to poor
economic growth performance.

Specifically, the Arab governments provide attractive job opportunities without proper discrimination of scholastic performance such
as grade point average or the choice of major studies. As a result,
students often select easy majors and earn an easy grade, knowing
that they will eventually join the ranks of government employees like
everyone else. Arab countries' spending on the public sector is unreason-
ably high, with wages and salaries around 9 percent higher than that
of other developing countries (Bangura, 2000). The resultant lack of
incentive for private sector development, coupled with a failing education system, have given rise to a sizeable section of overeducated
Arabs, who are not able to find jobs as per their skills and aspirations.

The public sector has furthermore become difficult to reduce in
size or scope, simply as a result of the interests and expectations of the
vast population it employs. Just as economies suffer when there is
excessive unemployment over a long period of time (from a loss of
output and atrophy of skills), economies also suffer when there is a long
period of overemployment (from complacency and a lack of alternative employment options). The dominance of the public sector in
Arab countries has also resulted in a lack of investment opportunities
in foreign and domestic capital. During the 1980s, the average central government spending was 39 percent of the GDP in Arab countries. This was the highest in the world, compared to 25 percent in

South Asia, 26 percent in Latin America, and 35 percent in industrialized countries on an average (Bangura, 2000). The labor market has encouraged investors to substitute capital for labor rather than offering incentives to create jobs. Low-paying jobs are crucial in reducing poverty, but are no substitute for high-wage employment.

Furthermore, the public sector systematically misallocates labor. High government wages attract the most qualified personnel to the public sector, while measures designed to protect existing jobs make it difficult for entrepreneurs to start and sustain dynamic businesses. At the present time, the revenue-raising aspect of privatization in Arab economies is very slow, involving mainly small and medium-size enterprises. It is the lowest in the world about 3,510 millions between 1990–96 compared to 82,641 millions in Latin America (Bangura, 2000).

In the past, the issues of sufficient representation, participation, and accountability were not central to the economic growth of a nation. But today, reform in the public sector needs to focus on restructuring, wage reform, privatization, and decentralization. Ironically, and to compound the challenge, reform will be difficult to implement without professional civil services, because it may fragment the state systems and encourage corruption.

OVERINVESTMENT IN TECHNOLOGY

Arab countries have often fixed their attention on emerging technologies—advanced and labor-saving, but expensive and with intensive demands in operation and maintenance. Such technologies are usually recommended by the labor elite (local workers trained abroad), as well as by the foreign consultants. This often results in islands of modernity in an ocean of backwardness, providing limited employment opportunities and causing considerable displacement in the private sector. In turn, the labor shortages make the choice of sophisticated technologies both feasible and necessary. As a result of the choice to employ technology rather than workers, labor markets in oil-producing countries have experienced a qualitative dependence on migrant laborers who possess particular qualifications and skills, and who have left their home countries for higher wages. Thus, a large portion of the national workforce has remained in rural and traditional sectors, and has not participated in the modern sector's development.

EDUCATIONAL SHORTSIGHTEDNESS

Research on educational achievement indicates that the Arab World lags behind in several areas. There is little evidence that education has contributed to the economic growth of the Arab nations, despite the fact that human capital has become vital to compete in the global economy. And yet, Arab countries spend a higher percentage of their GDP on education than other countries. Why the discrepancy? Because (*a*) the choices of major studies is distorted by public sector hiring and promotion policies, and consequently, deviates sharply from the mix of skills and the basic knowledge required by the private sector; and (*b*) hiring nationals in the public sector as a means of distributing oil dividends has led to overstaffing, overemployment and underutilization of these important human resources (Girgis, 2002).

One of the major problems facing Arab countries is of graduates who are unemployable due to a lack of basic skills and/or the appropriate educational background. Also, there is a significant gender gap in the completion rate for primary school, as more girls drop out of schools. This gap widens even further in secondary enrollment. As a result, nearly a quarter of the region's women are illiterate, compared with fewer than 10 percent of men (Mkandawire and Rodriguez, 2000).

THE LACK OF FEMALE PARTICIPATION

The evidence is clear: education empowers and allows a broader and more effective participation in an economy, policymaking, administration, and government. More specifically, evidence shows that governments and businesses alike are more ethically run when women participate in them actively. Despite this evidence, Arab nations rank last in the world in terms of female participation in the workforce. This remains a serious issue facing the potential development and economic growth of the region.

AN ABSENCE OF NON-OIL EXPORTS

For decades, high oil-prices and bountiful oil-revenues, especially in the Gulf Cooperation Council (GCC) countries, encouraged lavish spending and also led the non-oil-producing countries to a culture of dependency. A cushy welfare system and a culture of entitlement in GCC countries stifled entrepreneurship, work ethics, and the development of alternative exports. In non-oil-producing countries, labor migration and loans to and from oil-producing countries substituted for local development.

Thus, a current structural problem in the Arab infrastructure is its lack of non-oil exports; these nations are unable to keep their national capital at home (capital from the region that is held abroad figures about $350 billion), and have been generally unsuccessful at attracting foreign investors. The total volume of exports is simply too small. In fact, non-oil exports from all the Arab countries (with 284 million people) are fewer than the exports of Finland (a country of only 5 million people). The share of the Arab economy in the world trade is only about 3.4 percent. To make matters worse, this figure is based primarily on the sale of oil. Currently, these economies are deriving their GDP from oil, gas, and mining, all of which are being exploited at unsustainable rates; also, their prices are unlikely to increase in real terms in the coming years. While oil exports currently account for more than 90 percent of their exports, the proven oil and gas reserves will be depleted within a maximum of 100 years. Moreover, the excessive reliance on volatile oil-exports not only increases vulnerability to external shocks, but has also led to a sharp fall in per capita income; while the total oil revenue for all Arab countries reached a record $297 billion in 1980, their populations surged, causing a decline in per capita income of around $1700 in the mid-1970s to $500 in 1995.

While this situation will be relatively easier to repair in non-oil-producing Arab countries compared to the oil-producing ones (which will require fundamental changes in policy and living standards), nevertheless, it is a serious concern for the entire region. Economic gains will be contingent on action and the implementation of policies that favor flexibility and change.

WIDESPREAD AND INCREASING POVERTY

Arab nations can reduce poverty to a great degree through economic growth; moving from 0 to 15 percent annual growth alone would reduce the number of poor in the Arab countries by 8 million people over the next decade. Without any changes in economic growth, the number of poor (those living on less than $1 a day) will rise to about 15 million by 2010 (World Bank, 1995). An annual employment growth rate in excess of the current 5 percent is needed in order to absorb the growing population. However, poverty reduction means more than simply increasing incomes. Policies have to become much more specific in targeting the real problems, one of which is an overwhelming lack of empowerment. Empowerment is both an inherent part of, and a means to, poverty reduction; with the ability to shape their own lives, citizens will gain the key to increased incomes and improved assets (both psychological and physical). Social protection can be seen as a dimension of empowerment, and is something much more than a short-run palliative. It is an essential underpinning of a market economy, one that helps it to function well and to involve poor people in the opportunities it creates. Without good social protection, poor people may be unable to take some of the risks necessary to participation in an economy. From this perspective, social protection is indeed a crucial element of empowerment. A growth in GDP alone actually has little impact on the quality of economic growth, for instance, GDP growth of 1 percent from 5 percent to 6 percent would reduce the number of poor by only 1.5 percent. Poverty must be reduced by a more significant and rapid economic growth brought on by reform.

A New Socioeconomic Contract

Every nation has a unique social system of cultural, political and social institutions in which its economy is embedded. The broad dimensions of those institutions must be considered when we discuss globalization, which encompasses these interconnected social systems. Although it is easy to focus simply on the economic institutions of Arab nations, we must examine political institutions, power relations, and cultures, in order to understand why their economies are in decline. Indeed, the current problems in the Arab economies are rooted in the socioeconomic, and political structures of the Arab societies. One of the unique benefits presented by globalization to Arab countries is that it provides the structural context for reform. These problems can't be resolved without serious attempts to overcome them. These serious attempts should include public-sector management, market-oriented management reform that promotes managerial efficiency, education reform, and public expenditure reform.

The World Summit for Social Development (1995) acknowledged that high economic growth is not in itself a sufficient means to achieve all the goals set by the summit; as far back as 1987, scholars like Elias

Tuma argued likewise. Tuma warns of the inadequacy of "standard" versions of the history of economic development in the region that were based, as he asserts, on a tendency to "measure development in quantitative terms, or evaluate change in segmented and partial aspects of the economy, or look at results in a short-term perspective only, or through the eyes of international agencies and developed countries, which have vested interests different from those of the Middle Eastern countries" (p. 33).

The dangers of reliance on economic factors alone as indicators of development have been widely recognized. Although faster growth will help to reduce poverty, the latter is affected by other important variables as well—notably by equality in income and asset distribution, stability of economic growth, and reformed fiscal policy. The quality of growth also matters—that is, it entails among other things, a more equal distribution of income, more and better paying jobs, more gender equality, and more gender inclusiveness. All were regarded as significant objectives in their own right, to which the World Summit attached great importance (Singh, 2000). One could be tempted to label the new era as "Globalization with a Human Face."

Steve Vago (1999) argued that there is a striking difference between how we as a nation assess our economic well-being, and our social well-being. We are greatly concerned with economic performance figures, such as the GDP and Index of Leading Economic Indicators. In contrast, the social well-being of the nation is reported much less frequently and without an overall view of the nation's social performance.

Although slow economic growth remains a major cause of poverty, growth alone does not ensure improvement in incomes or standard of living for the poor. Resources and opportunities generated by growth may not be utilized in ways that promote changes in social indicators that are usually associated with improved social-welfare and equity. While suspicion of hidden agendas of the developed world and those international agencies that sing the praises of globalization has now become a cliché, globalization doesn't occur in a vacuum. In Arab countries, the forces of globalization, for better and for worse, come head to head with pre-existing patterns of economic decline and social imbalances that need to be addressed ever more urgently. Indeed, it may be said that one of globalization's primary benefits for the Arab world is that it provides reason and encouragement to examine these issues and take steps to remedy them. The basic priorities for policy in Arab countries need to be the creation of a virtuous cycle whereby economic growth promotes human development and vice versa.

The starting point for this process must be a return of focus on the people. Reforms in Arab nations will be difficult to implement without a professional civil service. Lacking this, market reforms may further fragment the state systems and encourage more corruption within them. A shared professional culture and common ethical standards are necessary for flexibility and de-concentrated administrative structures advocated by managerial reforms (Nickson, 1999). But the role of social policy in building, utilizing, and liberating people's capabilities remains critical. The Arab governments need to provide an enabling environment for broad-based political support and mobilization of the poor into both policy and market participation.

Culture and values are the soul of development. They provide its impetus, facilitate the means needed to further it, and substantially define people's vision of its purposes and ends. They are instruments in the sense that they help to shape people's daily hopes, fears, ambitions, attitudes, and actions. The values of democracy also have a part to play in the process of integrating Arab countries with the global system. Values relating to gender equality are important for human development. Human development is the development of the people, for the people and by the people. If development is to be people-centered, then participatory processes need to be central to its evolution. Participation takes many forms: political, economic, social and, cultural. The freedom deficit in Arab nations undermines human development and is one of the most painful manifestations of lagging political reform.

Among the most important tasks that the Arab governments currently face, in view of the preceding trends, is the creation of a political environment conducive to market and social development. This involves redefining the roles of the state, social partners, the private sector, and other groups in society; this redefinition can help build political commitment to economic, social, and political restructuring, provide an infrastructure, decentralize and democratize government, and strengthen financial and administrative capacities at local, urban, and national levels of government. Experience suggests that the long-term success of economic adjustment and development requires strong political will and determined leadership to direct the process of development and establishment of strong social institutions.

Because of the nature of political structures in the Arab world at the present time, the decision that shapes the future lies in the hands of governments and to a much lesser degree of its people. Arab governments must decide what direction reforms should take in order to ensure a prosperous future for their people and to maintain macroeconomic stability. Evidence from the outstanding economic successes of East Asian economies indicates the positive role of the government in institutionalizing structural reform and learning from the outside world. The well-being of Arab people will depend on realizing a development paradigm of growth that is rapid and that is widely shared throughout the entire Arab world. This means undertaking a critical mass of structural reform to improve resources allocation, facilitate international trade, encourage private inflows, and increase productive investments, jobs, and growth. Partial reform will not elicit much response if substantial impediments to reform remain in place.

Strong convergence is necessary if Arab countries are to maintain their equilibrium, steer themselves through difficulties, and respond creatively to the challenges and opportunities ahead. The governments must convince their people that developing a modern, efficient market economy is the only way to provide jobs and economic security, and to raise standards of living. Also, citizens need to be consulted and offered adequate information about the quantity and quality of public services to enable them to make rational decisions about whether to support such services or demand change in policies. Therefore, reform that focuses on public accountability should strongly include the self-organization of citizens to influence public polices and improve the delivery of government services. At the present time, Arab citizens are not included in such processes, and government officials believe they are doing society a favor by taking charge of services.

All Arab countries are entering the final phase of demographic transition (birth rates are slowing); as a result, there are decreasing numbers of children to support. This "demographic gift" is only an opportunity, however, and not a promise. The future depends on structural reform that is growth-oriented and widely shared across societies. Employment growth rates in excess of 4 percent annually are necessary for absorbing the growing population, allowing increased participation, and reducing unemployment. The operation and structure of the labor market must be adjusted so that there is a workforce and manufacturing infrastructure that will attract capital from an international market. This requires full participation from the population and relative equality within it.

Hope is, however, not yet lost. The great feature of today's global economy is that no country is destined to be poor due to a bad endowment of natural resources, an isolated location, or a concentration of certain products. Production, finance, and trade have changed to make human beings more valuable than natural resources, agility more crucial than location, and quality and innovation more important than mass production. The implication is that countries can choose, through their policies, to be rich or to be poor. Making this vision a reality is within the grasp of policymakers. Until recently, oil-revenues enabled Arab countries to postpone this reality of reform. The increasing globalization of the world's goods and capital market makes the need for reforms all the more pressing. Slow and steady decline now will lead to rising poverty and social polarization, and thus, must be arrested. But the reform path also presents new dangers so that policymakers need to make hard choices and find innovative solutions to difficult problems.

CONCLUSION

Globalization has its own problems and they are countless; it is a different stage of capitalism, and it has its own unique assets and liabilities. Their scope and magnitude are different for each country, and the problems will change over time. It has social, economic, and political costs, such as the displacement of workers. Furthermore, it exposes the social fissures between those with education, skills, and mobility and those without these problems.

The negative effects of globalization, then, are not unique to developing countries and certainly not to Arab countries. Truthfully, the experience of both developed and developing countries under globalization has so far been disappointing. As Singh (2000) notes, leading industrialized countries have been operating under a regime of more or less free trade, and more or less free movements of capital, since the early-1980s. But, contrary to expectations, the performance of the real economy of these advanced countries during this period has been less than impressive, as is indicated by the fact that productivity growth during the 1980s and 1990s has been half of what it was in the Golden Age. Also, GDP growth for the 1980s and 1990s under globalization is much less than that achieved in the illiberal and regulated Golden Age of the 1950s and 1960s. Lester Thurow (1999) stated that no nation does everything well. All, without exception, have strengths, things they do well, and weaknesses, things they do poorly. The central question is whether a nation has the ability to adapt to changing times.

The lack of a free and democratic civil society at large in Arab countries contributes significantly to their decline. Social capital, a country's stock of human connections such as trust, freedom, and a sense of community, will play a fundamental role in the future of Arab development. The mismanagement of public expenses, education, the public sector, and technology are all internal conditions that has led to the present decline in Arab economies.

The favorable record of the Arab economy during the 1970s (the reduction of poverty, education of large numbers of people, and the accumulation of substantial assets) was not the product of effective policy or efficient structure, but rather of high oil-revenues, expanding economies, and a smaller population size in oil-producing countries. The formula for economic growth during this period (dominant public sector, immigration, intensive technology investments) was not a rational policy. It was a recipe for decline. High oil-revenues simply delayed the inevitable. Even if there were no globalization today, Arab countries would face these same problems.

To be brief, Arab countries can thrive in the new global economy, but only if they combine economic openness with a clear domestic investment strategy and effective civil and political institutions. The traditional sources of growth in Arab countries will not provide the needed basis for sustained economic expansion. Indeed, these traditional sources are the cause of decline. The basic problem in Arab countries today is the population imbalance between supply and demand: the public sector has stopped hiring, the oil economy is slowing, and population, especially of working-age people, continues to grow. The result is that the labor market cannot be a strong source of growth in the future, and thus the economy is in danger of deteriorating even further.

Policymakers in the Arab world are yet to identify with a reasonable degree of certainty the correct and comprehensive answer to globalization's challenges; nor have they come up with a policy package that can steer Arab economies towards a high-growth path. The ability of Arab countries to garner the potential gains from globalization will depend primarily on the quality of their domestic policies—a quality critical to the speed of both integration and growth—and the mutually reinforcing relationships between them.

Arab countries must adjust quickly to the new reality by shifting from the old social contracts of immigration, labor-saving technology, and public sector jobs, to the new social contract, by implementing policies designed to maintain a stable macroeconomic environment, attract foreign capital, increase non-oil exports, create favorable conditions for private-sector development, and enhance human capital. What are needed now are benefits to a broader segment of the population that will fully utilize and expand human potential, and that will stabilize social tensions by formulating a set of policies that reduce dualism and equalize opportunities. The new social contract will also require income security, minimum wages, protection of female workers, and enhancement of the role of labor unions. Too, the quality of education must be upgraded to meet the demands of the 21st century.

The next 20 years will be crucial as Arab countries move away from dependence on oil revenues and find ways to diversify their economies. Their workforce development strategy will be key to their success in weathering this big change. People must be trained in up-to-date technology, but need also to be prepared psychologically for the changes and opportunities that globalization will bring. In order to cope with threats of cultural homogenization and the resulting backlash, all countries need to develop workforce strategies that will make their people self-reliant, and to create social and organizational structures that will empower them politically. If people are given the skills they need, if they are treated well as employees, and if the necessary political structures are in place to allow them to achieve their full intellectual and physical potential, they will be in the best possible position to make the most of opportunities that globalization offers, while also to counter its possible dangers.

REFERENCES

Abu- Lughod. 1989. Before European Hegemony: The World System A.D. 1250–1350. New York: Oxford University Press.

Ali, A. and Elbadawi, Ibrahim. 2000. Poverty and the Labor Market in the Arab World: The Role of Inequality and Growth. World Bank.

Alonso-Gamo, Patricia. 1997. Globalization and Growth Prospects in Arab Countries. IMF Working Paper, International Monetary Fund.

Alterman, Jon B. 2000. "The Middle East's Information Revolution" in Current History, January, pp. 21–26.

Bangura, Yusuf. 2000. Public Sector Restructuring. United Nations Research Institute for Social Development, Occasional Paper no. 3: Geneva, Switzerland.

Deacon, Bob. 2000. Globalization and Social Policy. New York: United Nations Research Institution for Social Development.

Girgis, Maurice. 2002. "Would Foreign Nationals and Asians Replace Arab Workers in the GCC", Unpublished Draft.

Keller, Jennifer and Mustapha K. Nabli. 2002. "The Macroeconomics of Labor Market Outcomes in MENA Over the 1990s," Mediterranian Development Forum, World Bank.

McMichael, Philip. 2000. *Development and Social Change: A Global Perspective*. Second edition. Thousand Oaks, CA: Pine Forge Press.

Mkandawire, T. and V. Rodriguez. 2000. *Globalization and Social Development after Copenhagen: Premises, Promises and Policies*. United Nations Research Institute for Social Development, Occasional Paper no. 10: Geneva, Switzerland.

Nickson, A. 1999. Public Sector Management in Latin America. Mimeograph. United Nations Research Institute for Social Development: Geneva, Switzerland.

Schumpeter, J.A. 1962. *Capitalism, Socialism and Democracy*. Third edition. New York: Harper.

Singh, Ajit. 2000. Global Economic Trends and Social Development, United Nations Research Institute for Social Development, Occasional Paper no. 3: Geneva, Switzerland.

Stephenson, Gail and Arvil Van Adams. (1992). Youth Unemployment in the Middle East and North Africa: Issues and Policies. PHREE mimeograph.

Tabb, William K. 1997. "Globalization is *An* Issue, The Power of Capital is *The* Issue" in *Monthly Review*, vol. 49, no. 2.

Tuma, Elias. 1987. *Economic and Political Change in the Middle East*. Palo Alto, CA: Pacific Books.

Thurow, Lester C. 1999. "The Boom that wasn't" in *New York Times*, January.

UNDP. 1999–2002. *Arab Human Development Reports*. New York: United Nations.

Vago, Steve. 1999. *Social Change*. 4th edition. New Jersey: Prentice-Hall.

World Bank. 1995. "Will Arab Workers Prosper or be Leftout in the 21st Century," World Development Report.

9

DISAFFECTED AND DISCONNECTED GENERATION—CONSEQUENCES OF GLOBALIZATION FOR AFRICAN SOCIETIES

Joy Asongazoh Alemazung

INTRODUCTION

Let me start with modernity. According to Anthony Giddens (1997), modernity refers to modes of social life or organization which emerged in Europe from about the 17th century onwards and subsequently became more or less worldwide in their influence. My reason for starting with modernity is to support the fact, often brought up by some historians and social science experts, that despite the upcoming and frequent usage of the concept of globalization, it is actually not a new phenomenon.

In the case of Africa, globalization beginning from Europe and spreading to other parts of the world, has had both positive and negative impact on the African societies. Globalization has its winners and losers. And, of course, Africa happens to be amongst its losers.

According to Ali Mazuri (1999), globalization of Africa began long ago, and the development of the West using the labor force of Africa was by itself a stage in the history of globalization. The word globalization may be new and present in almost every world agenda today, but the situation of the present world, that is, increasing similarities among the different societies of the world, the increasing domination of the world by a particular kind of ideology and civilization leading to a common world economy, and also technological success, are all the results of globalization that started over the past hundreds of years.

Globalization might have many different and even controversial definitions because of its many faces, but one thing remains clear—its influential transformation impacts the societies on the "receiving" end. These effects have mostly been negative considering the situation of Africa (Africa is known as the poorest continent) today. Among the most harmful consequences have been the contamination of the rich culture, traditions, and social values of African societies.

A Brief Historical Review

The Neglected Africa

When it comes to the topic of globalization, Africa is rarely heard. She has been very much left aside, the reasons being her "no control" and "no say" position in the world economy. As globalization and world power are mainly based on economic strength, those, who are important in this domain, and control it, will quite clearly omit Africa's role in the whole process. "Control" the economy is the key here, and not importance, because if that had been the case, then Africa would have been on the forefront of discussions about globalization, or at least in the historical introduction of such topics.

Many of the writings on globalization that I have come across, trace its roots to the changes that took place in West Europe during the 15th and 18th centuries, creating an industrial system that later on integrated other parts of the world. It set up a hegemonic network, which made every other member in the network—besides Europe, the dominant nation (later USA and other so-called First World countries)—less important and subordinate. In fact, to the Europeans, the underdeveloped world was their "discovery," and lived under their control.

Europe, and the other developed countries, are today great industrial nations, but it must not be forgotten that for their "take off" they relied greatly on Africa's resources—human and material. The slaves captured from Africa simultaneously provided labor force for the agrarian revolution in the Americas as well as supported European sugar industries.

Later on, an overproduction in the Americas led to a price-fall of sugar in Europe. The increase in charges for slaves and the inability of plantation owners in America to pay their loans taken from European banks, amongst many other issues, made matters worse. A new and more profitable opening was brought in place by the industrial revolution in Europe. The industries set up in Europe needed raw material from Africa. Africans would also provide markets for European finished products. Thus, there was a need to stop slavery not because of humane reasons but because of its economic disadvantages. Until this day, every one positive thing done to Africa has had many more positive rewards for those responsible for the act in the West.

DOMINATED AFRICA

In subsequent stages of globalization, Africa's role kept on changing. Africa became a raw material supplier from a human labor provider for Europe's agrarian generation. That Africa was very important, became clear in what is known in history as the "Scramble for Africa" (Shillington, 1995). One rarely scrambles for what is not of a great value. Those who needed it so much to survive in the famous Berlin Conference of 1884, then divided Africa, into various "sphere of influence"—fields of harvest—to the European nations involved in the colonization of Africa. Africa, thus, marked another significant point in history and in globalization. The colonial masters did not only dominate Africa, they ruled Africa controlling its material and immaterial aspects. While discussing this topic with a friend, I got a curious response from her. She said that if it were not for the mosquitoes and the tropical diseases, Europeans would have not only colonized, they would have migrated to and taken control of Africa, like they did to the New World and to South Africa. This is not far from truth, as acceptance of the leadership of Africa by Africans themselves needed the will, determination, strength and blood of millions of Africans.

The colonization of Africa brought many changes—political as well as cultural (see definition of culture later). Britain and France, while dividing territory arbitrarily in the Berlin Conference, stressed upon ethnic differences. This promoted feelings of hatred among the people (see Shillington, 1995). The French practised what they called the "policy of assimilation." The name of the policy was clear, assimilating their African colonial people into becoming French people in their way of life—their culture. This policy worked a great deal in distorting the original African culture and way of life. Africa fell under the powers of the Western nations whose single objective[1] was to exploit.

TRANSFORMED AFRICA

Most Africans today see their land as the "lost Africa". It is far from its true culture and identity, and even further from their dominators' culture as well. It cannot go back to its former self and likewise, it is far from completely imbibing the borrowed culture, which has contaminated its culture. Is there really a solution? Can globalization complete what it has started? The word "contaminate," as I have used it should not mislead the reader. It is used here not because all what comes in from the West is bad but because it has transformed Africa into worse ways. This has resulted in a disconnected and disaffected generation, which I will describe in this chapter as the youths of today.

The hegemonic globalization with the West in control, and the homogenizing tendency brought by it, has transformed Africa into a strange society, which Africans themselves cannot handle.

Globalization has had economic, political as well as cultural impacts. The effects of political globalization has been seen over the last decades in what has resulted in the struggle for power, wars, instability and high degrees of human right abuses to name a few. Effects of economic globalization can be seen in the situation of Africa today—the poorest continent in the world. Cultural globalization has somehow not been taken seriously because it may not seem important, but its effects are coming up seriously and we are already living them. Culturally, the generations have been changing creating strong boundary lines between the old and the new generations. Some of these points we are going to look into in the next section. First, however, let us see what we mean by culture.

Bailey and Peoples (2002) formally defined culture as the socially transmitted knowledge and behavior shared by some group of people. They took into considerations other important definitions like that of E.B. Taylor (1871), who defined culture as that complex whole which includes belief, art, morals, law, customs, and any other capabilities and habits acquired by member of a society. Lastly, Ralph Linton defined culture as the sum total of knowledge, attitudes, and habitual behavior patterns shared by the members of a particular society. In the next section we shall see how all the different components in culture have been influenced and/or transformed through globalization.

Some of the questions one could ask are: What has changed in the beliefs, art, morals, laws, customs, behavior shared by societies in Africa? Are the changes due to globalization? In looking at the uprooted youth and tracing the cause to the process of globalization, the mention of the word Africa or Cameroonian culture actually means everything about how Africa/Cameroonian live, their family and social life, their religion, their values, their economy, government, agriculture and so on, which of course differentiates them from Germans, British, Americans, French etc.

THE NEW AFRICAN GENERATIONS

The colonial impact in Africa had generated urbanization without industrialization, had fostered Western consumption patterns without Western productive techniques, Western tastes without Western skills, and had initiated secularization without the scientific spirit. The stage was set for the marginalization of Africa in the era of globalization.

Looking at the new Africa it would be better if we begin with the traditional leadership, which also plays an important role in Africa's changing culture as a result of the marginalization of Africa. Not only has the traditional leaderships forms in Africa been transformed to something else, future generations are in little or no better position to preserve and continue with it. In the next sections, we shall see how some forms of foreign intervention, foreign knowledge, and foreign ways of government has distorted Africa's ruling forms and future generations.

AFRICA'S RULING SYSTEM GONE WITH THE WIND

Before the Europeans entered Africa, it was a continent with a typical traditional ruling system, the type described by Max Weber (Weber, 1925). Traditional leadership rest on an established belief in the sanctity of immemorial traditions and the legitimacy of those exercising authority as per their stipulations. With this system the different ethnic groups in Africa sustained their societies with the obvious and traditional differences, disputes, and tribal wars, which were and are common with traditional societies all over the world. The possibility of a coup were non-existent, for instance with the case of an ethnic group in Cameroon[2] like the Bamilekes because there was no chance of the coup leader taking of the chieftaincy[3] since it was something hereditary. Such an attempt could lead to one being banished from that society. The system functioned relatively better and law and order were maintained in the societies. The chief was responsible for protecting the laws and traditional values of the people, as well as the people. He was respected and obeyed by everybody in the village[4] and had his advisors on whom he relied. Of course, like any system, arose there traditionally dictatorial leaders who did not care about getting advice from their notables and cared very little about the well-being of his people. But those were very rare cases, as the whole leadership system was and is, in some cases today, based on strict traditional customs and rituals, which had severe mystical consequences in case of non-compliance. With the fading away of tradition and the uprising of offsprings who care less about their traditional values and customs and stand for foreign ways of lives, which are unidentical to their way of life, the cultural meanings, values, and powers of these traditions is disappearing. For example, children of traditional leaders studying the "White Man's book" at home or in the West sometime give a damn about the traditional rites and customs governing their throne or simply are not well-informed about it. Some of the successors are sometimes scared by the responsibilities and traditional rules guiding them like inheriting their fathers' wives (as practised by some cultures) and having children with them.

These systems also had their bad sides when some chiefs decided to abuse their powers, like in cases where a chief moving around his village (his jurisdiction) could just see a young girl and said he wanted her for his wife. This was something nobody could object, not even the girl's parents. Sometimes the parents even rejoice over the fact that their child would be getting married to the chief because it meant a link from the chieftaincy to the family. Also, a son from their daughter could come to have a title and may become the next chief depending upon which of the wives' sons had the right to succeed the father. This particular succession aspect varies from one tribe to the other. In some cases, it was automatically the first son of the man's own first wife (since a chief usually inherited the wives of his father also), in other cases, he decided as per his personal choice and told his notables, who made it known when he was dead and so on.

However, some parents resented their daughters getting married to the chief, and such parents were usually exiled from the village or suffered punishment. Such incidents, however, were witnessed after the Europeans came in with formal education and some parents sent their girl children to school. Some parents also refused marriage proposals of the chiefs—most of the time due to a great age difference between the chief and the girl.

This was, however, not a problem for most parents because the girl child would anyway one day leave the house for another man, and the chief, of course, was the highest authority and thus the best person one could get for his daughter.

The Western formation of states in Africa, which brought together people from different ethnic groups into one nation did not only force upon the people a new form of governance but also changed the original ruling forms in Africa, wiped them out, and subsequently also their respective cultures. For example, when multiparty democracy was introduced in Cameroon in the early 1990s chiefs as well as their subject had the right to chose their different parties. Since according to most traditions the people loved, respected, and obeyed the will of their chiefs, the ruling party thought it could use the chiefs to get the votes of the people. No doubt, it was out of the question that people should disobey their traditional leaders, but in most cases where they were for the opposition parties there were cultural problems which arose as a result of the chiefs trying to force the people to support the ruling party. There were rumors of chiefs getting corrupted in favor of the government and wooing their own people to support it. When such chiefs attempted to force the people using their traditional prerogative they often met with resistance from their subject. There were cases where an individual slapped the chief who was trying to use his traditional authority for forcing the people to support the ruling party. This individual then declared that he did not slap the chief as a chief, as a militant against the ruling party. All such situations brought rebellion to most chieftaincy, as most chiefs were believed to have been bought away by the ruling party in its attempt to exploit the traditional authority to their political advantage. Most subject lost faith in their chiefs, and the chiefs in most cases gained greater administrative power from the governments. Traditional and cultural values were traded for political and foreign values. The question one can ask here is: Will the subsequent generations be able to continue or bring back the worthy values of their parent generations? This is almost impossible since the type of beliefs, art, morals, law, customs, and capabilities and habits acquired by the present generations are not the same as their parent generations. The present laws, customs, morals and the way of life transmitted to and accepted by the present generations being transmitted to the future generations is completely different from the older Africa.

SOME INDICATORS OF A DISAPPEARING CULTURE

Cameroon and Germany, the two countries where I have had the opportunity to live in are contrasted here. Cameroon as an example of a loser in globalization and Germany as a winner. Few years before setting off for studies in Germany, I spent time observing the severe changes that were taking place in my society and prepared a questionnaire on the "degrading[5] situation of the youth today." This had been due to the result of what I realized as the increasingly great value attached to western ideologies and ways of life by the youth. The effect was fading away of our true culture and identity in favor of a borrowed one. Some of the indicators and results of the new way of life were increasing unwanted pregnancies amongst young girls. Dating[6] amongst young girls and boys became the order of the day and those who were not involved were regarded as "misfits" or the weak ones. These were even sometimes molested and insulted to the extend that they often felt provoked to take up the challenge. Parents were/are worried and lamented, and are still lamenting, the situation of this generations because according to them, not only were such things uncalled for in their own youth, they were in fact, taboos.

The parent generations found this very unbecoming especially in cases where the saying that "you do not have to spare the rod and spoil the child" could not do any good. Most often they would curse their youth, accusing them of being spoilt by the "White Man's ideas and way of life:" Visiting of nightclubs and drinking spots by youth was fast becoming the order of the day. The number of drinking spots increased massively until in most cases one could find up to five successive bars in one place, all of them filled with students in their school uniforms. Until the late 1980s the situation had been that when students were in this situation and they saw their parents, teacher(s), or an elderly person who knew their parents, they would run away for fear of immediate sanction or being reported to their parents for eventual punishment.

I posed myself and many of my friends these questions:

- what type of world are we making of that inherited from our parents?;
- What type of world are we preparing for subsequent generations?

The obvious answers were not encouraging. For instance, their were increasing cases of young girls getting pregnant, and some also dying in crude abortion attempts. This situation grew worse with failing economy and introduction of democracy. I was almost convinced that a situation like this could result in a society lacking leadership and guidance for the present generation.

It was clear that Africa was moving from a rooted, strictly originally cultured society, to one oriented to pleasure and to ways of life dominant in the West. These are some of the "loser effects" of globalization on the African society brought in place by the "goodwill" enculturation of Africa by the West through slavery, colonization, formal education, western media, cinemas and so on.

INDUSTRIAL WINNER—GERMANY vs NON-INDUSTRIAL LOSER—CAMEROON

According to the CIA World Fact Book 2002, Germany, a post-war industrial nation has about 83 million people consisting of about 34 percent Protestants, 34 percent Roman Catholics, 3.7 percent Muslims and 28.3 percent unaffiliated or others. The present German society has undergone vast changes in recent years, especially after television became common, which for example, has done a great deal in causing homogenization (globalization within national borders) of a popular culture bringing urban ways of life to the rural areas.

Cameroon, unlike Germany is a non-industrial nation with a relatively small population of about 16 million people divided into these different religious proportions: Christians 40 percent (20 percent Catholics and 20 percent Protestants), 20 percent Muslims and 40 percent indigenous beliefs. The percentage of indigenous beliefs has reduced over the years and keeps doing so with an increase in the literate population which is mainly made up of newer generation of youth who in turn dislike and abandon traditional customs and beliefs.

Unlike in Germany the 16 million inhabitants of Cameroon is composed of a heterogeneous mixture of over 200 different ethnic groups with different languages, traditional rites, and customs, culture etc.

In my observation of both societies I noticed some important similarities and differences especially in my area of interest—the uprooted generation, the youths—most of which were the consequences of globalization.

SOME VALUES HELD BY BOTH SOCIETIES

RESPECT AND OBEDIENCE

In a typical African society great emphasis is laid upon difference among classes of people (chiefs, "quarter-head," nobles, elders etc.), male and female, different age groups and so on. These are relatively well-defined codes of conduct based upon socially accepted hierarchy. For instance, its not common for children to answer back to their parents and elders without being considered extremely impolite.

In Germany, I observed a different situation (now spreading over to Africa) in my last five years. A child answers back to his/her parents or worse to a stranger if they attempt to reproach or correct him/her. It is even common to see children call the police because their parents beat or sanction them. More so with those who have attained the age of 18 and by law are considered mature enough to decide for themselves. Parents and children are seen engaging in arguments on TV talk shows about children's freedom and timings of outdoor activities. Some habits, e.g., smoking, is normal for both the old and young, boys and girls. Children even share cigarettes with their parents. African students who return from holidays in Europe, share these stories to the shock of their parents.

Unfortunately, African students living in Europe cultivate such habits and take them over to Africa. Even those who live in Africa, learn from western films, media, literature try to adopt such borrowed and poor habits. One thing, which is still noticeable, is the fact that unlike their European counterparts, a African youth who smokes, will hide it from his parent, elder or caretakers. To the Africans, respect for and obedience to the elders, is part of our culture because the older person is believed to have more experience and wisdom than the younger pupil. There exists an old adage: what an old man can see sitting down, a young man cannot see while standing.

However, the degree of respect for elders, and consequently adherence to our traditional beliefs and customs is rapidly fading away. Developing societies, such as Cameroon, are quickly changing and becoming more like our western example, the German society. This change is heightened by the permanently increasing number of Africans who move to Europe and America for studies and jobs and adopt the lifestyle of the people of these societies.

I realize that certain reasons allow both societies to function the way they are, for example:

The Application of the Law

If a child is beaten and bullied even by his/her parents in Germany, and the incident is reported to authorities, the parent could be cautioned or even sanctioned under the German Law, unlike in Cameroon where there is no sanction accompanying such acts (You do not have to spare the rod and spoil the child as they say). Furthermore, the youth in Germany are well-informed about these laws and put them into effect when need be. In Cameroon, the youth mostly have no idea about such laws and even if they do, the law would hardly sanction a parent dealing sternly with their children. One notes the fact that the West had set up a system in Africa which did not curb the problems generated by indirected freedom.

Economic Reason

Those children who have attained the age of 18 and do not want to pursue formal education, are able to get unskilled jobs most often in Germany. Besides, they can simply undergo training (*Ausbildung*) or advanced training (*Weiterbildung*) provided by the type of educational order in their country. It offers a mixture of business, academic or handwork training advanced training for the majority of youth who do not want to pursue university studies. In developing countries on the contrary, such economic independence does not exist. The reason is clear that western colonial urbanization of Africa was not accompanied with industrialization. The industries were created in Europe from raw materials from Africa. Africans was assimilated into European ways and taste so that they would continue to desire and be dependent upon the finished products from Europe. Paradoxically, the system developed in Africa did not provide for him to be able to make the money he would need for the goods made out of the raw materials from his land.

FREEDOM AND RESPONSIBILITY

This change from a deeply rooted society that even Germans had at one point, is accompanied by a kind of freedom. Freedom for the younger generation. Freedom to do what they want, how they want it and when they want. With the older generation in Germany, it was always the rule: You are allowed to do everything but not everything is good for you, and those things that are not good for you are prohibited and kept out of your life by your parents or caretaker or elders who know better than you. Today this is no longer so in Germany where the youth, especially above 18, are free to decide almost everything for themselves. In Cameroon, despite this same tendency among about making their own decisions, there is still a great number of them, who still respect the old culture, way of life, and traditional norms. These are those who have continued to receive the same "behavioral pattern," socially transmitted from their grandparents to their parents. Its not uncommon to find girls who do not allow their male friends to visit them without prior information of their parents/guardians. I myself have experienced the same thing in my life.

Me and my fiancée, despite our plans to get married could not live together for a long time. Our German neighborhood found it strange and funny (but appreciated it). Nevertheless, many German parents told me that it was like that in Germany in the past even up to their generation. Most of them in fact, regretted that they have reached this stage. A globalized world is like a family, with each unit having its own special and positive talent. They could all bring together their talents for a happier family. If the elder and more powerful think they cannot learn from the young, they fail to gain their support when needed. Some of their ways would certainly not be agreeable to the juniors and forcing them would distort the family. Some of their ways may simply need to be reformed and adapted to the values of their juniors before it could be agreed upon by them.

In developmental politics the most important part is the development and globalization from below. There is nothing wrong with Africa that cannot be made right with Africa already has. Africa can be made rich with its own resources. It has made other continents and nations rich in the past, it can do it for itself!

THE FAMILY UNIT

This is another very interesting aspect when one is discussing about these two societies. In Africa, the family is extended to two generations working very closely together. At times even regardless of how distant the relationship could be it is simply defined in terms the immediate family. These extended families, can at times have more than 100 members due to the presence of polygamy, which is legal in Cameroon (not legal in Germany) and is practised by many. On the contrary, in Germany family is simply of the nuclear type i.e., on an average there are 1.5 children per family. One fends just for the nuclear family and may not be able to do more than that due to the economic demands and level of individualism of the society. In Africa the extended family is also a support network. The well-off member in the family has a duty to look after every member of the family, as far as possible. It is almost like an obligation. However, these aspects of our families are changing in our generation bringing us on par with our German counterparts. Our youth prefer, lesser children, and under the pressures of modern society, the extended family is fading away. It is not uncommon to find Cameroonian families facing polar positions between the parents and children over the member of children.

THE ROLE OF GLOBALIZATION IN MARRIAGE

In Cameroon, unlike Germany, monogamy and polygamy both are legal. Polygamy, however, is fading away, as the old reasons for polygamy no longer hold. Polygamy was a normal thing during our grandparents' age, as a big family meant strength, wealth (a strong labor force), security and honor and was easier to sustain than today. Mothers were responsible for their children's upbringing. With the introduction of formal education, which in the beginning was restricted to males (in Germany and Cameroon alike), things began to change. As money was needed for their education, males were given preference over girls, because they were anyway to be married off. This also reduced the level of say women had in family. Marriage at that time was strictly restricted within one's ethnic group. Parents generally selected the brides for their sons and later the sons had to agree. Things have change now. Parents are gradually accepting interethnic marriages and also allow their children to choose their partners. Nevertheless, their consent is still needed, and the negotiation and marriage procedures are actually initiated and carried out by them.

The national boundaries (enclosing several ethnic groups, as in Cameroon) and the legal system has facilitated interethnic marriages. Children from different ethnic groups now have a chance to mix and work together. This may be good for the establishment of a good national and social network amongst the different ethnic group; but is harmful for the individual culture. As the interethnic married couples come from different ethnic origins, they do not share the same mother tongue and communicate either in English or French or both[7]. This also means that their children would most probably not speak either French or English. This situation has led to a crisis for the local languages. Language being a very important factor of culture we can say that it is a serious setback for the local cultures.

There is the practice of bride price in most African societies that is absent in Germany. This is a kind of "compensation" or "thank you" from the boy's family to the girl's for allowing them to take their daughter into their family. Europeans misinterpreted this in the past and used to say that African men buy their wives, which was and is totally false. The marriages usually take the following course: Parents of the boy visit the girl's parents to tell them their son loves their daughter and would like to ask her in marriage. The girl's parent are given time to think. During this time they probe into the life and history of the boy's family making sure there are no scandals or curse like a member of this family having committed suicide or killed someone (there were beliefs about conduct being hereditary), sickness like epilepsy, elephantiasis etc., linked to the family. If any of this is traced in the history of the boy's family this can result to a rejection from their part. In such a case, the couple cannot get married, or if they do so, may be disowned by their parents. However, young people nowadays do get married even when their parents disagree with their choice. In the case of a positive response from the girl's family the two families come together for a traditional marriage.[8] How this is performed and the rites involved, varies from one ethnic group to another. The couple still has to proceed to a court or legal marriage, which was introduced by the Cameroon Law shortly after independence in 1961.

Living together without being officially married, which has become a common thing in Germany, is still something new to African culture. In Cameroon, it would bring bad name for the family, and thus, will not be allowed by parents. These are some of the worldviews held by Africans that are gradually changing under Western influence.

In the German society, it was the girl whose parent brought what they call "Mitgift" for the boy's family. The opposite of bride price. In their own interpretation of bride price, then one could say that in Germany, women buy their husbands. Thus, what is been transmitted to the African generation is a mixture of African and western culture. The western component is evidently the dominant one today.

Both the German and Cameroonian society have undergone a lot of changes over the last centuries. Some people believe (when they look at the trends in both the societies) that African societies are undergoing what the western societies had undergone in the past. They will soon reach the same levels as Europe is in now—not necessarily in industrial and technological terms, but at least in terms of social life and way of living and thinking.

Africans strongly believe that development does not lie only in materialism, industries, and capitalism. Solidarity, brotherly love, and assisting the underprivileged, are parts of development, and in this domain Africa is far more developed than most of her Western counterparts. The West has material wealth but most often lacks even the time to enjoy it with their families due to the ever increasing demands of a world which has no room for incompetence, failures and incapability. Such people are labelled as misfits in society and have nothing to get. Such is the type of society that has reduced human beings to mere machines, who are thrown out after they can no longer bring in any economic profits (the presence of old age homes is an example). This is not the type of development Africa needs. It is economic but not social development. It needs development which caters to the well-being of people.

CONCLUSION

African cultures and tradition are undergoing transformations which leave them distorted. Transformation which Africans themselves cannot stop. The media represents an exaggerated and unrealistic western culture. Adopting their lifestyle is like living above other Africans, as the colonial masters have left behind an image of western superiority over Africans. Some, who think they are living the way white people live, often proudly tell others, "I live a whiteman's life." Such people are often envied by others, giving this lifestyle undue importance and making it attractive for the next generation. Thus, cultural knowledge (ideas, beliefs, attitudes, assumptions about the world and other mental phenomena) with components of cultural knowledge like norms, values, collective understanding, world views (Bailey and Peoples, 2002) etc., have moved from African origins to something imported, which does not actually suit our environment and people. The attractive image of the West is very much welcomed by the youth, because they see in it a kind of liberation from parental control and direction. This foreign way of life is often used by the youth to justify their doing some of the things their parents would classify under delinquency.

It is indeed a sad situation for the parent generation but they can do nothing. The situation is even heightened by the thousands of youths leaving their homeland every year for studies abroad, and come back with a completely different way of life. Thus, the effect of globalization on Africa as we have seen in this chapter is irreversible.

Finally, globalization as it is, does not only do away with Africa's culture but also renders Africa limited access to development and the economic gains from it.

I will end this chapter with what the Nigerian President Olusegun Obasanjo once said,

> Globalization has failed to spur economic recovery, faster growth, greater employment opportunities and poverty eradication in developing countries. Rather it has exhibited a tendency to accentuate the income and welfare gaps between the rich and the poor among and within countries and regions... the North reluctance to address the growing impoverishment in the South constitutes a major threat to international peace and security.

NOTES

1. Europeans brought in many positive things into Africa but their objectives behind these were more exploitative (providing chance for further exploitation) than humanitarian.
2. Cameroon has over 200 different ethnic group and each group has its own language and culture.
3. The subjects and the area of jurisdiction of the chief. It is like King and Kingdom.
4. Normally people of the same origin or ethnic group (the same language, culture etc.) live in small groupings in villages led by the chief. But there are now a days many villages with mixed ethnic groups (metropolitan villages). Most often a village may just be a chieftaincy but there are sometime chieftaincies including more than one village.
5. That was my personal observation and opinion and has no scientific backing.
6. Dating here as most of the parents regretted in their answers to the questionnaire did not end at the platonic level, as was the case in their days.
7. Cameroon was colonized by France and England, thus the two official languages are French and English.
8. Marriage in the African context is a family matter. The two families become one family through the marriage of their children. This accounts for stability in most African marriages.

REFERENCES

Bailey, Garrick and James Peoples. 2002. *Essentials of Cultural Anthropology*. Belmont: Wadsworth.

Giddens, Anthony. 1997. *Consequences of Modernity*. Cambridge: Polity Press.

Mazuri, Ali. 1999. "From Slave Ships to Space Ship: Africa between Marginalization and Globalization" in *African Studies Quarterly*, vol. 2, no. 4.

Shillington, Kevin. 1995. *In History of Africa*. New York: St. Martin's Press.

Taylor, E.B. 1871 [1877]. *Premitive Culture: Researches into the Development of Mythology, Philosophy, Religion, Language, Art and Custom*. 2 Volumes. New York: Henry Holt.

Weber, Max. 1925[1978]. *Economy and Society*. Berkeley: University of California Press.

10

NEO-LIBERAL GLOBALIZATION MEETS GLOBAL RESISTANCE: THE SIGNIFICANCE OF "ANTI-GLOBALIZATION" PROTEST

Ray Kiely

The last few years have seen the rise of so-called anti-capitalist and anti-globalization[1] protest in the western world.

However, many parts of the former Third World have experienced direct action protest for much longer (Walton and Seddon, 1994), but in the western world, the 1999 events in Seattle and subsequent protests have brought such protests into the wider public sphere. Movements such as the Peoples Global Action, Global Exchange, Direct Action Network, Jubilee 2000/Movement International, the International Forum on Globalization (Starr, 2000); campaigns against sweat shops, Third World debt and intensive farming; protests in Washington, Prague, Melbourne, Davos, Nice and Quebec; books such as *No Logo: The Silent Takeover;* and *Captive State* (Hertz, 2001; Klein, 2000; and Monbiot, 2000)—all these reflect a growing awareness of and movement against corporate globalization.

This chapter discusses the emergence and the politics of these movements. I start by outlining the emergence of a neo-liberal, flexible, global capitalism, which developed out of the breakdown of the post-World War II Fordist era. I relate this change to the "newer" forms of resistance in the current era, and draw on Polanyi's notion of the "double movement" to examine the ways in which anti-globalization movements have emerged in response to the tendency of capital to dominate all aspects of social life. My second section then moves on to a more detailed analysis of the politics of the anti-globalization movements. I focus on two key questions: the critique of globalization from above, and the role of direct action and non-hierarchical organization within the movements. These questions are linked to the key problem of solidarity with movements in the South that are challenging neo-liberal globalization.

The chapter focuses on the dilemmas of these movements, arguing that at present, there is a precarious balancing act going on between potential and actual strengths and weaknesses. For example, the non-hierarchical mode of organization of global resistance can be seen as a strength, but this has taken place in part on the basis of a flawed account of the character of neo-liberal globalization. Similarly, while direct action is important in avoiding the hierarchies associated with formal politics, attempts to by-pass formal political institutions can easily lead to a politics of escapism rather than transcendence.

THE HISTORICAL EMERGENCE OF "ANTI-GLOBALIZATION" MOVEMENTS

THE BREAKDOWN OF NEO-KEYNESIAN FORDISM

The post-World War II political settlement emerged in the context of US dominance of the world order, the Cold War, and decolonization. The United States administration was largely committed to free trade but—fearing communist "expansion"—was prepared to compromise in the face of international pressure from weaker capitalist powers and pressure from powerful domestic interests such as the farmers. The organizations that emerged from the 1944 Agreement at Bretton Woods, USA—the World Bank, IMF, and the GATT forum for inter-national trade—largely reflected this compromise. On the one hand, there was a long-term commitment to international free trade, which was reflected in the successive rounds of GATT talks that lowered tariffs at various levels. On the other, the weaker capitalist powers had sufficient space to develop their "national economies." This applied to the European powers weakened by the war, and the countries that were beginning to win independence from the colonial powers.

In the "advanced" capitalist world, the post-war order, was thus based on "labor friendly" regimes (Silver and Arrighi, 2001: 53). While labor was far from experiencing a level playing field with capital, the former did win important concessions from state managed capital-isms—and maintained these through strong labor organization. These concessions included commitments to full employment, welfare rights, and improved living standards. This development occurred in the context of the increased generalization of Fordist production methods, whereby standardized goods were manufactured on a mass basis (Harvey, 1989: 129–33). Workers were allocated strictly demarcated tasks and they utilized specialist machinery for each particular good produced (Dicken, 1992: 16). Production was focused primarily on the national market, which was usually protected from foreign competition, although there was still considerable scope for exports to, or investment in the foreign markets. Profitability was derived from the economies of scale of production, which meant that the costs decreased as the amount produced of a particular good increased.

In the developing world, labor did not win such concessions and was often subordinated in the quest for rapid development. States in the Third World did have at least some scope for "national development" and attempted modernization through import substitution industrialization. Nation states protected infant industry from foreign competition in order to develop a strong industrial base and thus, reduce dependence on expensive manufactured imports (Kiely, 1998a: chs. 6 and 8). Thus, while neo-Keynesian capitalism in the "advanced" world was labor friendly, neo-Keynesianism in the Third World could be described as "development friendly" (Silver and Arrighi, 2001: 53). In the case of the former, labor organizations such as the trade union movement and social democratic parties, were crucial in preserving and improving living standards; in the case of the latter, the state was deemed to play this role (though whether it always did is another question).

By the late 1960s and early 1970s, the post-War order had been undermined. The monotony of work and the sexual division of labor were increasingly challenged, by both Fordist men and women (Brown and Lauder, 2001: ch. 4). Profit rates began to slowly decline, and in the early 1970s, the United States abandoned the system of fixed exchange rates agreed at the Bretton Woods, thus allowing for a system of floating exchange rates and the start of the deregulation of international finance. The increase in oil prices in 1973–74 aggravated these problems as oil exporters deposited windfall profits (petrodollars) in western banks. Already facing a glut of dollars passed on by a United States government whose military spending soared in an attempt to win the war in Vietnam, the advanced capitalist countries fell into a stagflationary recession. In the Third World—particularly (though not exclusively) among oil importers—states borrowed money in an effort to maintain high rates of growth. This culminated in the debt crisis of the 1980s when, faced with increasing rates of interest payments on debts, several Third World countries threatened default.

A "New Era" of Capitalism: Neo-Liberalism, Flexible Accumulation, Informational Capitalism, and Globalization

Many writers have argued that there has been a change in the "regime of accumulation" since the early 1970s. A regime of accumulation "describes the stabilization over a long period of the allocation of the net product between consumption and accumulation; it implies some correspondence between the transformation of both the conditions of production and the conditions of reproduction of wage earners." (Lipietz, 1986: 19) For such a regime of accumulation to work effectively there must also exist, "a materialization of the regime of accumulation taking the form of norms, habits, laws, regulating networks and so on that ensure the unity of the process"—a mode of regulation. The new regime of accumulation has been described as "disorganised capitalism" (Lash and Urry, 1987), "flexible accumulation" (Harvey, 1989), "post-Fordism" (Amin, 1994) and the "network society" (Castells, 1996). Although there are differences over specific details, all agree that this restructured capitalism is based on a neo-liberal mode of regulation and flexible regime of accumulation.

Neo-liberalism can be identified in the ways in which nation states have (to some extent) moved away from a welfare to a competition state (Cerny, 2000). This can be seen in state strategies to deregulate economies to promote the supposed efficiency of market forces (as in Thatcher's Britain), promote global competitiveness through promotion of education appropriate to the "knowledge economy" (as in Blair's Britain). In much of the former Second and Third Worlds, it can be seen in the (uneven) implementation of Structural Adjustment polices, designed to open up former protected economies to the forces of global competition. These policies are designed to allow each country to exercise their respective comparative advantage in a global system of free trade.

The promotion of such a "global free market" developed through successive rounds of GATT talks since 1949, which led to a gradual reduction in tariff rates (Dunkley, 2000: 32). The Uruguay Round of talks led to the formation of the more formal World Trade Organization (WTO) in 1995. The WTO has a wider remit than GATT, including an expansion into services and intellectual property, as well as promoting free trade in agriculture and textiles. There is also a more formal Dispute Settlement system, where disputes are settled more quickly and not necessarily on the basis of joint consensus (Panos Briefing, 1999: 6).

Flexible accumulation refers to the new organizational forms, which have developed out of the contradictions of Fordism. Output and productivity declined substantially in the 1970s (Harvey, 1989: 132), and so capital responded by experimenting with new forms of work organization. The fundamental weakness of Fordism was its rigidity. Production techniques, consumer markets, and labor markets could not be changed quickly or easily. Flexible production, on the other hand, is based on "forms of production characterized by a well-developed ability both to shift promptly from one process and/or product configuration to another (dynamic flexibility) and to adjust quantities of output rapidly up or down over the short run without any strongly deleterious effects on levels of efficiency (static flexibility)." (Storper, 1991: 107) Crucial to such flexibility is one or more of the following: flexible technologies; flexible relationships between core firms and suppliers; and flexible organization of the labor process (Kiely, 1998a: 146–50).

Flexible, computer based technology, contains information that allows manufacturing plants to shift from one product line to another relatively quickly and cheaply. Though the actual flexibility of such technology has been exaggerated (Amin, 1994; Kiely, 1998b), changes have occurred and their importance is best seen in the case of retailing. The bar code potentially overcomes problems of under (loss of market share) or overproduction (too much stock), as computerized accounting of stocks allows firms to order or produce supplies that coincide with demand (Murray, 1989: 42–43). In turn, this allows firms to produce or sell relatively small batches, and so in some sectors at least, niche markets replace mass markets.

This system was also applied to relations between core firms and their suppliers. In Japan, Toyota developed a system in which they ordered supplies according to daily need, enabling them to speed up the passage of products through the factory system and eliminate waste in the process. The company drew on a hierarchical system of supply networks, with around 230 first-tier suppliers, 5,000 second-tier suppliers, and around 20,000 third and fourth-tier suppliers (Ruigrok and van Tulder, 1995: 53). Profits—and wages and job stability—tended to decline the lower one's place in the hierarchy. The labor market thus has a minority of core workers who enjoy high wages, relative job stability, full-time work, and who are expected to show some skills and degree of self-management of the flexible assembly line. On the other hand, the majority secondary labor market has far worse job conditions, low wages, work is often part-time, job security is low and unemployment high.[2]

Central to this process is the increasing importance of information. Manuel Castells (1996: 13–22) has argued that a new "socio-technical paradigm" has facilitated the globalization of economic activity. Due to advances in computing and transportability there is a need to locate engineering and design close to manufacturing, except for pilot production. The result is that almost all economic activities can be outsourced. Companies have therefore decentralized into flexible networks in which core firms control design, marketing, research and development and finance functions, while other functions are contracted out to suppliers. Companies like Nike and The Gap—often the targets of contemporary anti-capitalist protest—own no manufacturing facilities at all, and instead draw on a large global network of subcontractors. This is an example of what Gereffi (1994: 219) calls a buyer driven global commodity chain in which the bulk of profits are made at the brand name merchandizing and retail levels "where companies invest considerable sums in product development, advertising and computerized store networks to create and sell these items."

The move from Fordist to flexible accumulation has enormous implications, for labour and development friendly regimes have ended.[3] This argument exaggerates the extent to which mass production has ended, which has important political implications, particularly for organized labor, which I return to later in the text. Nevertheless, important changes have taken place, which leads Castells (1997: 475) to argue that "labour is disaggregated in its performance, fragmented in its organization, diversified in its existence, divided in its collective action." This fragmentation and division is reflected—at least in the "advanced" capitalist world—in falling union membership and density, ageing membership, and difficulties of unionizing in smaller workplaces and among part-time workers. Union membership, as a percentage of wage and salary earners, had fallen by 1995 in the UK to 33 percent (from 46 percent in 1985), in Germany to 29 percent (35 percent in 1985), and in France to 9 percent (15 percent in 1985) (Jefferys, 2001: 154). In the US, 36 percent of the private sector workforce was unionized in 1953; by 1994 the proportion had declined to just

11 percent (Danaher 1996: 19). Such figures reflect the end of the post-War "labor friendly consensus."

"Development friendly" regimes have met with a similar fate, and Castells argues that the network society has produced a global economy, not in the sense of a level playing field between free and equal producers, but in the sense that it has "the capacity to operate as a unit in real time on a planetary basis." (1996: 92) He reiterates the view that the global economy, "is not a planetary economy. In other words, the global economy does not embrace all economic processes in the planet, it does not include all territories, and it does not include all people in its workings, although it does affect directly or indirectly the livelihoods of the entire humankind. While its effects reach out to the whole planet, its actual operation and structure concern only segments of economic structures, countries, and regions, in proportions that vary according to the particular position of a country or region in the international division of labour." (Castells, 1996: 102; also Carnoy et al., 1993).

This fragmentation means that both labor movements and developmental states have been undermined. For Castells (1997: 360), "the labor movement does not seem fit to generate by itself and from itself a project identity able to reconstruct social control and to rebuild social institutions in the Information Age." Instead, it is social movements—ecologists, feminists, religious fundamentalists, nationalists and localists—who resist particular aspects of "globalization, capitalist restructuring, organizational networking, uncontrolled informationalism, and patriarchalism" and so constitute (albeit in a fragmented way) "the embryos of a new society" (Castells, 1997: 360–62; see also Arrighi et al., 1989). These "new social movements" do not simply fill the space of resistance left by the decline of old labor, not least because many of them—especially postcolonial and feminists struggles—arose during the contradictions of the Fordist era. Nevertheless, with the decline of organized labor, these movements have taken on an even greater significance in the post-Fordist world.

Such social movements are often characterized by the fact that they are not concerned with winning direct contol over, or access to, state power. Giddens (1991: ch. 7) has argued that in the West at least, social movements since the 1960s have been principally concerned with "life politics" as opposed to "emancipatory politics" (Giddens, 1991: ch. 7; see also Habermas, 1981). The latter was principally concerned with struggles against structural inequalities that constrained people's "life chances." The former is principally concerned with how we use particular freedoms once they have been won. This distinction could be challenged on the grounds that it separates too rigidly, a politics of (material) distribution from a politics of (cultural) recognition (see Fraser, 1997; Young, 1997),[4] but what is of more immediate interest here is that the current direction of a number of social movements in an explicitly anti-capitalist direction—including, and indeed especially, in the West.[5]

One particularly fruitful way of understanding this development is by utilizing the work of Karl Polanyi, and in particular his 1944 classic, *The Great Transformation*. In this work, Polanyi argued that the rise of the "market system" was distinct from the market as one means of allocating resources. This market system did not arise naturally or spontaneously but was actually the deliberate creation of the state. A separate market economy was thus the product of historical social struggles such as the enclosure of land. Once a "separate" economic sphere was created, it tended to dominate all aspects of social life—"instead of economy being embedded in social relations, social relations are embedded in the economic system" (Polanyi, 1957: 57). Profit maximization thus becomes the main goal of economic activity and capital tends to commodify more and more aspects of social life, with destructive consequences. As Polanyi (1957: 73) argued, "to allow the market mechanism to be sole director of the fate of human beings and their natural environment...would result in the demolition of society." Unsurprisingly, this tendency for capital to penetrate into new areas was resisted in the 19th century, and attempts were made to "re-embed" the economy into wider social relations. There was thus what Polanyi (1957: 76) called a "double movement":

> While on the one hand markets spread all over the globe and the amount of goods involved grew to unbelievable proportions, on the other hand a network of measures and policies was integrated into powerful institutions designed to check the action of the market relative to labour, land and money.

So in the first stage of the double movement the market became separated from social control, which led to conflict, while in phase two, society restored some control over the market economy. Such means of control included universal suffrage, the rise of "mass politics," trade unions and so on. The 1930s saw a challenge to the democratic potential of the double movement, in the shape of Stalinism and Fascism, but the post-World War II period constituted a renewal of this second movement.

With the breakdown of the neo-Keynesian welfare and developmental states, and the resurgence of a global "market economy," post-Fordist, neo-liberal capitalism can be regarded as the first phase of a new double movement (Hettne, 1995; Harriss, 2000). The rise of the anti-globalization movements is thus the second phase of a new double movement, in which these movements are attempting "to reassert social control over the movement towards the unfettered power of capital in determining the possibilities for social choice" (Gill, 1995: 66). Thus protests against Structural Adjustment policies and the IMF and the World Bank, the proposed Multilateral Agreement on Investment, and the WTO meeting at Seattle, are clearly part of a protest against the tendency of capital to become disembedded from wider social relations. Placards at May Day anti-globalization protests at Sydney and Melbourne in 2001 read, "We live in a Society, not an Economy" (*Daily News*, May 2, 2001).

So, to summarise. Current anti-globalization protest can be situated in the context of a protest against the increasingly unfettered power of capital, promoted by flexible accumulation and neo-liberal state policies. In what ways do these movements seek to challenge corporate globalization and re-embed the market in wider social relations? To answer this question we need to look at the politics of these movements in greater detail.

THE POLITICS OF "ANTI-GLOBALIZATION"

This section provides a broad overview of the politics of "anti-capitalism." I cannot possibly hope to do justice to the broad variety of movements that are currently resisting "globalization from above," and so here I will present just two broad, and interrelated themes—the critique of corporate globalization, and the emergence of "postmodern" politics. Some—not least many in the anti-capitalist movement—may find the search for "unifying themes" to be desperately old fashioned in that it attempts to impose a false universalism when there are in fact many different struggles. I think that such a critique is misplaced and that part of the reason for identifying some broad themes is to show the significance of these differences, as well as similarities. More contentiously, I also hope to show that not all the differences within the movements are productive, and indeed not all the political positions adopted are progressive. While the anti-capitalist movement should be commended for its reluctance to accept the certainties of Leninist politics, I remain unconvinced that a "postmodern" politics constitutes a significant advance, and that autonomy or direct action can represent an escape from, rather than an engagement with, politics. These abstract points will hopefully become clearer in the discussion that follows. I proceed by focusing on the two broad themes identified above, and attempt to show the connections between them, and the political implications that follow. I conclude by arguing for the continued importance of a "critical modernist" politics.

THE CRITIQUE OF "GLOBALIZATION FROM ABOVE": AN OUTLINE

Anti-globalization protest movements are united around the belief that globalization represents a new period of capitalist development. This is based on a restructuring of capitalism, the increased commodification of different areas of social life, increased mobility of global capital flows, and the increased importance of multilateral institutions such as the IMF, World Bank and the IMF, and regional agreements such as the North American Free Trade Agreement and the Free Trade Area for the Americas.

Roger Burbach (2001: 25), one of the most influential figures at the Seattle protests, has argued that globalization constitutes a new period of capitalism with a transnational bourgeoisie at the apex of the social order. He places great emphasis on the increases in direct foreign investment from 1983–87, and from 1993–97, and of the former Third World's increasing global share of this investment—an increase from 17 percent (1986–90) to 40 percent (1996). He draws the conclusion that:

> The global mobility of capital has allowed for the integration around the world of vast chains of production and distribution, the instantaneous movement of values, and the unprecedented concentration and centralisation of worldwide economic management, control and decision making power in transnational capital (Burbach, 2001: 28).

This global capital can easily move from one part of the world to another and thereby undermine state and labor controls over the unfettered power of capital (Burbach, 2001: 29). As outlined earlier, trade unions and nation states have been weakened by these changes.

The World Bank (cited in Munck, 1998: 8) has recently pointed out
that in the mid-1970s, two-thirds of the world's workforce lived in
countries weakly linked to international markets, but by 2000 this
had declined to just 10 percent. By the turn of the century, about 70
percent of goods made in the US were subject to foreign competition
(Brown and Lauder, 2001: 100). Richard Barnet (1996: 37) draws
the conclusion, "A global pool of bargain labor is available to companies making virtually anything and, increasingly, to corporations selling insurance, data of every description and legal, engineering and
accounting services." Capital mobility also allows transnational companies to avoid paying taxes. The co-founder of the influential Global
Exchange Movement Kevin Danaher (1996: 24; see also Burbach,
2001: 45) has pointed out that in the US in the early 1950s, companies paid 76 cents in taxes for every $1 paid by families and individu-
als; by the early 1990s, they paid only 21 cents for every dollar paid
by families and individuals.

The result of these changes is said to be a global "race to the bottom"
(Korten, 1995: 229–37; Rinehart, 1996: 95) as states and localities
compete to gain some share of an ever decreasing slice of the cake.
David Korten (1996: 50) argues:

> as you erase national economic borders, and integrate national econo-
> mies into a global economy in which companies are free to move their
> money and goods without restraints, the real competition is far less
> among firms—which are managing competition among themselves with
> mergers and acquisitions and strategic alliances. The real competition
> is among people and communities for a declining pool of jobs, and
> they compete by offering the lowest wages, the poorest working con-
> ditions and the least environmental restraint.

Thus, global capital is based on limited competition "between oli-
gopolist clusters in a transnational environment" (Burbach, 2001: 45).
The more intense—and harmful—competition is between national
states and national labor for access to capital investment, but this is
inevitably on terms favorable to hyper-mobile capital. Burbach (2001:
39) draws the conclusion that the old Core-Periphery, "First World/
Third World" divide is less significant, and that contemporary Core/
Periphery relations are more social than geographical. The United States
is a 20:80 society in which the living standards for the bottom 80
percent have declined since the 1970s—the "Third World" now exists
in the "First." In this way, the protests at Seattle could be interpreted

as a global class struggle in which the exploited and oppressed of the world lined up against the transnational bourgeoisie and the WTO that represented its interests.

THE CRITIQUE OF "GLOBALIZATION FROM ABOVE": AN ASSESSMENT

The anti-capitalist movement has faced a lot of criticism both before and after Seattle, particularly (but not exclusively) from neo-liberals (*The Economist,* 1999; WTO, 2000). Here I present a sympathetic critique, which essentially argues that the rejection of neo-liberalism (including in its modified form) is correct but that the movement has not fully grasped the complexities of corporate globalization, and that this has significant political implications.

Some on the Left, such as (Lord) Meghnad Desai, have used Marx's account of the progressiveness of capitalism to reject anti-capitalist protest as an obstacle to the needs of the developing world. He argues that globalization constitutes a bigger threat to the "advanced" capitalist world, and that the fastest way for the developing world to industrialise is to embrace the global economy. For Desai (2000: 44):

> Countries which have not yet received foreign investment, especially those in sub-Saharan Africa, need to integrate into the global order or they will be left even further behind. The Third World needs capitalism because capitalism alone will lead to its growth. No other plausible, feasible alternative has yet been found.

He then explicitly links this contention to the radical development debates of the 1970s, and rightly rejects Andre Gunder Frank's contention that monopoly capitalism could only underdevelop the Third World. Desai (2000: 44) argues that "only Bill Warren has challenged that view…. It is clear that capitalism can lead to growth in countries which are willing to trade and that, far from monopoly capital stifling growth in countries, capital goes wherever it will make profits." Finally, he argues that the historical evidence *favors* globalization as the last 25 years have seen a decline in global inequalities.[6]

Desai's (2000: 44) evidence for this last claim is that Organization for Economic Co-operation and Development (OECD) countries' share of global GDP has declined from 80 percent in 1975 to 70 percent in 2000. This figure is of course highly selective and abstracts from the different economic performances of former Third World countries, inequalities within countries, and ignores different rates of population increases across country groups. If we measure developing country, *per capita* income as a proportion of OECD countries income, a very different picture emerges. Comparing the years 1961–65 with 1996–97, the ratio of sub-Saharan African income to OECD income fell from 3.4 percent to 1.5 percent; for Latin America the ratio fell from 15 to 11 percent; for South Asia the ratio fell from 2 to 1.8 percent. In North Africa and the Middle East, per capita growth has been continually below OECD average since the 1970s (Weeks, 2001: 20, 22). There has been any significant improvement only in East and Southeast Asia.

The decline in the share of OECD countries' GDP can therefore be explained by the rise of the East Asian newly industrializing countries. Desai's claim ignores the fact that in the so-called global era, outside of these countries, the developing world as a whole has experienced declining rates of participation in global trade and investment. Thus, the share of developing countries in world exports was 27.7 percent in 1995, up from 18.9 percent in 1970 (though still down from 33 percent in 1950). However, the share of the first-tier newly industrializing countries increased from 2 percent in 1970 to 10.4 percent by 1995. For Latin America, the share fell from 12.1 percent in 1950 (and 5.5 percent in 1970) to just 4.4 percent in 1995; in Africa, the share had fallen from 5.3 percent in 1950 (2 percent in 1970) to 1.5 percent in 1995 (Hoogvelt, 2001: 73). Investment is also highly concentrated in specific parts of the "developing world." While there has been a substantial increase in DFI flows in the 1990s, China accounted for a third of the DFI flow for all developing countries, and this is concentrated in eight coastal provinces and Beijing. Hirst and Thompson (1999: 73–74) have added up the populations of the coastal provinces and Beijing, together with the populations of the nine other main developing country recipients of DFI, plus the populations of the Triad countries (North America, the European Union, and Japan). Together these populations make up around 30 percent of the world's population. In the first-half of the 1990s, they received 86 percent of all global direct investment. In the 1990s, the percapita incomes of over 80 countries actually fell, representing for many in these cases an intensification of absolute as well as relative poverty. Inequalities have also increased within countries, not least in the United States where real wages were lower in the mid-1990s than they were in the late-1960s (Sassen, 2000: 130; Kaplinsky, 2001: 48). Between 1987–98 (a period of growing global integration) the number of people living below the official poverty line ($1 a day at 1985 prices) was effectively unchanged at around 1.2 billion people (Kaplinsky, 2001: 49–50). Income and wealth gaps between the richest 20 percent and poorest 20 percent of the world's population increased from 30:1 in 1960 to 60:1 by 1990 and 74:1 in 1999 (*Guardian*, July 12, 1999). Today, the net worth of the top 200 billionaires is the equivalent of 41 percent of the world's population (Hoogvelt, 2001: 91).

Of course, global integration may not be the main reason for these problems, but it is equally clear that it has not alleviated them. Desai and the WTO appear to believe that simply embracing the global economy will lead to an improvement in living standards, but this is not the case. Participating in the world economy is neither inherently "developmental" nor "underdevelopmental" (Kiely, 1995: ch. 3). Bill Warren's critique of Frank was correct, but he then tended to assume that capitalist development would automatically take place irrespective of specific conditions within particular countries, and in the world economy at a particular point in time. He also assumed that capitalism took one concrete form, and that this was determined by an evolutionary logic outside of the actions of human beings. Warren died in 1978, a few years before the establishment of neo-liberal hegemony in the world economy. Had he lived, it is unlikely that he would have advocated developing country participation without considerable protection for some economic sectors, the very thing that the WTO partially undermines.[7] Without strong restrictions on capital, competition between capitals tends to take the form of extracting absolute surplus value through low wages and raising the intensity of labor—rather than through technological change or government legislation to facilitate social development such as better work conditions or health care.

The effects of freer trade are thus more contradictory than Desai suggests. In agriculture it is likely to have devastating effects on production for some developing countries. At the WTO talks, weaker agrarian producers have sided with the European Union against the US and stronger agrarian producers (for example, the Cairns group) over the extent to which protectionist measures should persist. Similarly, the expansion into Trade Related Intellectual Property Rights favors more established producers. TRIPs give a company the right to hold a patent for a minimum of 20 years and for copyright, 50 years (Panos Briefing, 1999: 17). The technological diffusion that previous late developers enjoyed, regulated by a protectionist developmental state, is seriously undermined, as the monopoly power of earlier industrializers is reinforced. The clear implication is that "free trade" unequally benefits those countries with stronger structures of production who monopolize technology and Research and Development, establish economies of scale and scope, labor skills and so on. Investment too, is likely to concentrate more in those areas (Dunkley, 2000: ch. 6; Kiely, 1998a: chs. 5 and 9).

These comments imply that neo-liberal interpretations of the theory of comparative advantage are misplaced. But the above comments also have implications for the anti-capitalist movement's critique of corporate globalization, and in particular the contention that a global free market represents a "race to the bottom." In some sectors, there is a race to the bottom in which capital (local and foreign) utilizes cheap sweat shop labor and/or takes advantage of a lack of environmental regulations. Anti-corporate campaigns—brilliantly documented by Naomi Klein (2000; see also, Ross, 1997)—have done an excellent job in publicizing struggles over work conditions and wages. However, these sweat shops tend to be in labor intensive manufacturing where capital can easily shift production facilities. This is not the case in many capital intensive or high-tech sectors and these continue to be concentrated in established areas of accumulation (the US, EU, Japan and the first-tier Newly Industrialized Countries [NICS]), as the investment figures above make clear. Capital is not as mobile as key thinkers in the anti-capitalist movement imply, and that is because of the sunk costs involved in capital investment. Neil Smith (1990: 88–89) rightly argues that:

> It is all very well that $500 million can be whizzed around the world at the push of a button, but it must come from somewhere and be en route to somewhere. This somewhere is the production process, where in order to produce surplus value it is necessary that vast quantities of productive capital be spatially immobilised for relatively long periods in the form of factories, machinery, transport routes, warehouses, and a host of other facilities.

This is not to deny that living standards and real wages have fallen—including for many in the advanced capitalist world (see above). The end of Fordist–Keynesian capitalism has increased the levels of marginalization in the advanced capitalist world, and in this respect we can talk about a Core-Periphery divide and the "Third Worldization" of the First World. Nor is it to deny that there has been a significant restructuring of production in which a group of factories make separate parts for a single finished good (see earlier text in this chapter on Toyota and post-Fordism). What is at issue is whether capital is as mobile as the "race to the bottom" argument implies, and whether global uneven development *between* as well as *within* countries has ended. As the figures above make clear, capital on the whole continues to concentrate in advanced countries and not disperse to take advantage of cheap labor elsewhere. Indeed, post-Fordist practices reinforce such concentration, as suppliers must locate close to the final producer (or retailer) to ensure that their supplies arrive "just in time" (Kiely, 1998b). Lower real wages are therefore the result of restructuring within the advanced capitalist world, rather than a product of a global race to the bottom. It could be argued that this restructuring is carried out to remain competitive in the face of potential competition from low-wage producers abroad, but (except in a few labor intensive industries or from a few higher-wage first-tier NICs) there is no evidence of a large increase in "First World" import of "Third World" goods. In the early 1990s, OECD manufactured imports from the developing world were of a value equivalent to only 2.3 percent of OECD countries' GDP (Thompson, 2000: 119). Both state and capital may justify restructuring through notions of global competitiveness, but the underlying reasons for this practice are to restore profits and regulate labor. Above all, this is done by increasing labor productivity through investment in new technology. In other words, industries in the United States may face increasing competition from other countries but it does not follow that workers will lose their jobs to lower wage workers in the developing countries. The (small) decline in manufacturing employment, the rise of unemployment, and the increase in part-time, low-paid work in the First World has been caused by capitalist restructuring rather than the global relocation of capital.

This emphasis on uneven development leads to a different interpretation of the collapse of the WTO talks at Seattle. While the protests outside were important in highlighting the growing intensity of global corporate power, they were not the sole (or even main) reason for the collapse of the talks. The Millennium round of talks at Seattle collapsed because of the continued importance of competition between capitalist states. The United States advocated more free market reforms in agriculture and further liberalization of trade in services; Japan rejected further liberalization; the European Union wanted developing countries to open their markets further to agricultural goods; and many

developing countries wanted to enforce Special and Differential Treatment clauses (such as preferential access for their exports as had been
agreed at previous GATT talks). The US administration also attempted
to place labor standards on to the agenda, which was opposed by
delegates from the developing world and the European Union. There
was also much resentment at the setting up of special Green Room
meetings where key issues were discussed among representatives from
a select minority of countries. These differences suggest that competition between capitalist states remains a key factor in the world economy,
and that Burbach's contention that globalization has united a
transnational capitalist class is misplaced.[8]

Summary

The anti-capitalist movement tends to argue that the globalization of
capital has led to a new global class-divide between a transnational
bourgeoisie, which enjoys unprecedented capital mobility, and the
exploited "mass." In this respect convergence has taken place across
nations and so anti-globalization struggles can take similar forms
throughout the world. I have questioned these contentions by arguing
that global capital—measured in terms of investment, trade, income
and so on—has not led to a convergence but has actually intensified
uneven development. The struggle against global capital is likely to
take different forms in different parts of the world. In saying this, I
am not arguing that there is simply a plurality of struggles and there
can be no common unity, a point I return to below. Neither am I saying
that the division of the world continues to be a basic, North–South
divide—I have argued elsewhere that geographical Core-Periphery
models have *never* been accurate (Kiely, 1995: ch. 7). What I am
arguing however is that a global politics of anti-capitalist resistance
must at least recognize the complexities and unevenness of global capitalism and the struggles against it, and that differences must be recognized. These issues—and related shortcomings—are addressed below.

Anti-capitalism, Autonomy and Direct Action

I have already emphasized the great diversity of interests and politics
that have been embraced under the anti-capitalist umbrella. This diversity is linked to the claim that these movements represent a novel

form of politics based on non-hierarchy. Burbach (2001: 2) describes such anti-hierarchical organization as a form of postmodern politics. Postmodernism here refers to a "de-centered" politics, "with a wide variety of groups coming together on any given issue to challenge the established order." Globalization has undermined modern politics based on national political parties and the nation state, and instead a new "grassroots" politics has emerged. For Burbach:

the opposition is postmodern in the sense that it has no clear rationale or logic to its activities while it instinctively recognises that it cannot be effective by working through a 'modern' political party, or by taking state power. It functions from below as an almost permanent rebellion, placing continuous demands on all the powers that be (2001: 11).

This emphasis on the organizational form of "postmodern politics" has close parallels with academic literature on "new" social movements. Touraine (1986; also Castells, 1997) sees post-1968 social movements as a response to changes in the social structure of the advanced capitalist societies, and in particular a move to a "post-industrial society." The major struggle in these societies is over the control of information and lifestyle. Melucci (1989) takes this argument a step further, arguing that movements have no meaning outside of the perceptions of those involved in a particular action. What is crucial is "the organizational forms of movements [which] are not just 'instrumental' for their goals, they are a goal in themselves. Since collective action is focussed on cultural codes, the *form* of the movement is itself a message, a symbolic challenge to the dominant codes" (1989: 60). These movements are often contrasted to the hierarchical mode of organizing, which is characteristic of political parties and organized labor movements. The former are said to focus on civil society rather than the state, on signs and cultural codes rather than material factors, and on grassroots rather than hierarchical organization (Touraine, 1981, 1986; Melucci, 1989; and Boggs, 1995).

This direct action politics now transcends national boundaries, as networks of resistance emerge through the Internet and relatively cheap and fast international travel (Cohen and Rai, 2000). Naomi Klein (2001a: 147) has argued that the Net is significant not only because it allows for the rapid global spread of information, but also because:

mobilizations are able to unfold with sparse bureaucracy and minimal hierarchy; forced consensus and labored manifestos are fading into the

background, replaced instead by a culture of constant, loosely structured and sometimes compulsive information swapping. What emerged
on the streets of Seattle and Washington was an activist model that
mirrors the organic, decentralized, interlinked pathways of the
Internet—the Internet come to life.

The anti-capitalist movement is thus not one, but many movements. Protests at Seattle and elsewhere "were activist hubs, made up
of hundreds, possibly thousands, of autonomous spokes" (Klein,
2001a: 147). Such networking was crucial in exposing OECD plans
to liberalize investment regulations through the Multilateral Agreement on Investment, and which were put on hold in early 1999.

This emphasis on the *how* of resistance is important. The Far Left
have since 1917 been dominated by a Leninist vanguardism which
assumed that the political party had *the* correct knowledge, and that it
was only a matter of time before the working class—currently suffering from "false consciousness"—would be converted to the party line.
In this way politics was reduced to the demonstration of the theoretical truth, without any recognition that "the leadership" may actually
have something to learn from those it was claiming to represent. The
anti-hierarchical way in which social movements construct their politics (or at least attempt to) is important, as it allows the views of those
people engaged in these movements to be taken seriously (see Melucci,
discussed earlier), rather than subordinated to the correct views of the
leadership. A politics based on simplistic accusations of false consciousness wish away that which needs to be explained, as it really amounts
to a disappointment with the way that people actually behave, and an
expectation of how they should behave. On the other hand, to reduce
analyses of social movements to participants' actions and ideas (as
does Melucci), is too limited. Critique remains important "because it
is a way of distinguishing between ideas which are effective in transforming people's circumstances and those which are not" (Harriss,
1994: 192). There is a need to take account of people's perceptions
but there is also a need for theoretical work that is concerned with
demonstrating the existence of underlying structures, which may not
be immediately observable (Wainwright, 1994: 104). Focusing too
much on the *how* of resistance (non-hierarchical organization, direct
action) leads to a failure to address questions around *what* is being
resisted, *who* is doing the resisting, and *why* they are doing so.[9]

Naomi Klein has herself pointed to the limitations of direct action.
She describes how in April 2000 a blockade of the streets surrounding

the IMF and World Bank headquarters in Washington collapsed as each intersection of the blockade declared autonomy. The effect was that some continued the blockade while others did not, which made it completely ineffective—delegates to the official meetings simply went down a street which was no longer blockaded. For Klein (2001a: 152) this was a metaphor for the strengths and weaknesses of the movement, arguing that the activist network around websites and e-mails "is better at speed and volume than at synthesis." For the anti-capitalist movement, the challenge to corporate globalization could easily turn into "a movement of meeting stalkers, following the trade bureaucrats as if they were the Grateful Dead" (Klein, 2001a: 152; also Brecher et al., 2000: 86–88). WTO meetings may not last as long as an interminable Grateful Dead jam, but capitalism has out-lived Jerry Garcia.

The problem then is that an excessive focus on direct action becomes a *replacement* for, rather than an engagement with, transformative politics (Kiely, 2000: 1067–68; see also McKay, 1998: 11–12; Gilbert and Pearson, 1999: 172). There is a need then for a wider engage-ment with politics. Anti-capitalist movements have "named the enemy" (Starr, 2000) and so questions need to be asked about their potential to challenge global capitalism, and some of the alternative visions that are embraced—and whether some of these should be rejected. Diversity in the movement is one thing; incoherence and lack of effectiveness is another. I illustrate this further through a discussion of two related issues: the focus on local autonomy and progressive politics; and, through a discussion of organized labor, a brief assessment of some of the problems of challenging globalization from above.

LOCALISM VERSUS GLOBALIZATION: PROGRESSIVE OR REACTIONARY?

One of the most influential campaigners at Seattle was the Indian ecofeminist Vandana Shiva. Along with a number of anti or "post-development" theorists, she supports the development of local agrar-ian societies based on subsistence production (Shiva, 1989; also Esteva and Prakash, 1997). She argues that precolonial India was character-ized by sustainable agriculture and population growth, where people were closer to nature and genuine community existed (Shiva, 1989, 2000a). Korten (1995: 269; see also Hines, 2000) also argues for the development of "locally rooted, self-reliant economies" supported by enabling global structures.

While there is nothing intrinsically wrong with some forms of localism, there are problems with how these particular ones are imagined. Shiva's populism is based on a romanticization of a mythical, pre-industrial past.[10] For Shiva, the Golden Age was pre-colonial India, an era of massive social inequalities, caste oppression and famine (Jackson, 1994; Nanda, 1991). She also refers to India as a predominantly Hindu society, and backs the ban on the slaughter of cows (Shiva, 2000b), a measure used by Hindu communalists to discriminate against Muslims. The politics of other populists may not be so questionable, but their "progressive" credentials need to be scrutinized. Korten (1995: 307) argues that his vision of sustainability is "actively pro-business and pro-market" but it favors "local over global businesses and markets." This latest version of "small is beautiful" champions the virtues of local communities, small-scale industry and peasant agriculture. Populists tend to argue that peasant communities are exploited by outside forces such as the state and the urban classes (Lipton, 1977). This argument, also made by the World Bank (Schiff and Valdes, 1992), abstracts from class and gender differentiation *within* communities. Differentiation is internal to the peasantry and poorer peasants "are unable to reproduce their means of production in the face of multiple pressures—including competition with other peasants over land, labour, access to inputs, to credit or to markets" (Bernstein, 1990: 73). This leads to marginalization and ultimately dispossession. On the other hand, rich peasants are able to accumulate and employ the labor of others.[11] Small-scale development is thus not intrinsically progressive—local or national capitalists are likely to be as exploitative as large-scale transnational capital, and differentiation (among peasants or owners of small industries) will occur in conditions of supposedly perfect competition. Marx (cited in Kitching, 1982: 32) rightly criticized Proudhon and the like minded populists when he argued that "(t)hey all want the impossible, namely the conditions of bourgeois existence without the necessary consequences of these conditions."

In some respects contemporary populists are worse, as they combine a focus on scale with a deep ecology critique of industrialization. This often leads to a resource pessimism that provides no grounds for examining the ways in which technologies may utilize resources efficiently or discover new ones, and even develop environmentally friendly methods of production. Capitalist industrialization is in many ways destructive of the environment but contemporary populism tends to see this as a "zero sum" game. This can lead to a neo-Malthusian perspective in which people are considered a burden as they consume the limited resources of "Mother Earth." Korten (1995: 34–35) appears to approvingly cite studies which propose reducing the world's population. He does at least recognize that these studies may have "controversial assumptions," but he later (pp. 290–91) approvingly cites an awful study based on the division of the world into three socioecological classes—overconsumers, sustainers, and the marginalized. The 3.3 billion sustainers (US $700 to $75,000 per capita incomes) are in some ways a model, as these people are meeting their basic needs in relatively sustainable ways. In these societies people travel by bicycle, eat healthy unpackaged foods, and recycle. For Korten (1995: 280) "(a)lthough their lifestyles do not correspond to our vision of consumer affluence, neither is it a vision of hardship...." This breathtaking statement completely ignores the massive inequalities in these societies, not to mention overcrowded roads (clearly some people do not cycle), low life-expectancy, low female-literacy rates, high infant-mortality rates—and, it should be stressed high rates of population growth. Korten's patronizing romanticism betrays the contemporary populist's distrust of technology (Kiely, 1999: 40–41), and with it a reluctance to recognize that development can have desirable results, such as increases in life-expectancy and improvements in health care. There are, of course, massive inequalities in the distribution of these benefits but this is a product of the uneven development of global capitalism rather than the undesirable consequences of industrial technology.

Other thinkers in the anti-capitalist movement do not repeat the populist fallacies of Shiva, Korten and deep ecologists, but localism is still overemphasized. Escobar (1995: 223) and Burbach (2001) both recognize that global capitalism has in some respects marginalized certain localities, but argue that this should be regarded as an opportunity rather than a danger. Burbach (2001: 94) states that "the very process of globalization marginalizes more and more people as incomes and even jobs are concentrated in fewer and fewer hands, leaving little else for many but the informal economy and alternative economic endeavors." Such initiatives may include cooperatives and Local Exchange Trading Schemes (LETS) based on people in local communities exchanging skills and services. These schemes represent an alternative mechanism of economic integration to the market, based on "socially embedded forms of exchange in small scale symmetrical communities" (Hettne, 1995: 4–5)—what Polanyi (1957: 47–50) called "reciprocity." Such schemes can lead to the kind of differentiation discussed above, this is not inevitable and they can be important to those marginalized by global (and local) capitalism.[12] However, they at best provide important means of distribution in situations of resource deprivation. In addition to such initiatives then, more attention needs to be paid to what Polanyi (1957: 48, 50–52) identified as a third mechanism of economic integration—that of redistribution.

This is a key question and it is one that a politics, based principally on autonomy and direct action, largely ignores. Such a policy involves a politics that goes beyond mere negation, and which constructively engages with the need for (global, national, local) institutions to facilitate this process. I return to this point here. A politics which overemphasises autonomy can easily descend into one that advocates local delinking or, on a personal level, a politics of "dropping out" rather than changing the system (Pieterse, 2000: 192). Politics based on autonomy must also address the question of what this autonomy means for different people (Jordan, 1994: 50). In other words, as I argued in my discussion of globalization from above, anti-capitalism must address the complexities and ambiguities of corporate globalization in ways that go beyond mere negation.

RESISTING GLOBALIZATION FROM ABOVE: ALLIANCES, DIFFERENCES, AND THE CASE OF ORGANIZED LABOR

Earlier I criticized the view that globalization had led to a convergence between different parts of the world. Apologists such as the WTO and Meghnad Desai argue that globalization entails a potential "levelling up," while critics argue that it has led to a "levelling down." Instead I argued two crucial points: (a) that insofar as there has been a levelling down in the "advanced" capitalist countries, this has been caused by competition between advanced capitals and defeats of organised labor, rather than being a product of the supposed hypermobility of capital; (b) uneven development has intensified, leading to a *divergence* rather than convergence between countries, regions, and so on.[13] I want to finish this chapter by drawing out one or two of the political implications for a progressive global politics. In particular I want to return to some of the issues outlined at the start of the article, which related to the collapse of "labor and development friendly" regimes (Silver and Arrighi, 2001), and relate this to my discussion of the limitations of direct action politics.

As I have already outlined, organized labor is in many respects in crisis. This has led many to conclude that it is no longer a significant social and political force. Two reasons are cited. First, that changes in employment patterns have undermined the significance of work. Second, that even if the first argument is rejected, the fragmentation of labor is too great and so the most significant agents of change are the new social movements. The first claim, often associated with the work of Jeremy Rifkin (1995), is that automation is displacing workers in the North and that this technological development, and the low costs and fast delivery of these products has made it impossible for the South to compete. However, the figures for manufacturing employment alone undermine this claim. The number of industrial workers in the 24 leading economies was 51 million in 1900; 88 million in 1950; 120 million by 1971; and 112 million by 1998. In the United States manufacturing employment actually increased from 26 million in 1971 to 31 million in 1998 (Feinstein, 2000: 53). In addition there has been a massive expansion of urban (and industrial) employment in the former Third World, and in the 1980s and 1990s, the biggest job creators were the United States and Japan—the most technologically advanced societies (Castells, 1996: 251–64). These jobs—often poorly paid service work—may not be of a high quality, but the fact that they exist hardly entails "the end of work."

As to the second claim, it is true that in the "advanced" capitalist countries at least, labor movements have declined in significance in recent years. However, whether this is a terminal decline is another question. Labor was slow to respond to capitalist restructuring in the late 19th century and it took 25 years to recover from this process (Arrighi, 1996). In this case then, the decline was a cyclical and not a terminal one. For labor to recover in the current period then, new strategies have to be developed to adapt to new situations. Unions have made some progress in this respect, organizing workers in new sectors and focusing on issues wider than just wage demands. Trade unions in parts of the former Third World have set an example in this respect, as they have consciously formed alliances with social movements, thus breaking down the false "oppositions between workplace and community, economic and political struggles, and between formal sector workers and the working poor" (Munck, 2000: 93). In May–June 2000 alone, there were six massive strikes (in India, Argentina, Nigeria, South Korea, South Africa and Uruguay) explicitly opposed to global neo-liberalism, each of which made alliances beyond the immediate workplace (Moody, 2000).

One area in which such adaptation is needed, and which is most relevant for our purposes, is that of global labor solidarity. Some analyses going back to the 1970s (Frobel et al., 1980), argued that the globalization of production has created the material basis for such solidarity. The decline of industrial employment and rise in unemployment in the core was said to be accompanied by the "super-exploitation" of low-wage workers in the former periphery. The creation of a global labor market was said to create a common interest among workers— resisting unemployment in the core, resisting "super-exploitation" in the periphery. This scenario is clearly implicit in the views of anti-globalizers, who argue that a race to the bottom has occurred which has been caused by the global mobility of capital (see earlier discussion). It should be clear that I reject this argument because such a "race to the bottom" does not occur evenly throughout the world economy, and is not primarily caused by the relocation of productive capital to low-wage areas. Moreover, even if we accept the scenario outlined above—that is, a zero sum game between employment in Core and Peripheral capitalist countries—then it is equally likely to encourage calls for protectionism and even worse. The AFL–CIO's Campaign for Global Fairness was established in part to oppose China joining the WTO. Its main motivation appears to have been fear of cheap imports rather than concern with human rights abuses in that country. Moreover, despite high rates of exploitation, workers in the developing world do not want to lose their jobs in factories. A progressive position—and one that is contrary to the views of Vandana Shiva for instance—is not one that closes the factories but one that shows solidarity with the fight for better conditions, wages (and perhaps ultimately, wider social transformation).

There have been intense debates around these issues, and particularly over the question of whether there should be social clauses embedded in trade agreements. From outside of the movement, critics like Desai (2000) argue that such calls represent protectionist interests in the "First World," which are intent on depriving the Third World of the right to develop. Such views are echoed by many thinkers within the movement. For instance, David Bacon (2000: 127–28) argues that the Clinton administration's (admittedly half-hearted) support for labor standards ignores the fact that successive US administrations have pursued policies that help to maintain global inequalities. Social clauses therefore only address the symptoms and not the causes of world poverty. On the other hand Bacon (2000: 126) at times appears to reject the need for independent trade unions in China for example, and thus displays a blind faith in local production, which will automatically promote development.[14] Moreover, on their own low labor-costs do not guarantee investment as my discussion of investment flows above made clear.

One alternative strategy promoted by anti-globalization campaigners is a grassroots mobilization of trade unionists promoting global solidarity, often through the Internet (Waterman, 1998: 72–73). Such a strategy may be useful, as in the case of the Liverpool dockers' struggle of 1995–96. Grassroots organization is crucial to the development of a solidarity that moves beyond both abstract internationalist rhetoric and an economism that focuses narrowly on immediate wage demands. Demonstrating that technological progress is responsible for more job losses than relocation to the South is important, but the fact remains that competition in some sectors does exist between workers of different countries of the North, and often the newly industrializing countries too. Grassroots solidarity therefore can only be developed through longer term goals based on labour's independence from capital, rather than immediate wage demands.

This perspective based on struggle from below has undoubtedly made some headway among sections of the North American working class for instance, and the anti-capitalist struggles deserve much of the credit for this development. However, grassroots struggles should not be fetishized and, on its own, such a strategy may suffer from the same weaknesses of direct action politics discussed above. Moreover, labor (and other) networks are vulnerable to charges that they lack democratic legitimacy as they are accountable to no one. What is also needed then is the expansion of (democratic) organizational structures in which long-term solidarity strategies can be developed. Such strategies must recognize the reality of both uneven development and poor working conditions. Thus for example "no sweat" campaigns could be linked to the promotion of debt reduction for the developing world. Remarkably even the AFL–CIO endorsed protests against the IMF and World Bank in April 2000 (Brecher et al., 2000: 93). It is also both likely and desirable that trade unionists will also continue to pressurize and not just bypass existing institutions, including their own trade union and the nation state. These comments therefore imply that global networks represent an important mobilizing strategy for labor solidarity, but that this does not mean that existing institutions should simply be ignored.

CONCLUSION

Anti-capitalist movements have historically been Leninist in character. Key thinkers in the current movement have stressed the novelty of anti-globalization protest and stressed its non-hierarchical character, and its autonomy from existing institutions. But there are problems with an overemphasis on direct action, both in terms of organization *per se*, and in terms of the critique of corporate globalization. A politics that focuses solely on local initiatives effectively means delinking which, on its own, is a recipe for underdevelopment or "dropping out". A politics that simply attempts to by-pass established institutions through the construction of a global civil society, supposedly totally independent of states and markets, similarly leads to a politics of escapism. Leninist politics recognizes these problems, and suggests that single-issue campaigns must be linked in ways that criticize the system as a whole. While there is some truth to this argument, the problem with this position is that it leads to an ultra-leftist politics proposing an "impossiblist" revolution whereby capitalism is simply "smashed."

An alternative politics must develop the strengths and move beyond the weaknesses of the contemporary anti-capitalist movement. The undoubted strengths are its critique of neo-liberalism, its recognition of the need to regulate capitalism, the development of a global consciousness and solidarity, a recognition of the need to develop genuinely democratic organization, and a redefintion and widening of the meaning of politics. Existing institutions work "on impoverished definitions of what constitutes legitimate 'politics,' which themselves 'depoliticize' other arenas and issues" (Corrigan and Sayer, 1991: 206). Revolution is not simply the capture of (state) power but involves the creation of new subjectivities.

However—against the voluntarism of much of the anti-capitalist movement—radical change must be done on the basis of current resources, which in part means an engagement with, rather than outright rejection of, existing institutions.[15] The purity of Leninism ("smash the institutions") must be rejected, but so too must the purity of autonomism ("autonomy from the institutions"). As Bromley (2001: 10) argues, "if the protests are...ultimately about a politics that 'embraces globalization but seeks to wrest it from the multinationals,'[16] then if it is not through...multilateral forums (in combination with political pressure at the national level), where is the social and democratic re-regulation of neo-liberal capitalism to be located?" The second phase of Polanyi's double movement requires local, national, and global regulation (and possibly transcendence) of neo-liberal capitalism. In fairness there is a great deal of recognition of these problems among key thinkers within the various movements, but a pervasive localism persists.

These comments imply moving beyond either/or politics: it is not local versus the global; civil society versus the state; rejectionism versus engagement; reform versus revolution; autonomy versus integration. Many in the anti-capitalist movement will accept this argument (Brecher et al., 2000), but may also ignore the ways in which many activists embrace such either/or positions. The key question is, thus, the terms on which such positions are embraced. Hence, the need to develop perspective that effectively critiques globalization from above. Such a critique can form a basis for concrete and coherent political programs—which is not the same as a rigid blueprint. Naomi Klein (2001b: 2) has argued that since Seattle, the movement has began to "recast itself as a pro-democracy movement." If this is the case, then the movement is committed to general goals, orientations and policies that unite people across specific differences. And this implies something that the anti-capitalist movement cannot evade—an engagement with (modern, ideological) politics.

NOTES

1. The terms anti-globalization and anti-capitalist are not without problems, especially as it has allowed critics to represent the movement as hostile to all forms of globalization. I use these terms for ease of recognition only. This chapter was written before September 11, 2001. I explore the question of the relationship between "anti-globalization" and "anti-war" positions—and the simultaneous rejection of Third Way and fundamentalist anti-imperialism in Kiely 2003.
2. Unemployment increased in the West from the 1970s, but was less of a problem in Japan until the 1990s.
3. Some qualifications will be made to this Fordism/flexibility dichotomy later in the text. Similarly, my discussion of the politics of anti-capitalist movements will suggest that the defeat of labor—and possibly development—is far from total. Nevertheless, the tendency towards a new era of capitalist development (things *have* changed, though not as much as some of the writers discussed imply) needs to be recognized.
4. This is not to say that such a distinction cannot be made, but that Giddens' separation is too rigid, and that may be one reason for the absence of any serious discussion of inequality in his current work. The questions of inequality and difference are touched on further in the text, with particular reference to the question of "the local."

5. The question of whether these movements are anti-capitalist—and indeed what we mean by anti-capitalist—is discussed further in the text.

6. Desai also makes some more specific arguments concerning social and environmental clauses in trade agreements. I examine these debates in more detail later in the text.

7. In their critique of the World Bank, Sender and Smith (1985), whose work owes a clear debt to Warren (1980), reject delinking from the world economy, but still advocate some protection for agriculture and/or industry. Desai replicates the "inevitable developmentalism" weakness of Warren's work and applies this to a period of (neo-liberal) capitalism in which it is even more inappropriate.

8. In this respect Burbach's theory of globalization is similar to Kautsky's equally misplaced theory of "ultra-imperialism."

9. Post-structuralists also evade important questions about social movements. Escobar (2001: 2) for instance argues that social movements are "historically privileged spaces" which can challenge the established order. He further argues that this argument is founded on a "political desire to find in social movements sources of alternatives, hopes and theories of how the world can be made differently." The problem with this argument is that it is politically opportunist and tautological—he wants to see in social movements the potential for autonomous spaces, and so he then proceeds to represent them in this way. Some social movements may be progressive in the ways that Escobar hopes (though whether any can be completely autonomous from dominant discourses is questionable) but this must be demonstrated rather than hoped for. Escobar's (2001: 2) position is derived from a wish to move beyond "the realist position that representation is constrained by the real," which allows him to use arguments, concepts and so on in any way that he (rather than the real world) sees fit.

10. Golden Age myths are not new. In the 1930s, the Leavis' lamented the loss of community at the turn of the century; in the 1890s, Hardy wrote of the lost England of the 1830s; in the 1830s Cobbett regarded the 1770s as a golden age. As Raymond Williams points out (1993) each of these periods was one of "exploitation of a most thoroughgoing kind."

11. These comments do not imply that such differentiation takes place in exactly the same way, irrespective of time and place (see Bernstein, 1990, 1994, 2001; and Byres, 1991).

12. I have only touched on the issue of class formation and capitalist development in this chapter. Marxists rightly point to the reality of class differentiation in local settings. In stressing such differentiation a potential problem arises. Capitalism may be conceptualized in such an all-embracing way that it is difficult to see any social transformation without a mythical "smashing" of the total system. In conceptualizing capitalism in such a totalizing way, and proposing only an impossiblist revolution as an alternative, capitalism's opponents can contribute to its continued (eternal) hegemony (Gibson-Graham, 1996). On the other hand attempts to transcend capitalism through an overemphasis on discourse or the search for "autonomous spaces" can ignore "the dull compulsion of economic relations." In many ways, this is what is at stake in current arguments between Marxists and poststructuralists, and radical and postdevelopment theory. There are also close parallels with development debates of the 1970s, between Marxists and neo-populists—see for instance Kitching, 1982; Kiely, 1995, 1998a, 1999; and Cowen, 2001.

13. On uneven development see Shaikh, 1978; Kiely, 1998b; Weeks, 2001. Kay (1975)—often wrongly described as a Warrenite analysis—is also crucial.

14. See further my comments on local production.
15. In contrast to the ultra-left voluntarism of Cleaver (1989) for example, who demands nothing less than the immediate abolition of debt, closure of the IMF, and end of development.
16. The quote within a quote—one that again shows the tendency to champion the local over the global—is from Naomi Klein's *No Logo*. This criticism notwithstanding, Klein's book remains by far the best book to come out of the movement.

REFERENCES

Amin, A. (ed.). 1994. *Post-Fordism: A Reader.* Oxford: Blackwell.
Arrighi, G. 1996. "Workers of the World at Century's End" in *Review.* vol. 19, no. 3.
Arrighi, G., T. Hopkins and I. Wallerstein. 1989. *Anti-Systemic Movements.* London: Verso.
Bacon, D. 2000. "Will a Social Clause in Trade Agreements Advance International Solidarity" in K. Danaher and R. Burbach (eds) 2000. *Globalize This!* Monroe: Common Courage, pp.124–28.
Barnet, R. 1996. "Stateless Corporations: Lords of the Global Economy" in K. Danaher (ed.) 1996. *Corporations are Gonna Get Your Mama.* Maine: Common Courage Press, pp. 35–42.
Bernstein, H. 1990. "Taking the Part of Peasants?" in H. Bernstein et al. 1990. *The Food Question.* London: Earthscan, pp. 69–79.
_____. 1994. "Agrarian Classes in Capitalist Development" in L. Sklair (ed.) 1994. *Capitalism and Development.* London: Routledge, pp. 40–71.
_____. 2001. "'The Peasantry' in Global Capitalism: Who, Where and Why?" in *The Socialist Register,* London: Merlin, pp. 25–52.
Boggs, C. 1995. "Rethinking the Sixties Legacy: From New Left to Social Movements" in S. M. Lyman (ed.). 1995. *Social Movements: Critiques, Concepts, Case Studies.* London: Macmillan, pp. 331–35.
Brecher, J., T. Costello and B. Smith. 2000. *Globalization from Below.* Cambridge, Mass.: South End Press.
Briefing, Panos. 1999. "More Power to the World Trade Organization?", no. 37, *www.oneworld.org./panos/briefing.*
Bromley, S. 2001. "The golden straightjacket" in *Radical Philosophy,* no. 107, pp. 5–10.
Brown, P. and H. Lauder. 2001. *Capitalism and Social Progress.* London: Palgrave.
Burbach, R. 2001. *Globalization and Postmodern Politics.* London: Pluto.
Byres, T. 1991. "The Agrarian Question and Differing Forms of Capitalist Agrarian Transition: An Essay with Reference to Asia" in J. Breman and S. Mundle (eds) 1991. *Rural Transformation in Asia.* Oxford: Oxford University Press, pp. 5–72.
Carnoy, M., M. Castells, S. Cohen and F. H. Cardoso. 1993. *The New Global Economy in the Information Age.* Pennsylvania: Pennsylvania State University Press.
Castells, M. 1996. *The Rise of the Network Society.* Oxford: Blackwell.
_____. 1997. *The Power of Identity.* Oxford: Blackwell.
Cerny, P. 2000. "Restructuring the Political Arena: Globalization and the Paradoxes of the Competition State" in R. Germain (ed.) 2000. *Globalization and its Critics.* London: Mamillan, pp. 117–38.

Cleaver, H. 1989. "Close the IMF, Abolish Debt, and End Development" in *Capital and Class*, vol. 39, pp. 17–39.

Cohen, R. and S. Rai (eds). 2000. *Global Social Movements*. London: Athlone.

Corrigan, P. and D. Sayer. 1991. *The Great Arch*. Oxford: Blackwell.

Cowen, M. 2001. "Quakes of Development" in *Historical Materialism*, no. 6, pp. 149–214.

Daily News, May 2, 2001 (Sri Lanka).

Danaher, K. 1996. "Introduction: Corporate Power and the Quality of Life" in K. Danaher (ed.). 1996. *Corporations are Gonna Get Your Mama*. Monroe: Common Courage Press, pp. 15–31.

Desai, M. 2000. "Seattle: A Tragi-Comedy" in B. Gunnell and D. Timms (eds) 2000. *After Seattle*. London: Catalyst, pp. 41–45.

Dicken, P. 1992. *Global Shift*. London: Paul Chapman.

Dunkley, G. 2000. *The Free Trade Adventure*. London: Zed.

Escobar, A. 1995. *Encountering Development*. Princeton: Princeton University Press.

——. 2001. "A brief response to Ray Kiely's 'Reply to Escobar'" in *Development*, vol. 43, no. 4, online, *www.sidint.org/journal/online/Escobar434.htm*.

Esteva, G. and M. Prakash. 1997. "From Global Thinking to Local Thinking" in M. Rahnema and V. Bawtree (eds). 1997. *The Post-Development Reader*. London: Zed, pp. 277–89.

Feinstein, C. 2000. "Structural Change in the Developed Countries in the Twentieth Century" in *Oxford Review of Economics*, no. 1.

Fraser, N. 1997. *Justice Interruptus: Critical Reflections on the 'Postsocialist' Condition*. London: Routledge.

Frobel, F., J. Heinrichs and O. Kreye. 1980. *The New International Division of Labour*. Cambridge: Cambridge University Press.

Gereffi, G. 1994. "Capitalism, Development and Global Commodity Chains" in L. Sklair (ed.). *Capitalism and Development*. London: Routledge, pp. 211–41.

Gibson-Graham, J. K. 1996. *The End of Capitalism (as we knew it)*. Oxford: Blackwell.

Giddens, A. 1991. *The Consequences of Modernity*. Cambridge: Polity.

Gilbert, J. and E. Pearson. 1999. *Discographies*. London: Routledge.

Gill, S. 1995. "Theorizing the Interregnum: The Double Movement and Global Politics in the 1990s" in B. Hettne (ed.) 1995. *International Political Economy*. London: Zed, pp. 65–99.

Habermas, J. 1981. "New social movements" in *Telos*, vol. 49, pp. 33–37.

Harriss, J. 1994. Between Economism and Postmodernism: Reflections on Research on 'Agrarian Change' in India", in D. Booth (ed.). 1994. *Rethinking Social Movement*. London: Longman, pp. 172–96.

——. 2000. "The second 'great transformation'? Capitalism at the end of the twentieth century" in T. Allen and A. Thomas (eds). 2000. *Poverty and Development ino the Twenty First Century*. Oxford: Oxford University Press, pp. 325–42.

Harvey, D. 1989. *The Condition of Postmodernity*. Oxford: Blackwell.

Hertz, N. 2001. *The Silent Takeover*. London: Heinemann.

Hettne, B. 1995. "Introduction: The International Political Economy of Transformation" in B. Hettne (ed.). 1995. *International Political Economy*. London: Zed, pp. 1–30.

Hines, C. 2000. *Localization: A Global Manifesto*. London: Zed.

Hirst, P. and G. Thompson. 1999. *Globalization in Question*. Second Edition. Cambridge: Polity.

Hoogvelt, A. 2001. *Globalization and the Postcolonial World*. London: Palgrave.

Jackson, C. 1994. "Gender Analysis and Environmentalisms" in M. Redclift and T. Benton (eds). *Social Theory and the Environment*. London: Routledge, pp. 113–49.

Jefferys, S. 2001. "Western European Trade Unionism at 2000" in *The Socialist Register*. London: Merlin, pp. 143–69.

Jordan, T. 1994. *Reinventing Revolution*. Aldershot: Avebury.

Kaplinsky, R. 2001. "Is globalization all it is cracked up to be?" in *Review of International Political Economy*, vol. 8, no. 1, pp. 45–65.

Kay, G. 1975. *Development and Underdevelopment*. London: Macmillan.

Kiely, R. 1995. *Sociology and Development: The Impasse and Beyond*. London: UCL Press.

_____. 1998a. *Industrialization and Development: A Comparative Analysis*. London: UCL Press.

_____. 1998b. "Globalization, post-Fordism, and the Contemporary Context of Development" in *International Sociology*, vol. 13, no. 1, pp. 95–114.

_____. 1999. "The Last Refuge of the Noble Savage? A Critical Account of Post-Development" in *European Journal of Development Research*, vol. 11, no. 1, pp. 30–55.

_____. 2000. "Globalization: From Domination to Resistance" in *Third World Quarterly*.

_____. 2003. "The Race to the Bottom and International Labour Solidarity" in *Review*, vol. 26, no. 1, pp. 67–88.

Kitching, G. 1982. *Development and Underdevelopment in Historical Perspective*. London: Methuen.

Klein, N. 2000. *No Logo*. London: Flamingo.

_____. 2001a. "The Vision Thing: Are the Protests Unfocused or are Critics Missing the Point?" in K. Danaher (ed.) 2001. *Democratizing the Global Economy*. Monroe: Common Courage Press, pp. 145–55.

_____. 2001b. "A Fete for the End of the End of History" *www.nologo.org*.

Korten, D. 1995. *When Corporations Rule the World*. London: Earthscan.

_____. 1996. "When Corporations Rule the World" in K. Danaher (ed.). 1996. *Corporations are Gonna Get Your Mama*. Monroe: Common Courage Press, pp. 49–56.

Lash, S. and J. Urry. 1987. *The End of Organised Capitalism*. Cambridge: Polity.

Lipietz, A. 1986. "New Tendencies in the International Division of Labour: Regimes of Accumulation and Modes of Regulation" in A. Scott and M. Storper (eds). *Production, Work, Territory*. London: Allen and Unwin, pp. 16–40.

Lipton, M. 1977. *Why Poor People Stay Poor*. London: Temple Smith.

McKay, G. (ed.). 1998. *DIY Culture*. London: Verso.

Melucci, A. 1989. *Nomads of the Present: Social Movements and Individual Needs in Contemporary Society*. Philadelphia: Temple University Press.

Monbiot, G. 2000. *The Captive State*. London: Macmillan.

Moody, K. 2000. "Mass Strike Around the World: Global Labor Stands Up to Global Capital" in *Labor Notes*, no. 256.

Munck, R. 1998. Labour Dilemmas and Labour Futures", in R. Munck and P. Waterman (eds). 1998. *Labour Worldwide in the Era of Globalization*. London: Macmillan, pp. 3–21.

_____. 2000. "Labour in the Global", in R. Cohen and S. Rai (eds). *Global Social Movements*. London: Athlone Press, pp. 83–100.

Murray, R. 1989. "Fordism and Post-Fordism" in S. Hall and M. Jacques (eds). 1989. *New Times*. London: Lawrence and Wishart, pp. 38–52.

Nanda, M. 1991. Is Modern Science a Western Patriarchal Myth?" in *South Asia Bulletin*, vol. 11, no. 1–2, pp. 32–61.

Pieterse, J. N. 2000. "Globalization and Emancipation: From Local Empowerment to Global Reform" in B. Gills (eds). 2000. *Globalization and the Politics of Resistance*. London: Macmillan, pp. 189–206.

Polanyi, K. 1957. The Great Transformation. New York: Beacon.

Rifkin, J. 1995. *The End of Work*. New York: Putnam.

Rinehart, J. 1996. "The Ideology of Competitiveness: Pitting Worker Against Worker" in K. Danaher (ed.). 1996. *Corporations are Gonna Get Your Mama*. Maine: Common Courage Press, pp. 87–96.

Ross, A. (ed.). 1997. *No Sweat*! London: Verso.

Ruigrok, W. and R. van Tulder. 1995. *The Logic of International Restructuring*. London: Routledge.

Sassen, S. 2000. *Cities in a World Economy* (Second Edition). Thousand Oaks: Pine Forge.

Schiff, M. and Valdes. 1992. *The Plunder of Agriculture in Developing Countries*. Washington: World Bank.

Sender, J. and S. Smith. 1985. "What's Right with the Berg Report and What's Left of its Critics" in *Capital and Class*, vol. 24, pp. 125–46.

Shaikh, A. 1978. "Foreign Trade and the Law of Value" in *Science and Society*, vol. 44, pp. 27–57.

Shiva, V. 1989. *Staying Alive*. London: Zed.

————. **2000a.** *Poverty and Globalization*, BBC Reith Lecture, *www.news.bbc.co.uk/hi/english/static/events/reith_2000/lecture5.stm*.

————. **2000b.** *Stolen Harvest*, Cambridge, Mass.: South End Press.

Silver, B. and G. Arrighi. 2001. "Workers North and South" in *The Socialist Register*. London: Merlin, pp. 53–77.

Smith, N. 1990. *Uneven Development* (Second Edition). Oxford: Blackwell.

Starr, A. 2000. *Naming the Enemy*. London: Zed.

Storper, M. 1991. *Industrialization, Economic Development and the Regional Question in the Third World*. London: Pion.

The Economist, **1999,** Editorial: Clueless in Seattle, Dec. 6.

Thompson, G. 2000. "Economic globalization?" in D. Held (ed.). *A Globalizing World? Culture, Economics, Politics*. London: Routledge, pp. 85–126.

Touraine, A. 1981. *The Voice and the Eye: An Analysis of Social Movements*. Cambridge: Cambridge University Press.

————. **1986.** "Unionism as a Social Movement" in S.M. Lipset (ed.). *Unions in Transition*. San Francisco: ICS Press.

Wainwright, H. 1994. *Arguments for a New Left*. Oxford: Blackwell.

Walton J. and Seddon D. 1994. *Free Markets and Food Riots*. Oxford: Blackwell.

Warren, B. 1980. *Imperialism: Pioneer of Capitalism*. London: Verso.

Waterman, P. 1998. *Globalization, Social Movements and the New Internationalism*. London: Mansell.

Weeks, J. 2001. "The Expansion of Capital and Uneven Development on a World Scale" in *Capital and Class*, no.74, pp. 9–30.

Williams, R. 1993. *The Country and the City*. London: Hogarth.

World Trade Organisation. 2000. "Seven Common Misunderstandings about the WTO" in F. Lechner and J. Boli (eds). 2000. *The Globalization Reader*. Oxford: Blackwell, pp. 236–39.

Young, I. 1997. "Unruly Categories: A Critique of Nancy Fraser's Dual Systems Theory" in *New Left Review*, no. 222, pp. 147–60.

11

THE GLOBALIZATION OF NOTHING

George Ritzer and Michael Ryan

While social theorists have long been interested in globalization, there has been an explosion of work on the topic in recent years. The flowering of such theories is a reflection of the fact that globalization is of great concern to, and of enormous significance for, much of the world's population. See for instance, Bauman (1998); Beck (2000); Giddens (2000); and Kellener, (2002). Virtually every nation and the lives of billions of people throughout the world are being transformed, often quite dramatically, by globalization.[1] The degree and significance of its impact can be seen virtually everywhere one looks (e.g., in the shopping malls that increasingly dot many areas of the developed world, the vast array of franchises found in them, and the goods and services offered by those franchises), most visibly in the now-commonplace protests that accompany high-level meetings of such key global organizations as the World Trade Organization (WTO), the International Monetary Fund (IMF) and the World Bank (WB). As is made clear by the magnitude of the issues before these organizations, the level of protest against them, and the fact that these protests have taken place in widely dispersed geographic areas, people throughout the world feel very strongly that they are confronting matters of great importance.

They feel deeply about many things, including the fact that not only they may not be profiting economically from globalization, in fact, they may be further disadvantaged by it. They may also balk over the external control over their lives by international agencies (such as the IMF) and other nations (especially the United States). Furthermore, there is a fear that indigenous culture is being undermined and over-whelmed by either a global culture or one associated with another nation (again, especially that of the United States). Of course, this opposition is not found everywhere. Developed nations that clearly gain from globalization are less likely to be opposed than less developed nations that feel disadvantaged by it.

Given the public furor, and the enormous academic attention to the topic, the title of this essay seems, to put it mildly, counter-intuitive. In fact, since globalization is so clearly something of great importance (dealing with issues such as greater choice versus lost identity; homogeneity versus heterogeneity), how can we dare to discuss the globalization of nothing? The wording is important here. We are *not* arguing that globalization *is* nothing, but rather that there is a globalization *of* nothing and, further, that this form of globalization, like the process in general, is of enormous importance.

This chapter will focus on globalization in the realm of consumption, but that is not to say that similar arguments could not be made about other areas of the economy (especially production), as well as about politics, religion, medicine, and so on. Furthermore, consumption is an integral part of these other social institutions (e.g., the consumption of medical services, the voter as consumer, and so on). Finally, the focus here is on consumption because of its growing importance not only in the United States, but throughout much of the rest of the developed world. However, issues of production are important in this analysis, especially the difference between that which is mass-produced and that which is more individualized.

NOTHING AND SOMETHING

Before we can proceed further, we need some basic definitions. *Nothing* is defined as a *social form that is generally[2] centrally[3] conceived, controlled and comparatively devoid of distinctive substantive content*. This leads to a definition of *something* as a *social form that is generally[4] indigenously conceived, controlled and comparatively rich in distinctive substantive content*. This makes it clear that neither *nothing* nor *something* exists independently of each other, *each makes sense only when paired with, and contrasted to the other*. While presented as a dichotomy,[5] this implies a *continuum* from *something* to *nothing* and that is precisely the way the concepts will be employed here—as the two poles of that continuum.

Thus, for example, in the realm of consumption (our focal concern in this chapter), the Mills corporation (and others like it) create and control shopping malls (e.g., Potomac Mills in Virginia, Sawgrass

Mills in Florida) as forms, as structures that, in themselves, have little, if any, distinctive content (except, perhaps, for comparatively minor variations in structural design and architectural nuance); the content of any given mall depends on what (particular shops, goods, restaurants, employees, customers, and so on) happens to be in it. A mall in one part of the world (say, London or Hong Kong) may be structured much like that in another location (Chicago or Mexico City, for example), but there will be innumerable differences in their specific contents. More importantly, people use the mall in countless ways, many of which may not have been anticipated by the mall designers and owners, and their behaviors will vary greatly in different parts of the globe. The basic structure of the mall is repeated over and over, but the contents will vary, especially in different parts of the world.

If, within the confines of this analysis, the shopping mall is an example of *nothing* (or at least as lying toward that end of the continuum), then we can think of a local farmers' market as something (flea markets, craft fairs, cooperatives are other examples). That is, it is locally conceived and controlled and each one has a great deal of distinctive content. To this day, a farmers' market is created anew each time the farmers, who happen at that particular time to have produce to sell, arrive at the appointed place. There is no pre-set structure into which farmers must fit, although they may, by custom, sell particular things in particular spots. Which farmers are there, and what they offer for sale, will vary greatly from one time (especially season) to another. Most importantly, once the market has ended for the day, whatever structure has been created will be dismantled and then created again, perhaps somewhat differently, the next market day. And, the farmers' market is no mere throwback to an earlier time period; it remains viable not only in many areas of the United States, but even more commonly in most other parts of the world, including the highly developed countries of western Europe.

GLOBALIZATION: GLOCALIZATION AND GROBALIZATION

Globalization can be defined as "the compression of the world and the intensification of consciousness of the world as a whole" (Robertson, 1992). As it has come to be used, globalization encompasses a number of trans-national processes that, while they can be seen as global in reach, are separable from each other. It is beyond the scope of this

chapter to deal with the full range (~~~~~~~
Antonio and Bonanno, 2000), but two broad ~~~~~~~
glocalization and *grobalization*—will be of interest here. The concept
of glocalization gets to the heart of what most contemporary theorists associated with globalization theory think about the nature of
transnational processes.[6] *Glocalization* can be defined as *the interpenetration of the global and the local resulting in unique outcomes in different geographic areas*. The concept of *grobalization*, coined here for the
first time as a much-needed companion to the notion of glocalization,[7]
focuses on *the imperialistic ambitions of nations, corporations, organizations, and the like and their desire, indeed need, to impose themselves on
various geographic areas*.[8] Their main interest is in seeing their power,
influence, and in many cases profits grow (hence the term *grobalization*)
throughout the world. No necessary value judgment is implied here,
there can be negatives associated with the glocal (lack of openness to
some useful grobal inputs) and positives tied to the grobal (the delivery of new medications and medical technologies).

It is argued that grobalization tends to be associated with the proliferation of nothing (e.g., the shopping mall), while glocalization
tends to be tied more to something (e.g., the farmer's market) and
therefore stands opposed, at least partially (and along with the local
itself), to the spread of nothing. It is a fact that these two processes
coexist under the broad heading of globalization, and because they
are, at least to some degree, in conflict in terms of their implications
for the spread of nothingness around the world, that globalization as
a whole does not have a unidirectional effect on the spread of nothingness. That is, in some of its aspects (those involved in grobalization)
globalization favors the spread of nothing, but in others (those related to glocalization) it tends toward the dissemination of something.

Those who emphasize glocalization tend to see it as militating against
the globalization of nothing and, in fact, view it as leading to the
creation of a wide array of new, "glocal" forms of something. In contrast,
those who emphasize grobalization see it as a powerful contributor to
the spread of nothingness throughout the world. This being said, it
must be noted that there are important similarities and differences
between glocalization and grobalization and their roles in the globalization of nothing and they must be delineated as we proceed.

The concept of grobalization is at odds, to some degree, with the
thrust of globalization theory—especially glocalization—that have the
greatest cache today. At the risk of being reductive, this divide amounts

to a difference in vision between those who see a world that is becoming increasingly grobalized[9] more homogeneous, Americanized, rationalized, codified, and restricted and those who view it as growing increasingly glocalized—more heterogeneous, diverse, effervescent, and free. Of course, this is a matter of emphasis and both processes are occurring simultaneously, and in varying degrees, in different parts of the world.

While our focal concern is with the globalization of nothing, that linkage can only be dealt with within the broader context of a discussion of the relationship between grobalization/glocalization and something/nothing. Figure 11.1 offers the four basic possibilities (with a few representative examples) that emerge when we cross-cut the grobalization–glocalization and something–nothing continua. It should be noted that while this yields four "ideal types," there are no hard-and-fast lines between them. This is reflected in the use of both dotted lines and of multidirectional arrows in Figure 11.1.

Quadrants one and four in Figure 11.1 are of greatest importance,[10] at least for the purposes of this analysis because their relationship to one another represents a key point of tension and conflict in the world

Figure 11.1: The Relationship between Glocal–Grobal and Something–Nothing
(with a few representative examples in each quadrant)

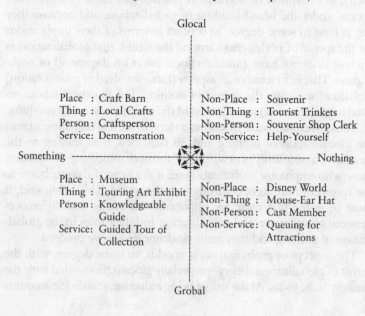

Glocal

Place : Craft Barn	Non-Place : Souvenir
Thing : Local Crafts	Non-Thing : Tourist Trinkets
Person : Craftsperson	Non-Person : Souvenir Shop Clerk
Service : Demonstration	Non-Service : Help-Yourself

Something ———————————————————————————— Nothing

Place : Museum	
Thing : Touring Art Exhibit	Non-Place : Disney World
Person : Knowledgeable	Non-Thing : Mouse-Ear Hat
Guide	Non-Person : Cast Member
Service : Guided Tour of	Non-Service : Queuing for
Collection	Attractions

Grobal

today. Clearly, there is great pressure to grobalize *nothing* (from, for example, entrepreneurs) and, often, all that stands in its way in terms of achieving global hegemony is the glocalization of *something* (and those seeking to defend and further it). We will return to this conflict and its implications for our analysis below.

It should be noted that there is an ongoing process by which *something* is, over time, transformed into *nothing*, and vice versa. On the one hand, traditional works of art (for example, *Kokopellis* from the American Southwest and *Matryoshka* dolls from Russia) that were at one time *something*, have been transformed into mass-produced *kitsch* for the grobal consumer and tourist. On the other hand, the toys given away or sold by McDonald's over the years have come, in some cases, to be collector's items.

The close and centrally important relationship between (*a*) grobalization and nothing and (*b*) glocalization and something leads to the view that there is what Max Weber called an *elective affinity*[11] between the two elements of each of these pairs.[12] Neither in the case of grobalization and *nothing* nor of glocalization and *something* do one of these elements "cause" the other to come into existence. Rather, the development and diffusion of one tends to go hand-in-hand with the other (see Howe, 1978). Thus, it is far easier to grobalize *nothing* than *something*; the development of grobalization creates a favorable ground for the development and spread of *nothing* (and *nothing* is easily grobalized). Similarly, it is far easier to glocalize *something* than *nothing*; the development of glocalization creates a favorable ground for the development and proliferation of *something* (and *something* is easily glocalized).

However, the situation is more complex than this since we can also see support for the argument that grobalization can, at times, involve *something* (e.g., art exhibits that move among art galleries throughout the world; Italian exports of food like Parmiagiano Reggiano and Culatella ham; touring symphony orchestras and bands that perform in venues throughout the world) and that glocalization can sometimes involve *nothing* (e.g., the production of local souvenirs and trinkets for tourists from around the world).

Grobalization, by its very nature, generally requires large numbers of that which is to be disseminated throughout the globe. It is far easier to centrally conceive, construct, and reproduce many times over, that which is derived from a "bare bones" model with minimal content (or to put it another way, a model that is far more *form* than *content*), than it is from a complex model that has rich and elaborate distinctive content. That is, a minimalist phenomenon, or one that comes as close as possible to it, is far easier to centrally create, reproduce and disseminate widely than one that is rich in content. Furthermore, once the basic model of a minimal phenomenon has been constructed, all iterations that follow are easy to produce since there is so little substance to the model. Also easing the way toward the proliferation of the model is the fact that only minor variations and deviations over time and across space are permitted. The proliferation of nullities (that which exists at or near the *nothing* end of the *something–nothing* continuum) obviously assumes the existence of entrepreneurs (in the broadest sense of the term—e.g., the corporate officials at McDonald's or Gucci; government leaders) who are interested, for financial and/ or myriad other reasons, in the expansion of such minimalist creations and their exportation to other parts of the world.

However, it should be noted that some entrepreneurs do create phenomena that are rich, elaborate, distinctive and idiosyncratic, or develop those already in existence, and export them, often successfully (the grobalization of something). But the very nature of these complex phenomena serves to limit their numbers and hence their global proliferation. There are just so many world-class ballet companies, gymnastic teams, and rock groups and the profit potential of such groups, if that is indeed the objective, is highly limited, to put it mildly. This is not the case with nothing which, precisely because it is devoid of such characteristics, is far easier to produce in large numbers and to distribute globally.

In contrast, things derived from the glocal are, almost by definition, much more complex and therefore likely to be produced in more limited numbers. The complexity of the glocal comes from the fact that it involves an idiosyncratic mix of the global and the local. There are innumerable such combinations in many areas of the world with subtle differences in each area in the ways in which global and local elements are combined. It is difficult to produce such complex combinations in great numbers and, in any case, the many different combinations (for example, slight differences in the food served in different parts of Provence in southern France) speak of the likelihood of small-batch, rather than mass-production. Furthermore, there is likely to be only a minimal demand for such idiosyncratic products (e.g., only relatively small numbers of people outside France are likely to be interested in, and able to afford, Provencal food). Finally, that which is glocal in character is almost by definition produced and marketed in a limited geographic area and this means that low levels of production might be hard-pressed to satisfy even the local demand, let alone a global market. Thus, the most famous restaurants in Provence are booked long in advance and the Provencal food served in most French restaurants throughout the world has little resemblance to that served in Provence.

In contrast, because they are so content-less, nullities are easier to extract from the given locality in which they were created and to export to other, sometimes very different, locales. As a result, it is relatively easy to grobalize that which is relatively devoid of distinctive content. In contrast, elaborate and distinctive phenomena may be too tied to a specific locale to be extracted from it and their complex distinctiveness may make it difficult for them to take root in other locales. Thus, Parmigiano Reggiano is a very distinctive cheese product of a region of Italy and while it is available globally, at least on a limited scale, its market potential in locales outside of Italy dominated by other cuisines is limited. For example, it is questionable, to put it mildly, how well such a distinctive cheese would go with a Tex-Mex dish, an Indian curry or a Chinese stir-fry?[13] In contrast, Coca Cola, and more generally colas of any brand or even no-name versions, have proven easier to extract from their American roots, fit with virtually every cuisine (it could be, and is, consumed with Tex-Mex, curry or stir-fry), and have, as a result, been exported successfully throughout the world; in other words, cola, especially Coca Cola, has been grobalized.[14] In fact, a WW II soldier said he was fighting for "the right to buy Coca Cola again" and an advertising campaign in the 1990s proclaimed, "If you don't know what it [Coca Cola] is, Welcome to Planet Earth" (Pavitt, 2001: 4).

For many of the same reasons, nullities are also easier to extract from the given time period in which they were created and to be at home in other time periods. For example, stemming from an era in which there was greater tolerance, and less awareness, of drugs and the problems associated with them, Coca Cola originally had small amounts of cocaine, but times changed and it quickly became clear that such a drug had no place in a soft drink and it was removed. Coca Cola with cocaine would be impossible to sell today, but with the offending drug removed, it is saleable almost everywhere. More generally, there is a tendency to modify products of a given time period, remove much of what makes them distinctive, so that they can be marketed in a different time period. The taco may have deep roots in the history of Mexican culture, but much of what was originally involved in the creation of tacos (especially the way they were made, the extremely hot chilies that gave, and continue to give, traditional tacos their spiciness) has been removed (at least outside indigenous areas where the original taco is still made and consumed) to make it the kind of time-less generic product that chains like Taco Bell can market today around the world. It is far easier to distribute such products globally—to grobalize them—than it is those that retain deep ties to a specific epoch (and local area).

Because they lack ties to any place (or time), nullities can more easily be modified to adapt to different places (or times). While the core elements of the model can and must remain in place, some elements can be safely dropped and others can be grafted on depending on the nature of the specific place (or time) to which the nullity is being exported. The fast-food restaurant is a good example of this and a prime model for the process of grobalization. The basic model was developed in the United States by the mid-20th century, but it has now been exported to virtually every corner of the world and has proven very adaptable to many different locales. For example, McDonald's might sell a few different things in various settings (e.g., beer in German McDonald's, McFalafel in Egypt, Teriyaki Burger in Japan), or it might adapt its functioning in various ways (customers in Asian settings are encouraged to linger), but the basic model remains intact and seems to function quite nicely (*Washington Post*, December 2, 2002).

The fact that there is a basic model, and minor adaptations are made to that model, means that the costs of producing and modifying grobal settings, products and so forth can be kept to a minimum in comparison to creating such things anew in many different places and times. And this means, of course, that higher profits are possible (in those cases in which profit-making organizations are being discussed) where a simple, basic model is employed. There is no need to make massive expenditures in learning about the detailed requirements of each new time and place. Many technologies, procedures and recipes that work in one place (or time) can simply be reproduced in many other locales (and time periods) and this makes for great economies of scale. Personnel costs are kept low because relatively unskilled and poorly paid workers can be fitted into these systems and are able to perform at reasonably high levels because of system imperatives. Thus, for example, the automatic French Fry machines turn out large numbers of perfectly cooked fries no matter who happens to be put in-charge of them. Such cost advantages (and many others) aid in the grobalization of these nullities in comparison to that of phenomena with far more content. The grobal has a huge competitive advantage over the glocal.

This means, of course, that there are great cost disadvantages in seeking to grobalize the glocal. There are innumerable models for the glocal; that is, the integration of local and grobal elements differs from one locale to another. Because each form of the glocal is different from every other, the glocal lacks the cost advantages of the grobal models. Thus, even if efforts were made to grobalize the glocal, they would be at great cost disadvantages relative to that which is easily amenable to grobalization.

Of course, the success of any new glocal phenomenon is likely to attract the attention of entrepreneurs interested in expanding the market for it. In order to reach other markets, perhaps even one that is global in magnitude, the familiar dialectic occurs and an effort is made to create a paired-down version of the glocal phenomenon that is likely to be attractive to a broad clientele in many different geographic settings. In the process, of course, the glocal is transformed into the grobal and *something* is transformed into *nothing*.

Finally, the converse point is that it is far more difficult and expensive to create *something* (in contrast to *nothing*), especially from some central location in time or space, and then to be able to export it widely and successfully to other times and places. Thus, a fine gourmet restaurant is hard to create and establish and relatively few succeed, at least for very long. Even more difficult is the creation of a model for a gourmet restaurant that can be exported to other times and places. Unlike fast-food restaurants, each gourmet restaurant is expensive to create and maintain. More importantly, it has proven almost impossible to create a chain of such restaurants and to manage them from some central location making sure that the high quality is consistently maintained in all locations. This is not to say that this never occurs. For example, famous chefs like France's Alain Ducasse have opened gourmet restaurants in several different locales. However, the presence of such "chains" in the global marketplace is insignificant in comparison to the global proliferation of fast-food restaurants. Nevertheless, there is no doubt that such gourmet chains will seek to become an ever-greater presence in the world market.

THE ULTIMATE EXAMPLE OF THE GLOBALIZATION OF NOTHING—CONSUMPTION ON THE INTERNET

So far, a strong case has been made for the utility of the concept of *nothing* (and *something*), and the elective affinity between these nullities and grobalization. However, the fact is that a discussion of what, in many ways, is the most persuasive example of *nothing* and its globalization—*most* large-scale consumption sites on the Internet (e.g., Amazon.com, Expedia.com, Wal-mart.com, Fidelity.com)—have been held in abeyance. If the reader is already convinced of the existence and importance of the grobalization of *nothing*, then this section will offer little more than another set of examples of this process. However, if the reader has not been persuaded by the argument to this point, this example, and an extended discussion of it, should prove compelling. After all, most large-scale Internet consumption sites are perfect examples of nothing as empty form(s) and they are by their very nature global.[15]

Following the basic definition of *nothing* employed in this chapter, we will discuss large-scale Internet consumption sites in the sense that they are *forms*, in fact a potentially infinite number of *forms*, that are centrally conceived and controlled, and are largely lacking in distinctive content. There is a great deal about the Internet that involves consumption. Indeed, one often hears the argument that much of its potential has been undermined by the fact that so much of it has come under the sway of businesses pushing innumerable types of consumption. Nevertheless, much that characterizes the Internet is omitted because of this singular focus on consumption, although we believe that many of the points to be made later about consumption on the Internet, can be extended to other things to be found on, and transpiring on, the World Wide Web (WWW).

As already mentioned, the totality of consumption sites on the Internet (and it is a constantly growing and changing totality) can be seen as a vast field that encompasses, among many other things, an enormous number of centrally conceived and controlled *forms*, most of which are, in themselves, largely, if not totally, devoid of distinctive content. The brick-and-mortar shopping mall, to take our earlier example in this chapter, is clearly such a *form* and since that is the case, then it is certainly even more true of Internet shopping malls. While both the brick-and-mortar and the Internet mall are centrally conceived and controlled, such conception and control is greater in the latter than the former. On-site managers (and other personnel) of brick-and-mortar malls can reconceptualize matters (at least to some degree), and should the need arise, they can alter the nature and level of control on a moment-to-moment basis. However, since no humans are present at the Internet mall, everything must be conceptualized in advance and controls cannot be altered at a moment's notice as the need arises. It is for this reason that Internet malls need to be conceptualized far more carefully and in far greater detail in advance and much more extensive controls need to be in place. It is certainly the case that, after the fact, the Internet mall can be rethought and new controls put in place, perhaps overnight (see later section), but that cannot be accomplished on-the-fly as it might by a brick-and-mortar mall manager.

Because it is empty, a wide range of specific content can be included in a brick-and-mortar shopping mall, but the immateriality of an equally empty Internet mall eliminates virtually all barriers and makes an even wider range of content possible. This is true quantitatively and qualitatively. Quantitatively, the immateriality of the Internet mall makes it infinitely expandable, while the material structure of a brick-and-mortar mall, and even the totality of such malls, makes for comparatively severe restrictions on the amount and variety of content to be included.[16] Qualitatively, the Internet mall's immateriality allows for experiences that may not be possible in a "real-world" mall. For example, Amazon.com offers its users free alerts to new products and services, free e-cards, and the possibility of not only buying at its mall, but selling one's own things there, as well.

More generally, an Internet address, even one devoted to consumption, is a form that can lead one to literally virtually any type of content.[17] Furthermore, even within the context of a specific Internet address, a wide array of content can be offered. Amazon.com became known for the million-plus book titles available through its Website, but now it offers a wide array of other types of products for sale. More generally, a portal like Yahoo.com, or one of its many alternatives, offers entry into what is literally a world of alternatives, an increasing number of which relate to consumption. Even more alternatives are to be found on Google.com which has concentrated on continually expanding its content (Levy, 2002). That content has become so extensive that it is used by Yahoo and others. Furthermore, recently Google itself has moved more in the direction of consumption (Walker, 2002).

A related point is that because they are virtual realities, Internet malls can easily, literally overnight, transform what they have to sell and how they sell it, an option not open to brick-and-mortar malls.[18] As a result of their comparative inability to adapt, many such malls, especially the older strip-malls, have become ghost towns (Chung et al., 2001). Again, the best example is Amazon.com, which has, in recent years, added and sometimes eliminated product lines with great rapidity. For example, at the moment, among its featured "stores" are those dedicated to health and beauty, magazine subscriptions, home and garden, kitchen and housewares, and so on. These are quite distant from the Website's roots in the book business.

The growth and continual transformation of Internet malls lends support, of course, to this chapter's most general grand narrative—the dramatic proliferation of nothing—in this case in and through large-scale consumption sites on the Internet. The roots of the Internet lie in Arpanet, founded in 1969 as a conduit for messages between defense laboratories and universities. It is startling to realize that the Internet itself is, as we write this, not yet 15 years old, having been founded in 1988 on the basis of Arpanet technology. And, of course, the Internet did not truly take-off for several years, with the result that wide-scale use of it is only a decade (or less) old. The big names in consumption on the Internet (Amazon.com) did not begin operations until the mid-1990s and the entry of the brick-and-mortar firms (e.g., Wal-Mart.com) into Internet commerce came slightly later (in Wal-Mart's case, 1996). Many of the start-ups that made a big splash on the Internet in the 1990s (those that existed only online) have disappeared or been downsized substantially in the dot.com crash of the early 21st century. While some of the "irrational exuberance" (an expression made famous by Federal Reserve Chairman Alan Greenspan, during the height of the stock market bubble of the late 1990s) has disappeared from consumer business on the Internet; there is no question that it is not only here to stay, but likely to expand enormously in the coming years (Ritzer, 2001).

While the case for the relationship between large-scale Internet consumption sites and nothing requires considerable argumentation, no such detailed discussion is needed to make the case for the association between the Internet (and those sites) and globalization. Theoretically, anyone, anywhere in the world can log onto and consume on the Internet (assuming electricity, phone lines, credit cards, and so on). Because it is so immaterial, there are no geographic barriers to the dissemination of messages, information, and transactions across the Internet. A nation may try to block this or that (as China does on occasion), but in the main there is little that can be done about global transmissions on the Internet. Indeed, one of the hallmarks of the Internet is that it is entirely possible that one does not know, and may never know, the geographic location of a person or site with which one is dealing. The Internet is global and the size and magnitude of the globe pose few, if any, barriers to communication through, and making purchases on, it.

All of the other examples of globalization used in this chapter, especially as they relate to consumption, pale in comparison to the global nature of the Internet. For example, the ability to send packages quickly to virtually any place in the world via carriers like FedEx is impressive, but it is child's play in comparison to the ability to purchase and obtain stock shares (for example, on Fidelity.com) or airline tickets (on Expedia.com, and other similar sites) over the Internet. The wedding of the immateriality of the WWW with various immaterial goods like stock positions or airline reservations, makes the Internet and consumption on it the ultimate examples of globalization as it relates to consumption. After all, everyone with a computer, a modem, and a credit card anywhere in the world can engage in such transactions and almost instantaneously obtain what they are looking for.

Of course, it is true that some aspects of the Internet, and especially consumption on it, are not so immaterial with the result that global barriers remain as impediments, at least to some degree. For example, all of the steps leading up to the purchase of, say, a book on Amazon.com are immaterial and therefore easily globalized. However, once the purchase is complete, the book (or some other product) must be sent to the purchaser (or a third party) and here the materiality of the book itself limits globalization. In effect, the more nearly limitless character of the Internet is stymied by limits associated with, for example, FedEx and its ability, no matter how great, to deliver a book that exists in a material form. While I might receive a book overnight from a nearby Amazon.com warehouse, residents in remote areas of the United States and the world may have to wait days and even weeks (and some may not be able to get the book at all). Nonetheless, Amazon.com has succeeded in making the book business (and others) a far more global business than it ever was before.

While there is a strong association between consumption on the Internet and globalization, it is also the case that the Internet is an important site and resource for both anti-consumption and anti-globalization forces. Large-scale anti-globalization demonstrations have relied, to a large degree, on the Internet to organize participants from around the world. Adbusters is an example of an anti-consumption organization that uses the Internet to great advantage for its activities, including organizing "buy nothing day (www.adbusters.org/home/).

On a related note, let us take a look at the issue of making *something* out of *nothing* as it applies to large-scale consumption sites on the Internet. It is certainly the case that on Internet Websites, especially those that permit interaction between and among people on the Web, the emptiness of *forms* does not prevent people from making *something* out of them, perhaps something quite important to them and others. Thus, a chat room would be a good example of a Website which, while it is formally empty, can be made into something quite important by those who happen to be participating at any given time. However, large-scale consumption sites tend to offer little or nothing in the way of interaction with the result that the ability to transform them into *something* is much more limited. Furthermore, such consumption Websites are centrally created and controlled. As a result, they are crammed full of preprogramed mechanisms that involve set responses to actions taken by consumers on the Website. This often seems like interaction, but it is one-sided and there is little possibility of a meaningful relationship developing between consumers and a "dumb" Website.

Of course, those who are deeply enmeshed in the computer, and the life possible on and through it, will find large-scale consumer Websites as one more component of what is to them a quite meaningful way of life. While some might question how meaningful such an isolated life can be, the fact remains that many do find meaning there. There is no question that it is possible to turn the Internet into quite something, and large-scale consumer Websites can be part of that meaningful life.

Certainly, those who find meaning in consumption, and who are deeply enmeshed in such a life, will find the huge variety of Websites available to them quite meaningful and an important addition to the many other ways of consuming. For those who simply find that they must purchase something—a new car, a new house, insurance, and so on—the Internet can be *something* in the sense that it puts an unprecedented amount of information and power in the hands of the consumer. For example, for someone in the market for a new car, the Internet provides a near limitless amount of information that can be of great help to the consumer—list price, invoice price, stock on hand in a particular dealership, automobile specifications, expert reviews as well as the views of owners of the car in question. More generally, comparison-shopping services like DealTime, BizRate, and My Simon allow people to be knowledgeable consumers of a wide range of things by providing them with prices (ranked by lowest price), as well as taxes and shipping costs. The Internet makes it possible for people to be far more knowledgeable consumers. Furthermore, it gives them much more power in the negotiating process. Prices can be solicited over the Internet from a number of dealers and the consumer can pit one dealer against the others. Negotiations can be conducted over the Internet with the result that the consumer is less likely to fall victim to the various interpersonal sales devices at the disposal of a salesperson (Browne, 1973). Successfully completing a purchase through the Internet at the best possible price can certainly mean something to the consumer. Indeed, it can free people from what many consider the most odious aspects of consumption, such as negotiating in person with automobile salespeople.

However, while the Internet can be used to the advantage of the consumer, it can, as pointed out before, also make it easy for the consumer to plunge into the depths of the void associated with the *nothingness* of consumption. That is, it is all-too-easy to consume over the Internet at all times of the day and night and on every day of the year. One who is already involved in hyperconsumption can easily find Internet consumption irresistible . . . and it is all likely to be made easier, and for some insidious, because the preferred mode of payment on the Internet is the credit card.

CONCLUSION

As pointed out earlier, one of the central aspects of this work is the argument that the/a key dynamic under the broad heading of globalization is the conflict between grobalization and glocalization. This is a very different view than *any* of the conventional perspectives on global conflict. For example, we think a large number of observers have tended to see the defining conflict, where one is seen to exist, as that between globalization and the local. However, the perspective offered here differs from that perspective on several crucial points.

First, globalization does not represent one side in the central conflict. It is far too broad a concept encompassing, as it does, all trans-national processes. It needs further refinement to be useful in this context such as the distinction between grobalization and glocalization. When that differentiation is made, it is clear that the broad process of globalization already encompasses important conflicting processes. Since globalization contains the key poles in the conflict, it therefore is not, and cannot be, one position in that conflict.

Second, the other side of the traditional view of that conflict—the local—is relegated to secondary importance in this conceptualization. That is, the local, to the degree that it continues to exist, is seen as increasingly insignificant and not a key player in the dynamics of glo-balization. Little of the local remains that has been untouched by the global. Thus, much of what we often think of as the local is, in reality, the glocal. As the grobal increasingly penetrates the local, less and less of the latter will remain free of grobal influences. That which does, will be relegated to the peripheries and interstices of the local com-munity. The bulk of that which remains is much better described as glocal than local.

In community after community, the real struggle is between the more purely grobal versus the glocal. One absolutely crucial implication is that *it is increasingly difficult to find anything in the world untouched by globalization*. The major alternative in an increasing portion of the world seems to be the choice between that which is inherently and deeply globalized—grobalization—and that in which global and vestiges of local elements intermingle—glocalization. This clearly implies the near-total triumph of the global throughout the world.

Ironically, then, the hope for those opposed to grobalization seems to lie in an alternative form of globalization—glocalization. This is hardly a stirring hope as far as most opponents of globalization are concerned, but it is the most realistic and viable one available. The implication is that those who wish to oppose globalization, specifi-cally grobalization, must support and align themselves with the other major form of globalization–glocalization.

Yet, glocalization does represent some measure of hope. For one thing, it is the last outpost of most lingering, if already adulterated (by grobalization), forms of the local. That is, important vestiges of the local remain in the glocal. For another, the interaction of the grobal and the local produces unique phenomena that are not reducible to either the grobal or the local. If the local alone is no longer the source that it once was for uniqueness, at least some of the slack has been picked up by the glocal. It is even conceivable that the glocal is, or at least can be, a significant source of uniqueness and innovation. Another source of hope lies in two or more glocal forms interacting to produce that which is distinctive in content.

Those who oppose globalization can continue to support the local as an alternative to it. However, this analysis leads to the conclusion that this effort is likely to fail because of the progressive disappearance of the local unaffected by globalization. A more successful strategy might be to support the glocal as an alternative to the grobal. While this does concede the field to globalization, it at least gives great importance to that aspect of it still affected by the local. Furthermore, it involves a recognition of the fact that the glocal is likely to be an increasingly important source of not only cultural diversity, but also cultural innovation. In addition, it allows us to see that globalization is not monolithic and that while in some ways it might be deeply troubling, in others it can offer some hope.

NOTES

1. As we will see, the meaning of this concept is not unambiguous. An effort will be made to sort this out in the ensuing discussion.
2. However, there are some forms of nothing that are locally conceived and/or controlled.
3. That is, by, for example, the headquarters of a multinational corporation or a national government.
4. As in the case of the caveat about the definition of nothing, there are some forms of something that are centrally conceived and/or controlled.
5. For a critique of dichotomous thinking see (Mudimbe-Boyi, 2002).
6. See, Robertson (2001: 458–71). Globalization not only goes to the heart of Robertson's own approach, but it is central to that of many others. The most notable is Appadurai's view that (see, Arjun Appadurai, 1996). While John Tomlinson uses other terms, he sees glocalization as "friendly" to his own orientation (see, Tomlinson, 1999).
7. We feel apologetic about adding yet another neologism, especially such an ungainly one, to a field already rife with jargon. However, the existence and popularity of the concept of glocalization requires the creation of the parallel notion of grobalization in order to emphasize that which the former concept ignores or downplays.
8. We are combining a number of different entities under this heading (nations, corporations, a wide range of organizations, and so on), but it should be clear that there are profound differences among them including the degree to which, and the ways in which, they seek to grobalize.
9. Although everyone recognizes that grobalization, and more generally globalization, play themselves out differently in various local and national contexts (see, Mudimbe-Boyi, 2002).

10. While the other two quadrants (two and three) are residual in nature and of secondary significance, it is important to recognize that there is, at least to some degree, a glocalization of *nothing* (quadrant two) and a grobalization of *something* (quadrant three). Their empirical manifestations are not only not nearly as common as those associated with the other two possibilities, but whatever tensions may exist between them are of far less significance than that between the grobalization of *nothing* and the glocalization of *something*. However, the existence of the glocalization of *nothing* and the grobalization of *something* makes it clear that grobalization is not an unmitigated source of *nothing* (it can involve *something*) and glocalization is not to be seen solely as a source of *something* (it can involve *nothing*).

11. And there is not an *elective affinity* between grobalization and *something*, and glocalization and *nothing*.

12. Indeed, it is difficult to accept the view that there are *any* such relationships in the social world.

13. However, new, eclectic cuisines and cookery do involve the combination of the most unlikely of foods. Nonetheless, such combinations are unlikely to be attractive to a large, global population of consumers, or at least one as large and global as that for, say, Coca Cola.

14. An apparent exception is the uproar over "Coca Colonization" in France after World War II, but that quickly died out and today Coca Cola is only one of many nonthings widely accepted in France. See, for example, Kuisel, 1993.

15. Of course, there are many areas of the world with little or no access to the Internet in general and these large-scale consumption sites in particular. Further, those who do not understand English also lack such access.

16. Although traditional malls, and the shops in them, have sought to become more flexible (*Boston Globe*, October 22, 2002).

17. One broad type of restriction is the nature of the ending of an address (.com, .org, .gov, .edu and so on). However, even within each of those broadly restricted categories, a great quantity and diversity of content is available.

18. This seems to contradict the preceding point about Internet sites not being able to respond immediately and therefore requiring greater prior conceptualization and preset methods of control. However, this is a different point. On the one hand, because no humans are on duty, Internet sites are not as adaptable as brick-and-mortar malls. On the other hand, because they are immaterial, Internet malls can be altered dramatically literally overnight (although this might require much preplanning), while traditional malls are very difficult and time-consuming to alter because of their materiality.

References

Antonio, Roberto J. and Alessandro Bonanno. 2000. "A New Global Capitalism? From 'Americanism' and 'Fordism' to 'Americanization–Globalization'" in *American Studies*, vol. 41, pp. 33–77.

Appadurai, Arjun. 1996. *Modernity at Large: Cultural Dimensions of Globalization*. Mineapolis: University of Minnesota Press.

Bauman, Zygmunt. 1998. *Globalization: The Human Consequences*. New York: Columbia University Press.

Beck, Ulrich. 2000. *What is Globalization?* Cambridge: Polity Press.

Boston Globe, October 22, 2002, p.C1.

Browne, J. 1973. *The Used Car Game: A Sociology of Bargain*. Lexington MA.: Lexington Books.

Chung, C.J. et al. 2001. *Harvard Design School Guide to Shopping*. Koln: Taschen.

Giddens, Anthony. 2000. *The Runaway World: How Globalization is Reshaping Our Lives*. New York: Routledge.

Howe, Robert Herbert, 1978. "Max Weber's Elective Affinities: Sociology Within the Bounds of Pure Reason" in *American Journal of Sociology*, vol. 84, pp. 366–85.

Kellner, Douglas. 2002. "Theorizing Globalization" in *Sociological Theory*, vol. 20, pp. 285–305.

Kuisel, Richard, 1993. *Seducing the French: The Dilemma of Americanization*. Berkeley: University of California Press.

Levy, S. 2002. "The World According to Google" in *Newsweek*, December 16, pp. 46–51.

Mudimbe-Boyi, Elisabeth (ed.). 2002. *Beyond Dichotomies: Histories, Identities, Cultures, and the Challenge of Globalization*. Albany: Stage University of New York Press.

Pavitt, Jane. 2001. "Branded: A Brief History of Brands: 1 Coca Cola" in *Guardian*, July 9, p. 4.

Ritzer, G. 2001. "Ensnared in the E-Net: The Future Belongs to the Immaterial Means of Consumption" in G. Ritzer (ed.). *Explorations in the Sociology of Consumption: Fastfood Restaurants, Credit Cards and Casinos*. London: Sage, pp. 145–49.

Robertson, Roland. 1992. *Globalization: Social Theory and Global Culture*. London: Sage.

_____. 2001. "Globalization Theory 2000: Major problematics" in George Ritzer and Barry Swart (eds). *Handbook of Social Theory*. London: Sage.

Tomilson, John. 1999. *Globalization and Culture*. Chicago: University of Chicago Press.

Walker, L. 2002. "Google turns its Gaze to Online Shopping," *Washington Post Business*, December 15, p. H7.

Washington Post, "Kiwi Burger to Go, Hold the Fried Egg", December 2, 2002.

ABOUT THE EDITOR AND CONTRIBUTORS

EDITOR

Samir Dasgupta is Professor, Department of Sociology, University of Kalyani, West Bengal. A D.Litt in sociology, he has published extensively on development studies, gender studies, urban studies, and sociology of globalization. His books include *A Short History of Sociological Thought; Economic Sociology; Globalization and Development*; and *History of Western Sociology* (in Bengali), and *Sociology Through Objective Mirror;* and *Global Malady in the Third World—A Reflection*.

CONTRIBUTORS

Joy Asongazoh Alemazung is at the Department of Sociology, University of Erlangen-Nuremberg. He is the Chairman of Pan-African Organization for Information and Humanity Service Erlangen and Moderator of *Africa Panorama*, the first Africa radio program on Radio Z Nuremberg (program is in German language).

Kaushik Chattopadhyay, PhD, teaches at the Department of Sociology, Kalyani Mahavidyalaya. He has published a number of articles on the issues of development studies and sociology of globalization. He is the co-author of the volume *Global Malady in the Third World—A Reflection* and *Globalization and Development* (Bengali version).

Sing C. Chew is Professor and Chairperson of the Department of Sociology at Humboldt State University, Arcata, California, USA. His most recent book is *World Ecological Degradation (Accumulation, Urbanization, and Deforestation) 3000 B.C.–A.D. 2000*, and *The Underdevelopment of Development* (eds).

Verghese Chirayath, a sociologist with interests in labor issues, regularly offers a course on Corporate Deviance based on case studies of corporations involved in unlawful activities. He has been a sociology faculty at John Carroll University since 1970, and has taught courses in white-collar crime, social theory, ethnicity, and global social problems.

Robyn Bateman Driskell is an Assistant Professor of sociology at Baylor University. Her research interests include issues related to women's empowerment, community, racial and ethnic groups, and Latino studies. Recent publications include topics related to minority women in the labor force, communities in cyberspace, and the lost community. She also continues to explore the issues of gender role reconstruction, Mexican American women's wage inequality, and community in cyberspace.

Ray Kiely, Senior Lecturer in Development Studies, School of Oriental Studies, University of London, WC1H 0XG, England. E-mail: rk14@soas.ac.uk. His recent books include *Industrialisation and Development: A Comparative Analysis* and *Globalization and the Third World* (ed.).

Abbas Mehdi originally from Iraq, was a resident of UK since 1974–82, arrived in the United States in 1982, and became a US citizen in 1995. He graduated in economics in 1974 from the Baghdad University, Iraq, and earned an MA in Management in 1982 from the School of Management, Bath University, England. He has a Ph.D. in comparative organizations and sociology from Ohio State University, USA. Abbas Mehdi's academic background involves multidisciplinary and cross-cultural approaches to his areas of specialization: comparative management and complex organization. His work emphasizes both the external relationship between the organization and its environment and the internal process of organizational adaptation and change.

He has been Professor of organization and sociology at St. Cloud State University, Minnesota, since 1988. Between 1991 and 1997, he was also Adjunct Professor in the Department of Strategic Management and Organization in the Graduate School Program of the Carlson School of Management at the University of Minnesota. He is currently advisor and board member for various local and international organizations: he has been a member of the Board and Council of the International Research Foundation for Development since 1999 (this body has consultancy status with the United Nations); Board member of the Minnesota International Center since 1997. And distinguished Resource Person, International Fellowship Programs, Hubert H. Humphrey Institute of Public Affairs, Minneapolis, MN, USA (1997–2002). Between 1996 and 1997 he acted as an advisor for the St. Cloud Chamber of Commerce, and he is a consultant on Middle East affairs for several American and European organizations.

He is also Founder and Chairman of the Union of Independent Iraqis, an international organization that promotes democracy and the replacement of the present government in Iraq. Abbas Mehdi is an internationally recognized speaker and expert on issues involving the Middle East, and is frequently interviewed and quoted by local, regional, and international reporters.

Elvira del Pozo is a doctoral student in the Department of Sociology at the University of Valencia, Spain. She received her undergraduate degree in law and her MA in sociology, the latter at Eastern Michigan University. Her MA thesis focused on Amnesty International (AI) and the extent to which its members and volunteers are altruistically motivated. She plans to continue this work in her Ph.D. dissertation research, for which she will survey several non-governmental organizations—possibly including a restudy of AI.

George Ritzer, is Distinguished University Professor of Sociology at the University of Maryland. He has served as Chair of the American Sociological Association's sections on Theoretical Sociology and Organizations and Occupations. Professor Ritzer is the author of *The Classical Sociological Theory; The Modern Sociological Theory; The McDonaldization of Society; Enchanting a Disenchanted World: Revolutionizing The Means of Consumption,* and is the editor of the forthcoming *Encyclopedia of Social Theory* (two volumes).

Michael Ryan is a graduate student at the University of Maryland. He is a C. Wright Mills Fellow, working towards a PhD in sociology. His interests include social theory, sexuality, consumption, and globalization.

Immanuel Wallerstein is a well-known and distinguished sociologist. He earned his Ph.D. from Columbia University and D.Litt. from York University. He held a number of Chairs in different universities of the world. He was Professor of sociology at McGill and Columbia Universties. He was a Visiting Professor at the Alicante, Amsterdam, Chinese, British Columbia, Illinois, Montpellier, Ottawa, and Texas, Universities.

Jay Weinstein, Professor, Department of Sociology at Eastern Michigan University and private research consultant specializing in statistical analysis and community development. He helped to establish the first-ever degree program in social science at Georgia Institute of Technology and has actively championed the cause of applied sociology throughout his career. He is author of numerous publications, including the groundbreaking monograph, *Sociology/Technology: Foundations of Postacademic Social Science* and his most recent book *Demography: The Science of Population*. In 1998, he received the Michigan Sociological Association (MSA) Charles Horton Cooley Award for Scholarly Contributions; and in 2000, he received that organization's Marvin Olsen Award for Service. He has served as Executive Board Member, Vice-President, and President (2002–03) of the Society for Applied Sociology; Executive Board Member of the North Central Sociological Association; and Executive Board Member and the President of the Michigan Sociological Association.

Ernest De Zolt, is a sociologist with an interest in criminology, and regularly offers a course in deviant behavior with an emphasis on power. He has been a sociology faculty at John Carroll University since 1989, and has taught courses in introductory sociology, deviant behavior, criminology, social stratification, law and social policy, and criminal justice systems, writing about Iraq.

INDEX